PREFACE.

This Manual has been prepared, in order to present, in compact and convenient form, the important Political Facts of the period to which it refers. It will be found to contain Messages, Proclamations, Orders, Telegrams, Speeches, Bills, Propositions, Reports, Constitutional Amendments, Votes, Platforms, and sundry Miscellaneous Matters required to make the Record complete.

It is necessarily confined to those facts which illustrate the positions of parties; and to those propositions upon which votes were taken, and to the more significant of the latter class. Much material, interesting in itself as part of the history of the times, and as showing the precise views of persons, has been omitted, in obedience to this rule. I hope, in a future work, to develop these various features of current history.

The action of all parties on Reconstruction will be found full, and especially pertinent to present issues. This Record covers the agency of the President, the responses of the people of the lately insurrectionary States, and the judgment of Congress, with the elaborated views of each.

The Tabular Statements at the close of the Volume have been prepared with direct reference to the topics to be discussed this fall. That giving the Votes on each Tariff since, and including that of, 1816, by States and Sections, will be conceded to be a valuable and interesting contribution to the history of the subject; and that respecting Representation, and the effect of proposed Amendments to the Constitution, will be of highest utility.

A glance at the Table of Contents will show the scope of the Work, and the variety of facts embraced. In the votes given, the names of Democrats are placed in *italic*, that results may be readily analyzed.

The whole Manual, it is hoped, will be found adapted to the purposes which prompted its preparation.

EDWARD McPHERSON.

WASHINGTON CITY, *July* 12, 1866.

POLITICAL MANUAL FOR 1866,

INCLUDING A CLASSIFIED SUMMARY OF THE IMPORTANT

EXECUTIVE, LEGISLATIVE, AND POLITICO-MILITARY FACTS OF THE PERIOD,

FROM

PRESIDENT JOHNSON'S ACCESSION,

APRIL 15, 1865, TO JULY 4, 1866;

AND CONTAINING A FULL RECORD OF THE

ACTION OF EACH BRANCH OF THE GOVERNMENT

ON

RECONSTRUCTION.

BY EDWARD McPHERSON,
Clerk of the House of Representatives of the United States.

WASHINGTON, D. C.:
PHILP & SOLOMONS.
1866.

Stereotyped by
McGILL & WITHEROW,
Washington, D. C.

TABLE OF CONTENTS.

I. Constitution of the United States—Mr. Seward's Certificate of the Ratification of the Anti-Slavery Amendment 1-6

II President Johnson's Orders and Proclamations 7-18

Respecting Commercial Intercourse—Trial and Punishment of the Assassins of Abraham Lincoln—Arrest of Jefferson Davis, Clement C. Clay, and others—To re-establish the Authority of the United States in Virginia—Equality of Rights with Maritime Nations—The Blockade—Amnesty—Appointing Provisional Governor for North Carolina, and other Insurrectionary States—Freedmen—Suppression of Rebellion in Tennessee—Paroled Prisoners—Martial Law withdrawn from Kentucky—Annulling the Suspension of the *Habeas Corpus*—Declaring the Rebellion Ended—Appointments to Office—Trials by Military Courts—Against the Fenian Invasion of Canada.

III. Action of the Conventions and Legislatures of the Lately Insurrectionary States 18-28

Proclamations of Provisional Governors—Elections of Conventions and Ordinances thereof—Enactments of Legislatures—Telegrams of President Johnson and Secretary Seward respecting the Rebel Debt, Colored Suffrage, Anti-Slavery Amendment, Admission to Congress of Senators and Representatives elect—President Lincoln's Letter to Governor Hahn, March 13, 1864, on Colored Suffrage, and his Telegram of April 12, 1865, prohibiting the meeting of the rebel legislature of Virginia.

IV. Legislation respecting Freedmen 29-44

In North Carolina—Mississippi—Georgia—Alabama—South Carolina, and General Sickles's Order relative thereto—Florida—Virginia, and General Terry's Order suspending the Vagrant Act—Tennessee—Texas—Louisiana.

V. President Johnson's Interviews and Speeches 44-63

Remarks to citizens of Indiana—Nashville Speech, June 9, 1864—To Virginia Refugees—Interview with George L. Stearns—Address to Colored Soldiers, October 10, 1865—Interview with Senator Dixon—With Colored Delegation respecting Suffrage, with Reply of—Remarks to Committee of the Virginia Legislature—Speech of February 22, 1866—To the Colored People of the District of Columbia.

VI. Annual, Special, and Veto Messages of President Johnson, with Copies of the Vetoed Bills, and the Votes on them 64-84

Annual Message, December 4, 1865—

Messages of President Johnson—*Continued.*

On the condition of the late Insurrectionary States, and General Grant's accompanying Report—Veto of the Freedmen's Bureau Bill, with Copy, and Votes—Veto of the Civil Rights Bill, with Copy, and Votes—Veto of the Colorado Bill, with Copy, and Votes—Message on the proposed Constitutional Amendment.

VII. Majority and Minority Reports of the Joint Committee on Reconstruction 84-101

VIII. Votes on Proposed Constitutional Amendments 102-106

On Constitutional Amendment as finally adopted—The Accompanying Bills—The Amendment on Representation and Direct Taxes—On Representation—On Immunities of Citizens—On Tennessee—On Rebel Debt.

IX. Members of the Cabinet of President Johnson, and of the 39th Congress, and of Claimants of Seats therein 107-109

X. Votes in the House of Representatives on Political Resolutions 109-114

On Public Debt—Punishment of Treason—Representation of lately Insurrectionary States—Elective Franchise in the States—Test Oath—Test Oath for Lawyers—Endorsement of the President's Policy—Withdrawal of Military Forces—Legal Effect of Rebellion—Duty of Congress—Writ of *Habeas Corpus*—Thanks to the President—Recognition of State Government of North Carolina—Trial of Jefferson Davis—Neutrality—The Fenians.

XI. Votes on Political Bills 114-117

Suffrage in District of Columbia—Extending the Homestead Act—*Habeas Corpus*—West Virginia Bill—Elective Franchise in the Territories.

XII. Political and Military Miscellaneous 117-124

Union National Platform of 1864—Democratic National Platform of 1864—Call for National Union Convention, 1866—Address of Democratic Members of Congress, 1866—Elections of 1866—Lee's Surrender to Grant—The Sherman-Johnston Agreement, and its Disapproval—Grant's Orders—Pennsylvania and Maryland Platforms of 1866—Convention of Southern Unionists.

XIII. Tabular Statements on Representation, Tariff, and the Public Debt 125-126

Census Tables showing Population, Voting Population, Present Apportionment, and effect of proposed changes—Table of Votes, by States and Sections, on the Tariffs of 1816, 1824, 1828, 1832, 1842, 1846, 1857, 1861, 1864, and the Bill of 1866—The Public Debt, June 1, 1866.

POLITICAL MANUAL FOR 1866.

I.

CONSTITUTION OF THE UNITED STATES.

We the People of the United States, in order to form a more perfect Union, establish Justice, insure domestic Tranquillity, provide for the common defence, promote the general Welfare, and secure the Blessings of Liberty to ourselves and our Posterity, do ordain and establish this Constitution for the United States of America.

Article I.

Section 1. All legislative Powers herein granted shall be vested in a Congress of the United States, which shall consist of a Senate and House of Representatives.

Sec. 2. The House of Representatives shall be composed of Members chosen every second Year by the People of the several States, and the Electors in each State shall have the Qualifications requisite for Electors of the most numerous Branch of the State Legislature.

No Person shall be a Representative who shall not have attained to the Age of twenty-five Years, and been seven Years a Citizen of the United States, and who shall not, when elected, be an Inhabitant of that State in which he shall be chosen.

Representatives and direct Taxes shall be apportioned among the several States which may be included within this Union, according to their respective Numbers, which shall be determined by adding to the whole Number of free Persons, including those bound to Service for a Term of Years, and excluding Indians not taxed, three fifths of all other Persons. The actual Enumeration shall be made within three Years after the first Meeting of the Congress of the United States, and within every subsequent Term of ten Years, in such Manner as they shall by Law direct. The Number of Representatives shall not exceed one for every thirty Thousand, but each State shall have at Least one Representative; and until such enumeration shall be made, the State of New Hampshire shall be entitled to chuse three, Massachusetts eight, Rhode Island and Providence Plantations one, Connecticut five, New York six, New Jersey four, Pennsylvania eight, Delaware one, Maryland six, Virginia ten, North Carolina five, South Carolina five, and Georgia three.

When vacancies happen in the Representation from any State, the Executive Authority thereof shall issue Writs of Election to fill such Vacancies.

The House of Representatives shall chuse their Speaker and other Officers; and shall have the sole Power of Impeachment.

Sec. 3. The Senate of the United States shall be composed of two Senators from each State, chosen by the Legislature thereof, for six Years; and each Senator shall have one Vote.

Immediately after they shall be assembled in Consequence of the first Election, they shall be divided as equally as may be into three Classes. The Seats of the Senators of the first Class shall be vacated at the Expiration of the second Year, of the second Class at the Expiration of the fourth Year, and of the third Class at the Expiration of the sixth Year, so that one-third may be chosen every second Year; and if Vacancies happen by Resignation, or otherwise, during the Recess of the Legislature of any State, the Executive thereof may make temporary Appointments until the next Meeting of the Legislature, which shall then fill such Vacancies.

No Person shall be a Senator who shall not have attained to the Age of thirty Years, and been nine Years a Citizen of the United States, and who shall not, when elected, be an Inhabitant of that State for which he shall be chosen.

The Vice President of the United States shall be President of the Senate, but shall have no Vote, unless they be equally divided.

The Senate shall chuse their other Officers, and also a President pro tempore, in the Absence of the Vice President, or when he shall exercise the Office of President of the United States.

The Senate shall have the sole Power to try all Impeachments. When sitting for that Purpose, they shall be on Oath or Affirmation. When the President of the United States is tried, the Chief Justice shall preside: And no Person shall be convicted without the Concurrence of two thirds of the Members present.

Judgment in Cases of Impeachment shall not extend further than to removal from Office, and Disqualification to hold and enjoy any Office of honour, Trust or Profit under the United States: but the Party convicted shall nevertheless be liable and subject to Indictment, Trial, Judgment and Punishment, according to Law.

Sec. 4. The Times, Places and Manner of holding Elections for Senators and Representatives, shall be prescribed in each State by the Legislature thereof; but the Congress may at any time by Law make or alter such Regulations, except as to the place of chusing Senators.

The Congress shall assemble at least once in every Year, and such Meeting shall be on the first Monday in December, unless they shall by Law appoint a different Day.

SEC. 5. Each House shall be the Judge of the Elections, Returns and Qualifications of its own Members, and a Majority of each shall constitute a Quorum to do Business; but a smaller Number may adjourn from day to day, and may be authorized to compel the Attendance of absent Members, in such Manner, and under such Penalties as each House may provide.

Each House may determine the Rules of its Proceedings, punish its Members for disorderly Behaviour, and, with the Concurrence of two thirds, expel a Member.

Each House shall keep a Journal of its Proceedings, and from time to time publish the same, excepting such Parts as may in their Judgment require Secrecy; and the Yeas and Nays of the Members of either House on any question shall, at the Desire of one fifth of those Present, be entered on the Journal.

Neither House, during the Session of Congress, shall, without the Consent of the other, adjourn for more than three days, nor to any other Place than that in which the two Houses shall be sitting.

SEC. 6. The Senators and Representatives shall receive a Compensation for their Services, to be ascertained by Law, and paid out of the Treasury of the United States. They shall in all Cases, except Treason, Felony and Breach of the Peace, be privileged from Arrest during their Attendance at the Session of their respective Houses, and in going to and returning from the same; and for any Speech or Debate in either House, they shall not be questioned in any other Place.

No Senator or Representative shall, during the Time for which he was elected, be appointed to any civil Office under the Authority of the United States, which shall have been created, or the Emoluments whereof shall have been encreased during such time; and no Person holding any Office under the United States, shall be a Member of either House during his Continuance in Office.

SEC. 7. All Bills for raising Revenue shall originate in the House of Representatives; but the Senate may propose or concur with Amendments as on other Bills.

Every Bill which shall have passed the House of Representatives and the Senate, shall, before it becomes a Law, be presented to the President of the United States; If he approve he shall sign it, but if not he shall return it, with his Objections to that House in which it shall have originated, who shall enter the Objections at large on their Journal, and proceed to reconsider it. If after such Reconsideration two thirds of that House shall agree to pass the Bill, it shall be sent, together with the Objections, to the other House, by which it shall likewise be reconsidered, and if approved by two thirds of that House, it shall become a Law. But in all such Cases the Votes of both Houses shall be determined by yeas and Nays, and the Names of the Persons voting for and against the Bill shall be entered on the Journal of each House respectively. If any Bill shall not be returned by the President within ten Days (Sundays excepted) after it shall have been presented to him, the Same shall be a law, in like Manner as if he had signed it, unless the Congress by their Adjournment prevent its return, in which Case it shall not be a Law.

Every Order, Resolution, or Vote to which the Concurrence of the Senate and House of Representatives may be necessary (except on a question of Adjournment) shall be presented to the President of the United States; and before the Same shall take Effect, shall be approved by him, or being disapproved by him, shall be repassed by two-thirds of the Senate and House of Representatives, according to the Rules and Limitations prescribed in the Case of a Bill.

SEC. 8. The Congress shall have Power

To lay and collect Taxes, Duties, Imposts and Excises, to pay the Debts and provide for the common Defence and general Welfare of the United States; but all Duties, Imposts and Excises shall be uniform throughout the United States;

To borrow Money on the credit of the United States;

To regulate Commerce with foreign Nations, and among the several States, and with the Indian Tribes;

To establish an uniform Rule of Naturalization, and uniform Laws on the subject of Bankruptcies throughout the United States;

To coin Money, regulate the Value thereof, and of foreign Coin, and fix the Standard of Weights and Measures;

To provide for the Punishment of counterfeiting the Securities and current Coin of the United States;

To establish Post Offices and post Roads;

To promote the progress of Science and useful Arts, by securing for limited Times to Authors and Inventors the exclusive Right to their respective Writings and Discoveries;

To constitute Tribunals inferior to the supreme Court;

To define and punish Piracies and Felonies committed on the high Seas, and Offences against the Law of Nations;

To declare War, grant Letters of Marque and Reprisal, and make Rules concerning Captures on Land and Water;

To raise and support Armies, but no Appropriation of Money to that Use shall be for a longer Term than two years;

To provide and maintain a Navy;

To make Rules for the Government and Regulation of the land and naval Forces;

To provide for calling forth the Militia to execute the Laws of the Union, suppress Insurrections and repel Invasions;

To provide for organizing, arming, and disciplining, the Militia, and for governing such Part of them as may be employed in the Service of the United States, reserving to the States respectively, the Appointment of the Officers, and the Authority of training the Militia according to the Discipline prescribed by Congress;

To exercise exclusive Legislation in all Cases whatsoever, over such District (not exceeding ten Miles square) as may, by Cession of particular States, and the Acceptance of Congress, become the Seat of the Government of the United States, and to exercise like Authority over all Places purchased by the Consent of the Legislature of the State in which the Same shall be, for the Erection of Forts, Magazines, Arsenals, Dock-Yards, and other needful Buildings;—And

To make all Laws which shall be necessary and proper for carrying into Execution the foregoing Powers, and all other Powers vested by this Constitution in the Government of the United States, or in any Department or Officer thereof.

SEC. 9. The Migration or Importation of such Persons as any of the States now existing shall think proper to admit, shall not be prohibited by the Congress prior to the Year one thousand eight hundred and eight, but a Tax or Duty may be imposed on such Importation, not exceeding ten dollars for each Person.

The Privilege of the Writ of Habeas Corpus shall not be suspended, unless when in Cases of Rebellion or Invasion the public Safety may require it.

No Bill of Attainder or ex post facto Law shall be passed.

No Capitation, or other direct, Tax shall be laid, unless in Proportion to the Census or Enumeration herein before directed to be taken.

No Tax or Duty shall be laid on Articles exported from any State.

No Preference shall be given by any Regulation of Commerce or Revenue to the Ports of one State over those of another; nor shall Vessels bound to, or from, one State, be obliged to enter, clear, or pay Duties in another.

No Money shall be drawn from the Treasury, but in Consequence of Appropriations made by Law; and a regular Statement and Account of the Receipts and Expenditures of all public Money shall be published from time to time.

No Title of Nobility shall be granted by the United States: and no Person holding any Office of Profit or Trust under them, shall, without the Consent of the Congress, accept of any present, Emolument, Office, or Title, of any kind whatever, from any King, Prince, or foreign State.

SEC. 10. No State shall enter into any Treaty, Alliance, or Confederation; grant Letters of Marque and Reprisal; coin Money; emit Bills of Credit; make any Thing but gold and silver Coin a Tender in Payment of Debts; pass any Bill of Attainder, ex post facto Law, or Law impairing the Obligation of Contracts, or grant any Title of Nobility.

No State shall, without the consent of the Congress, lay any Imposts or Duties on Imports or Exports, except what may be absolutely necessary for executing it's inspection Laws: and the net Produce of all Duties and Imposts, laid by any State on Imports or Exports, shall be for the Use of the Treasury of the United States; and all such Laws shall be subject to the Revision and Controul of the Congress.

No State shall, without the Consent of Congress, lay any Duty of Tonnage, keep Troops, or Ships of War in time of Peace, enter into any Agreement or Compact with another State, or with a foreign Power, or engage in War, unless actually invaded, or in such imminent Danger as will not admit of Delay.

ARTICLE II.

SEC. 1. The executive Power shall be vested in a President of the United States of America. He shall hold his Office during the Term of four Years, and, together with the Vice President, chosen for the same term, be elected as follows

Each State shall appoint, in such Manner as the Legislature thereof may direct, a Number of Electors, equal to the whole Number of Senators and Representatives to which the State may be entitled in the Congress: but no Senator or Representative, or person holding an Office of Trust or Profit under the United States, shall be appointed an Elector.

[The Electors shall meet in their respective States, and vote by Ballot for two Persons, of whom one at least shall not be an Inhabitant of the same State with themselves. And they shall make a list of all the Persons voted for, and of the Number of Votes for each; which List they shall sign and certify, and transmit sealed to the Seat of the Government of the United States, directed to the President of the Senate. The President of the Senate shall, in the Presence of the Senate and House of Representatives, open all the Certificates, and the Votes shall then be counted. The Person having the greatest Number of Votes shall be the President, if such Number be a Majority of the whole Number of Electors appointed; and if there be more than one who have such Majority, and have an equal Number of Votes, then the House of Representatives shall immediately chuse by Ballot one of them for President; and if no Person have a Majority, then from the five highest on the List the said House shall in like Manner chuse the President. But in chusing the President, the Votes shall be taken by States, the Representation from each State having one Vote; A Quorum for this Purpose shall consist of a Member or Members from two-thirds of the States, and a Majority of all the States shall be necessary to a Choice. In every Case, after the Choice of the President, the Person having the greatest Number of Votes of the Electors shall be the Vice President. But if there should remain two or more who have equal Votes, the Senate shall chuse from them by Ballot the Vice President.*]

The Congress may determine the Time of chusing the Electors, and the Day on which they shall give their Votes; which Day shall be the same throughout the United States.

No Person except a natural born Citizen, or a Citizen of the United States, at the time of the Adoption of this Constitution, shall be eligible to the Office of President; neither shall any Person be eligible to that Office who shall not have attained to the Age of thirty-five Years, and been fourteen Years a Resident within the United States.

In Case of the Removal of the President from Office, or of his Death, Resignation, or Inability

* This clause of the Constitution has been annulled. See twelfth article of the Amendments.

to discharge the Powers and Duties of the said Office, the same shall devolve on the Vice President, and the Congress may by Law provide for the Case of Removal, Death, Resignation, or Inability, both of the President and Vice President, declaring what Officer shall then act as President, and such Officer shall act accordingly, until the Disability be removed, or a President shall be elected.

The President shall, at stated Times, receive for his Services, a Compensation, which shall neither be encreased nor diminished during the Period for which he shall have been elected, and he shall not receive within that Period any other Emolument from the United States, or any of them.

Before he enter on the Execution of his Office, he shall take the following Oath or Affirmation:—

"I do solemnly swear (or affirm) that I will faithfully execute the Office of President of the United States, and will to the best of my Ability, preserve, protect and defend the Constitution of the United States."

Sec. 2. The President shall be Commander in Chief of the Army and Navy of the United States, and of the Militia of the several States, when called into the actual Service of the United States; he may require the Opinion, in writing, of the principal Officer in each of the executive Departments, upon any Subject relating to the Duties of their respective Offices, and he shall have Power to grant Reprieves and Pardons for Offences against the United States, except in Cases of Impeachment.

He shall have Power, by and with the Advice and Consent of the Senate, to make Treaties, provided two thirds of the Senators present concur; and he shall nominate, and by and with the Advice and Consent of the Senate, shall appoint Ambassadors, other public Ministers and Consuls, Judges of the supreme Court, and all other Officers of the United States, whose Appointments are not herein otherwise provided for, and which shall be established by Law: but the Congress may by Law vest the Appointment of such inferior Officers, as they think proper, in the President alone, in the Courts of Law, or in the Heads of Departments.

The President shall have Power to fill up all Vacancies that may happen during the Recess of the Senate, by granting Commissions which shall expire at the End of their next Session.

Sec. 3. He shall from time to time give to the Congress Information of the State of the Union, and recommend to their Consideration such Measures as he shall judge necessary and expedient; he may, on extraordinary Occasions, convene both Houses, or either of them, and in Case of Disagreement between them, with Respect to the Time of Adjournment, he may adjourn them to such Time as he shall think proper; he shall receive Ambassadors and other public Ministers; and he shall take Care that the Laws be faithfully executed, and he shall Commission all the officers of the United States.

Sec. 4. The President, Vice President and all civil Officers of the United States, shall be removed from Office on Impeachment for, and Conviction of, Treason, Bribery, or other high Crimes and Misdemeanors.

Article III.

Sec. 1. The judicial Power of the United States, shall be vested in one supreme Court, and in such inferior Courts as the Congress may from time to time ordain and establish. The Judges, both of the supreme and inferior Courts, shall hold their Offices during good Behavior, and shall, at stated Times, receive for their Services, a Compensation, which shall not be diminished during their Continuance in Office.

Sec. 2. The judicial Power shall extend to all cases, in Law and Equity, arising under this Constitution, the Laws of the United States, and Treaties made, or which shall be made, under their Authority;—to all Cases affecting Ambassadors, other public Ministers, and Consuls;—to all Cases of admiralty and maritime Jurisdiction;—to Controversies to which the United States shall be a Party;—to Controversies between two or more States;—between a State and Citizens of another State;—between Citizens of different States,—between Citizens of the same State claiming Lands under Grants of different States, and between a State or the Citizens thereof, and foreign States, Citizens or Subjects.

In all Cases affecting Ambassadors, other public Ministers and Consuls, and those in which a State shall be Party, the supreme Court shall have original Jurisdiction. In all the other Cases before mentioned, the supreme Court shall have appellate Jurisdiction, both as to Law and Fact, with such Exceptions, and under such Regulations as the Congress shall make.

The Trial of all Crimes, except in Cases of Impeachment, shall be by Jury; and such Trial shall be held in the State where the said Crimes shall have been committed; but when not committed within any State, the Trial shall be at such Place or Places as the Congress may by Law have directed.

Sec. 3. Treason against the United States, shall consist only in levying War against them, or in adhering to their Enemies, giving them Aid and Comfort. No Person shall be convicted of Treason unless on the Testimony of two Witnesses to the same overt Act, or on Confession in open Court.

The Congress shall have Power to declare the Punishment of Treason, but no Attainder of Treason shall work Corruption of Blood, or Forfeiture except during the Life of the Person attainted.

Article IV.

Sec. 1. Full Faith and Credit shall by given in each State to the public Acts, Records, and judicial Proceedings of every other State. And the Congress may by general Laws prescribe the Manner in which such Acts, Records and Proceedings shall be proved, and the Effect thereof.

Sec. 2. The Citizens of each State shall be entitled to all Privileges and Immunities of Citizens in the several States.

A Person charged in any State with Treason, Felony, or other Crime, who shall flee from Justice, and be found in another State, shall on Demand of the executive Authority of the State from which he fled, be delivered up, to be removed to the State having Jurisdiction of the Crime.

No Person held to Service or Labour in one

State, under the Laws thereof, escaping into another, shall, in Consequence of any Law or Regulation therein, be discharged from such Service or Labour, but shall be delivered up on Claim of the Party to whom such Service or Labour may be due.

SEC. 3. New States may be admitted by the Congress into this Union; but no new State shall be formed or erected within the Jurisdiction of any other State; nor any State formed by the Junction of two or more States, or Parts of States, without the Consent of the Legislatures of the States concerned as well as of the Congress.

The Congress shall have Power to dispose of and make all needful Rules and Regulations respecting the Territory or other Property belonging to the United States; and nothing in this Constitution shall be so construed as to Prejudice any Claims of the United States, or of any particular State.

SEC. 4. The United States shall guarantee to every State in this Union a Republican Form of Government, and shall protect each of them against Invasion; and on Application of the Legislature, or of the Executive (when the Leislature cannot be convened) against domestic Violence.

ARTICLE V.

The Congress, whenever two thirds of both Houses shall deem it necessary, shall propose Amendments to this Constitution, or, on the Application of the Legislatures of two thirds of the several States, shall call a Convention for proposing Amendments, which, in either Case, shall be valid to all Intents and Purposes, as Part of this Constitution, when ratified by the Legislatures of three fourths of the several States, or by Conventions in three fourths thereof, as the one or the other Mode of Ratification may be proposed by the Congress; Provided that no Amendment which may be made prior to the Year one thousand eight hundred and eight shall in any Manner affect the first and fourth Clauses in the Ninth Section of the first Article; and that no State, without its Consent, shall be deprived of its equal Suffrage in the Senate.

ARTICLE VI.

All Debts contracted and Engagements entered into, before the Adoption of this Constitution, shall be as valid against the United States under this Constitution, as under the Confederation.

This Constitution, and the Laws of the United States which shall be made in Pursuance thereof; and all Treaties made, or which shall be made, under the authority of the United States, shall be the supreme Law of the Land; and the Judges in every State shall be bound thereby, any Thing in the Constitution or Laws of any State to the Contrary notwithstanding.

The Senators and Representatives before mentioned, and the Members of the several State Legislatures, and all executive and judicial Officers, both of the United States and of the several States, shall be bound by Oath or Affirmation, to support this Constitution; but no religious Test shall ever be required as a Qualification to any Office or public Trust under the United States.

ARTICLE VII.

The Ratification of the Conventions of nine States, shall be sufficient for the Establishment of this Constitution between the States so ratifying the Same.

Amendments.

ART. 1. Congress shall make no law respecting an establishment of religion, or prohibiting the free exercise thereof; or abridging the freedom of speech, or of the press; or the right of the people peaceably to assemble, and to petition the Government for a redress of grievances.

ART. 2. A well regulated Militia, being necessary to the security of a free State, the right of the people to keep and bear Arms, shall not be infringed.

ART. 3. No Soldier shall, in time of peace be quartered in any house, without the consent of the Owner, nor in time of war, but in a manner to be prescribed by law.

ART. 4. The right of the people to be secure in their persons, houses, papers, and effects, against unreasonable searches and seizures, shall not be violated, and no Warrants shall issue, but upon probable cause, supported by Oath or affirmation, and particularly describing the place to be searched, and the persons or things to be seized.

ART. 5. No person shall be held to answer for a capital, or otherwise infamous crime, unless on a presentment or indictment of a Grand Jury, except in cases arising in the land or naval forces, or in the Militia, when in actual service in time of War or public danger; nor shall any person be subject for the same offence to be twice put in jeopardy of life or limb; nor shall be compelled in any Criminal Case to be a witness against himself, nor be deprived of life, liberty, or property, without due process of law; nor shall private property be taken for public use, without just compensation.

ART. 6. In all criminal prosecutions, the accused shall enjoy the right to a speedy and public trial, by an impartial jury of the State and district wherein the crime shall have been committed, which district shall have been previously ascertained by law, and to be informed of the nature and cause of the accusation; to be confronted with the witnesses against him; to have Compulsory process for obtaining Witnesses in his favour, and to have the Assistance of Counsel for his defence.

ART. 7. In Suits at common law, where the value in controversy shall exceed twenty dollars, the right of trial by jury shall be preserved, and no fact tried by a jury shall be otherwise re-examined in any Court of the United States, than according to the rules of the common law.

ART. 8. Excessive bail shall not be required, nor excessive fines be imposed, nor cruel and unusual punishments inflicted.

ART. 9. The enumeration in the Constitution, of certain rights, shall not be construed to deny or disparage others retained by the people.

ART. 10. The powers not delegated to the United States by the Constitution, nor prohibited by it to the States, are reserved to the States respectively, or to the people.

ART. 11. The Judicial power of the United

States shall not be construed to extend to any suit in law or equity, commenced or prosecuted against one of the United States by Citizens of another State, or by Citizens or Subjects of any Foreign State.

ART. 12. The Electors shall meet in their respective states, and vote by ballot for President and Vice-President, one of whom, at least, shall not be an inhabitant of the same state with themselves; they shall name in their ballots the person voted for as President, and in distinct ballots the person voted for as Vice-President, and they shall make distinct lists of all persons voted for as President, and of all persons voted for as Vice-President, and of the number of votes for each, which lists they shall sign and certify, and transmit sealed to the seat of the government of the United States, directed to the President of the Senate;—The President of the Senate shall, in presence of the Senate and House of Representatives, open all the certificates and the votes shall then be counted;—The person having the greatest number of votes for President, shall be the President, if such number be a majority of the whole number of Electors appointed; and if no person have such majority, then from the persons having the highest numbers not exceeding three on the list of those voted for as President, the House of Representatives shall choose immediately, by ballot, the President. But in choosing the President, the votes shall be taken by states, the representation from each state having one vote; a quorum for this purpose shall consist of a member or members from two thirds of the states, and a majority of all the states shall be necessary to a choice. And if the House of Representatives shall not choose a President whenever the right of choice shall devolve upon them, before the fourth day of March next following, then the Vice-President shall act as President, as in the case of the death or other constitutional disability of the President. The person having the greatest number of votes as Vice-President, shall be the Vice-President, if such number be a majority of the whole number of Electors appointed, and if no person have a majority, then from the two highest numbers on the list, the Senate shall choose the Vice-President; a quorum for the purpose shall consist of two thirds of the whole number of Senators, and a majority of the whole number shall be necessary to a choice. But no person constitutionally ineligible to the office of President shall be eligible to that of Vice-President of the United States.

Mr. Seward's Certificate of the Anti-Slavery Amendment, known as the 13th Amendment.

WILLIAM H. SEWARD, SECRETARY OF STATE OF THE UNITED STATES,

To all to whom these presents may come, greeting:

Know ye, that whereas the Congress of the United States on the 1st of February last passed a resolution which is in the words following, namely:

"A resolution submitting to the Legislatures of the several States a proposition to amend the Constitution of the United States.

"*Resolved by the Senate and House of Representatives of the United States of America in Congress assembled, (two-thirds of both Houses concurring,)* That the following article be proposed to the Legislatures of the several States as an amendment to the Constitution of the United States, which, when ratified by three fourths of said Legislatures, shall be valid, to all intents and purposes, as a part of the said Constitution, namely:

ARTICLE XIII.

"SEC. 1. Neither slavery nor involuntary servitude, except as a punishment for crime, whereof the party shall have been duly convicted, shall exist within the United States, or any place subject to their jurisdiction.

"SEC. 2. Congress shall have power to enforce this article by appropriate legislation."

And whereas it appears from official documents on file in this Department that the amendment to the Constitution of the United States, proposed as aforesaid, has been ratified by the Legislatures of the States of Illinois, Rhode Island, Michigan, Maryland, New York, West Virginia, Maine, Kansas, Massachusetts, Pennsylvania, Virginia, Ohio, Missouri, Nevada, Indiana, Louisiana, Minnesota, Wisconsin, Vermont, Tennessee, Arkansas, Connecticut, New Hampshire, South Carolina, Alabama, North Carolina, and Georgia—in all, twenty-seven States;

And whereas the whole number of States in the United States is thirty-six, and whereas the before specially-named States, whose Legislatures have ratified the said proposed amendment, constitute three-fourths of the whole number of States in the United States:

Now, therefore, be it known that I, William H. Seward, Secretary of State of the United States, by virtue and in pursuance of the second section of the act of Congress approved the twentieth of April, eighteen hundred and eighteen, entitled "An act to provide for the publication of the laws of the United States and for other purposes," do hereby certify that the amendment aforesaid has become valid, to all intents and purposes, as a part of the Constitution of the United States.

In testimony whereof I have hereunto set my hand and caused the seal of the Department of State to be affixed.

Done at the city of Washington this eighteenth day of December, in the year of our Lord [SEAL] one thousand eight hundred and sixty-five, and of the Independence of the United States of America the ninetieth.

WILLIAM H. SEWARD,
Secretary of State.

[New Jersey, Oregon, California and Iowa ratified subsequently to the date of this certificate, as did Florida in the same form as South Carolina and Alabama.]

II.

PRESIDENT JOHNSON'S ORDERS AND PROCLAMATIONS.

Respecting Commercial Intercourse with Insurrectionary States, April 29, 1865.

EXECUTIVE CHAMBER,
WASHINGTON, *April* 29, 1865.

Being desirous to relieve all loyal citizens and well-disposed persons, residing in insurrectionary States, from unnecessary commercial restrictions, and to encourage them to return to peaceful pursuits, *It is hereby ordered:*

I. That all restrictions upon internal, domestic, and coastwise commercial intercourse be discontinued in such parts of the States of Tennessee, Virginia, North Carolina, South Carolina, Georgia, Florida, Alabama, Mississippi, and so much of Louisiana as lies east of the Mississippi river, as shall be embraced within the lines of national military occupation, excepting only such restrictions as are imposed by acts of Congress and regulations in pursuance thereof, prescribed by the Secretary of the Treasury, and approved by the President; and excepting also from the effect of this order the following articles contraband of war, to wit: arms, ammunition, all articles from which ammunition is manufactured, gray uniforms and cloth, locomotives, cars, railroad iron, and machinery for operating railroads, telegraph wires, insulators, and instruments for operating telegraphic lines.

II. All existing military and naval orders in any manner restricting internal, domestic, and coastwise commercial intercourse and trade with or in the localities above named be, and the same are hereby revoked; and that no military or naval officer, in any manner, interrupt or interfere with the same, or with any boats or other vessels engaged therein, under proper authority, pursuant to the regulations of the Secretary of the Treasury.

ANDREW JOHNSON.

Executive Order for the Trial of the Alleged Assassins of President Lincoln, May 1, 1865.

EXECUTIVE CHAMBER,
WASHINGTON CITY, *May* 1, 1865.

Whereas, the Attorney General of the United States hath given his opinion:

That the persons implicated in the murder of the late President, Abraham Lincoln, and the attempted assassination of the Honorable William H. Seward, Secretary of State, and in an alleged conspiracy to assassinate other officers of the Federal Government at Washington city, and their aiders and abettors, are subject to the jurisdiction of, and lawfully triable before, a military commission:

It is *Ordered*: 1st, That the Assistant Adjutant General detail nine competent military officers to serve as a commission for the trial of said parties, and that the Judge Advocate General proceed to prefer charges against said parties for their alleged offences, and bring them to trial before said military commission; that said trial or trials be conducted by the said Judge Advocate General, and as recorder thereof, in person, aided by such assistant and special judge advocates as he may designate; and that said trials be conducted with all diligence consistent with the ends of justice: the said commission to sit without regard to hours.

2d. That Brevet Major General Hartranft be assigned to duty as special provost marshal general, for the purpose of said trial, and attendance upon said commission, and the execution of its mandates.

3d. That the said commission establish such order or rules of proceedings as may avoid unnecessary delay, and conduce to the ends of public justice.

ANDREW JOHNSON.

ORDER FOR THE EXECUTION OF THE SENTENCE OF THE COMMISSION.

EXECUTIVE MANSION, *July* 5, 1865.

The foregoing sentences in the cases of David E. Herold, G. A. Atzerodt, Lewis Payne, Michael O'Laughlin, Edward Spangler, Samuel Arnold, Mary E. Surratt and Samuel A. Mudd, are hereby approved, and it is ordered that the sentences of said David E. Herold, G. A. Atzerodt, Lewis Payne, Mary E. Surratt and Samuel A. Mudd, be carried into execution by the proper military authority, under the direction of the Secretary of War, on the 7th day of July, 1865, between the hours of 10 o'clock, a. m., and 2 o'clock, p. m., of that day. It is further ordered, that the prisoners, Samuel Arnold, Samuel A. Mudd, Edward Spangler, and Michael O'Laughlin be confined at hard labor in the Penitentiary at Albany, New York, during the period designated in their respective sentences.

ANDREW JOHNSON, *President*,

[By an order dated July 15, the place of confinement, as to the four last mentioned, was changed to the "military prison at Dry Tortugas, Florida."]

For the Arrest of Jefferson Davis, Clement C. Clay, and others, May 2, 1865.

Whereas it appears from evidence in the Bureau of Military Justice that the atrocious murder of the late President, Abraham Lincoln, and the attempted assassination of the Honorable William H. Seward, Secretary of State, were incited, concerted, and procured by and between Jefferson Davis, late of Richmond, Virginia, and Jacob Thompson, Clement C. Clay, Beverly Tucker, George N. Saunders, William C. Cleary, and other rebels and traitors against the Government of the United States, harbored in Canada:

Now, therefore, to the end that justice may be done, I, Andrew Johnson, President of the United States, do offer and promise for the arrest of said persons, or either of them, within the limits of the United States, so that they can be brought to trial, the following rewards:

One hundred thousand dollars for the arrest of Jefferson Davis.

Twenty-five thousand dollars for the arrest of Clement C. Clay.*

Twenty-five thousand dollars for the arrest of Jacob Thompson, late of Mississippi.

Twenty-five thousand dollars for the arrest of George N. Sanders.

Twenty-five thousand dollars for the arrest of Beverly Tucker.

Ten thousand dollars for the arrest of William C. Cleary, late clerk of Clement C. Clay.

The Provost Marshal General of the United States is directed to cause a description of said persons, with notice of the above rewards, to be published.

In testimony whereof, I have hereunto set my hand and caused the seal of the United States to be affixed.

Done at the city of Washington this second day of May, in the year of our Lord one thousand eight hundred and sixty-five, and of the Independence of the United States of America the eighty-ninth.

[L. S.]

ANDREW JOHNSON.

By the President:

W. HUNTER, Acting Secretary of State.

Executive Order to Re-establish the Authority of the United States, and Execute the Laws within the Geographical Limits known as the State of Virginia.

EXECUTIVE CHAMBER,
WASHINGTON CITY, *May* 9, 1865.

ORDERED—*First*. That all acts and proceedings of the political, military, and civil organizations which have been in a state of insurrection and rebellion, within the State of Virginia, against the authority and laws of the United States, and of which Jefferson Davis, John Letcher, and William Smith were late the respective chiefs, are declared null and void. All persons who shall exercise, claim, pretend, or attempt to exercise any political, military, or civil power, authority, jurisdiction, or right, by, through, or under Jefferson Davis, late of the city of Richmond, and his confederates, or under John Letcher or William Smith and their confederates, or under any pretended political, military, or civil commission or authority issued by them, or either of them, since the 17th day of April, 1861, shall be deemed and taken as in rebellion against the United States, and shall be dealt with accordingly.

Second. That the Secretary of State proceed to put in force all laws of the United States, the administration whereof belongs to the Department of State, applicable to the geographical limits aforesaid.

Third. That the Secretary of the Treasury proceed, without delay, to nominate for appointment, assessors of taxes and collectors of customs and internal revenue, and such other officers of the Treasury Department as are authorized by law, and shall put into execution the revenue laws of the United States within the geographical limits aforesaid. In making appointments, the preference shall be given to qualified loyal persons residing within the districts where their respective duties are to be performed. But if suitable persons shall not be found residents of the districts, then persons residing in other States or districts shall be appointed.

Fourth. That the Postmaster General shall proceed to establish post offices and post routes, and put into execution the postal laws of the United States within the said States, giving to loyal residents the preference of appointment; but if suitable persons are not found, then to appoint agents, &c., from other States.

Fifth. That the district judge of said district proceed to hold courts within said State, in accordance with the provisions of the acts of Congress. The Attorney General will instruct the proper officers to libel and bring to judgment, confiscation, and sale, property subject to confiscation, and enforce the administration of justice within said State, in all matters civil and criminal within the cognizance and jurisdiction of the Federal courts.

Sixth. That the Secretary of War assign such assistant provost marshal general, and such provost marshals in each district of said State as he may deem necessary.

Seventh. The Secretary of the Navy will take possession of all public property belonging to the Navy Department within said geographical limits, and put in operation all acts of Congress in relation to naval affairs having application to the said State.

Eighth. The Secretary of the Interior will also put in force the laws relating to the Department of the Interior.

Ninth. That to carry into effect the guarantee of the Federal Constitution of a republican form of State government, and afford the advantage and security of domestic laws, as well as to complete the re-establishment of the authority of the laws of the United States, and the full and complete restoration of peace within the limits aforesaid, Francis H. Pierpoint, Governor of the State of Virginia, will be aided by the Federal Government, so far as may be necessary, in the lawful measures which he may take for the extension and administration of the State Government throughout the geographical limits of said State.

*Mr. CLAY was released under this order:

WAR DEPARTMENT, ADJUTANT GENERAL'S OFFICE,
WASHINGTON, *April* 17, 1866.

Maj. Gen. N. A. MILES, *Commanding, &c., Fortress Monroe, Virginia:*

Ordered, That Clement C. Clay, Jr., is hereby released from confinement, and permitted to return to and remain in the State of Alabama, and to visit such other places in the United States as his personal business may render absolutely necessary, upon the following conditions, viz: that he takes the oath of allegiance to the United States, and gives his parole of honor to conduct himself as a loyal citizen of the same, and to report himself in person at any time and place to answer any charges that may hereafter be prepared against him by the United States.

Please report receipt and execution of this order.

By order of the President of the United States:

E. D. TOWNSEND,
Assistant Adjutant General.

In testimony whereof, I have hereunto set my hand and caused the seal of the United States to be affixed. [SEAL.]

ANDREW JOHNSON.

By the President:

W. HUNTER, *Acting Secretary of State.*

Equality of Rights with all Maritime Nations, May 10, 1865.

Whereas the President of the United States, by his proclamation of the nineteenth day of April, one thousand eight hundred and sixty-one, did declare certain States therein mentioned in insurrection against the Government of the United States;

And whereas armed resistance to the authority of this Government in the said insurrectionary States may be regarded as virtually at an end, and the persons by whom that resistance, as well as the operations of insurgent cruisers, were directed, are fugitives or captives;

And whereas it is understood that some of those cruisers are still infesting the high seas, and others are preparing to capture, burn, and destroy vessels of the United States:

Now, therefore, be it known, that I, Andrew Johnson, President of the United States, hereby enjoin all naval, military, and civil officers of the United States, diligently to endeavor, by all lawful means, to arrest the said cruisers, and to bring them into a port of the United States, in order that they may be prevented from committing further depredations on commerce, and that the persons on board of them may no longer enjoy impunity for their crimes.

And I further proclaim and declare, that if, after a reasonable time shall have elapsed for this proclamation to become known in the ports of nations claiming to have been neutrals, the said insurgent cruisers and the persons on board of them shall continue to receive hospitality in the said ports, this Government will deem itself justified in refusing hospitality to the public vessels of such nations in ports of the United States, and in adopting such other measures as may be deemed advisable towards vindicating the national sovereignty.

In witness whereof, I have hereunto set my hand and caused the seal of the United States to be affixed.

Done at the city of Washington, this tenth day of May, in the year of our Lord one thousand eight hundred and sixty-five, and of the independence of the United States of America the eighty-ninth. [L. S.]

ANDREW JOHNSON.

By the President:

W. HUNTER, *Acting Secretary of State.*

Commercial Intercourse and the Blockade, May 22, 1865.

Whereas, by the proclamation of the President of the eleventh day of April last, certain ports of the United States therein specified, which had previously been subject to blockade, were, for objects of public safety, declared, in conformity with previous special legislation of Congress, to be closed against foreign commerce during the national will, to be thereafter expressed and made known by the President; and whereas events and circumstances have since occurred which, in my judgment, render it expedient to remove that restriction, except as to the ports of Galveston, La Salle, Brazos de Santiago (Point Isabel,) and Brownsville, in the State of Texas:

Now, therefore, be it known that I, Andrew Johnson, President of the United States, do hereby declare that the ports aforesaid, not excepted as above, shall be open to foreign commerce from and after the first day of July, next; that commercial intercourse with the said ports may, from that time, be carried on, subject to the laws of the United States, and in pursuance of such regulations as may be prescribed by the Secretary of the Treasury. If, however, any vessel from a foreign port shall enter any of the before-named excepted ports in the State of Texas, she will continue to be held liable to the penalties prescribed by the act of Congress approved on the thirteenth day of July, eighteen hundred and sixty-one, and the persons on board of her to such penalties as may be incurred, pursuant to the laws of war, for trading, or attempting to trade, with an enemy.

And I, Andrew Johnson, President of the United States, do hereby declare and make known that the United States of America do, henceforth, disallow to all persons trading, or attempting to trade, in any ports of the United States in violation of the laws thereof, all pretence of belligerent rights and privileges, and I give notice that, from the date of this proclamation, all such offenders will be held and dealt with as pirates.

It is also ordered that all restrictions upon trade heretofore imposed in the territory of the United States east of the Mississippi river, save those relating to contraband of war, to the reservation of the rights of the United States to property purchased in the territory of an enemy, and to the twenty-five per cent. upon purchases of cotton, are removed. All provisions of the internal revenue law will be carried into effect under the proper officers.

In witness whereof I have hereunto set my hand and caused the seal of the United States to be affixed.

Done at the city of Washington, this twenty-second day of May, in the year of our Lord one thousand eight hundred and sixty-five, and of the Independence of the United States of America the eighty-ninth. [SEAL.]

ANDREW JOHNSON.

By the President:

W. HUNTER, *Acting Secretary of State.*

Of Amnesty, May 29, 1865.

WHEREAS the President of the United States, on the 8th day of December, A. D. eighteen hundred and sixty-three, and on the 26th day of March, A. D. eighteen hundred and sixty-four, did, with the object to suppress the existing rebellion, to induce all persons to return to their loyalty, and to restore the authority of the United States, issue proclamations offering amnesty and pardon to certain persons who had directly, or by implication, participated in the said rebellion; and whereas many persons who had so engaged in said rebellion, have, since the issuance of said proclamations, failed or neglected to take the benefits offered thereby; and whereas many persons who have been justly deprived of all claim to amnesty and pardon thereunder by reason of their participation, directly or by implication, in said rebellion, and continued hostility to the Government of the United States since the date of said proclamations, now desire to apply for and obtain amnesty and pardon:

To the end, therefore, that the authority of the Government of the United States may be restored, and that peace, order, and freedom may be established, I, Andrew Johnson, President of the United States, do proclaim and declare that I hereby grant to all persons who have, directly or indirectly, participated in the existing rebellion, except as hereinafter excepted, amnesty and pardon, with restoration of all rights of property, except as to slaves, and except in cases where legal proceedings, under the laws of the United States providing for the confiscation of property of persons engaged in rebellion, have been instituted; but upon the condition, nevertheless, that every such person shall take and subscribe the following oath (or affirmation), and thenceforward keep and maintain said oath inviolate; and which oath shall be registered for permanent preservation, and shall be of the tenor and effect following, to wit:

"I, ——— ———, do solemnly swear (or affirm), in presence of Almighty God, that I will henceforth faithfully support, protect, and defend the Constitution of the United States, and the union of the States thereunder; and that I will, in like manner, abide by and faithfully support all laws and proclamations which have been made during the existing rebellion, with reference to the emancipation of slaves: So help me God."

The following classes of persons are excepted from the benefits of this proclamation:

1st. All who are or shall have been pretended civil or diplomatic officers or otherwise domestic or foreign agents of the pretended government.

2d. All who left judicial stations under the United States to aid the rebellion.

3d. All who shall have been military or naval officers of said pretended confederate government above the rank of colonel in the army, or lieutenant in the navy.

4th. All who left seats in the Congress of the United States to aid the rebellion.

5th. All who resigned or tendered resignations of their commissions in the army or navy of the United States, to evade duty in resisting the rebellion.

6th. All who have engaged in any way in treating otherwise than lawfully as prisoners of war, persons found in the United States service as officers, soldiers, seamen, or in other capacities.

7th. All persons who have been or are absentees from the United States for the purpose of aiding the rebellion.

8th. All military and naval officers, in the rebel service, who were educated by the Government in the Military Academy at West Point or the United States Naval Academy.

9th. All persons who held the pretended offices of governors of States in insurrection against the United States.

10th. All persons who left their homes within the jurisdiction and protection of the United States, and passed beyond the Federal military lines into the pretended confederate States for the purpose of aiding the rebellion.

11th. All persons who have been engaged in the destruction of the commerce of the United States upon the high seas, and all persons who have made raids into the United States from Canada, or been engaged in destroying the commerce of the United States upon the lakes and rivers that separate the British Provinces from the United States.

12th. All persons who, at the time when they seek to obtain the benefits hereof by taking the oath herein prescribed, are in military, naval, or civil confinement, or custody, or under bonds of the civil, military, or naval authorities, or agents of the United States, as prisoners of war, or persons detained for offences of any kind, either before or after conviction.

13th. All persons who have voluntarily participated in said rebellion, and the estimated value of whose taxable property is over twenty thousand dollars.

14th. All persons who have taken the oath of amnesty as prescribed in the President's proclamation of December 8, A. D. 1863, or an oath of allegiance to the Government of the United States since the date of said proclamation, and who thenceforward kept and maintained the same inviolate.

Provided, That special application may be made to the President for pardon by any person belonging to the excepted classes; and such clemency will be liberally extended as may be consistent with the facts of the case and the peace and dignity of the United States.

The Secretary of State will establish rules and regulations for administering and recording said amnesty oath, so as to insure its benefit to the people, and guard the Government against fraud.

In testimony whereof, I have hereunto set my hand, and caused the seal of the United States to be affixed.

Done at the City of Washington, the twenty-ninth day of May, in the year of our Lord one thousand eight hundred and sixty-five, andof the Independence of the United States the eighty-ninth.

[SEAL.]

ANDREW JOHNSON.

By the President:

WILLIAM H. SEWARD, *Secretary of State.*

CIRCULAR.

DEPARTMENT OF STATE,
WASHINGTON, *May* 29, 1865.

SIR: A copy of the President's amnesty proclamation of this date is herewith appended. By a clause in the instrument, the Secretary of State is directed to establish rules and regulations for administering and recording the amnesty oath, so as to insure its benefit to the people and guard the Government against fraud. Pursuant to this injunction, you are informed that the oath prescribed in the proclamation may be taken and subscribed before any commissioned officer, civil, military, or naval, in the service of the United States, or any civil or military officer of a loyal State or Territory, who, by the laws thereof, may be qualified for administering oaths. All officers who receive such oaths are hereby authorized to give certified copies thereof to the persons respectively by whom they were made. And such officers are hereby required to transmit the originals of such oaths, at as early a day as may be convenient, to this Department, where they will be deposited, and remain in the archives of the Government. A register thereof will be kept in the Department, and on application, in proper cases, certificates will be issued of such records in the customary form of official certificates.

I am, sir, your obedient servant,

WILLIAM H. SEWARD.

Appointing William W. Holden Provisional Governor of North Carolina, May 29, 1865.

Whereas the fourth section of the fourth article of the Constitution of the United States declares that the United States shall guarantee to every State in the Union a republican form of government, and shall protect each of them against invasion and domestic violence; and whereas the President of the United States is, by the Constitution, made commander-in-chief of the army and navy, as well as chief civil executive officer of the United States, and is bound by solemn oath faithfully to execute the office of President of the United States, and to take care that the laws be faithfully executed; and whereas the rebellion, which has been waged by a portion of the people of the United States against the properly constituted authorities of the Government thereof, in the most violent and revolting form, but whose organized and armed forces have now been almost entirely overcome, has, in its revolutionary progress, deprived the people of the State of North Carolina of all civil government; and whereas it becomes necessary and proper to carry out and enforce the obligations of the United States to the people of North Carolina, in securing them in the enjoyment of a republican form of government:

Now, therefore, in obedience to the high and solemn duties imposed upon me by the Constitution of the United States, and for the purpose of enabling the loyal people of said State to organize a State government, whereby justice may be established, domestic tranquillity insured, and loyal citizens protected in all their rights of life, liberty, and property, I, Andrew Johnson, President of the United States, and Commander-in-Chief of the army and navy of the United States, do hereby appoint William W. Holden Provisional Governor of the State of North Carolina, whose duty it shall be, at the earliest practicable period, to prescribe such rules and regulations as may be necessary and proper for convening a convention, composed of delegates to be chosen by that portion of the people of said State who are loyal to the United States, and no others, for the purpose of altering or amending the constitution thereof; and with authority to exercise, within the limits of said State, all the powers necessary and proper to enable such loyal people of the State of North Carolina to restore said State to its constitutional relations to the Federal Government, and to present such a republican form of State government as will entitle the State to the guarantee of the United States therefor, and its people to protection by the United States against invasion, insurrection, and domestic violence; *Provided*, that in any election that may be hereafter held for choosing delegates to any State convention, as aforesaid, no person shall be qualified as an elector, or shall be eligible as a member of such convention, unless he shall have previously taken the oath of amnesty, as set forth in the President's proclamation of May 29, A. D. 1865, and is a voter qualified as prescribed by the Constitution and laws of the State of North Carolina, in force immediately before the 20th day of May, 1861, the date of the so-called ordinance of secession; and the said convention when convened, or the Legislature that may be thereafter assembled, will prescribe the qualification of electors, and the eligibility of persons to hold office under the Constitution and laws of the State, a power the people of the several States composing the Federal Union have rightfully exercised from the origin of the Government to the present time.

And I do hereby direct:

First. That the military commander of the Department, and all officers and persons in the military and naval service aid and assist the said Provisional Governor in carrying into effect this proclamation, and they are enjoined to abstain from, in any way, hindering, impeding, or discouraging the loyal people from the organization of a State Government, as herein authorized.

Second. That the Secretary of State proceed to put in force all laws of the United States, the administration whereof belongs to the State Department, applicable to the geographical limits aforesaid.

Third. That the Secretary of the Treasury proceed to nominate for appointment assessors of taxes and collectors of customs and internal revenue, and such other officers of the Treasury Department as are authorized by law, and put in execution the revenue laws of the United States within the geographical limits aforesaid. In making appointments, the preference shall be given to qualified loyal persons residing within the districts where their respective duties are to be performed. But, if suitable residents of the districts shall not be found, then persons residing in other States or districts shall be appointed.

Fourth. That the Postmaster General proceed to establish post offices and post routes, and put into execution the postal laws of the United States within the said State, giving to loyal residents the preference of appointment; but if suitable residents are not found, then to appoint agents, &c., from other States.

Fifth. That the district judge for the judicial district in which North Carolina is included proceed to hold courts within said State, in accordance with the provisions of the act of Congress. The Attorney General will instruct the proper officers to libel, and bring to judgment, confiscation and sale, property subject to confiscation, and enforce the administration of justice within said State in all matters within the cognizance and jurisdiction of the Federal courts.

Sixth. That the Secretary of the Navy take possession of all public property belonging to the Navy Department, within said geographical limits, and put in operation all acts of Congress in relation to naval affairs having application to the said State.

Seventh. That the Secretary of the Interior put in force the laws relating to the Interior Department, applicable to the geographical limits aforesaid.

In testimony whereof, I have hereunto set my hand and caused the great seal of the United States to be affixed.

[L. S.] Done at the city of Washington, this twenty-ninth day of May, in the year of our Lord one thousand eight hundred and sixty-five, and of the Independence of the United States the eighty-ninth.

ANDREW JOHNSON.

By the President:

WILLIAM H. SEWARD, *Secretary of State.*

1865, June 13—A like proclamation was issued, appointing WILLIAM L. SHARKEY, Provisional Governor of Mississippi.

1865, June 17—JAMES JOHNSON appointed Provisional Governor of Georgia.

1865, June 17—ANDREW J. HAMILTON appointed Provisional Governor of Texas.

1865, June 21—LEWIS E. PARSONS appointed Provisional Governor of Alabama.

1865, June 30—BENJAMIN F. PERRY appointed Provisional Governor of South Carolina.

1865, July 13—WILLIAM MARVIN appointed Provisional Governor of Florida.

Orders Respecting Freedmen.

EXECUTIVE MANSION,
WASHINGTON, D. C., *June* 2, 1865.

Whereas, By an act of Congress, approved March 3, 1865, there was established in the War Department a Bureau of Refugees, Freedmen, and Abandoned Lands, and to which, in accordance with the said act of Congress, is committed the supervision and management of all abandoned lands, and the control of all subjects relating to refugees and freedmen from rebel States, or from any district of country within the territory embraced in the operations of the army, under such rules and regulations as may be prescribed by the head of the bureau, and approved by the President; and whereas, it appears that the management of abandoned lands, and subjects relating to refugees and freedmen, as aforesaid, have been, and still are, by orders based on military exigencies, or legislation based on previous statutes, partly in the hands of military officers disconnected with said bureau, and partly in charge of officers of the Treasury Department; it is therefore *Ordered*, That all officers of the Treasury Department, all military officers and others in the service of the United States, turn over to the authorized officers of said bureau all abandoned lands and property contemplated in said act of Congress, approved March third, eighteen hundred and sixty-five, establishing the Bureau of Refugees, Freedmen, and Abandoned Lands, that may now be under or within their control. They will also turn over to such officers all funds collected by tax or otherwise for the benefit of refugees or freedmen, or accruing from abandoned lands or property set apart for their use, and will transfer to them all official records connected with the administration of affairs which pertain to said Bureau.

ANDREW JOHNSON.

By order of the Secretary of War:

E. D. TOWNSEND, *Ass't Adj't General.*

CIRCULAR NO. 15.

WAR DEPARTMENT,
BUREAU REFUGEES, FREEDMEN,
AND ABANDONED LANDS,
WASHINGTON, D. C., *September* 12, 1865.

I. Circular No. 13, of July 28, 1865, from this bureau, and all portions of circulars from this bureau conflicting with the provisions of this circular, are hereby rescinded.

II. This bureau has charge of such "tracts of land within the insurrectionary States as shall have been abandoned, or to which the United States shall have acquired title by confiscation or sale, or otherwise," and no such lands now in its possession shall be surrendered to any claimant except as hereinafter provided.

III. Abandoned lands are defined in section 2 of the act of Congress approved July 2, 1864, as lands, "the lawful owner whereof shall be voluntarily absent therefrom, and engaged either in arms or otherwise in aiding or encouraging the rebellion."

IV. Land will not be regarded as confiscated until it has been condemned and sold by decree of the United States court for the district in which the property may be found, and the title thereto thus vested in the United States.

V. Upon its appearing satisfactorily to any assistant commissioner that any property under his control is not abandoned as above defined, and that the United States has acquired no title to it by confiscation, sale or otherwise, he will formally surrender it to the authorized claimant or claimants, promptly reporting his action to the Commissioner.

VI. Assistant commissioners will prepare accurate descriptions of all confiscated and abandoned lands under their control, keeping a record thereof themselves, and forwarding monthly to the Commissioner copies of these descriptions in the manner prescribed in circular No. 10, of July 11, 1865, from this bureau.

They will set apart so much of said lands as is necessary for the immediate use of loyal refugees and freedmen, being careful to select for this purpose those lands which most clearly fall under the control of this bureau, which selection must be submitted to the Commissioner for his approval.

The specific division of lands so set apart into lots, and the rental or sale thereof, according to section 4 of the law establishing the bureau, will be completed as soon as practicable, and reported to the Commissioner.

VII. Abandoned lands held by this bureau may be restored to owners pardoned by the President, by the assistant commissioners, to whom applications for such restoration should be forwarded, so far as practicable, through the superintendents of the districts in which the lands are situated.

Each application must be accompanied by—

1st. Evidence of special pardon by the President, or a copy of the oath of amnesty prescribed in the President's proclamation of May 29, 1865, when the applicant is not included in any of the classes therein excepted from the benefits of said oath.

2d. Proof of title.

Officers of the bureau through whom the application passes will indorse thereon such facts as may assist the assistant commissioner in his decision, stating especially the use made by the bureau of the land.

VIII. No land under cultivation by loyal refugees or freedmen will be restored under this circular, until the crops now growing shall be secured for the benefit of the cultivators, unless full and just compensation be made for their labor and its products, and for their expenditures.

O. O. HOWARD,
Major General, Commissioner.

Approved: ANDREW JOHNSON,
President of the United States.

For the Return to Persons Pardoned, of their Property.

EXECUTIVE OFFICE, *August* 16, 1865.

Respectfully returned to the Commissioner of Bureau Refugees, Freedmen, &c. The records of this office show that B. B. Leake was specially pardoned by the President on the 27th ultimo, and was thereby restored to all his rights of property, except as to slaves. Notwithstanding this, it is understood that the possession of his property is withheld from him. I have, therefore, to direct that General Fisk, assistant commissioner at Nashville, Tennessee, be instructed by the Chief Commissioner of Bureau of Freedmen, &c., to relinquish possession of the property of Mr. Leake, held by him as assistant commissioner, &c., and that the same be immediately restored to the said Leake. The same action will be had in all similar cases.*

ANDREW JOHNSON,
President United States.

To O. O. HOWARD,
Maj. General, Com'r Freedmen's Affairs.

Respecting Commercial Intercourse, and the Suppression of the Rebellion in the State of Tennessee, June 13, 1865.

Whereas by my proclamation of the twenty-ninth of April, one thousand eight hundred and sixty-five, all restrictions upon internal, domestic, and commercial intercourse, with certain exceptions therein specified and set forth, were removed "in such parts of the States of Tennessee, Virginia, North Carolina, South Carolina, Georgia, Florida, Alabama, Mississippi, and so much of Louisiana as lies east of the Mississippi river, as shall be embraced within the lines of national military occupation; * *"

And whereas by my proclamation of the twenty-second of May, one thousand eight hundred and sixty-five, for reasons therein given, it was declared that certain ports of the United States which had been previously closed against foreign commerce, should, with certain specified exceptions, be reopened to such commerce, on and after the first day of July next, subject to the laws of the United States, and in pursuance of such regulations as might be prescribed by the Secretary of the Treasury;

And whereas I am satisfactorily informed, that dangerous combinations against the laws of the United States no longer exist within the State of Tennessee; that the insurrection heretofore existing within said State has been suppressed; that within the boundaries thereof the authority of the United States is undisputed; and that such officers of the United States as have been duly commissioned are in the undisturbed exercise of their official functions:

Now, therefore, be it known that I, Andrew Johnson, President of the United States, do hereby declare that all restrictions upon internal, domestic, and coastwise intercourse and trade, and upon the removal of products of States heretofore declared in insurrection, reserving and excepting only those relating to contraband of war, as hereinafter recited, and also those which relate to the reservation of the rights of the United States to property purchased in the territory of an enemy, heretofore imposed in the territory of the United States east of the Mississippi river, are annulled, and I do hereby direct that they be forthwith removed; and that on and after the first day of July next all restriction upon foreign commerce with said ports, with the exception and reservation aforesaid, be likewise removed; and that the commerce of such States shall be conducted under the supervision of the regularly appointed officers of the customs provided by law; and such officers of the customs shall receive any captured and abandoned property that may be turned over to them, under the law, by the military or naval forces of the United States, and dispose of such property as shall be directed by the Secretary of the Treasury.

The following articles contraband of war are excepted from the effect of this proclamation: arms, ammunition, all articles from which ammunition is made, and gray uniforms and cloth.

And I hereby also proclaim and declare that the insurrection, so far as it relates to, and within the State of Tennessee, and the inhabitants of the said State of Tennessee as re-organized and constituted under their recently adopted constitution and re organization, and accepted by them, is suppressed, and therefore, also, that all the disabilities and disqualifications attaching to said State and the inhabitants thereof

*Extract from letter of General Howard, April 23, 1866, in reply to resolution of the House of Representatives of March 5, 1866:

"In complying with these definite instructions, the bureau has been compelled to part with the greater portion of the property once under its control. Except in the very few cases where property has been actually sold under the act of July 17, 1862, and in that portion of South Carolina and Georgia embraced in the provisions of General Sherman's Field Order No. 15, its tenure of property has been too uncertain to justify allotments to freedmen.

	Acres.
Property seized under act of July, 1862, and restored by this bureau	15,452
Abandoned property allotted to freedmen and restored by this bureau	14,652
Abandoned property not allotted to freedmen restored by this bureau	400,000
Total	430,104"

consequent upon any proclamations, issued by virtue of the fifth section of the act entitled "An act further to provide for the collection of duties on imports and for other purposes," approved the thirteenth day of July, one thousand eight hundred and sixty-one, are removed.

But nothing herein contained shall be considered or construed as in any wise changing or impairing any of the penalties and forfeitures for treason heretofore incurred under the laws of the United States, or any of the provisions, restrictions, or disabilities set forth in my proclamation, bearing date the twenty-ninth day of May, one thousand eight hundred and sixty-five, or as impairing existing regulations for the suspension of the habeas corpus, and the exercise of military law in cases where it shall be necessary for the general public safety and welfare during the existing insurrection; nor shall this proclamation affect, or in any way impair, any laws heretofore passed by Congress, and duly approved by the President, or any proclamations or orders, issued by him, during the aforesaid insurrection, abolishing slavery, or in any way affecting the relations of slavery, whether of persons or of property; but on the contrary, all such laws and proclamations heretofore made or issued are expressly saved, and declared to be in full force and virtue.

In testimony whereof, I have hereunto set my hand, and caused the seal of the United States to be affixed.

Done at the city of Washington, this thirteenth day of June, in the year of our Lord one thousand eight hundred and [SEAL.] sixty-five, and of the independence of the United States of America the eighty-ninth.

ANDREW JOHNSON.

By the President:

WILLIAM H. SEWARD, *Secretary of State*.

Blockade Rescinded, June 23, 1865.

Whereas by the proclamation of the President of the fifteenth and twenty-seventh of April, eighteen hundred and sixty-one, a blockade of certain ports of the United States was set on foot; but whereas the reasons for that measure have ceased to exist:

Now, therefore, be it known that I, Andrew Johnson, President of the United States, do hereby declare and proclaim the blockade aforesaid to be rescinded as to all the ports aforesaid, including that of Galveston and other ports west of the Mississippi river, which ports will be open to foreign commerce on the first of July next, on the terms and conditions set forth in my proclamation of the twenty-second of May last.

It is to be understood, however, that the blockade thus rescinded was an international measure for the purpose of protecting the sovereign rights of the United States. The greater or less subversion of civil authority in the region to which it applied, and the impracticability of at once restoring that in due efficiency, may, for a season, make it advisable to employ the army and navy of the United States towards carrying the laws into effect, wherever such employment may be necessary.

In testimony whereof, I have hereunto set my hand and caused the seal of the United States to be affixed.

Done at the city of Washington this twenty-third day of June, in the year of our [L. S.] Lord one thousand eight hundred and sixty-five, and of the Independence of the United States the eighty-ninth.

ANDREW JOHNSON.

By the President:

W. HUNTER, *Acting Secretary of State*.

Further Removal of Restrictions, August 29, 1865.

Whereas by my proclamations of the thirteenth and twenty-fourth of June, one thousand eight hundred and sixty-five, removing restrictions, in part, upon internal, domestic, and coastwise intercourse and trade with those States recently declared in insurrection, certain articles were excepted from the effect of said proclamations as contraband of war; and whereas the necessity for restricting trade in said articles has now, in a great measure, ceased: It is hereby ordered, that on and after the 1st day of September, 1865, all restrictions aforesaid be removed, so that the articles declared by the said proclamations to be contraband of war may be imported into and sold in said States, subject only to such regulations as the Secretary of the Treasury may prescribe.

In testimony whereof, I have hereunto set my hand and caused the seal of the United States to be affixed.

Done at the city of Washington this twenty-ninth day of August, in the year of our [L. S.] Lord one thousand eight hundred and sixty-five, and of the Independence of the United States of America the ninetieth.

ANDREW JOHNSON.

By the President:

WILLIAM H. SEWARD, *Secretary of State*.

Passports for Paroled Prisoners.

DEPARTMENT OF STATE,
WASHINGTON, *August* 25, 1865.

Paroled prisoners asking passports as citizens of the United States, and against whom no special charges may be pending, will be furnished with passports upon application therefor to the Department of State in the usual form. Such passports will, however, be issued upon the condition that the applicants do not return to the United States without leave of the President. Other persons implicated in the rebellion, who may wish to go abroad, will apply to the Department of State for passports, and the applications will be disposed of according to the merits of the several cases.

By the President of the United States.

WILLIAM H. SEWARD.

Paroling certain State Prisoners.

EXECUTIVE OFFICE,
WASHINGTON, *October* 11, 1865.

Whereas the following named persons, to wit: John A. Campbell, of Alabama; John H. Reagan, of Texas; Alexander H. Stephens, of Georgia; George A. Trenholm, of South Carolina; and Charles Clark, of Mississippi, lately engaged in rebellion against the United States Government, who are now in close custody, have made their submission to the authority of the United States and applied to the President for pardon under his proclamation; and whereas, the authority of the Federal Government is sufficiently restored in the aforesaid States to admit of the enlargement of said persons from close custody, it is ordered that they be released on giving their respective paroles to appear at such time and place as the President may designate, to answer any charge that he may direct to be preferred against them; and also that they will respectively abide until further orders in the places herein designated, and not depart therefrom: John A. Campbell, in the State of Alabama; John H. Reagan, in the State of Texas; Alexander H. Stephens, in the State of Georgia; George A. Trenholm, in the State of South Carolina; and Charles Clark, in the State of Mississippi. And if the President should grant his pardon to any of said persons, such person's parole will be thereby discharged.

ANDREW JOHNSON,
President.

Martial Law Withdrawn from Kentucky, October 12, 1865.

Whereas by a proclamation of the fifth day of July, one thousand eight hundred and sixty-four, the President of the United States, when the civil war was flagrant, and when combinations were in progress in Kentucky for the purpose of inciting insurgent raids into that State, directed that the proclamation suspending the writ of *habeas corpus* should be made effectual in Kentucky, and that martial law should be established there and continue until said proclamation should be revoked or modified;

And whereas since then the danger of insurgent raids into Kentucky has substantially passed away:

Now, therefore, be it known that I, Andrew Johnson, President of the United States, by virtue of the authority vested in me by the Constitution, do hereby declare that the said proclamation of the fifth day of July, one thousand eight hundred and sixty-four, shall be, and is hereby, modified in so far that martial law shall be no longer in force in Kentucky from and after the date hereof.

In testimony whereof, I have hereunto set my hand and caused the seal of the United States to be affixed.

Done at the city of Washington this twelfth day of October, in the year of our Lord one thousand eight hundred and sixty-five, and of the Independence of the United States of America the ninetieth. [L. S.]

ANDREW JOHNSON.

By the President:
W. HUNTER, *Acting Secretary of State.*

Annulling the Suspension of the Habeas Corpus, December 1, 1865

Whereas by the proclamation of the President of the United States of the fifteenth day of September, one thousand eight hundred and sixty-three, the privilege of the writ of *habeas corpus* was, in certain cases therein set forth, suspended throughout the United States;

And whereas the reasons for that suspension may be regarded as having ceased in some of the States and Territories:

Now, therefore, be it known that I, Andrew Johnson, President of the United States, do hereby proclaim and declare that the suspension aforesaid, and all other proclamations and orders suspending the privilege of the writ of *habeas corpus* in the States and Territories of the United States, are revoked and annulled excepting as to the States of Virginia, Kentucky, Tennessee, North Carolina, South Carolina, Georgia, Florida, Alabama, Mississippi, Louisiana, Arkansas, and Texas, the District of Columbia, and the Territories of New Mexico and Arizona.

In witness whereof, I have hereunto set my hand and caused the seal of the United States to be affixed.

Done at the city of Washington this first day of December, in the year of our Lord one thousand eight hundred and sixty-five, and of the Independence of the United States of America the ninetieth. [L. S.]

ANDREW JOHNSON.

By the President:
WILLIAM H. SEWARD, *Secretary of State.*

Announcing that the Rebellion has ended, April 2, 1866.

Whereas, by proclamations of the fifteenth and nineteenth of April, one thousand eight hundred and sixty-one, the President of the United States, in virtue of the power vested in him by the Constitution and the laws, declared that the laws of the United States were opposed, and the execution thereof obstructed in the States of South Carolina, Georgia, Alabama, Florida, Mississippi, Louisiana, and Texas, by combinations too powerful to be suppressed by the ordinary course of judicial proceedings, or by the powers vested in the marshals by law;

And whereas, by another proclamation made on the sixteenth day of August, in the same year, in pursuance of an act of Congress approved July thirteenth, one thousand eight hundred and sixty-one, the inhabitants of the States of Georgia, South Carolina, Virginia, North Carolina, Tennessee, Alabama, Louisiana, Texas, Arkansas, Mississippi, and Florida (except the inhabitants of that part of the State of Virginia lying west of the Alleghany mountains, and to such other parts of that State and the other States before named, as might maintain a loyal adhesion to the Union and the Constitution, or might be from time to time occupied and controlled by forces of the United States engaged in the dispersion of insurgents) were declared to be in a state of insurrection against the United States;

And whereas, by another proclamation of the first day of July, one thousand eight hundred and sixty-two, issued in pursuance of an act of Congress approved June 7, in the same year, the insurrection was declared to be still existing in the States aforesaid, with the exception of certain specified counties in the State of Virginia;

And whereas, by another proclamation made on the second day of April, one thousand eight hundred and sixty-three, in pursuance of the act of Congress of July 13, one thousand eight hundred and sixty-one, the exceptions named in the proclamation of August 16, one thousand eight hundred and sixty-one were revoked, and the inhabitants of the States of Georgia, South Carolina, North Carolina, Tennessee, Alabama, Louisiana, Texas, Arkansas, Mississippi, Florida, and Virginia, (except the forty-eight counties of Virginia designated as West Virginia, and the ports of New Orleans, Key West, Port Royal, and Beaufort, in South Carolina,) were declared to be still in a state of insurrection against the United States.

And whereas the House of Representatives, on the 22d day of July, one thousand eight hundred and sixty-one, adopted a resolution in the words following, namely:

"*Resolved by the House of Representatives of the Congress of the United States*, That the present deplorable civil war has been forced upon the country by the disunionists of the southern States, now in revolt against the constitutional Government, and in arms around the capital; that in this national emergency Congress, banishing all feelings of mere passion or resentment, will recollect only its duty to the whole country; that this war is not waged on our part in any spirit of oppression, nor for any purpose of conquest or subjugation, nor purpose of overthrowing or interfering with the rights or established institutions of those States; but to defend and maintain the supremacy of the Constitution and to preserve the Union with all the dignity, equality, and rights of the several States unimpaired; that as soon as these objects are accomplished, the war ought to cease."

And whereas the Senate of the United States, on the 25th day of July, one thousand eight hundred and sixty-one, adopted a resolution in the words following, to wit:

"*Resolved*, That the present deplorable civil war has been forced upon the country by the disunionists of the southern States, now in revolt against the constitutional Government, and in arms around the capital; that in this national emergency Congress, banishing all feeling of mere passion or resentment, will recollect only its duty to the whole country; that this war is not prosecuted on our part in any spirit of oppression nor for any purpose of conquest or subjugation, nor purpose of overthrowing or interfering with the rights or established institutions of those States, but to defend and maintain the supremacy of the Constitution and all laws made in pursuance thereof, and to preserve the Union with all the dignity, equality, and rights of the several States unimpaired; that as soon as these objects are accomplished, the war ought to cease."

And whereas these resolutions, though not joint or concurrent in form, are substantially identical, and as such may be regarded as having expressed the sense of Congress upon the subject to which they relate;

And whereas, by my proclamation of the thirteenth day of June last, the insurrection in the State of Tennessee was declared to have been suppressed, the authority of the United States therein to be undisputed, and such United States officers as had been duly commissioned to be in the undisputed exercise of their official functions;

And whereas there now exists no organized armed resistance of misguided citizens or others to the authority of the United States in the States of Georgia, South Carolina, Virginia, North Carolina, Tennessee, Alabama, Louisiana, Arkansas, Mississippi, and Florida, and the laws can be sustained and enforced therein by the proper civil authority, State or Federal, and the people of the said States are well and loyally disposed, and have conformed or will conform in their legislation to the condition of affairs growing out of the amendment to the Constitution of the United States, prohibiting slavery within the limits and jurisdiction of the United States;

And whereas, in view of the before recited premises, it is the manifest determination of the American people that no State, of its own will, has the right or the power to go out of, or separate itself from, or be separated from the American Union, and that therefore each State ought to remain and constitute an integral part of the United States;

And whereas the people of the several beforementioned States have, in the manner aforesaid, given satisfactory evidence that they acquiesce in this sovereign and important resolution of national unity;

And whereas it is believed to be a fundamental principle of government that people who have revolted, and who have been overcome and subdued, must either be dealt with so as to induce them voluntarily to become friends, or else they must be held by absolute military power, or devastated, so as to prevent them from ever again doing harm as enemies, which last-named policy is abhorrent to humanity and freedom;

And whereas the Constitution of the United States provides for constituent communities only as States and not as Territories, dependencies, provinces, or protectorates;

And whereas such constituent States must necessarily be and by the Constitution and laws of the United States are made equals and placed upon a like footing as to political rights, immunities, dignity, and power, with the several States with which they are united;

And whereas the observance of political equality as a principle of right and justice is well calculated to encourage the people of the aforesaid States to be and become more and more constant and persevering in their renewed allegiance;

And whereas standing armies, military occupation, martial law, military tribunals, and the suspension of the privilege of the writ of *habeas corpus* are, in time of peace, dangerous to public liberty, incompatible with the individual rights of the citizen, contrary to the genius and spirit of our free institutions, and exhaustive of the national resources, and ought not, therefore, to be sanctioned or allowed, except in cases of actual necessity, for repelling invasion or suppressing insurrection or rebellion;

And whereas the policy of the Government of the United States, from the beginning of the insurrection to its overthrow and final suppression, has been in conformity with the principles herein set forth and enumerated:

Now, therefore, I, Andrew Johnson, President of the United States, do hereby proclaim and declare that the insurrection which heretofore existed in the States of Georgia, South Carolina, Virginia, North Carolina, Tennessee,

Alabama, Louisiana, Arkansas, Mississippi and Florida is at an end, and is henceforth to be so regarded.*

In testimony whereof, I have hereunto set my hand, and caused the seal of the United States to be affixed.

Done at the city of Washington, the second day of April, in the year of our Lord one thousand eight hundred and sixty-six, and of the Independence of the United States of America the ninetieth.

[SEAL.]

ANDREW JOHNSON.

By the President:

WM. H. SEWARD, *Secretary of State.*

Order in Relation to Appointments to Office.

EXECUTIVE MANSION, *April* 7, 1866.

It is eminently right and proper that the Government of the United States should give earnest and substantial evidence of its just appreciation of the services of the patriotic men who, when the life of the nation was imperiled, entered the army and navy to preserve the integrity of the Union, defend the Government, and maintain and perpetuate unimpaired its free institutions. It is therefore directed:

First. That in appointments to office in the several executive departments of the General Government and the various branches of the public service connected with said departments, preference shall be given to such meritorious and honorably discharged soldiers and sailors, particularly those who have been disabled by wounds received or diseases contracted in the line of duty, as may possess the proper qualifications.

Second. That in all promotions in said departments and the several branches of the public service connected therewith, such persons shall have preference, when equally eligible and qualified, over those who have not faithfully and honorably served in the land and naval forces of the United States.

ANDREW JOHNSON.

Order in Relation to Trials by Military Courts and Commissions.

WAR DEPARTMENT,
ADJUTANT GENERAL'S OFFICE,
WASHINGTON, *May* 1, 1866.

General Orders No. 26:

Whereas some military commanders are embarrassed by doubts as to the operation of the proclamation of the President, dated the 2d day of April, 1866, upon trials by military courts-martial and military offenses, to remove such doubts, it is ordered by the President that—

Hereafter, whenever offenses committed by civilians are to be tried where civil tribunals are in existence which can try them, their cases are not authorized to be, and will not be, brought before military courts-martial or commissions, but will be committed to the proper civil authorities. This order is not applicable to camp followers, as provided for under the 60th Article of War, or to contractors and others specified in section 16, act of July 17, 1862, and sections 1 and 2, act of March 2, 1863. Persons and offenses cognizable by the Rules and Articles of War, and by the acts of Congress above cited, will continue to be tried and punished by military tribunals as prescribed by the Rules and Articles of War and acts of Congress, hereinafter cited, to wit:

Sixtieth of the Rules and Articles of War. All sutlers and retainers to the camp, and all persons whatsoever serving with the armies of the United States in the field, though not enlisted soldiers, are to be subject to orders according to the rules and discipline of war. * * *

By order of the Secretary of War:

E. D. TOWNSEND,
Assistant Adjutant General.

Against the Fenian Invasion of Canada, June 6, 1866.

Whereas it has become known to me that certain evil-disposed persons have, within the territory and jurisdiction of the United States, begun and set on foot, and have provided and prepared, and are still engaged in providing and preparing, means for a military expedition and enterprise, which expedition and enterprise is to be carried on from the territory and jurisdiction of the United States against colonies, districts, and people of British North America, within the dominions of the United Kingdom of Great Britain and Ireland, with which said colonies, districts, and people, and kingdom the United States are at peace;

And whereas the proceedings aforesaid constitute a high misdemeanor, forbidden by the laws of the United States, as well as by the law of nations:

Now, therefore, for the purpose of preventing the carrying on of the unlawful expedition and enterprise aforesaid, from the territory and jurisdiction of the United States, and to maintain the public peace, as well as the national honor, and enforce obedience and respect to the

* The following official telegraphic correspondence shows the scope of the proclamation, in the opinion of the President:

AUGUSTA, GA., *April* 7, 1866.

Maj. Gen. O. O. HOWARD:

Does the President's recent proclamation remove martial law in this State? If so, Gen. Brannan does not feel authorized to arrest parties who have committed outrages on freed people or Union refugees. Please answer by telegraph.

DAVIS TILLSON,
Brig. Gen. of Vols.

[Answer.]

ADJUTANT GENERAL'S OFFICE, WAR DEPARTMENT,
WASHINGTON, *April* 17, 1866.

The President's proclamation does not remove martial law, or operate in any way upon the Freedmen's Bureau in the exercise of its *legitimate* jurisdiction. It is not expedient, however, to resort to military tribunal in any case where justice can be attained through the medium of civil authority. E. D. TOWNSEND, A. A. G.

TO GOVERNOR WORTH, OF NORTH CAROLINA.

WASHINGTON, D. C., *April* 27, 1866.

To Gov. WORTH: I am directed by the President to inform you that by his proclamation of April 2, 1866, it was not intended to interfere with military commissions at that time or previously organized, or trials then pending before such commissions, unless by special instructions the accused were to be turned over the civil authorities. General Ruger has been instructed to proceed with the trial to which you refer; but before the execution of any sentence rendered by said commission, to report all the proceedings to the War Department for examination and revision. There has been an order this day prepared, and which will soon be issued, which will relieve and settle all embarrassment growing out of a misconstruction of the proclamation, of which I will send you a copy.

EDWARD COOPER,
Acting Private Secretary to the President.

laws of the United States, I, Andrew Johnson, President of the United States, do admonish and warn all good citizens of the United States against taking part in or in any wise aiding, countenancing, or abetting said unlawful proceedings, and I do exhort all judges, magistrates, marshals, and officers in the service of the United States, to employ all their awful authority and power to prevent and defeat the aforesaid unlawful proceedings, and to arrest and bring to justice all persons who may be engaged therein.*

And, pursuant to the act of Congress in such case made and provided, I do furthermore authorize and empower Major General George G. Meade, commander of the Military Division of the Atlantic, to employ the land and naval forces of the United States and the militia thereof, to arrest and prevent the setting on foot and carrying on the expedition and enterprise aforesaid.

In testimony whereof, I have hereunto set my hand, and caused the seal of the United States to be affixed.

Done at the city of Washington the sixth day of June, in the year of our Lord one thousand eight hundred and sixty-six, and of the Independence of the United States the ninetieth. [SEAL.]

ANDREW JOHNSON.

By the President:

WILLIAM H. SEWARD, *Secretary of State.*

---

* *Circular to the District Attorneys and Marshals of the United States.*

ATTORNEY GENERAL'S OFFICE, WASHINGTON, D. C., June 5, 1866.—By direction of the President you are hereby instructed to cause the arrest of all prominent, leading, or conspicuous persons called Fenians, whom you may have probable cause to believe have been or may be guilty of violations of the neutrality laws of the United States.

JAMES SPEED,
Attorney General.

III.

ACTION OF THE CONVENTIONS AND LEGISLATURES OF THE LATELY INSURRECTIONARY STATES.

NORTH CAROLINA.

1865, April 27—Gen. Schofield announced the cessation of hostilities within that State.

April 28—Gen. Schofield issued an order that, under the emancipation proclamation, all persons heretofore held as slaves are now free, and that it is the duty of the army to maintain their freedom.

May 29—William W. Holden appointed Provisional Governor.

June 12—Provisional Governor Holden issued his proclamation announcing his purpose to order an election for a convention, and to appoint justices of the peace to administer the oath of allegiance and conduct the election, &c.

July —President Johnson ordered the cotton of the State to be restored to her, and the proceeds of all that had been sold to be paid to her agents.

August 8—Provisional Governor Holden fixed Thursday, September 21, for the election of a convention.

Voters' qualifications are thus prescribed:

"No person will be allowed to vote who is not a voter qualified as prescribed by the constitution and laws of the State in force immediately before the 20th day of May, 1861, except that the payment of poll tax shall not be required.

"All paroled soldiers of the army and navy of the pretended Confederate States, or of this State, and all paroled officers of the army and navy of the pretended Confederate States, or of this State, under and including the rank of colonel, if of the army, and under and including the rank of lieutenant, if of the navy, will be allowed to vote, provided they are not included in any of the fourteen excluded classes of the President's amnesty proclamation; and, provided further, that they are citizens of the State in accordance with the terms prescribed in the preceding paragraph.

"No person will be allowed to vote who does not exhibit to the inspectors a copy of the amnesty oath, as contained in the President's proclamation of May 29, 1865, signed by himself and certified by at least two justices of the peace."

The convention to meet October 2.

September 29—The colored people of the State met in convention in Raleigh, and petitioned for legislation to secure compensation for labor, and enable them to educate their children, and asking protection for the family relation, and for the repeal of oppressive laws making unjust discriminations on account of race or color.

October 2—Convention met.

October 7—The secession ordinance declared "null and void."

October 9—An ordinance passed, declaring slavery forever prohibited within the State.

October 10—Ordinance passed, providing for an election for Governor, members of the Legislature, and seven members of Congress November 9, the Provisional Governor to give the certificates. Each member of the Legislature, and each voter to be qualified "according to the now existing constitution of the State": *Provided*, That no one shall be eligible to a seat, or be capable of voting, who, being free in all respects, shall not, before May 29, 1865, have taken President Lincoln's amnesty oath, or have taken President Johnson's oath, and who shall not in either case be of the excepted classes. All persons who have preferred petitions for pardon shall be deemed to have been pardoned if the fact of being pardoned shall be announced by the Governor, although the pardon may not have been received. The payment of a public tax shall not be required as a qualification of the voter in the elections in November next.

October 12—Convention tabled a proposition to prohibit the payment of the war debt created by the State in aid of the rebellion.

October 16—Ordinance passed, dividing the State into seven congressional districts.

October 17—Resolution adopted, requesting Congress to repeal the "test-oath."

October 18—President Johnson sent this telegram:

EXECUTIVE OFFICE,
WASHINGTON, D. C., *October* 18, 1865.

W. W. HOLDEN, *Provisional Governor:*

Every dollar of the debt created to aid the rebellion against the United States should be repudiated finally and forever. The great mass of the people should not be taxed to pay a debt to aid in carrying on a rebellion which they in fact, if left to themselves, were opposed to. Let those who have given their means for the obligations of the State look to that power they tried to establish in violation of law, constitution, and will of the people. They must meet their fate. It is their misfortune, and cannot be recognized by the people of any State professing themselves loyal to the government of the United States and in the Union. I repeat that the loyal people of North Carolina should be exonerated from the payment of every dollar of indebtedness created to aid in carrying on the rebellion. I trust and hope that the people of North Carolina will wash their hands of everything that partakes in the slightest degree of the rebellion, which has been so recently crushed by the strong arm of the Government in carrying out the obligations imposed by the Constitution of the Union. ANDREW JOHNSON,
President of the United States.

October 19—Ordinance passed, that no officer of this State who may have taken an oath of office to support the constitution of the Confederate States, shall be capable of holding under the State any office of trust or profit which he held when he took such oath, until he may be appointed or re-elected to the same; and all the offices lately held by such persons are hereby declared vacant.

October 19—Convention—yeas 84, nays 12—passed an ordinance prohibiting the assumption of the State debt created in aid of the rebellion. An amendment to refer this question to a vote of the people, lost.

November 9—Election of State officers and Representatives in Congress. Same day, ordinances repealing secession ordinance and anti-slavery ordinance, submitted to popular vote, and approved.

November 13—Legislature met.

December 1—The Legislature ratified, with six dissenting voices, the anti-slavery amendment.

December 9—Jonathan Worth declared elected Governor, by a vote of 32,529 to 25,809 for Prov. Gov. Holden.

December 15—Governor Worth qualified.

1866, May 24—The Convention re-assembled. A motion to adjourn *sine die* was tabled, 61 to 30.

MISSISSIPPI.

1865, May 10—Governor Clark called an extra session of the Legislature for the 18th, to order a State Convention.

May 21—Major General Canby telegraphed as follows to Major General Warren, commanding the department: "By direction of the President, you will not recognize any officer of the Confederate or State government, within the limits of your command, as authorized to exercise in any manner whatever the functions of their late offices. You will prevent, by force if necessary, any attempt of any of the legislatures of the States in insurrection to assemble for legislative purposes, and will imprison any members or other persons who may attempt to exercise these functions in opposition to your orders."

June 13—William L. Sharkey appointed Provisional Governor.

July 1—Prov. Gov. Sharkey issued a proclamation, appointing local officers, and fixing an election for a Convention—August 7th—voters to have these qualifications:

"Voters for delegates to this convention must possess the qualifications required by the constitution and laws as they existed prior to the 9th day of January, 1861, and must also produce a certificate that they have taken, before a competent officer, the amnesty oath prescribed by the proclamation of the 29th of May, 1865, which certificate shall be attached to or accompanied by a copy of the oath, and no one will be eligible as a member of this convention who has not also taken this oath."

August 14—Convention met.

August 15—President Johnson sent this telegram:

EXECUTIVE OFFICE,
WASHINGTON, D. C., *August* 15, 1865.

Governor W. L. SHARKEY, *Jackson, Miss.:*

I am gratified to see that you have organized your Convention without difficulty. I hope that without delay your Convention will amend your State constitution, abolishing slavery and denying to all future legislatures the power to legislate that there is property in man; also that they will adopt the amendment to the Constitution of the United States abolishing slavery. If you could extend the elective franchise to all persons of color who can read the Constitution of the United States in English and write their names, and to all persons of color who own real estate valued at not less than two hundred and fifty dollars, and pay taxes thereon, you would completely disarm the adversary and set an example the other States will follow. This you can do with perfect safety, and you thus place the southern States, in reference to free persons of color, upon the same basis with the free States. I hope and trust your convention will do this, and, as a consequence, the radicals, who are wild upon negro franchise, will be completely foiled in their attempt to keep the southern States from renewing their relations to the Union by not accepting their senators and representatives.*

ANDREW JOHNSON, *President of the U. S.*

August 21—Ordinance passed that "the institution of slavery having been destroyed in the State of Mississippi," neither slavery nor involuntary servitude, &c., shall hereafter exist in the State.

August 21—An election ordered for first Monday in October for State and county officers, and Representatives in Congress in the several congressional districts as they were fixed by the legislature in 1857.

August 22—Secession ordinance declared null and void.

October 7—The colored citizens of Mississippi met in convention, and protested against the reactionary policy prevailing, and expressing the fear that the Legislature will pass such proscriptive laws as will drive the freedmen from the State, or practically re-enslave them.

October 16—Legislature met.

October 17—Benjamin G. Humphreys inaugurated Governor.

November 20—Governor Humphreys sent a message recommending that negroes be permitted to sue and be sued, and give testimony, and that the freedmen be encouraged to engage in pursuits of industry, and that a militia bill be passed, "to protect our people against insurrection, or any possible combination of vicious white men and negroes."

November 24—Bill passed "reserving twenty per cent. of the revenue of the State as a fund for the relief of destitute disabled Confederate and State soldiers, and their widows, and for the support and education of indigent children of deceased or disabled Confederate or State soldiers, to be distributed annually," &c.

November 27—The joint committee reported against ratifying the anti-slavery amendment, for reasons given; and the Legislature adopted it.

November 29—The Legislature adopted a memorial to the Congress of the United States, asking for the repeal of the "test oath." November 22, one for the pardon of Jacob Thompson. November 8, one for the pardon of Jefferson Davis.

December 1—The name of Jones county changed to Davis.

December 5—Bill passed, taxing each male inhabitant of the State, between 21 and 60, $1, and authorizing any person having in his or her employ any one subject to the tax, to pay it and charge it to the person for whom paid. All officers and enlisted men who have herefore received pensions, and have forfeited the same by taking a part in the late war against the United States, shall be exempt from poll tax.

GEORGIA.

1865, May 3—Gov. Joseph E. Brown issued a proclamation calling an extra meeting of the Legislature for 22d.

May 14—Maj. Gen. Gillmore issued an order annulling this proclamation, and directing the persons interested not to heed it.

June 17—James Johnson appointed Provisional Governor.

July 13—Prov. Gov. Johnson issued a proclamation fixing the first Wednesday in October for an election for delegates to a Convention—these to be the qualifications of voters:

"That no person at such election shall be qualified as an elector, or shall be eligible as a member of such convention, unless he shall have previously thereto taken and subscribed to the oath of amnesty, as set forth in the President's proclamation of May 29, A. D. 1865, and is a voter qualified as prescribed by the constitution and laws of the State of Georgia, in force immediately before the 19th of January, A. D. 1861, the date of the so-called ordinance of secession."

October 7—Names of members elect requiring pardons sent to the President, and pardons returned, as in each of the other States.

October 25—Convention met.

October 30—Secession ordinance repealed; ordinance passed dividing the State into seven congressional districts.

November 4—Slavery declared abolished, "the Government of the United States having, as a war measure, proclaimed all slaves held or owned in this State emancipated from slavery, and having carried that proclamation into full practical effect." "*Provided*, That acquiescence in the action of the Government of the United States is not intended to operate as a relinquishment, or waiver, or estoppel, of such claim for compensation of loss sustained by reason of the emancipation of his slaves, as any citizen of Georgia may hereafter make upon the justice and magnanimity of that Government."

November 8—The State debt of Georgia, incurred in aid of the rebellion, declared null and void—yeas 133, nays 117. Pending this proposition these telegrams were sent:

MILLEDGEVILLE, GA., *October* 27, 1865.

His Excellency ANDREW JOHNSON,

President of the United States:

We need some aid to repeal the war debt. Send me word on the subject. What should the Convention do? J. JOHNSON,

Provisional Governor of Georgia.

EXECUTIVE OFFICE,

WASHINGTON, D. C., *October* 28, 1865.

JAMES JOHNSON, *Provisional Governor:*

Your despatch has been received. The people of Georgia should not hesitate one single moment in repudiating every single dollar of debt created for the purpose of aiding the rebellion against the Government of the United States. It will not do to levy and collect taxes from a State and people that are loyal and in the Union, to pay a debt that was created to aid in an effort to take

---

* As bearing upon this point, this letter from the late President Lincoln, on a similar occasion, has value:

EXECUTIVE MANSION,
WASHINGTON, *March* 13, 1864.

Hon. MICHAEL HAHN:

MY DEAR SIR: I congratulate you on having fixed your name in history as the first free State Governor of Louisiana. Now you are about to have a convention, which, among other things, will probably define the elective franchise. I barely suggest, for your private consideration, whether some of the colored people may not be let in, as, for instance, the very intelligent, and especially those who have fought gallantly in our ranks. They would probably help, in some trying time to come, to keep the jewel of liberty in the family of freedom. But this is only a suggestion, not to the public, but to you alone.

Truly yours, A. LINCOLN.

them out, and thereby subvert the Constitution of the United States. I do not believe the great mass of the people of the State of Georgia, when left uninfluenced, will ever submit to the payment of a debt which was the main cause of bringing on their past and present suffering, the result of the rebellion. Those who vested their capital in the creation of this debt must meet their fate, and take it as one of the inevitable results of the rebellion, though it may seem hard to them. It should at once be made known at home and abroad, that no debt contracted for the purpose of dissolving the Union of the States can or ever will be paid by taxes levied on the people for such purpose.

ANDREW JOHNSON,
President of the United States.

—

Hon. W. H. SEWARD:

We are pressed on the war debt. What should the Convention do? J. JOHNSON,
Provisional Governor of Georgia.

MILLEDGEVILLE, *October* 27, 1865.

—

His Excellency JAMES JOHNSON,
Provisional Governor of Georgia:

Your several telegrams have been received. The President of the United States cannot recognize the people of any State as having resumed the relations of loyalty to the Union that admits as legal, obligations contracted or debts created in their name, to promote the war of the rebellion. WILLIAM H. SEWARD.

WASHINGTON, *October* 28, 1865.

November 8—Convention adjourned.

November 15—Election held for State officers and Representatives in Congress.

December 4—Legislature met.

December 5—Legislature ratified the anti-slavery amendment.

1866, January—A convention of colored persons at Augusta advocated a proposition to give those who could write and read well, and possessed a certain property qualification, the right of suffrage.

March 10—Bill passed legislature, authorizing an extra tax, the amount to be fixed by the grand juries, but not to exceed two per cent. upon the State tax, for the benefit of indigent soldiers, and the indigent families of deceased soldiers of the Confederate and State troops. Artificial arms and legs to be furnished disabled soldiers.

ALABAMA.

1865, June 21—Lewis E. Parsons appointed Provisional Governor.

July 20—Provisional Governor Parsons issued a proclamation, fixing August 31 for an election for a Convention, under these restrictions: "But no person can vote in said election, or be a candidate for election, who is not a legal voter as the law was on that day; and if he is excepted from the benefit of annesty, under the President's proclamation of the 29th May, 1865, he must have obtained a pardon.

"Every person must vote in the county of his residence, and, before he is allowed to do so, must take and subscribe the oath of amnesty prescribed in the President's proclamation of the 29th of May, 1865, before some one of the officers hereinafter appointed for that purpose in the county where he offers to vote; and any person offering to vote in violation of these rules or the laws of Alabama on the 11th of January, 1861, will be punished.

September 12—Convention met.

September 18—Election for State officers fixed for first Monday in November—the Provisional Governor authorized to order an election for Representatives in Congress.

September 20—Slavery abolished, "as the institution of slavery has been destroyed in the State of Alabama." Secession ordinance declared "null and void." Rebel State debt repudiated, 60 to 19.

September 30—Convention adjourned.

November 20—Legislature met.

December 2—Anti-slavery amendment ratified in this form:

1st. That the foregoing amendment to the Constitution of the United States be, and the same is hereby, ratified, to all intents and purposes, as part of the Constitution of the United States.

2d. That this amendment to the Constitution of the United States is adopted by the Legislature of Alabama with the understanding that it does not confer upon Congress the power to legislate upon the political status of freedmen in this State.

3d. That the governor of the State be, and he is hereby, requested to forward to the President of the United States an authenticated copy of the foregoing preamble and resolutions.

December 5—The President sent this response:

His Excellency L. E. PARSONS,
Provisional Governor:

The President congratulates you and the country upon the acceptance of the congressional amendment of the Constitution of the United States by the State of Alabama, which vote, being the twenty-seventh, fills up the complement of two-thirds, and gives the amendment finishing effect as a part of the organic law of the land. WILLIAM H. SEWARD.

WASHINGTON, *December* 5, 1865."

1866, January 8—The Legislature re-assembled.

Gov. R. M. Patton vetoed three bills. He vetoed the bill to regulate contracts with freedmen, because no special law is necessary. He adds:

"Information from various parts of the State shows that negroes are everywhere making contracts for the present year upon terms that are entirely satisfactory to the employers. They are also entering faithfully upon the discharge of the obligations contracted. There is every prospect that the engagement formed will be observed with perfect good faith. I therefore think that special laws for regulating contracts between whites and freedmen would accomplish no good, and might result in much harm."

Governor Patton has also vetoed the bill "to extend the criminal laws of the State, applicable to free persons of color, to freedmen, free negroes and mulattoes." He says:

"The bill proposes to apply to the freedmen a system of laws enacted for the government of free negroes residing in a community where slavery existed. I have carefully examined the laws which, under this bill, would be applied to the freedmen; and I think that a mere recital of some of their provisions will show the impolicy and injustice of enforcing them upon the negroes in their new condition."

Governor Patton has also vetoed "a bill entitled an act to regulate the relations of master and apprentice, as relate to freedmen, free negroes and mulattoes," because he deems the present laws amply sufficient for all purposes of apprenticeship, without operating upon a particular class of persons.

The Legislature passed a tax bill, of which these are two sections:

"12. To sell, or expose for sale, for one year, at any one place, any pictorial or illustrated weekly, or any monthly paper, periodical or magazine, *published outside the limits of this State, and not in a foreign country*, and to vend the same on the streets, or on boats or railroad cars, *fifty* dollars."

"13. To keep a news depot for one year, in any city, town or village, for the sale of any newspaper, periodical or magazine, not including pictorials provided for in the preceding paragraph, ten dollars."

The Legislature passed some joint resolutions on the state of the Union, of which this, the fourth, is the most important:

"That Alabama will not voluntarily consent to change the adjustment of political power as fixed by the Constitution of the United States, and to constrain her to do so, in her present prostrate and helpless condition, with no voice in the councils of the nation, would be an unjustifiable breach of faith; and that her earnest thanks are due to the President for the firm stand he has taken against amendments to the Constitution forced through in the present condition of affairs."

The code became operative June 1st, under a proclamation of Governor Patton.

SOUTH CAROLINA.

1865, May 2—Gov. Magrath issued a proclamation that the confederate stores within the State should be turned over to State officers, to be distributed among the people.

May 8—Gov. Magrath summoned the State officers to Columbia to resume their duties.

May 14—Maj. Gen. Gillmore issued an order annulling the Governor's acts, and notifying the persons interested not to heed his proclamations.

June 30—Benjamin F. Perry was appointed Provisional Governor.

July 20—Prov. Gov. Perry issued a proclamation fixing the first Monday of September for an election for a State Convention—the qualifications of voters being thus prescribed:

Every loyal citizen who had taken the amnesty oath, and not within the excepted classes in the President's proclamation, will be entitled to vote, provided he was a legal voter under the constitution as it stood prior to the secession of South Carolina. And all who are within the excepted classes must take the oath and apply for a pardon, in order to entitle them to vote or become members of the convention.

September 13—Convention met.

September 15—Secession ordinance repealed, 107 to 3.

September 19—Slavery declared abolished, "the slaves in South Carolina having been emancipated by the action of the United States authorities."

September 27—Election ordered for third Wednesday in October, for State officers. Ordinance passed, creating four congressional districts.

September 29—Convention adjourned.

October 18—James L. Orr elected Governor.

October —Legislature met.

This telegraphic correspondence occurred:

EXECUTIVE OFFICE,
WASHINGTON, D. C., *October* 28, 1865.

B. F. PERRY, *Provisional Governor:*

Your last two despatches have been received and the pardons suggested have been ordered. I hope that your Legislature will have no hesitancy in adopting the amendment to the Constitution of the United States abolishing slavery. It will set an example which will no doubt be followed by the other States, and place South Carolina in a most favorable attitude before the nation. I trust in God that it will be done. The nation and State will then be left free and untrammeled to take that course which sound policy, wisdom, and humanity may suggest.

ANDREW JOHNSON, *President.*

EXECUTIVE OFFICE,
WASHINGTON, D. C., *October* 31, 1865.

B. F. PERRY, *Provisional Governor*:

There is a deep interest felt as to what course the Legislature will take in regard to the adoption of the amendment to the Constitution of the United States abolishing slavery, and the assumption of the debt created to aid in the rebellion against the government of the United States. If the action of the convention was in good faith, why hesitate in making it a part of the Constitution of the United States?

I trust in God that restoration of the Union will not now be defeated, and all that has so far been well done thrown away. I still have faith that all will come out right yet.

This opportunity ought to be understood and appreciated by the people of the southern States. If I know my own heart and every passion which enters it, my earnest desire is to restore the blessings of the Union, and tie up and heal every bleeding wound which has been caused by this fratricidal war. Let us be guided by love and wisdom from on high, and Union and peace will once more reign throughout the land.

ANDREW JOHNSON.

COLUMBIA, S. C., *November* 1, 1865.

His Excellency ANDREW JOHNSON,
President United States:

I will send you to-day the whole proceedings of the State Convention, properly certified, as you request.

The debt contracted by South Carolina during the rebellion is very inconsiderable. Her expenditures for war purposes were paid by the confederate government. She has assumed no debt, or any part of any debt, of that government. Her whole State debt at this time is only about six millions, and that is mostly for railroads and building new State-house prior to the war. The members of the Legislature say they have received no official information of the amendment of the Federal Constitution abolishing slavery. They have no objection to adopting the first section of the amendment proposed; but they fear that the second section may be construed to give Congress power of local legislation over the negroes, and white men, too, after the abolishment of slavery. In good faith South Carolina has abolished slavery, and never will wish to restore it again.

The Legislature is passing a code of laws providing ample and complete protection for the negro. There is a sincere desire to do everything necessary to a restoration of the Union, and tie up and heal every bleeding wound which has been caused by this fratricidal war. I was elected United States Senator by a very flattering vote. The other Senator will be elected to-day.
B. F. PERRY,
Provisional Governor.

—

WASHINGTON, *November* 6, 1865.
His Excellency B. F. PERRY, *Prov. Gov.*:

Your despatch to the President of November 4 has been received. He is not entirely satisfied with the explanations it contains. He deems necessary the passage of adequate ordinances declaring that all insurrectionary proceedings in the State were unlawful and void *ab initio*. Neither the Constitution nor laws direct official information to the State of amendments to the Constitution submitted by Congress. Notices of the amendment by Congress abolishing slavery were nevertheless given by the Secretary of State at the time to the States which were then in communication with this Government. Formal notice will immediately be given to those States which were then in insurrection.

The objection you mention to the last clause of the constitutional amendment is regarded as querulous and unreasonable, because that clause is really restraining in its effect, instead of enlarging the powers of Congress. The President considers the acceptance of the amendment by South Carolina as indispensable to a restoration of her relations with the other States of the Union.
WILLIAM H. SEWARD.

November 7—Provisional Governor Perry sent a message communicating these telegrams, and recommending the ratification, and that they "place on record the construction which had been given to the amendment by the executive department of the Federal Government."

November 13—The Legislature ratified the anti-slavery amendment, in this form:

1. *Resolved, &c.*, That the aforesaid proposed amendment of the Constitution of the United States be, and the same is hereby, accepted, and adopted and ratified by this State.

2. That a certified copy of the foregoing preamble and resolution be forwarded by his excellency the Provisional Governor to the President of the United States, and also to the Secretary of State of the United States.

3. That any attempt by Congress towards legislating upon the political status of former slaves, or their civil relations, would be contrary to the Constitution of the United States as it now is, or as it would be altered by the proposed amendment, in conflict with the policy of the President, declared in his amnesty proclamation, and with the restoration of that harmony upon which depend the vital interests of the American Union.

Respecting the repudiation of the rebel State debt, this telegraphic correspondence took place:

DEPARTMENT OF STATE,
WASHINGTON, *Nov.* 20, 1865.
His Excellency B. F. PERRY,
Provisional Governor:

Your despatch of this date was received at half-past 10 o'clock this morning. This freedom of loyal intercourse between South Carolina and her sister States is manifestly much better and wiser than separation. The President and the whole country are gratified that South Carolina has accepted the congressional amendment to the Constitution abolishing slavery. Upon reflection South Carolina herself would not care to come again into the councils of the Union incumbered and clogged with debts and obligations which had been assumed in her name in a vain attempt to subvert it. The President trusts that she will lose no time in making an effective organic declaration, disavowing all debts and obligations created or assumed in her name or behalf in aid of the rebellion. The President waits further events in South Carolina with deep interest.

You will remain in the exercise of your functions of provisional governor until relieved by his express directions.
WM. H. SEWARD.

—

COLUMBIA, *November* 27, 1865.

HON. W. H. SEWARD: Your telegram of the 20th instant was not received in due time, owing to my absence from Columbia. The Convention having been dissolved, it is impracticable to enact any organic law in regard to the war debt. That debt is very small, as the expenditures of South Carolina were reimbursed by the confederate government. The debt is so mixed up with the ordinary expenses of the State that it cannot be separated. In South Carolina all were guilty of aiding the rebellion, and no one can complain of being taxed to pay the trifling debt incurred by his own assent in perfect good faith. The Convention did all that the President advised to be done, and I thought it wrong to keep a revolutionary body in existence and advised their immediate dissolution, which was done. There is now no power in the Legislature to repudiate the debt if it were possible to separate it from the other debts of the State. Even then it would fall on widows and orphans whose estates were invested in it for safety.
B. F. PERRY,
Provisional Governor.

—

DEPARTMENT OF STATE,
WASHINGTON, *November* 30, 1865.

SIR: I have the honor to acknowledge the receipt of your telegram of the 27th instant, informing me, that as the Convention had been dissolved, it was impossible to adopt the President's suggesstion to repudiate the insurgent debt, and to inform you that while the objections which you urge to the adoption of that proceeding are of a serious nature, the President cannot refrain from awaiting with interest an official expression upon that subject from the Legislature.*

I have the honor to be, sir, your obedient servant, WILLIAM H. SEWARD.

His Excellency B. F. PERRY.

November—The colored State Convention addressed a memorial to Congress, asking that equal suffrage be conferred upon them in common with the white men of the State.

November 22—Election held for Representatives in Congress.

Respecting their admission there was this telegraphic correspondence:

COLUMBIA, S. C., *November* 27, 1865.

President JOHNSON:

Will you please inform me whether the South Carolina members of Congress should be in Washington at the organization of the House. Will the Clerk of the House call their names if their credentials are presented to him? Will the test oath be required, or will it be refused by Congress? If the members are not allowed to take their seats they do not wish to incur the trouble and expense of going on, and the mortification of being rejected. Do give your views and wishes.

B. F. PERRY,
Provisional Governor.

EXECUTIVE OFFICE,
Washington, D. C., November 27, 1865.

B. F. PERRY, *Provisional Governor:*

I do not think it necessary for the members elect from South Carolina to be present at the organization of Congress. On the contrary, it will be better policy to present their certificates of election after the two Houses are organized, and then it will be a simple question under the Constitution of the members taking their seats. Each House must judge for itself the election, returns, and qualifications of its own members. As to what the two Houses will do in reference to the oath now required to be taken before the members can take their seats is unknown to me, and I do not like to predict; but, upon the whole, I am of opinion that it would be better for the question to come up and be disposed of after the two Houses have been organized.

I hope that your Legislature will adopt a code in reference to free persons of color that will be acceptable to the country, at the same time doing justice to the white and colored population.

ANDREW JOHNSON,
President of the United States.

FLORIDA.

1865, April 8—Abraham K. Allison, President of the rebel Senate, of Florida, announced the death of John Milton, rebel Governor, and appointed June 7 for election of a successor.

May 14—Major General Gillmore issued an order annulling this proclamation, and commanding the people to give it no heed whatever.

July 13—William Marvin appointed Provisional Governor.

August 3—Provisional Governor Marvin called an election for delegates to a convention for October 10th—these provisions governing the election:

"Every free white male person of the age of twenty-one years and upwards, and who shall be at the time of offering to vote a citizen of the United States, and who shall have resided and had his home in this State for one year next preceding the election, and for six months in the county in which he may offer to vote, and who shall have taken and subscribed the oath of amnesty, as set forth in the President's proclamation of amnesty of the 29th day of May, 1865, and if he comes within the exceptions contained in said proclamation, shall have taken said oath, and have been specially pardoned by the President, shall be entitled to vote in the county where he resides, and shall be eligible as a member of said convention, and none others. Where the person offering to vote comes within the exceptions contained in the amnesty proclamation, and shall have taken the amnesty oath, and shall have made application to the President for a special pardon through the Provisional Governor, and shall have been recommended by him for such pardon, the inspectors or judges of the election may, in most instances, properly presume that such pardon has been granted, though, owing to the want of mail facilities, it may not have been received by the party at the time of the election.

"Free white soldiers, seamen, and marines in the army or navy of the United States, who were qualified by their residence to vote in said State at the time of their respective enlistments, and who shall have taken and subscribed the amnesty oath, shall be entitled to vote in the county where they respectively reside. But no soldier, seaman, or marine not a resident in the State at the time of his enlistment shall be allowed to vote."

October 25—Convention met.

October 28.—Secession ordinance annulled.

November 6—Slavery abolished—"slavery having been destroyed in the State by the Government of the United States." Same ordinance gives colored people the right to testify in all cases where the person or property of such person is involved, but denies them the right to testify where the interest of the white class are involved.

Same day—Rebel State debt repudiated. A bill was first passed submitting this question to a vote of the people; but this was reconsidered, on finding this was a condition of recognition by the executive branch of the government, and the direct repudiation adopted.

November 29—Election held under an ordinance of the Convention for State officers and Representative in Congress.

December 18—Legislature met.

December 28—Anti-slavery amendment ratified, with this declaratory resolution a part of the ratifying instrument:

"*Resolved*, That this amendment to the Con-

* December 21—Before adjourning, the subject of the repudiation of the war debt was referred to the Committee on Federal Relations, who recommended the appointment of a special joint committee of both Houses to inquire into the amount of such debt due by the State, and to whom due; and to report at the next regular session of the Legislature, which will be in November, 1866.

stitution of the United States is adopted by the Legislature of the State of Florida, with the understanding that it does not confer upon the Congress the power to legislate upon the political status of the freedmen in this State."

Pending this action, this telegraphic correspondence took place:

DEPARTMENT OF STATE,
WASHINGTON, *September* 12, 1865.

SIR: Your excellency's letter of the 29th ultimo, with the accompanying proclamation, has been received and submitted to the President. The steps to which it refers, towards reorganizing the government of Florida, seem to be in the main judicious, and good results from them may be hoped for. The presumption to which the proclamation refers, however, in favor of insurgents who may wish to vote, and who may have applied for, but not received, their pardons, is not entirely approved. All applications for pardons will be duly considered, and will be disposed of as soon as may be practicable. It must, however, be distinctly understood that the restoration to which your proclamation refers will be subject to the decision of Congress.

I have the honor to be, your excellency's obedient servant, WILLIAM H. SEWARD.

His Excellency WILLIAM MARVIN.

—

OFFICE OF THE PROVISIONAL GOVERNOR,
TALLAHASSEE, FLA., *October* 7, 1865.

* * * I have said that the Convention will, in good faith, abolish slavery; but I think it probable that the Legislature, which will be elected and convened at an early period, will feel some reluctance against ratifying the proposed amendment to the Constitution of the United States. The principal argument urged against the ratification is, that the Legislature will thereby assist to impose abolition on Kentucky and Delaware, which have not yet abolished slavery. If the President should think it desirable that the Legislature should ratify the proposed amendment, either with a view to promote a more complete reconciliation between the North and the South, or for any other reason, he possibly may not deem it amiss to communicate to me his wishes on the subject. His wishes on the subject would be very potent in the State.

The military authorities in the State, under the command of Major General Foster, are rendering me every possible assistance in sending out notices and proclamations of the election, in the absence of mail facilities, and no disagreements exist between us.

I have the honor to be, very respectfully, your obedient servant,

WM. MARVIN, *Provisional Governor.*

Hon. W. H. SEWARD, *Secretary of State.*

—

DEPARTMENT OF STATE,
WASHINGTON, *November* 1, 1865.

His Excellency WILLIAM MARVIN,
Provisional Governor:

Your letter of October 7 was received and submitted to the President. He is gratified with the favorable progress towards reorganization in Florida, and directs me to say that he regards the ratification by the Legislature of the congressional amendment of the Constitution of the United States as indispensable to a successful restoration of the true legal relations between Florida and the other States, and equally indispensable to the return of peace and harmony throughout the Republic.

WILLIAM H. SEWARD.

VIRGINIA.

1865, April 4—President Lincoln visited Richmond.

April 7—An informal meeting of private individuals, among whom were five or six members of the rebel legislature in Richmond, was had to consider a suggestion that the Legislature reassemble to call a Convention to restore Virginia to the Union, said to be with the concurrence of President Lincoln.

April 12—This address was published in the Richmond *Whig:*

ADDRESS TO THE PEOPLE OF VIRGINIA.

The undersigned, members of the Legislature of the State of Virginia, in connection with a number of the citizens of the State, whose names are attached to this paper, in view of the evacuation of the city of Richmond by the Confederate government and its occupation by the military authorities of the United States, the surrender of the army of northern Virginia, and the suspension of the jurisdiction of the civil power of the State, are of the opinion that an immediate meeting of the General Assembly of the State is called for by the exigencies of the situation. The consent of the military authorities of the United States to a session of the Legislature in Richmond, in connection with the Governor and Lieutenant Governor, to their free deliberation upon public affairs, and to the ingress and departure of all its members under safe conduct, has been obtained.

The United States authorities will afford transportation from any point under their control to any of the persons before mentioned.

The matters to be submitted to the Legislature are the restoration of peace to the State of Virginia, and the adjustment of the questions, involving life, liberty and property, that have arisen in the State as a consequence of war.

We, therefore, earnestly request the Governor, Lieutenant Governor, and members of the Legislature, to repair to this city by the 25th of April, instant.

We understand that full protection to persons and property will be afforded in the State, and we recommend to peaceful citizens to remain at their homes and pursue their usual avocations with confidence that they will not be interrupted.

We earnestly solicit the attendance in Richmond, on or before the 25th of April, instant, of the following persons, citizens of Virginia, to confer with us as to the best means of restoring peace to the State of Virginia. We have secured safe conduct from the military authorities of the United States for them to enter the city and depart without molestation:

Hons. R. M. T. Hunter, A. T. Caperton, Wm. C. Rives, John Letcher, A. H. H. Stuart, R. L. Montague, Fayette McMullen, J. P. Holcombe, Alex. Rives, B. Johnson Barbour, Jas. Barbour, Wm. L. Goggin, J. B. Baldwin, Thos. S. Gholson, Waller Staples, S. D. Miller, Thos. J. Randolph, Wm. T. Early, R. A. Claybrook, John Critcher Williams, T. H. Eppes, and those other persons for whom passports have been procured, and especially others whom we consider it unnecessary to mention. Signed—

A. J. Marshall, Senator from Fauquier.

John Wesson, Senator from Marion.

James Venable, Senator elect from Petersburg.

David J. Burr, of the House of Delegates, from Richmond.

David J. Saunders, of the House of Delegates, Richmond city.

L. S. Hall, of the House of Delegates, Wetzel county.

J. J. English, of the House of Delegates, Henrico county.

Wm. Ambers, of the House of Delegates, Chesterfield county.

A. M. Keetz, House Delegates, Petersburg.

H. W. Thomas, Second Auditor, Richmond.

Lieutenant L. L. Moncure, Chief Clerk, Second Auditor's office.

Joseph Mayo, Mayor, city of Richmond.

Robert S. Howard, Clerk Hustings Court, Richmond city.

Thomas W. Dudley, Sergeant, Richmond city.

Littleton Tazewell, Commonwealth's Attorney, Richmond city.

Wm. T. Jaynes, Judge of the Circuit Court, Petersburg.

John A. Meredith, Judge of the Circuit Court, Richmond.

Wm. H. Lyons, Judge of the Hustings Court, Richmond.

Wm. C. Wickham, Member of Congress, Richmond.

Benjamin S. Ewell, President of William and Mary College.

Nat. Tyler, editor Richmond *Enquirer*.

R. F. Walker, publisher, *Examiner*.

J. R. Anderson, Richmond.

R. R. Howison, Richmond.

W. Goddin, Richmond.

P. G. Bagley, Richmond.

F. J. Smith, Richmond.

Franklin Sterns, Henrico.

John Lyon, Petersburg.

Thomas B. Fisher, Fauquier.

Wm. M. Harrison, Charles City.

Cyrus Hall, Ritchie.

Thos. W. Garnett, King and Queen.

James A. Scott, Richmond.

I concur in the preceding recommendation.

J. A. CAMPBELL.

Approved for publication in the *Whig* and in handbill form. G. WEITZEL,

Major General Commanding.

RICHMOND, VA., *April* 11, 1865.

April 12—Said authority revoked in this telegram from President Lincoln to Major General Weitzel, being the last telegram ever transmitted by the former:

OFFICE U. S. MILITARY TELEGRAPH,
WAR DEPARTMENT,
WASHINGTON, D. C., *April* 12, 1865.

Major General WEITZEL, *Richmond, Va.*:

I have just seen Judge Campbell's letter to you of the 7th. He assumes, as appears to me, that I have called the insurgent Legislature of Virginia together, as the rightful Legislature of the State, to settle all differences with the United States. I have done no such thing. I spoke of them not as a legislature, but as "the gentlemen who have *acted*, as the Legislature of Virginia in support of the rebellion." I did this on purpose to exclude the assumption that I was recognizing them as a *rightful* body. I dealt with them as men having power *de facto* to do a specific thing, to wit, "to withdraw the Virginia troops and other support from resistance to the General Government," for which, in the paper handed to Judge Campbell, I promised a specific equivalent, to wit, a remission to the people of the State, except in certain cases, the confiscation of their property. I meant this and no more. Inasmuch, however, as Judge Campbell misconstrues this, and is still pressing for an armistice, contrary to the explicit statement of the paper I gave him; and particularly as Gen. Grant has since captured the Virginia troops, so that giving a consideration for their withdrawal is no longer applicable, let my letter to you and the paper to Judge Campbell both be withdrawn or countermanded, and he be notified of it. Do not now allow them to assemble; but if any have come, allow them safe return to their homes.

A. LINCOLN.

May 9—President Johnson issued an executive order recognizing the Pierpoint Administration as that of Virginia. (See President Johnson's Orders, p. 8.)

June 19—Legislature met.

June 20—Bill passed prescribing means by which persons who have been disfranchised by the third article of the constitution may be restored to the rights of voters. [It provides, substantially, that persons, otherwise qualified as voters, who take the amnesty oath and an oath to uphold the executive government of Virginia, shall be qualified as voters.]

June 21—Bill passed submitting to a vote of the people whether the legislature to be chosen at the next election should have power to alter or amend the third article of the constitution, which is in these words:

"No person shall vote or hold office under this constitution who has held office under the so-called Confederate government, or under any rebellious State government, or who has been a member of the so-called Confederate Congress, or a member of any State Legislature in rebellion against the authority of the United States, excepting therefrom the county officers."

June 23—Legislature adjourned.

October 12—Election held for Representatives in Congress. The vote on empowering the Legislature to alter the third article almost unanimously affirmative.

December 4—Legislature assembled. A bill passed, providing that all qualified voters heretofore identified with "the rebellion," and not excluded from the amnesty proclamation by President Johnson (with the exception of those embraced in the "$20,000 clause,") can appear before a notary public, or other persons authorized to administer oaths, under the restored Government, and recover the right of suffrage, by taking the amnesty oath of the 29th of May, 1865, an oath to support the restored Government of Virginia, and to protect and defend the Constitution of the United States. He also becomes eligible to office, unless he has "held office under the so-called Confederate government, or under any rebellious State government, or has been a member of the so-called Confederate Congress, or a member of any State Legislature in rebellion against the authority of the United States," excepting therefrom county officers.

TENNESSEE.

1865, March 4—William G. Brownlow elected Governor, under the organization effected by Andrew Johnson, Military Governor. Brownlow received 23,352 votes, scattering 37.

June 5—Franchise act passed, with these provisions:

SEC. 1. *Be it enacted, &c.*, That the following persons, to wit:

1. Every white man twenty-one years of age, a citizen of the United States and a citizen of the county wherein he may offer his vote six months next preceding the day of election, and publicly known to have entertained unconditional Union sentiments from the outbreak of the rebellion until the present time; and

2. Every white man, a citizen of the United States and a citizen of the county wherein he may offer his vote six months next preceding the day of election, having arrived at the age of twenty-one years since March 4, 1865: *Provided*, That he has not been engaged in armed rebellion against the authority of the United States voluntarily; and

3. Every white man of lawful age coming from another State, and being a citizen of the United States, on proof of loyalty to the United States, and being a citizen of the county wherein he may offer his vote six months next preceding the day of election; and

4. Every white man, a citizen of the United States and a citizen of this State, who has served as a soldier in the army of the United States, and has been or may be hereafter honorably discharged therefrom; and

5. Every white man of lawful age, a citizen of the United States and a citizen of the county wherein he may offer his vote six months next preceding the day of election, who was conscripted by force into the so-called confederate army, and was known to be a Union man, on proof of loyalty to the United States, established by the testimony of two voters under the previous clauses of this section; and

6. Every white man who voted in this State at the presidential election in November, 1864, or voted on the 22d of February, 1865, or voted on the 4th of March, 1865, in this State, and all others who had taken the "oath of allegiance" to the United States, and may be known by the judges of election to have been true friends to the Government of the United States, and would have voted in said previously mentioned elections if the same had been holden within their reach, shall be entitled to the privileges of the elective franchise.

SEC. 2. That all persons who are or shall have been civil or diplomatic officers or agents of the so-called Confederate States of America, or who have left judicial stations under the United States or the State of Tennessee to aid, in any way, the existing or recent rebellion against the authority of the United States, or who are or shall have been military or naval officers of the so-called Confederate States, above the rank of captain in the army or lieutenant in the navy; or who have left seats in the United States Congress or seats in the Legislature of the State of Tennessee, to aid in said rebellion, or have resigned commissions in the army or navy of the United States, and afterward have voluntarily given aid to said rebellion; or persons who have been engaged in treating otherwise than lawfully, as prisoners of war, persons found in the United States service as officers, soldiers, seamen, or in any other capacities; or persons who have been or are absentees from the United States for the purpose of aiding the rebellion; or persons who held pretended offices under the government of States in insurrection against the United States; or persons who left their homes within the jurisdiction and protection of the United States, or fled before the approach of the national forces and passed beyond the Federal military lines into the so-called Confederate States, for the purpose of aiding the rebellion, shall be denied and refused the privilege of the elective franchise in this State for the term of fifteen years from and after the passage of this act.

SEC. 3. That all other persons, except those mentioned in section one of this act, are hereby and henceforth excluded and denied the exercise of the privilege of the elective franchise in this State for the term of five years from and after the passage of this act.

SEC. 4. That all persons embraced in section three of this act, after the expiration of said five years, may be readmitted to the privilege of the elective franchise by petition to the circuit or chancery court, on proof of loyalty to the United States, in open court, upon the testimony of two or more loyal citizens of the United States.

July 15—President Johnson sent this telegram:

WASHINGTON, D. C.—3.50 P. M.,
July 16, 1865.

To Governor W. G. Brownlow:

I hope, as I have no doubt you will see, that the laws passed by the last Legislature are faithfully executed, and that all illegal voters in the approaching election be kept from the polls, and that the election of members of Congress be conducted fairly. Whenever it becomes necessary for the execution of the law and the protection of the ballot-box, you will call upon General Thomas for sufficient military force to sustain the civil authority of the State. I have just read your address, which I most heartily endorse.

ANDREW JOHNSON,
President U. S. A.

1866, April 12—An amendment to the franchise act passed the House, 41 to 15.

May 3—The Senate passed it, 13 to 6. Its principal provisions are:

SEC. 1. That every white male inhabitant of this State of the age of twenty-one years, a citizen of the United States and a resident of the county wherein he may offer his vote six months next preceding the day of election, shall be entitled to the privilege of the elective franchise, subject to the following exceptions and disqualifications, to wit:

First. Said voter shall have never borne arms against the Government of the United States for the purpose of aiding the late rebellion, nor have voluntarily given aid, comfort, countenance, counsel, or encouragement to any rebellion against the authority of the United States Government, nor aided, countenanced, or encouraged acts of hostility thereto.

Second. That said voter shall have never sought, or voluntarily accepted, any office, civil or military, or attempted to exercise the functions of any office, civil or military, under the authority or pretended authority of the so-called Confederate States of America, or of any insurrectionary State whatever, hostile or opposed to the authority of the United States Government, with the intent and desire to aid said rebellion or insurrectionary authority.

Third. That said voter shall have never voluntarily supported any pretended government, power, or authority hostile or inimical to the authority of the United States, by contributions in money or property, by persuasion or influence, or in any other way whatever: *Provided*, That the foregoing restrictions and disqualifications shall not apply to any white citizen who may have served in and been honorably discharged from the army or navy of the United States since the 1st day of January, 1862, nor to those who voted in the Presidential election in November, 1864, or voted in the election for "ratification or rejection" in February, 1865, or voted in the election held on the 4th day of March of the same year for Governor and members of the Legislature, nor to those who have been appointed to any civil or military office by Andrew Johnson, Military Governor, or William G. Brownlow, Governor of Tennessee, all of whom are hereby declared to be qualified voters upon their complying with the requirements of this act: *Provided*, That this latter clause shall not apply to any commission issued upon any election which may have been held.

SEC. 2. That the Governor of the State shall, within sixty days after the passage of this act, appoint a commissioner of registration for each and every county in the State, who shall, without delay, enter upon the discharge of his duties, and who shall have full power to administer the necessary oaths provided by this act.

May 19—A bill was passed to disqualify certain persons from holding office, civil or military. It excludes those persons who held civil or diplomatic offices, or were agents of the so called Confederate States, or who left judicial stations under the United States, or the State of Tennessee, to aid the rebellion, or who were military or naval officers of the so-called Confederate States, above the rank of captain in the army, or lieutenant in the navy, or who left seats in the United States Congress, or seats in the Legislature of the State of Tennessee, to aid the rebellion, or who resigned commissions in the army or navy of the United States and afterward gave voluntary aid to the rebellion, or who absented themselves from the State of Tennessee to give such aid, or who held offices under the States in insurrection against the United States with intent to aid the rebellion, or who ever held office in the State of Tennessee of legislative, judicial, or executive character, under an oath to support the constitution of the State of Tennessee, and who violated said oath, and gave voluntary aid or countenance to the rebellion, that each and all be excluded from all offices, State, county, or municipal.

It also provides that any qualified voter shall not be excluded from office by the provisions of this bill, as amended.

May —The Senate rejected a suffrage bill, 16 to 5, which proposed to allow all blacks and whites of legal age to vote, and exclude all, after 1875, who cannot read.

May 28—The Legislature adjourned until November 28.

TEXAS.

1865, June 17—Andrew J. Hamilton appointed Provisional Governor.

1866, March —Convention met.

April 2—Convention adjourned. The Constitution to be voted on, June 5. It abolishes slavery, and annuls the Secession Ordinance. The war debt has been repudiated. Five years residence required for eligibility to the Legislature. White population is the basis of representation for State purposes. An ordinance passed exempting all persons who, under authority of civil or military power, had inflicted injury upon persons during the war, from accountability therefor.

ARKANSAS.

1865, October 30—President Johnson sent this telegram to Governor Isaac Murphy, elected Governor under the free State organization formerly made.

EXECUTIVE OFFICE, WASHINGTON, D. C., *October* 30, 1865.

To GOV. MURPHY, Little Rock, Arkansas:

There will be no interference with your present organization of State government. I have learned from E. W. Gantt, Esq., and other sources, that all is working well, and you will proceed and resume the former relations with the Federal Government, and all the aid in the power of the Government will be given in restoring the State to its former relations.

ANDREW JOHNSON, *Pres't of the U. S.*

LOUISIANA.

There was no interference with the State organization formerly made.

1865, November —J. M. Wells was elected Governor, and Albert Voorhis, Lieut. Governor.

November 23—Legislature met in extra session again, under proclamation of the Governor.

December 22—Legislature adjourned.

1866, March —J. T. Monroe elected mayor of New Orleans, and James O. Nixon an alderman.

March 19—General Canby issued an order suspending them from the exercise of any of the functions of these offices until the pleasure of the President be made known—as they come within the excepted class of the President's proclamation. They were subsequently pardoned, on application, and took the offices.

IV.

LEGISLATION RESPECTING FREEDMEN.

NORTH CAROLINA.

1866, March 10—The act "concerning negroes, and persons of color, or of mixed blood," passed by the Legislature, declares that "negroes and their issue, even where one ancestor in each succeeding generation to the fourth inclusive, is white, shall be deemed persons of color." It gives them all the privileges of white persons before the courts in the mode of prosecuting, defending, continuing, removing, and transferring their suits at law and in equity, and makes them eligible as witnesses, when not otherwise incompetent, in "all controversies at law and in equity where the rights of persons or property of persons of color shall be put in issue, and would be concluded by the judgment or decree of court; and also in pleas of the State, where the violence, fraud, or injury alleged shall be charged to have been done by or to persons of color. In all other civil and criminal cases such evidence shall be deemed inadmissible, unless by consent of the parties of record: *Provided*, That this section shall not go into effect until jurisdiction in matters relating to freedmen shall be fully committed to the courts of this State: *Provided further*, That no person shall be deemed incompetent to bear testimony in such cases, because of being a party to the record or in interest."

The criminal laws of the State are extended in their operation to embrace persons of color, and the same punishment is inflicted on them as on the whites, except for rape, which, if a white female is the victim, is a capital crime for a black. The law regarding apprentices is so amended as to make its provisions applicable to blacks, but it gives the former masters the preference, and declares that they should be regarded as the most suitable persons. Provision is also made for legalizing the marriages of the blacks contracted during slavery, and for punishment of illicit cohabitation. All which is modified by a proviso that the act shall not take effect until after the Freedmen's Bureau is removed. Where men and women, lately slaves, now cohabit together in the relation of husband and wife, they shall be deemed to have been lawfully married at the time of the commencement of such cohabitation; and they are required to go before the clerk of the county court, acknowledge the cohabitation, of which record shall be made, and shall be *prima facie* evidence of the statements made.

All contracts between any persons whatever, whereof one or more of them shall be a person of color, for the sale or purchase of any horse, mule, ass, jennet, neat cattle, hog, sheep, or goat, whatever may be the value of such articles, and all contracts between such persons for any other article or articles of property whatever of the value of ten dollars or more, and all contracts executed or executory between such persons for the payment of money of the value of ten dollars or more, shall be void as to all persons whatever, unless the same be put in writing and signed by the vendors or debtors, and witnessed by a white person who can read and write.

Marriage between white persons and persons of color shall be void; and every person authorized to solemnize the rites of matrimony, who shall knowingly solemnize the same between such persons, and every clerk of a court who shall knowingly issue license for their marriage, shall be deemed guilty of a misdemeanor, and, moreover, shall pay a penalty of five hundred dollars to any person suing for the same.

MISSISSIPPI.

An Act to regulate the Relation of Master and Apprentice relative to Freedmen, Free Negroes, and Mulattoes, November 22, 1865.

SEC. 1 provides that it shall be the duty of all sheriffs, justices of the peace, and other civil officers of the several counties in this State to report to the probate courts of their respective counties semi-annually, at the January and July terms of said courts, all freedmen, free negroes, and mulattoes, under the age of eighteen, within their respective counties, beats, or districts, who are orphans, or whose parent or parents have not the means, or who refuse to provide for and support said minors, and thereupon it shall be the duty of said probate court to order the clerk of said court to apprentice said minors to some competent and suitable person, on such terms as the court may direct, having a particular care to the interest of said minors: *Provided*, That the former owner of said minors shall have the preference when, in the opinion of the court, he or she shall be a suitable person for that purpose.

SEC. 2 provides that the said court shall be fully satisfied that the person or persons to whom said minor shall be apprenticed shall be a suitable person to have the charge and care of said minor, and fully to protect the interest of said minor: *Provided*, That said apprentice shall be bound by indenture, in case of males until they are twenty-one years old, and in case of females until they are eighteen years old.

SEC. 3 provides that in the management and control of said apprentices said master or mistress shall have power to inflict such moderate corporeal chastisement as a father or guardian is allowed to inflict on his or her child or ward at common law: *Provided*, That in no case shall cruel or inhuman punishment be inflicted.

SEC. 4 provides that if any apprentice shall leave the employment of his or her master or mistress, without his or her consent, said master or mistress may pursue and recapture said apprentice, and bring him or her before any justice of the peace of the county, whose duty it shall be to remand said apprentice to the service of his or her master or mistress; and in the event of a refusal on the part of said apprentice so to return, then said justice shall commit said apprentice to the jail of said county, on failure to give bond, until the next term of the county court; and it shall be the duty of said court, at the first term thereafter, to investigate said case, and if the court shall be of opinion that said apprentice left the employment of his or her master or mistress without good cause, to order him or her to be punished, as provided for the punishment of hired freedmen, as may be from time to time provided for by law for desertion, until he or she shall agree to return to his or her master or mistress: *Provided*, That the court may grant continuances, as in other cases: *And provided further*, That if the court shall believe that said apprentice had good cause to quit his said master or mistress, the court shall discharge said apprentice from said indenture, and also enter a judgment against the master or mistress, for not more than one hundred dollars, for the use and benefit of said apprentice, to be collected on execution, as in other cases.

SEC. 5 provides that if any person entice away any apprentice from his or her master or mistress, or shall knowingly employ an apprentice, or furnish him or her food or clothing, without the written consent of his or her master or mistress, or shall sell or give said apprentice ardent spirits without such consent, said person so offending shall be deemed guilty of a high misdemeanor, and shall on conviction thereof before the county court, be punished as provided for the punishment of persons enticing from their employer hired freedmen, free negroes, or mulattoes.

SEC. 6 makes it the duty of all civil officers to report any minors within their respective counties to said probate court for apprenticeship.

SEC. 9 provides that it shall be lawful for any freedman, free negro, or mulatto, having a minor child or children, to apprentice the said minor child or children as provided for by this act.

SEC. 10 provides that in all cases where the age of the freedman, free negro, or mulatto cannot be ascertained by record testimony, the judge of the county court shall fix the age.

The Vagrant Act, November 24, 1865.

SEC. 1 defines who are vagrants.

SEC. 2 provides that all freedmen, free negroes, and mulattoes in this State, over the age of eighteen years, found on the second Monday in January, 1866, or thereafter, with no lawful employment or business, or found unlawfully assembling themselves together, either in the day or night time, and all white persons so assembling with freedmen, free negroes, or mulattoes, or usually associating with freedmen, free negroes, or mulattoes on terms of equality, or living in adultery or fornication with a freedwoman, free negro, or mulatto, shall be deemed vagrants, and on conviction thereof shall be fined in the sum of not exceeding, in the case of a freedman, free negro or mulatto, fifty dollars, and a white man two hundred dollars, and imprisoned, at the discretion of the court, the free negro not exceeding ten days, and the white man not exceeding six months.

SEC. 3 gives all justices of the peace, mayors, and aldermen jurisdiction to try all questions of vagrancy, and it is made their duty to arrest parties violating any provisions of this act, investigate the charges, and, on conviction, punish as provided. It is made the duty of all sheriffs, constables, town constables, city marshals, and all like officers, to report to some officer having jurisdiction all violations of any of the provisions of this act, and it is made the duty of the county courts to inquire if any officer has neglected any of these duties, and if guilty to fine him not exceeding $100, to be paid into the county treasury.

SEC. 5 provides that all fines and forfeitures collected under the provisions of this act shall be paid into the county treasury for general county purposes, and in case any freedman, free negro or mulatto, shall fail for five days after the imposition of any fine or forfeiture upon him or her, for violation of any of the provisions of this act to pay the same, that it shall be, and is hereby made, the duty of the sheriff of the proper county to hire out said freedman, free negro or mulatto, to any person who will, for the shortest period of service, pay said fine or forfeiture and all costs: *Provided*, A preference shall be given to the employer, if there be one, in which case the employer shall be entitled to deduct and retain the amount so paid from the wages of such freedman, free negro or mulatto, then due or to become due; and in case such freedman, free negro or mulatto cannot be hired out, he or she may be dealt with as a pauper.

SEC. 6 provides that the same duties and liabilities existing among white persons of this State shall attach to freedmen, free negroes and mulattoes, to support their indigent families and all colored paupers; and that in order to secure a support for such indigent freedmen, free negroes and mulattoes, it shall be lawful, and it is hereby made the duty of the boards of county police of each county in this State, to levy a poll or capitation tax on each and every freedman, free negro or mulatto, between the ages of eighteen and sixty years, not to exceed the sum of one dollar annually to each person so taxed, which tax when collected shall be paid into the county treasurer's hands, and constitute a fund to be called the freedmen's pauper fund, which shall be applied by the commissioners of the poor for the maintenance of the poor of the freedmen, free negroes and mulattoes, of this State, under such regulations as may be established by the boards of the county police in the respective counties of this State.

SEC. 7 provides that if any freedman, free negro or mulatto shall fail or refuse to pay any tax levied according to the provisions of the sixth section of this act, it shall be *prima facie* evidence of vagrancy, and it shall be the duty of the sheriff to arrest such freedman, free negro or mulatto, or such persons refusing or neglecting to pay such tax, and proceed at once to hire, for the shortest time, such delinquent tax-payer to any one who will pay the said tax, with the accruing costs, giving preference to the employer, if there be one.

An Act to confer Civil Rights on Freedmen, and for other Purposes, November 25, 1865.

SECTION 1 provides that all freedmen, free negroes and mulattoes may sue and be sued, implead and be impleaded in all the courts of law and equity of this State, and may acquire personal property and choses in action by descent or purchase, and may dispose of the same in the same manner and to the same extent that white persons may: *Provided*, That the provisions of this section shall not be so construed as to allow any freedman, free negro or mulatto to rent or lease any lands or tenements, except in incorporated towns or cities, in which places the corporate authorities shall control the same.

SEC. 2 provides that all freedmen, free negroes and mulattoes may intermarry with each other in the same manner and under the same regulations that are provided by law for white persons: *Provided*, That the clerk of probate shall keep separate records of the same.

SEC. 3 further provides that all freedmen, free negroes and mulattoes, who do now and have heretofore lived and cohabited together as husband and wife shall be taken and held in law as legally married, and the issue shall be taken and held as legitimate for all purposes. That it shall not be lawful for any freedman, free negro or mulatto to intermarry with any white person; nor for any white person to intermarry with any freedman, free negro or mulatto; and any person who shall so intermarry shall be deemed guilty of felony, and on conviction thereof, shall be confined in the State penitentiary for life; and those shall be deemed freedmen, free negroes and mulattoes who are of pure negro blood, and those descended from a negro to the third generation, inclusive, though one ancestor of each generation may have been a white person.

SEC. 4 provides that in addition to cases in which freedmen, free negroes and mulattoes are now by law competent witnesses, freedmen, free negroes and mulattoes shall be competent in civil cases, when a party or parties to the suit, either plaintiff or plaintiffs, defendant or defendants; also in cases where freedmen, free negroes and mulattoes are either plaintiff or plaintiffs, defendant or defendants, and a white person or white persons is or are the opposing party or parties, plaintiff or plaintiffs, defendant or defendants. They shall also be competent witnesses in all criminal prosecutions where the crime charged is alleged to have been committed by a white person upon or against the person or property of a freedman, free negro or mulatto: *Provided*, That in all cases said witnesses shall be examined in open court on the stand, except, however, they may be examined before the grand jury, and shall in all cases be subject to the rules and tests of the common law as to competency and credibility.

SEC. 5 provides that every freedman, free negro, and mulatto shall on the second Monday of January, one thousand eight hundred and sixty-six, and annually thereafter, have a lawful home or employment, and shall have written evidence thereof, as follows, to wit: If living in any incorporated city, town, or village, a license from the mayor thereof, and if living outside of any incorporated city, town, or village, from the member of the board of police of his beat, authorizing him or her to do irregular and job work, or a written contract, as provided in section six of this act; which licenses may be revoked for cause at any time by the authority granting the same.

SEC. 6 provides that all contracts for labor made with freedmen, free negroes, and mulattoes, for a longer period than one month, shall be in writing and in duplicate, attested and read to said freedman, free negro, or mulatto by a beat, city, or county officer or two disinterested white persons of the county in which the labor is to be performed, of which each party shall have one; and said contracts shall be taken and held as entire contracts, and if the laborer shall quit the service of the employer before the expiration of his term of service without good cause, he shall forfeit his wages for that year up to the time of quitting.

SEC. 7. provides that every civil officer shall, and every person may arrest and carry back to his or her legal employer any freedman, free negro, or mulatto who shall have quit the service of his or her employer before the expiration of his or her term of service without good cause; and said officer and person shall be entitled to receive for arresting and carrying back every deserting employé aforesaid the sum of five dollars, and ten cents per mile from the place of arrest to the place of delivery, and the same shall be paid by the employer and held as a set-off for so much against the wages of said deserting employé: *Provided*, That said arrested party after being so returned may appeal to a justice of the peace or member of the board of the police of the county, who, on notice to the alleged employer, shall try, summarily, whether said appellant is legally employed by the alleged employer and has good cause to quit said employer; either party shall have the right of appeal to the county court, pending which the alleged deserter shall be remanded to the alleged employer, or otherwise disposed of as shall be right and just; and the decision of the county court shall be final.

SEC. 8 provides that upon affidavit made by the employer of any freedman, free negro, or mulatto, or other credible person, before any justice of the peace or member of the board of police, that any freedman, free negro, or mulatto, legally employed by said employer, has illegally deserted said employment, such justice of the peace or member of the board of police shall issue his warrant or warrants, returnable before himself or other such officer, directed to any sheriff, constable, or special deputy, commanding him to arrest said deserter and return him or her to said employer, and the like proceedings shall be had as provided in the preceding section; and it shall be lawful for any officer to whom such warrant shall be directed to execute said warrant in any county of this State, and that said warrant may be transmitted without indorsement to any like officer of another county to be executed and returned as aforesaid, and the said employer shall pay the cost of said warrants and arrest and return, which shall be set off for so much against the wages of said deserter.

SEC. 9 provides that if any person shall persuade, or attempt to persuade, entice, or cause any freedman, free negro, or mulatto to desert from the legal employment of any person before the expiration of his or her term of service, or shall knowingly employ any such deserting freedman, free negro, or mulatto, or shall knowingly give or sell to any such deserting freedman, free negro, or mulatto any food, raiment, or other thing, he or she shall be guilty of a misdemeanor, and upon conviction shall be fined not less than twenty-five dollars and not more than two hundred dollars and the costs; and if said fine and costs shall not be immediately paid, the court shall sentence said convict to not exceeding two months' imprisonment in the county jail, and he or she shall, moreover, be liable to the party injured in damages: *Provided*, If any person shall, or shall attempt to, persuade, entice, or cause any freedman, free negro, or mulatto to desert from any legal employment of any person with the view to employ said freedman, free negro, or mulatto without the limits of this State, such person, on conviction, shall be fined not less than fifty dollars and not more than five hundred dollars and costs; and if said fine and costs shall not be immediately paid the court shall sentence said convict to not exceeding six months' imprisonment in the county jail.

SEC. 10 provides that it shall be lawful for any freedman, free negro, or mulatto to charge any white person, freedman, free negro, or mulatto, by affidavit, with any criminal offence against his or her person or property, and upon such affidavit the proper process shall be issued and executed as if said affidavit was made by a white person, and it shall be lawful for any freedman, free negro, or mulatto, in any action, suit, or controversy pending or about to be instituted in any court of law or equity in this State, to make all needful and lawful affidavits as shall be necessary for the institution, prosecution, or defence of such suit or controversy.

SEC. 11 provides that the penal laws of this State, in all cases not otherwise specially provided for, shall apply and extend to all freedmen, free negroes, and mulattoes.

An Act Supplementary to "An Act to confer Civil Rights upon Freedmen," and for other purposes, December 2, 1865.

SEC. 1 provides that in every case where any white person has been arrested and brought to trial, by virtue of the provisions of the tenth section of the above recited act, in any court in this State, upon sufficient proof being made to the court or jury, upon the trial before said court, that any freedman, free negro or mulatto has falsely and maliciously caused the arrest and trial of said white person or persons, the court shall render up a judgment against said freedman, free negro or mulatto for all costs of the case, and impose a fine not to exceed fifty dollars, and imprisonment in the county jail not to exceed twenty days; and for a failure of said freedmen, free negro or mulatto to pay, or cause to be paid, all costs, fines and jail fees, the sheriff of the county is hereby authorized and required, after giving ten days' public notice, to proceed to hire out at public outcry, at the court-house of the county, said freedman, free negro or mulatto, for the shortest time to raise the amount necessary to discharge said freedman, free negro or mulatto from all costs, fines, and jail fees aforesaid.

An Act to punish certain Offences therein named, and for other purposes, November 29, 1865.

SEC. 1. *Be it enacted, &c.*, That no freedman, free negro, or mulatto, not in the military service of the United States Government, and not licensed to do so by the board of police of his or her county, shall keep or carry fire-arms of any kind, or any ammunition, dirk, or bowie-knife; and on conviction thereof, in the county court, shall be punished by fine, not exceeding ten dollars, and pay the costs of such proceedings, and all such arms or ammunition shall be forfeited to the informer; and it shall be the duty of every civil and military officer to arrest any freedman, free negro, or mulatto found with any such arms or ammunition, and cause him to be committed for trial in default of bail.

SEC. 2. That any freedman, free negro, or mulatto, committing riots, routes, affrays, trespasses, malicious mischief and cruel treatment to animals, seditious speeches, insulting gestures, language, or acts, or assaults on any person, disturbance of the peace, exercising the functions of a minister of the gospel without a license from some regularly organized church, vending spirituous or intoxicating liquors, or committing any other misdemeanor, the punishment of which is not specifically provided for by law, shall, upon conviction thereof, in the county court, be fined not less than ten dollars, and not more than one hundred dollars, and may be imprisoned, at the discretion of the court, not exceeding thirty days.

SEC. 3. That if any white person shall sell, lend, or give to any freedman, free negro, or mulatto, any fire-arms, dirk, or bowie-knife, or ammunition, or any spirituous or intoxicating liquors, such person or persons so offending, upon conviction thereof, in the county court of his or her county, shall be fined not exceeding fifty dollars, and may be imprisoned, at the discretion of the court, not exceeding thirty days.

SEC. 4. That all the penal and criminal laws now in force in this State, defining offences, and prescribing the mode of punishment for crimes and misdemeanors committed by slaves, free negroes or mulattoes, be and the same are hereby re-enacted, and declared to be in full force and effect, against freedmen, free negroes, and mulattoes, except so far as the mode and manner of trial and punishment have been changed or altered by law.

SEC. 5. That if any freedman, free negro or mulatto, convicted of any of the misdemeanors provided against in this act, shall fail or refuse, for the space of five days after conviction, to pay the fine and costs imposed, such person shall be hired out by the sheriff or other officer, at public outcry, to any white person who will pay said fine and all costs, and take such convict for the shortest time.

GEORGIA.

1865, December 15—Free persons of color are made competent witnesses in all courts in cases where a free person of color is a party, or the offence charged is against the person or property of a free person of color. Persons of color now living as husband and wife are declared to be so, except a man has two or more reputed wives, or a wife two or more reputed husbands; in such event, they shall select one and the marriage ceremony be performed.

1866, Feb. 23—All male inhabitants, white and black, between sixteen and fifty, subject to work on the public roads, except such as are specially exempted.

March 7—Any officer knowingly issuing any marriage license to parties, either of whom is of African descent and the other a white person, shall be guilty of a misdemeanor, and on conviction be fined from two hundred to five hundred dollars, or imprisoned for three months, or both. Any officer or minister marrying such persons shall be fined from five hundred to one thousand dollars, and imprisoned six months, or both.

March 9—That among persons of color the parent shall be required to maintain his or her children, whether legitimate or illegitimate. That children shall be subjected to the same obligations, in relation to their parents, as those which existing relation to white persons. That every colored child hereafter born, is declared to be the legitimate child of his mother, and also of his colored father, if acknowledged by such father.

To Amend the Penal Code.

March 12—The 4,435th section of the Penal Code shall read as follows:

All persons wandering or strolling about in idleness, who are able to work, and who have no property to support them; all persons leading an idle, immoral, or profligate life, who have no property to support them, and are able to work and do not work; all persons able to work having no visible and known means of a fair, honest, and reputable livelihood; all persons having a fixed abode, who have no visible property to support them, and who live by stealing or by trading in, bartering for, or buying stolen property; and all professional gamblers living in idleness, shall be deemed and considered vagrants, and shall be indicted as such, and it shall be lawful for any person to arrest said vagrants and have them bound over for trial to the next term of the county court, and upon conviction, they shall be fined and imprisoned or sentenced to work on the public works, for not longer than a year, or shall, in the discretion of the court, be bound out to some person for a time not longer than one year, upon such valuable consideration as the court may prescribe; the person giving bond in a sum not exceeding $300, payable to said court and conditioned to clothe and feed, and provide said convict with medical attendance for and during said time: *Provided*, That the defendant may, at any time, before conviction, be discharged, upon paying costs and giving bond and security in a sum not exceeding $200, payable to said court, and condition for the good behavior and industry of defendant for one year.

March 8—The wilful and malicious burning of an occupied dwelling-house of another on a farm, or plantation, or elsewhere, shall be punished with death; also burglary in the night; also stealing a horse or mule, unless recommended by the jury to the mercy of the court.

March 17—County courts organized, as in other States, for hearing of "cases arising out of the relation of master and servant," &c. Where such cases shall go against the servant, the judgment for costs upon written notice to the master shall operate as a garnishment against him, and he shall retain a sufficient amount for the payment thereof, out of any wages due to said servant, or to become due during the period of service, and may be cited at any time by the collecting officer to make answer thereto.

March 17—Sec. 1. That all negroes, mulattoes, mestizoes, and their descendants having one eighth negro or African blood in their veins, shall be known in this State as "persons of color."

2. That persons of color shall have the right to make and enforce contracts, to sue, be sued, to be parties and give evidence, to inherit, to purchase, lease, sell, hold, and convey real and personal property, and to have full and equal benefit of all laws and proceedings for the security of person and estate, and shall not be subjected to any other or different punishment, pain or penalty, for the commission of any act or offense, than such as are prescribed for white persons committing like acts or offenses.

March 20—Crimes defined in certain sections named, as felonies are reduced below felonies, and all other crimes, punishable by fine or imprisonment or either, shall be likewise punishable by a fine not exceeding $1,000, imprisonment not exceeding six months, whipping not exceeding thirty-nine lashes, to work in a chain-gang on the public works not to exceed twelve months, and any one or more of these punishments may be ordered in the discretion of the judge.

ALABAMA.

December —Bill passed, "making it unlawful for any freedmen, mulatto, or free person of color in this State to own fire-arms, or carry about his person a pistol or other deadly weapon," under a penalty of a fine of $100 or imprisonment three months. Also, making it unlawful for any person to sell, give, or lend fire-arms or ammunition of any description whatever to any freedman, free negro, or mulatto, under a penalty of not less than $50 not more than $100 at the discretion of the jury.

December 9—This bill passed: That all freedmen, free negroes, and mulattoes, shall have the right to sue and be sued, plead and be impleaded in all the different and various courts of this State, to the same extent that white persons now have by law. And they shall be competent to testify only in open court, and only in cases in which freedmen, free negroes, and mulattoes are parties, either plaintiff or defendant, and in civil or criminal cases, for injuries in the persons and property of freedmen, free negroes, and mulattoes, and in all cases, civil or criminal, in which a freedman, free negro, or mulatto, is a witness against a white person, or a white person against a freedman, free negro, or mulatto, the parties shall be competent witnesses, and neither interest in the question or suit, nor marriage, shall disqualify any witness from testifying in open court.

1866, Febuary 16—A law was enacted, of

3

which section 1 provides that it shall not be lawful for any person to interfere with, hire, employ, or entice away, or induce to leave the service of another, any laborer or servant who shall have stipulated or contracted, in writing, to serve for any given number of days, weeks, or months, or for one year, so long as the said contract shall be and remain in force and binding upon the parties thereto, without the consent of the party employing or to whom said service is due and owing in writing, or in the presence of some veritable white person; and any person who shall knowingly interfere with, hire, employ, or entice away, or induce to leave the service aforesaid, without justifiable excuse therefor, before the expiration of said term of service so contracted and stipulated as aforesaid, shall be guilty of a misdemeanor, and on conviction thereof, must be fined in such sum, not less than fifty nor more than five hundred dollars, as the jury trying the same may assess, and in no case less than double the amount of the injury sustained by the party from whom such laborer or servant was induced to leave, one-half to go to the party injured and the other to the county as fines and forfeitures.

Sec. 2 provides that the party injured shall be a competent witness in all prosecutions under this act, notwithstanding his interest in the fine to be assessed.

Sec. 3 provides that when any laborer or servant, having contracted as provided in the first section of this act, shall afterward be found, before the termination of said contract, in the service or employment of another, that fact shall be *prima facie* evidence that such person is guilty of violation of this act, if he fail and refuse to forthwith discharge the said laborer or servant, after being notified and informed of such former contract and employment.

A new penal code was adopted.

The material changes introduced by the new penal code are briefly these:

First. Whipping and branding are abolished, as legal punishments, and a new punishment is introduced, entitled "hard labor for the county." This "hard labor for the county" is put under the control of the court of county commissioners, who are authorized to employ a superintendent of the convicts, to make regulations for their government and labor, to put them to work on the public roads, bridges, &c., or to hire them out to railroad companies or private individuals.

Second. For all offences which were heretofore punishable by fine, or by fine and imprisonment, either in the county jail or in the penitentiary, the jury may still impose a fine; to which the court, in its discretion, may superadd imprisonment or hard labor, within specified limits in each case.

Third. The dividing line between grand and petit larceny, is raised from twenty to one hundred dollars; grand larceny being made a felony, that is, it may be punished by imprisonment in the penitentiary; while petit larceny is only a misdemeanor, punishable by fine, or by fine and imprisonment in the county jail.

Fourth. A county court is established for the trial of misdemeanors.

Fifth. Justices of the peace have jurisdiction of a few minor offences, such as vagrancy, larceny of less than ten dollars, and assaults, affrays, &c., in which no weapon is used. The proceedings before them conform substantially to proceedings before the county court.

The new code makes no distinction on account of color, only marriages between white persons and negroes are prohibited. It went into effect June 1, 1866.

The Governor vetoed three bills referring to persons of color. See page —.

SOUTH CAROLINA.

An Act Preliminary to the Legislation induced by the Emancipation of Slaves, October 19, 1865.

Section 3 provides that all free negroes, mulattoes, and mestizoes, all freedwomen, and all descendants through either sex of any of these persons, shall be known as *persons of color*, except that every such descendant who may have of Caucasian blood seven eighths, or more, shall be deemed a white person.

Sec. 4 provides that the statutes and regulations concerning slaves are now inapplicable to persons of color; and although such persons are not entitled to social or political equality with white persons, they shall have the right to acquire, own, and dispose of property, to make contracts, to enjoy the fruits of their labor, to sue and be sued, and to receive protection under the law in their persons and property.

Sec. 5 provides that all rights and remedies respecting persons or property, and all duties and liabilities under laws, civil and criminal, which apply to white persons, are extended to persons of color, subject to the modifications made by this act and the other acts hereinbefore mentioned.

An Act to Amend the Criminal Law, December 19, 1865.

Section 1 provides that either of the crimes specified in this first section shall be felony, without benefit of clergy, to wit: For a person of color to commit any wilful homicide, unless in self-defence; for a person of color to commit an assault upon a white woman, with manifest intent to ravish her; for a person of color to have sexual intercourse with a white woman by personating her husband; for any person to raise an insurrection or rebellion in this State; for any person to furnish arms or ammunition to other persons who are in a state of actual insurrection or rebellion, or permit them to resort to his house for advancement of their evil purpose; for any person to administer, or cause to be take by any other person, any poison, chloroform, soporific, or other destructive thing, or to shoot at, stab, cut, or wound any other person, or by any means whatsoever to cause bodily injury to any other person, whereby, in any of these cases, a bodily injury dangerous to the life of any other person is caused, with intent, in any of these cases, to commit the crime of murder, or the crime of rape, or the crime of robbery, burglary, or larceny; for any person who had been transported under sentence to return to this State within the period of prohibition contained in the sentence; or for a person to steal a horse or mule, or cotton packed in a bale ready for market.

SEC. 10 provides that a person of color who is in the employment of a master engaged in husbandry shall not have the right to sell any corn, rice, peas, wheat, or other grain, any flour, cotton, fodder, hay, bacon, fresh meat of any kind, poultry of any kind, animal of any kind, or any other product of a farm, without having written evidence from such master, or some person authorized by him, or from the district judge or a magistrate, that he has the right to sell such product; and if any person shall, directly or indirectly, purchase any such product from such person of color without such written evidence, the purchaser and seller shall each be guilty of a misdemeanor.

SEC. 11 provides that it shall be a misdemeanor for any person not authorized to write or give to a person of color a writing which professes to show evidence of the right of that person of color to sell any product of a farm which, by the section last preceding, he is forbidden to sell without written evidence; and any person convicted of this misdemeanor shall be liable to the same extent as the purchaser in the section last preceding is made liable; and it shall be a misdemeanor for a person of color to exhibit as evidence of his right to sell any product a writing which he knows to be false or counterfeited, or to have been written or given by any person not authorized.

SEC. 13 states that persons of color constitute no part of the militia of the State, and no one of them shall, without permission in writing from the district judge or magistrate, be allowed to keep a fire-arm, sword, or other military weapon, except that one of them, who is the owner of a farm, may keep a shot-gun or rifle, such as is ordinarily used in hunting, but not a pistol, musket, or other fire-arm or weapon appropriate for purposes of war. The district judge or a magistrate may give an order, under which any weapon unlawfully kept may be seized and sold, the proceeds of sale to go into the district court fund. The possession of a weapon in violation of this act shall be a misdemeanor which shall be tried before a district court or a magistrate, and in case of conviction, shall be punished by a fine equal to twice the value of the weapon so unlawfully kept, and if that be not immediately paid, by corporeal punishment.

SEC. 14 provides that it shall not be lawful for a person of color to be the owner, in whole or in part, of any distillery where spirituous liquors of any kind are made, or of any establishment where spirituous liquors of any kind are sold by retail; nor for a person of color to be engaged in distilling any spirituous liquors, or in retailing the same in a shop or elsewhere. A person of color who shall do anything contrary to the prohibitions herein contained shall be guilty of a misdemeanor, and, upon conviction, may be punished by fine or corporeal punishment and hard labor, as to the district judge or magistrate before whom he may be tried shall seem meet.

SEC. 22 provides that no person of color shall migrate into and reside in this State, unless, within twenty days after his arrival within the same, he shall enter into a bond, with two freeholders as sureties, to be approved by the judge of the district court or a magistrate, in a penalty of one thousand dollars, conditioned for his good behavior, and for his support, if he should become unable to support himself.

SEC. 24 provides that when several persons of color are convicted of one capital offence, the jury which tries them may recommend one or more to mercy, for reasons which, in their opinion, mitigate the guilt; the district judge shall report the case, with his opinion, and the Governor shall do in the matter as seems to him meet. The same may be done when one only is convicted of capital offence. Before sentence of death shall be executed in any case, time for application to the Governor shall be allowed.

SEC. 27 provides that whenever, under any law, sentence imposing a fine is passed, if the fine and costs be not immediately paid, there shall be detention of the convict, and substitution of other punishment. If the offence should not involve the *crimen falsi*, and be infamous, the substitution shall be, in the case of a white person, imprisonment for a time proportioned to the fine, at the rate of one day for each dollar; and in the case of a person of color, enforced labor, without unnecessary pain or restraint, for a time proportioned to the fine, at the rate of one day for each dollar. But if the offence should be infamous, there shall be substituted for a fine, for imprisonment, or for both, hard labor, corporeal punishment, solitary confinement, and confinement in tread-mill or stocks, one or more, at the discretion of the judge of the superior court, the district judge, or the magistrate, who pronounces the sentence. In this act, and in respect to all crimes and misdemeanors, the term servants shall be understood to embrace an apprentice as well as a servant under contract.

SEC. 29 provides that, upon view of a misdemeanor committed by a person of color, or by a white person toward a person of color, a magistrate may arrest the offender, and, according to the nature of the case, punish the offender summarily, or bind him in recognizance with sufficient sureties to appear at the next monthly sitting of the district court, or commit him for trial before the district court.

SEC. 30 provides that, upon view of a misdemeanor committed by a person of color, any person present may arrest the offender and take him before a magistrate, to be dealt with as the case may require. In case of a misdemeanor committed by a white person toward a person of color, any person may complain to a magistrate, who shall cause the offender to be arressted, and, according to the nature of the case, to be brought before himself, or be taken for trial in the district court.

An Act to establish District Courts, December 19, 1865.

Courts are established to have "exclusive jurisdiction, subject to appeal, of all civil causes where one or both the parties are persons of color, and of all criminal cases wherein the accused is a person of color, and also of all cases of misdemeanors affecting the person or property of a person of color, and of all cases of bastardy, and of all cases of vagrancy, not tried before a magistrate."

An indictment against a white person for the homicide of a person of color shall be tried in the superior court of law, and so shall other indictments in which a white person is accused of a capital felony affecting the person or property of a person of color.

In every case, civil and criminal, in which a person of color is a party, or which affects the person or property of a person of color, persons of color shall be competent witnesses. The accused, in such a criminal case, and the parties in every such civil case, may be witnesses, and so may every other person who is a competent witness; and in every such case, either party may offer testimony as to his own character, or that of his adversary or of the prosecutor, or of the third person mentioned in an indictment.

December 21—"*An act to establish and regulate the domestic relations of persons of color, and to amend the law in relation to paupers and vagrancy*," establishes the relation of husband and wife, declares those now living as such to be husband and wife, and provides that persons of color desirous hereafter to marry shall have the contract duly solemnized. A parent may bind his child over two years of age as an apprentice to serve till 21 if a male, 18 if a female. All persons of color who make contracts for service or labor shall be known as servants, and those with whom they contract as masters.

"Colored children between 18 and 21, who have neither father nor mother *living in the district in which they are found*, or whose parents are paupers, or unable to afford them a comfortable maintenance, *or whose parents are not teaching them habits of industry and honesty*, or are persons of notoriously bad character, or are vagrants, or have been convicted of infamous offences, and colored children, *in all cases where they are in danger of moral contamination*, may be bound as apprentices by the district judge or one of the magistrates for the aforesaid term."

It "provides that no person of color shall pursue or practice the art, trade, or business of an artisan, mechanic, or shopkeeper, or any other trade, employment, or business, (besides that of husbandry, or that of a servant under a contract for service or labor,) on his own account and for his own benefit, or in partnership with a white person, or as agent or servant of any person, until he shall have obtained a license therefor from the judge of the district court, which license shall be good for one year only. This license the judge may grant upon petition of the applicant, and upon being satisfied of his skill and fitness, and of his good moral character, and upon payment by the applicant to the clerk of the district court of one hundred dollars if a shopkeeper or pedlar, to be paid annually, and ten dollars if a mechanic, artisan, or to engage in any other trade, also to be paid annually: *Provided, however*, That upon complaint being made and proved to the district judge of an abuse of such license, he shall revoke the same: *And provided, also*, That no person of color shall practice any mechanical art or trade unless he shows that he has served an apprenticeship in such trade or art, or is now practicing such trade or art."

Former slaves, now helpless, who were on a farm Nov. 10, 1865 and six months previous shall not be evicted by the owner from the house occupied by them before January 1, 1867.

It "provides that if the district court fund, after payment of the sums with which it is charged, on account of the salary of the judge of the district court, superintendent of convicts, jurors, and other expenses of the court and of convicts, shall be insufficient to support indigent persons of color, who may be proper charges on the public, the board aforesaid shall have power to impose for that purpose, whenever it may be required, a tax of one dollar on each male person of color between the ages of eighteen and fifty years, and fifty cents on each unmarried female person of color between the ages of eighteen and forty-five, to be collected in each precinct by a magistrate thereof: *Provided*, That the said imposition of a tax shall be approved in writing by the judge of the district court, and that his approval shall appear in the journals of that court."

Order of General Sickles, disregarding the Code, January 17, 1866.

1866, January 17—Major General Sickles issued this order:

HEADQ'RS DEP'T OF SOUTH CAROLINA,
January 17, 1866.

[G. O., No. 1.]—I. To the end that civil rights and immunities may be enjoyed; that kindly relations among the inhabitants of the State may be established; that the rights and duties of the employer and the free laborer respectively may be defined; that the soil may be cultivated and the system of free labor undertaken; that the owners of estates may be secure in the possession of their lands and tenements; that persons able and willing to work may have employment; that idleness and vagrancy may be discountenanced, and encouragement given to industry and thrift; and that humane provision may be made for the aged, infirm and destitute, the following regulations are established for the government of all concerned in this department.

II. All laws shall be applicable alike to all the inhabitants. No person shall be held incompetent to sue, make complaint, or to testify, because of color or caste.

III. All the employments of husbandry or the useful arts, and all lawful trades or callings, may be followed by all persons, irrespective of color or caste; nor shall any freedman be obliged to pay any tax or any fee for a license, nor be amenable to any municipal or parish ordinance, not imposed upon all other persons.

IV. The lawful industry of all persons who live under the protection of the United States, and owe obedience to its laws, being useful to the individual, and essential to the welfare of society, no person will be restrained from seeking employment when not bound by voluntary agreement, nor hindered from traveling from place to place, on lawful business. All combinations or agreements which are intended to hinder, or may so operate as to hinder, in any way, the employment of labor—or to limit compensation for labor—or to compel labor to be involuntarily performed in certain places or for certain persons; as well as all combinations or agreements to prevent the sale or hire of lands or tenements, are declared to be misdemeanors; and any person or persons convicted thereof shall be punished by fine not exceeding $500, or by imprisonment, not to exceed six months, or by both such fine and imprisonment.

V. Agreements for labor or personal service of any kind, or for the use and occupation of lands and tenements, or for any other lawful purpose, between freedmen and other persons, when fairly made, will be immediately enforced against either party violating the same.

VI. Freed persons, unable to labor, by reason of age or infirmity, and orphan children of tender years, shall have allotted to them by owners suitable quarters on the premises where they have been heretofore domiciled as slaves, until adequate provision, approved by the general commanding, be made for them by the State or local authorities, or otherwise; and they shall not be removed from the premises, unless for disorderly behavior, misdemeanor, or other offence committed by the head of a family or a member thereof.

VII. Able-bodied freedmen, when they leave the premises in which they may be domiciled, shall take with them and provide for such of their relatives as by the laws of South Carolina all citizens are obliged to maintain.

VIII. When a freed person, domiciled on a plantation, refuses to work there, after having been offered employment by the owner or lessee, on fair terms, approved by the agent of the Freedmen's Bureau, such freedman or woman shall remove from the premises within ten days after such offer and due notice to remove by the owner or occupant.

IX. When able-bodied freed persons are domiciled on premises where they have been heretofore held as slaves, and are not employed thereon or elsewhere, they shall be permitted to remain, on showing to the satisfaction of the commanding officer of the post that they have made diligent and proper efforts to obtain employment.

X. Freed persons occupying premises without the authority of the United States, or the permission of the owner, and who have not been heretofore held there as slaves, may be removed by the commanding officer of the post, on the complaint of the owner, and proof of the refusal of said freed persons to remove after ten days' notice.

XI. Any person employed or domiciled on a plantation or elsewhere, who may be rightfully dismissed by the terms of agreement, or expelled for misbehavior, shall leave the premises, and shall not return without the consent of the owner or tenant thereof.

XII. Commanding officers of districts will establish within their commands respectively suitable regulations for hiring out to labor, for a period not to exceed one year, all vagrants who cannot be advantageously employed on roads, fortifications and other public works. The proceeds of such labor shall be paid over to the assistant commissioner of the Freedmen's Bureau, to provide for aged and infirm refugees, indigent freed people and orphan children.

XIII. The vagrant laws of the State of South Carolina, applicable to free white persons, will be recognized as the only vagrant laws applicable to the freedmen; nevertheless, such laws shall not be considered applicable to persons who are without employment, if they shall prove that they have been unable to obtain employment, after diligent efforts to do so.

XIV. It shall be the duty of officers commanding posts to see that issues of rations to freedmen are confined to destitute persons who are unable to work because of infirmities arising from old age or chronic diseases, orphan children too young to work, and refugee freedmen returning to their homes with the sanction of the proper authorities; and in ordering their issues, commanding officers will be careful not to encourage idleness or vagrancy. District commanders will make consolidated reports of these issues tri-monthly.

XV. The proper authorities of the State in the several municipalities and districts shall proceed to make suitable provision for their poor, without distinction of color; in default of which the general commanding will levy an equitable tax on persons and property sufficient for the support of the poor.

XVI. The constitutional rights of all loyal and well-disposed inhabitants to bear arms will not be infringed; nevertheless this shall not be construed to sanction the unlawful practice of carrying concealed weapons, nor to authorize any person to enter with arms on the premises of another against his consent. No one shall bear arms who has borne arms against the United States, unless he shall have taken the amnesty oath prescribed in the proclamation of the President of the United States, dated May 20, 1865, or the oath of allegiance, prescribed in the proclamation of the President, dated December 8, 1863, within the time prescribed therein. And no disorderly person, vagrant, or disturber of the peace, shall be allowed to bear arms.

XVII. To secure the same equal justice and personal liberty to the freedmen as to other inhabitants, no penalties or punishments different from those to which all persons are amenable shall be imposed on freed people; and all crimes and offences which are prohibited under existing laws shall be understood as prohibited in the case of freedmen; and if committed by a freedman, shall, upon conviction, be punished in the same manner as if committed by a white man.

XVIII. Corporeal punishment shall not be inflicted upon any person other than a minor, and then only by the parent, guardian, teacher, or one to whom said minor is lawfully bound by indenture of apprenticeship.

XIX. Persons whose conduct tends to a breach of the peace may be required to give security for their good behavior, and in default thereof shall be held in custody.

XX. All injuries to the person or property committed by or upon freed persons shall be punished in the manner provided by the laws of South Carolina for like injuries to the persons or property of citizens thereof. If no provision be made by the laws of the State, then the punishment for such offences shall be according to the course of common law; and in the case of any injury to the person or property, not prohibited by the common law, or for which the punishment shall not be appropriate, such sentence shall be imposed as, in the discretion of the court before which the trial is had, shall be deemed proper, subject to the approval of the general commanding.

XXI. All arrests for whatever cause will be reported tri-monthly, with the proceedings thereupon, through the prescribed channel, to the general commanding.

XXII. Commanding officers of districts, sub-districts, and posts, within their commands respectively, in the absence of the duly-appointed agent, will perform any duty appertaining to the ordinary agents of the Bureau of Refugees, Freedmen, and Abandoned Lands, carefully observing for their guidance all orders published by the commissioner or assistant commissioner, or other competent authority.

XXIII. District commanders will enforce these regulations by suitable instructions to sub-district and post commanders, taking care that justice be done, that fair dealing between man and man be observed, and that no unnecessary hardship, and no cruel or unusual punishments be imposed upon any one.

By command of D. E. SICKLES, Major General.

Official: W. L. M. BURGER,
Assistant Adjutant General.

FLORIDA.

An Act to Establish and Organize a County Criminal Court, January 11, 1866.

SEC. 1 gives the court jurisdiction in cases of assault, assault and battery, assault with intent to kill, riot, affray, larceny, robbery, arson, burglary, malicious mischief, vagrancy, and all misdemeanors, and all offences against religion, chastity, morality, and decency: *Provided*, That the punishment of the same does not affect the life of the offender. The Governor to appoint the judge. In the proceedings, "no presentment, indictment, or written pleadings, shall be required." Where a fine is imposed, and not paid, the party may be put to such labor as the county commissioner may direct, the compensation for which to go in payment of the fine and cost of prosecution; "or the said county commissioner may hire out, at public outcry, the said party to any person who will take him or her for the shortest time, and pay the fine, forfeiture, and penalty imposed, and cost of prosecution."

An Act to Extend to all the Inhabitants of the State the Benefit of Courts of Justice, and the Processes thereof, January 11, 1866.

SEC. 1 provides that the judicial tribunals of this State, with the processes thereof, shall be accessible to all the inhabitants of the State, without distinction of color, for the prosecution and defence of all the rights of person and property, subject only to the restrictions contained in the constitution of the State.

SEC. 2 provides that all laws heretofore passed, with reference to slaves, free negroes, and mulattoes, except the act to prevent their migration into the State, and the act prohibiting the sale of fire-arms and ammunition to them, be, and the same are hereby, repealed; and all the criminal laws of this State applicable to white persons now in force, and not in conflict with, or modified by, the legislation of the present session of the General Assembly, shall be deemed and held to apply equally to all the inhabitants of the same without distinction of color.

An act to Establish and Enforce the Marriage Relation between Persons of Color, January 11, 1866.

SEC. 1 requires all the colored inhabitants, claiming to be living together in the relation of husband and wife, and who have not been joined as such agreeably to the laws, and who shall mutually desire to continue in that relation, within nine months from the passage of this act, to appear before some person legally authorized to perform the marriage ceremony, and be regularly joined in the holy bonds of matrimony.

SEC. 2 provides that the issue of such prior cohabitation shall be legitimated by the act of marriage so regularly contracted as aforesaid, and be thenceforth entitled to all the rights and privileges of a legitimate offspring.

SEC. 5 provides that after the expiration of the time limited in the first section, all laws applicable to or regulating the marriage relation between white persons shall deemed to apply to the same relation between the colored population of the State.

An Act in Addition to An Act concerning Marriage Licenses, January 12, 1866.

SEC. 1 provides that if any white female resident shall hereafter attempt to intermarry, or shall live in a state of adultery or fornication, with any negro, mulatto, or other person of color, she shall be deemed to be guilty of a misdemeanor, and upon conviction shall be fined in a sum not exceeding one thousand dollars, or be confined in the public jail not exceeding three months, or both, at the discretion of the jury; and shall, moreover, be disqualified to testify as a witness against any white person.

SEC. 2 provides that if any negro, mulatto, or other person of color, shall hereafter live in a state of adultery or fornication with any white female resident within the limits of this State, he shall be deemed to be guilty of a misdemeanor, and upon conviction shall be fined in a sum not exceeding one thousand dollars, or be made to stand in the pillory for one hour and be whipped not exceeding thirty-nine stripes, or both, at the discretion of the jury.

SEC. 3 provides that every person who shall have one eighth or more of negro blood shall be deemed and held to be a person of color.

SEC. 4 provides that in existing cases, upon petition to the circuit judge, parties coming within the provisions of this act and liable to be punished under the same, may by order and judgment of said judge be relieved from the penalties thereof, when in his opinion justice and equity shall so require.

SEC. 5 provides that in all cases where marriages have heretofore been contracted and solemnized between white persons and persons of color, and where the parties have continued to live as man and wife, the said marriages are hereby legalized, and neither of the parties shall be subject to the provisions of this or of any other act.

An Act to Require the Children of Destitute Persons to Provide for the Support of said Persons, January 11, 1866.

SEC. 1 requires the children of natural parents who are unable to support themselves to make provision for their support. In case of neglect, and proof before a justice of the peace or judge, that officer shall make an order of assessment on the children for the necessary amount, which order shall carry with it the right of enforcement by execution, and shall have the force of a writ of garnishment on the wages of such children.

An Act to Punish Vagrants and Vagabonds, January 12, 1866.

SEC. 1. Defines as a vagrant "every able-bodied person why has no visible means of living and shall not be employed at some labor to support himself or herself, or shall be leading an idle, immoral, or profligate course of life;" and may be arrested by any justice of the peace or judge of the county criminal court and be bound "in sufficient surety" for good behavior and future industry for one year. Upon refusing or failing to give such security, he or she may be committed for trial, and if convicted sentenced to labor or imprisonment not exceeding twelve months, by whipping not exceeding thirty-nine stripes, or being put in the pillory. If sentenced to labor, the "sheriff or other officer of said court shall hire out such person for the term to which he or she shall be sentenced, not exceeding twelve months aforesaid, and the proceeds of such hiring shall be paid into the county treasury." All vagrants going armed may be disarmed by the sheriff, constable, or police officer.

An Act in Relation to Contracts of Persons of Color, January 12, 1866.

SEC. 1 Provides that all contracts with persons of color shall be made in writing and fully explained to them before two credible witnesses, which contract shall be in duplicate, one copy to be retained by the employer and the other filed with some judicial officer of the State and county in which the parties may be residing at the date of the contract, with the affidavit of one or both witnesses, setting forth that the terms and effect of such contract were fully explained to the colored person, and that he, she, or they had voluntarily entered into and signed the contract and no contract shall be of any validity against any person of color unless so executed and filed: *Provided*, That contracts for service or labor may be made for less time than thirty days by parol.

SEC. 2 Provides, that whereas is is essential to the welfare and prosperity of the entire population of the State that the agricultural interest be sustained and placed upon a permanent basis, it is provided that when any person of color shall enter into a contract as aforesaid, to serve as a laborer for a year, or any other specified term, on any farm or plantation in this State, if he shall refuse or neglect to perform the stipulations of his contract by wilful disobedience of orders, wanton impudence or disrespect to his employer, or his authorized agent, failure or refusal to perform the work assigned to him, idleness, or abandonment of the premises or the employment of the party with whom the contract was made, he or she shall be liable, upon the complaint of his employer or his agent, made under oath before any justice of the peace of the county, to be arrested and tried before the criminal court of the county, and upon conviction shall be subject to all the pains and penalties prescribed for the punishment of vagrancy: *Provided*, That it shall be optional with the employer to require that such laborer be remanded to his service, instead of being subjected to the punishment aforesaid: *Provided, further*, That if it shall on such trial appear that the complaint made is not well founded, the court shall dismiss such complaint, and give judgment in favor of such laborer against the employer, for such sum as may appear to be due under the contract, and for such damages as may be assessed by the jury.

SEC. 3 provides that when any employé as aforesaid shall be in the occupancy of any house or room on the premises of the employer by virtue of his contract to labor, and he shall be adjudged to have violated his contract; or when any employé as aforesaid shall attempt to hold possession of such house or room beyond the term of his contract, against the consent of the employer, it shall be the duty of the judge of the criminal court, upon the application of the employer, and due proof made before him, to issue his writ to the sheriff of the court, commanding him forthwith to eject the said employé and to put the employer into full possession the premises: *Provided*, Three days' previous notice shall be given to the employé of the day of trial.

SEC. 4 provides that if any person employing the services or labor of another, under contract entered into as aforesaid, shall violate his contract by refusing or neglecting to pay the stipulated wages or compensation agreed upon, or any part thereof, or by turning off the employé before the expiration of the term, unless for sufficient cause, or unless such right is reserved by the contract, the party so employed may make complaint thereof before the judge of the criminal court, who shall at an early day, on reasonable notice to the other party, cause the same to be tried by a jury summoned for the purpose, who, in addition to the amount that may be proved to be due under the contract, may give such damages as they in their discretion may deem to be right and proper, and the judgment thereon shall be a first lien on the crops of all kinds in the cultivation of which such labor may have been employed: *Provided*, That either party shall be entitled to an appeal to the circuit court, as in case of appeal from justices of the peace.

SEC. 5 provides that if any person shall entice, induce, or otherwise persuade any laborer or employé to quit the service of another to which he was bound by contract, before the expiration of the term of service stipulated in said contract, he shall be guilty of a misdemeanor, and upon conviction shall be fined in a sum not exceeding one thousand dollars, or shall stand in the pillory not more than three hours, or be whipped not more than thirty-nine stripes on the bare back, at the discretion of the jury.

SEC. 6 applies the provisions of this act to all contracts between employers and employés relating to the lumber, rafting, or milling business, and to all other contracts with persons of color to do labor and to perform service.

An Act prescribing additional Penalties for the Commission of Offences against the State, and for other purposes, January 15, 1866.

SEC. 1 provides that whenever in the criminal laws of this State, heretofore enacted, the punishment of the offence is limited to fine and imprisonment, or to fine or imprisonment, there shall be superadded, as an alternative, the punishment of standing in the pillory for an hour, or whipping not exceeding thirty-nine stripes on the bare back, or both, at the discretion of the jury.

SEC. 3 makes a felony, punishable with death, the exciting, or attempting to excite, by writing, speaking, or by other means, an insurrection or sedition amongst any portion or class of the population.

SEC. 12 makes it unlawful for any negro, mulatto, or person of color to own, use, or keep in possession or under control any bowie-knife, dirk, sword, fire-arms, or ammunition of any kind, unless by license of the county judge of probate, under a penalty of forfeiting them to the informer, and of standing in the pillory one hour, or be whipped not exceeding thirty-nine stripes, or both, at the discretion of the jury.

SEC. 14 forbids colored and white persons respectively from intruding upon each other's public assemblies, religious or other, or public vehicle set apart for their exclusive use, under punishment of pillory or stripes, or both.

SEC. 15 provides that persons forming a military organization not authorized by law, or aiding or abetting it, shall be fined not exceeding $1,000 and imprisonment not exceeding six months, or be pilloried for one hour, and be whipped not exceeding thirty-nine stripes, at the discretion of the jury—the penalties to be threefold upon persons who accepted offices in such organizations.

SEC. 19 prohibits any person from hunting within the enclosure of another without his consent, under penalty of a fine of $1,000, or imprisonment not exceeding six months, or the pillory for one hour, and being whipped not exceeding thirty-nine stripes. So, if a person takes, rides, or uses any horse, mule, ass, or ox, without the consent of the owner, whether the person so using is in the employ of the owner or not: so, by SEC. 17, if a person shall move into any tenant house or other building without leave of the person in charge, or illegally take possession of any church or school-house, educational or charitable building, or cut down trees exceeding $1 in value, with a view to convert the same to his own use. Burglary is punishable with death, or fine of $1,000 and imprisonment not exceeding six months, or standing in the pillory one hour, and being whipped not exceeding thirty-nine stripes. An assault upon a white female, with intent to commit a rape, or being accessory thereto, is punishable with death.

An Act Prescribing additional Penalties for the Commission of Offenses against the State, January 15, 1866.

SEC. 12 provides that it shall not be lawful for any negro, mulatto, or other person of color, to own, use, or keep in his possession or under his control any bowie-knife, dirk, sword, fire-arms, or ammunition of any kind, unless he first obtain a license to do so from the judge of probate of the county in which he may be a resident for the time being; and the said judge of probate is hereby authorized to issue license, upon the recommendation of two respectable citizens of the county, certifying to the peaceful and orderly character of the applicant; and any negro, mulatto, or other person of color, so offending, shall be deemed to be guilty of a misdemeanor, and upon conviction shall forfeit to the use of the informer all such fire-arms and ammunition, and in addition thereto, shall be sentenced to stand in the pillory for one hour, or be whipped, not exceeding thirty-nine stripes, or both, at the discretion of the jury.

SEC. 14 provides that if any negro, mulatto, or other person of color, shall intrude himself into any religious or other public assembly of white persons, or into any railroad car or other public vehicle set apart for the exclusive accommodation of white people, he shall be deemed to be guilty of a misdemeanor, and upon conviction shall be sentenced to stand in the pillory for one hour, or be whipped, not exceeding thirty-nine stripes, or both, at the discretion of the jury; nor shall it be lawful for any white person to intrude himself into any religious or other public assembly of colored persons, or into any railroad car or other public vehicle, set apart for the exclusive accommodation of persons of color, under the same penalties.

An Act to Raise a Revenue for the State of Florida, January 16, 1866.

SECTION 1 imposes a yearly capitation tax of three dollars upon every male inhabitant between twenty-one and fifty-five, except paupers and insane or idiotic persons. In default of payment the tax collector is hereby authorized and required to seize the body of the said delinquent and hire him out, after five days' public notice, before the door of the public court-house, to any person who will pay the said tax and the costs incident to the proceedings growing out of said arrest, and take him into his service for the shortest period of time: *Provided*, That if said delinquent be in the employment of another the said employer may pay the tax and costs, and the said payment shall be good as a credit against the amount that may be due by the employer as wages to the said delinquent.

An Act Concerning Schools for Freedmen, January 16, 1866.

Provision is made for schools for freedmen—supported by a tax of one dollar upon all male persons of color between twenty-one and fifty-five, and a tuition fee to be collected from each pupil—the schools to be in charge of a superintendent and assistants; no person to teach without a certificate; and the fee, five dollars, to go to the school fund for freedmen, and the certificate good for one year, subject to be cancelled by the superintendent for incompetency, immorality or other sufficient cause. The superintendent "to establish schools for freedmen when the number of children of persons of color in any county or counties will warrant the same: *Provided*, The funds provided for shall be sufficient to meet the expenses thereof."

By another act, the interest from the school fund of the State is applied to the education of indigent white children.

An Act concerning Testimony, January 16, 1866.

SECTION 3 provides that this act shall not be construed to authorize the testimony of colored persons to be taken by depositions in writing or upon written interrogatories, otherwise than in such manner as will enable the court or jury to judge of the credibility of the witness.

VIRGINIA.

These are some of the provisions in the recently-enacted laws of Virginia respecting colored persons:

That no contract between a white person and a colored person, for the labor or service of the latter for a longer period than two months, shall be binding on such colored person, unless the contract be in writing, signed by such white person or his agent and by such colored person, and duly acknowledged before a justice or notary public, or clerk of the county or corporation court, or overseer of the poor, or two or more credible witnesses, in the county or corporation court in which the white person may reside, or in which the labor or service it to be performed. And it shall be the duty of the justice, notary, clerk or overseer of the poor, or the witnesses, to read and explain the contract to the colored person, before taking his acknowledgment thereof, and to state that this has been done in the certificate of acknowledgment of the contract.

"§ 5. The writing by which any minor is bound an apprentice, shall specify his age, and what art, trade, or business he is to be taught. The master, whether it is expressly provided therein or not, shall be bound to teach him the same, and shall also be bound to teach him reading, writing, and common arithmetic, including the rule of three."

The marital relation between colored persons is regulated by law. The colored person must procure a license the same as the whites, and persons celebrating a marriage are obliged to report it to the county clerks, and whether white or colored.

Where colored persons, before the passage of this act, shall have undertaken and agreed to occupy the relation to each other of husband and wife, and shall be cohabiting together as such at the time of its passage, whether the rites of marriage shall have been celebrated between them or not, they shall be deemed husband and wife, and be entitled to the rights and privileges, and subject to the duties and obligations, of that relation in like manner as if they had been duly married; and all their children shall be deemed legitimate, whether born before or after the passage of this act. And when the parties have ceased to cohabit before the passage of this act, in consequence of the death of the woman, or from any other cause, all the children of the woman, recognized by the man to be his, shall be deemed legitimate.

Bigamy, too, is punished in the case of the negro as of the white person, and also intermarriage within the prohibited degrees. And all persons officiating in the rites of marriage without due authority of law are punished by fine and imprisonment.

Under the old code these provisions applied only to white persons.

Be it enacted, That every person having one fourth or more of negro blood shall be deemed a colored person, and every person not a colored person having one fourth or more of Indian blood shall be deemed an Indian.

2. All laws in respect to crimes and punishments, and in respect to criminal proceedings, applicable to white persons, shall apply in like manner to colored persons and to Indians, unless when it is otherwise specially provided.

3. The following acts and parts of acts are hereby repealed, namely: All acts and parts of acts relating to slaves and slavery; chapter one hundred and seven of the code of eighteen hundred and sixty, relating to free negroes; chapter two hundred of said code relating to offences by negroes; chapter two hundred and twelve of said code, relating to proceedings against negroes; chapter ninety-eight of said code, relating to patrols; sections twenty-five to forty-seven, both inclusive, of chapter one hundred ninety-two of said code; sections twenty-six to thirty, both inclusive, and sections thirty-three to thirty-seven, both inclusive, of chapter one hundred and ninety-eight of said code; the fifth paragraph, as enumerated in section two of chapter two hundred and three, of said code; all acts and parts of acts imposing on negroes the penalty of stripes, where the same penalty is not imposed on white persons; and all other acts and parts of acts inconsistent with this act are hereby repealed.

January 24—General Terry issued this order:

The Virginia Vagrant Act—General Terry orders its Non-Enforcement.

GENERAL ORDERS—NO 4.

HEADQUARTERS, DEPARTMENT OF VA.,
RICHMOND, *January* 24, 1866.

By a statute passed at the present session of the Legislature of Virginia, entitled "A bill providing for the punishment of vagrants," it is enacted, among other things, that any justice of the peace, upon the complaint of any one of certain officers therein named, may issue his warrant for the apprehension of any person alleged to be a vagrant and cause such person to be apprehended and brought before him; and that if upon due examination said justice of the peace shall find that such person is a vagrant within the definition of vagrancy contained in said statute, he shall issue his warrant, directing such person to be employed for a term not exceeding three months, and by any constable of the county wherein the proceedings are had be hired out for the best wages which can be procured, his wages to be applied to the support of himself and his family. The said statute further provides, that in case any vagrant so hired shall, during his term of service, run away from his employer without sufficient cause, he shall be apprehended on the warrant of a justice of the peace and returned to the custody of his employer, who shall then have, free from any other hire, the services of such vagrant for one month in addition to the original terms of hiring, and that the employer shall then have power, if authorized by a justice of the peace, to work such vagrant with ball and chain. The said statute specifies the persons who shall be considered vagrants and liable to the penalties imposed by it. Among those declared to be vagrants are all persons who, not having the wherewith to support their families, live idly and without employment, and refuse to work for the usual and common wages given to other laborers in the like work in the place where they are.

In many counties of this State meetings of employers have been held, and unjust and wrongful combinations have been entered into for the purpose of depressing the wages of the freedmen below the real value of their labor, far below the prices formerly paid to masters for labor performed by their slaves. By reason of these combinations wages utterly inadequate to the support of themselves and families have, in many places, become the usual and common wages of the freedmen. The effect of the statute in question will be, therefore, to compel the freedmen, under penalty of punishment as criminals, to accept and labor for the wages established by these combinations of employers. It places them wholly in the power of their employers, and it is easy to foresee that, even where no such combination now exists, the temptation to form them offered by the statute will be too strong to be resisted, and that such inadequate wages will become the common and usual wages throughout the State. The ultimate effect of the statute will be to reduce the freedmen to a condition of servitude worse than that from which they have been emancipated—a condition which will be slavery in all but its name.

It is therefore ordered that no magistrate, civil officer or other person shall in any way or manner apply or attempt to apply the provisions of said statute to any colored person in this department.

By command of Major General A. H. TERRY,

ED. W. SMITH, *Assistant Adjutant General.*

January 26—President Johnson refused to interfere with this order. The Legislature took no further action on the question.

February 28—This bill passed in relation to the testimony of colored persons:

Be it enacted, That colored persons and Indians shall, if otherwise competent, and subject to the rules applicable to other persons, be admitted as witnesses in the following cases:

1. In all civil cases and proceedings at law or in equity, in which a colored person or an Indian is a party, or may be directly benefited or injured by the result.

2. In all criminal proceedings in which a colored person or an Indian is a party, or which arise out of an injury done, attempted, or threatened to the person, property, or rights of a colored person or Indian, or in which it is alleged in the presentment, information, or indictments, or in which the court is of opinion from the other evidence that there is probable cause to believe that the offence was committed by a white person in conjunction or co-operation with a colored person or Indian.

3. The testimony of colored persons shall, in all cases and proceedings, both at law and in equity, be given *ore tenus*, and not by deposition, and in suits in equity, and in all other cases in which the deposition of the witness would regularly be part of the record, the court shall, if desired by any party, or if deemed proper by itself, certify the facts proved by such witnesses, or the evidence given by him as far as credited by the court, as the one or the other may be proper under the rules of law applicable to the case, and such certificate shall be made part of the record.

March 4—The Legislature adjourned.

TENNESSEE.

1866, January 25—This bill became a law:

That persons of African and Indian descent are hereby declared to be competent witnesses in all the courts of this State, in as full a manner as such persons are by an act of Congress competent witnesses in all the courts of the United States, and all laws and parts of laws of the State excluding such persons from competency are hereby repealed: *Provided, however*, That this act shall not be so construed as to give colored persons the right to vote, hold office, or sit on juries in this State; and that this provision is inserted by virtue of the provision of the 9th section of the amended constitution, ratified February 22, 1865.

May 26—This bill became a law:

An act to define the term "persons of color," and to declare the rights of such persons.

SEC. 1. That all negroes, mulattoes, mestizoes, and their descendants, having any African blood in their veins, shall be known in this State as "persons of color."

SEC. 2. That persons of color shall have the right to make and enforce contracts, to sue and be sued, to be parties and give evidence, to inherit, and to have full and equal benefits of all laws and proceedings for the security of person and estate, and shall not be subject to any other or different punishment, pains, or penalty, for the commission of any act or offence than such as are prescribed for white persons committing like acts or offences.

SEC. 3. That all persons of color, being blind, deaf and dumb, lunatics, paupers, or apprentices, shall have the full and perfect benefit and application of all laws regulating and providing for white persons, being blind, or deaf and dumb, or lunatics or paupers, or either (in asylums for their benefit) and apprentices.

SEC. 4. That all acts or parts of acts or laws, inconsistent herewith, are hereby repealed: *Provided*, That nothing in this act shall be so construed as to admit persons of color to serve on a jury: *And provided further*, That the provisions of this act shall not be so construed as to require the education of colored and white children in the same school.

SEC. 5. That all free persons of color who were living together as husband and wife in this State while in a state of slavery are hereby declared to be man and wife, and their children legitimately entitled to an inheritance in any property heretofore acquired, or that may hereafter be acquired, by said parents, to as full an extent as the children of white citizens are now entitled by the existing laws of this State.

May 26—All the freedmen's courts in Tennessee were abolished by the assistant commander, the law of the State making colored persons competent witnesses in all civil courts.

TEXAS.

A colored man is permitted by the new constitution to testify orally where any one of his race is a party, allows him to hold property, and to sue and be sued.

LOUISIANA.

1865, December .—"An act to provide for and regulate labor contracts for agricultural pursuits" requires all such laborers to make labor contracts for the next year within the first ten days of January—the contracts to be in writing, to be with heads of families, to embrace the labor of all the members, and be binding on all minors thereof. Each laborer, after choosing his employer, "shall not be allowed to leave his place of employment until the fulfillment of his contract, unless by consent of his employer, or on account of harsh treatment, or breach of contract on the part of employer; and if they do so leave, without cause or permission, they shall forfeit all wages earned to the time of abandonment." Wages due shall be a lien upon the crops; and one half shall be paid at periods agreed by the parties, "but it shall be lawful for the employer to retain the other moiety until the completion of the contract." Employers failing to comply, are to be fined double the amount due to laborer. These are the eighth and ninth sections in full:

SEC. 8. That in case of sickness of the laborer, wages for the time lost shall be deducted, and where the sickness is feigned for purposes of idleness, and also on refusal to work according to contract, double the amount of wages shall be deducted for the time lost, and also where rations have been furnished; and should the refusal to work be continued beyond three days, the offender shalll be reported to a justice of the peace, and shall be forced to labor on roads, levees, and other public works, without pay, until the offender consents to return to his labor.

SEC. 9. That, when in health, the laborer shall work ten hours during the day in summer, and nine hours during the day in winter, unless otherwise stipulated in the labor contract; he shall obey all proper orders of his employer or his agent; take proper care of his work mules, horses, oxen, stock; also of all agricultural implements; and employers shall have the right to make a reasonable deduction from the laborer's wages for injuries done to animals or agricultural implements committed to his care, or for bad or negligent work. Bad work shall not be allowed. Failing to obey reasonable orders, neglect of duty, and leaving home without permission, will be deemed disobedience; impudence, swearing, or indecent language to or in the presence of the employer, his family or agent, or quarrelling and fighting with one another, shall be deemed disobedience. For any disobedience a fine of one dollar shall be imposed on the offender. For all lost time from work hours, unless in case of sickness, the laborer shall be fined twenty-five cents per hour. For all absence from home without leave the laborer will be fined at the rate of two dollars per day. Laborers will not be required to labor on the Sabbath except to take the necessary care of stock and other property on plantations and do the necessary cooking and household duties, unless by special contract. For all thefts of the laborer from the employer of agricultural products, hogs, sheep, poultry or any other property of the employer, or wilful destruction of property or injury, the laborer shall pay the employer double the amount of the value of the property stolen, destroyed or injured, one half to be paid to the employer and the other half to be placed in the general fund provided for in this section. No live stock shall be allowed to laborers without the permission of the employer. Laborers shall not receive visitors during work hours. All difficulties arising between the employers and laborers, under this section, shall be settled, and all fines be imposed, by the former; if not satisfactory to the laborers, an appeal may be had to the nearest justice of the peace and two freeholders, citizens, one of said citizens to be selected by the employer and the other by the laborer; and all fines imposed and collected under this section shall be deducted from the wages due, and shall be placed in a common fund, to be divided among the other laborers employed on the plantation at the time when their full wages fall due, except as provided for above.

December 21—This bill became a law:

SEC. 1. That any one who shall persuade or entice away, feed, harbor, or secrete any person who leaves his or her employer, with whom she or he has contracted, or is assigned to live, or any apprentice who is bound as an apprentice, without the permission of his or her employer, said person or persons so offending shall be liable for damages to the employer, and also, upon conviction thereof, shall be subject to pay a fine of not more than five hundred dollars, nor less than ten dollars, or imprisonment in the parish jail for not moro than twelve months nor less than ten days, or both, at the discretion of the court.

SEC. 2. That it shall be duty of the judges of this State to give this act especially in charge of the grand juries at each jury term of their respective courts.

A new vagrant act is thus condensed in the New Orleans *Picayune:*

It adopts the same definition of vagrancy as in the act of 1855, and provides that any person charged with vagrancy shall be arrested on the warrant of any judge or justice of the peace; and if said judge or justice of the peace shall be satisfied by the confession of the offender, or by competent testimony, that he is a vagrant within this said description, he shall make a certificate of the same, which shall be filed with the clerk of the court of the parish and in the city of New Orleans. The certificate shall be filed in the offices of the recorders, and the said justice or other officer shall require the party accused to enter into bond, payable to the Governor of Louisiana, or his successors in office, in such sums as said justice of the peace or other officer shall prescribe, with security, to be approved by said officer, for his good behavior and future industry for the period of one year; and upon his failing or refusing to give such bond and security, the justice or other officer shall issue his warrant to the sheriff or other officer, directing him to detain and to hire out such vagrant for a period not exceeding twelve months, or to cause him to labor on the public works, roads, and levees, under such regulations as shall be made by the municipal authorities: *Provided*, That if the accused be a person who has abandoned his employer before his contract expired, the preference shall be given to such employer of hiring the accused: *And provided further*, That in the city of New Orleans the accused may be committed to the work-house for a time not exceeding six months, there to be kept at hard labor on the public works, roads, or levees. The proceeds of hire in the cases herein provided for to be paid into the parish treasury for the benefit of paupers: *And provided further*, That the persons hiring such vagrant shall be compelled to furnish such clothing, food, and medical attention as they may furnish their other laborers.

V.

PRESIDENT JOHNSON'S INTERVIEWS AND SPEECHES.

1865, April 15—Andrew Johnson qualified as President, Chief Justice Chase administering the oath of office.

Remarks at an Interview with Citizens of Indiana.

1865, April 21—A delegation was introduced by Governor O. P. Morton, to whose address President Johnson responded, stating that he did not desire to make any expression of his future policy more than he had already made, and adding:

But in entering upon the discharge of the duties devolving upon me by the sad occurrence of the assassination of the Chief Magistrate of the nation, and as you are aware, in surrounding circumstances which are peculiarly embarrassing and responsible, I doubt whether you are aware how much I appreciate encouragement and countenance from my fellow-citizens of Indiana. The most courageous individual, the most determined will, might justly shrink from entering upon the discharge of that which lies before me; but were I a coward, or timid, to receive the countenance and encouragement I have from you, and from various other parts of the country, would make me a courageous and determined man. I mean in the proper sense of the term, for there is as much in moral courage and the firm, calm discharge of duty, as in physical courage. But, in entering upon the duties imposed upon me by this calamity, I require not only courage, but determined will, and I assure you that on this occasion your encouragement is peculiarly acceptable to me. In reference to what my administration will be, while I occupy my present position, I must refer you to the past. You may look back to it as evidence of what my course will be; and, in reference to this diabolical and fiendish rebellion sprung upon the country, all I have to do is to ask you to also go back and take my course in the past, and from that determine what my future will be. Mine has been but one straightforward and unswerving course, and I see no reason now why I should depart from it.

As to making a declaration, or manifesto, or message, or what you may please to call it, my past is a better foreshadowing of my future course than any statement on paper that might be made. Who, four years ago, looking down the stream of time, could have delineated that which has transpired since then? Had any one done so, and presented it, he would have been looked upon as insane, or it would have been thought a fable—fabulous as the stories of the Arabian Nights, as the wonders of the lamp of Aladdin, and would have been about as readily believed.

If we knew so little four years ago of what has passed since then, we know as little what events will arise in the next four years; but as these events arise I shall be controlled in the disposition of them by those rules and principles by which I have been guided heretofore. Had it not been for extraordinary efforts, in part owing to the machinery of the State, you would have had rebellion as rampant in Indiana as we had it in Tennessee. Treason is none the less treason whether it be in a free State or in a slave State; but if there could be any difference in such a crime, he who commits treason in a free State is a greater traitor than he who commits it in a slave State. There might be some little excuse in a man based on his possession of the peculiar property, but the traitor in a free State has no excuse, but simply to be a traitor.

Do not, however, understand me to mean by

this that any man should be exonerated from the penalties and punishments of the crime of treason. The time has arrived when the American people should understand what crime is, and that it should punished, and its penalties enforced and inflicted. We say in our statutes and courts that burglary is a crime, that murder is a crime, that arson is a crime, *and that treason is a crime;* and the Constitution of United States, and the laws of the United States, say that treason shall consist in levying war against them, and giving their enemies aid and comfort. I have just remarked that burglary is a crime and has its penalties, that murder is a crime and has its penalties, and so on through the long catalogue of crime.

To illustrate by a sad event, which is before the minds of all, and which has draped this land in mourning. Who is there here who would say if the assassin who has stricken from our midst one beloved and revered by all, and passed him from time to eternity, to that bourne whence no traveler returns, who, I repeat, who, here would say that the assassin, if taken, should not suffer the penalties of his crime? Then, if you take the life of one individual for the murder of another, and believe that his property should be confiscated, what should be done with one who is trying to assassinate this nation? What should be done with him or them who have attempted the life of a nation composed of thirty millions of people?

We were living at a time when the public mind had almost become oblivious of what treason is. The time has arrived, my countrymen, when the American people should be educated and taught what is crime, and that treason is a crime, and the highest crime known to the law and the Constitution. Yes, treason against a State, treason against all the States, treason against the Government of the United States, *is* the highest crime that can be committed, and those engaged in it should suffer all its penalties.

I know it is very easy to get up sympathy and sentiment where human blood is about to be shed, easy to acquire a reputation for leniency and kindness, but sometimes its effects and practical operations produce misery and woe to the mass of mankind. Sometimes an individual whom the law has overtaken, and on whom its penalties are about to be imposed, will appeal and plead with the Executive for the exercise of clemency. But before its exercise he ought to ascertain what is mercy and what is not mercy. It is a very important question, and one which deserves the consideration of those who moralize upon crime and the morals of a nation, whether in some cases action should not be suspended here and transferred to Him who controls all. There, if innocence has been invaded, if wrong has been done, the Controller and Giver of all good, one of whose attributes is mercy, will set it right.

It is not promulging anything that I have not heretofore said to say that traitors must be made odious, that treason must be made odious, that traitors must be punished and impoverished.

They must not only be punished, but their social power must be destroyed. If not, they will still maintain an ascendency, and may again become numerous and powerful; for, in the words of a former Senator of the United States, "When traitors become numerous enough, treason becomes respectable." And I say that, after making treason odious, every Union man and the Government should be remunerated out of the pockets of those who have inflicted this great suffering upon the country. But do not understand me as saying this in a spirit of anger, for, if I understand my own heart, the reverse is the case; and, while I say that the penalties of the law, in a stern and inflexible manner, should be executed upon conscious, intelligent, and influential traitors—the leaders, who have deceived thousands upon thousands of laboring men who have been drawn into this rebellion—and while I say, as to the leaders, *punishment*, I also say leniency, conciliation, and amnesty to the thousands whom they have misled and deceived; and in reference to this, as I remarked, I might have adopted your speech as my own.

As my honorable friend knows, I long since took the ground that this Government was sent upon a great mission among the nations of the earth; that it had a great work to perform, and that in starting it was started in perpetuity. Look back for one single moment to the Articles of Confederation, and then come down to 1787, when the Constitution was formed—what do you find? That we, "the people of the United States, in order to form a more perfect government," &c. Provision is made for the admission of new States, to be added to old ones embraced within the Union. Now, turn to the Constitution: we find that amendments may be made, by a recommendation of two thirds of the members of Congress, if ratified by three fourths of the States. Provision is made for the admission of new States; no provision is made for the secession of old ones.

The instrument was made to be good in perpetuity, and you can take hold of it, not to break up the Government, but to go on perfecting it more and more as it runs down the stream of time.

We find the Government composed of integral parts. An individual is an integer, and a number of individuals form a State; and a State itself is an integer, and the various States form the Union, which is itself an integer—they all making up the Government of the United States. Now we come to the point of my argumont, so far as concerns the perpetuity of the Government. We have seen that the Government is composed of parts, each essential to the whole, and the whole essential to each part. Now, if an individual (part of a State) declare war against the whole, in violation of the Constitution, he, as a citizen, has violated the law, and is responsible for the act as an individual. There may be more than one individual, it may go on till they become parts of States. Sometime the rebellion may go on increasing in numbers till the State machinery is overturned, and the country becomes like a man that is paralyzed on one side. But we find in the Constitution a great panacea provided. It provides that the United States (that is, the great integer) shall guarantee to each State (the integers composing the whole) in this Union a republican form of government. Yes, if rebellion had been rampant, and set aside the machinery of a State for a time, there stands the great law to remove the paralysis and revitalize it, and put it on its feet again. When we come to understand our system of government, though it be complex, we see how beautifully one part moves in harmony with another; then we see our Government is to be a perpetuity, there being no provision for pulling it down, the Union being its vitalizing power, imparting life to the whole of the States that move around it like planets round the sun, receiving thence light and heat and motion.

Upon this idea of destroying States, my position has been heretofore well known, and I see no cause to change it now, and I am glad to hear its reiteration on the present occasion. Some are satisfied with the idea that States are to be lost in territorial and other divisions; are to lose their character as States. But their life breath has been only suspended, and it is a high constitutional obligation we have to secure each of these States in the possession and enjoyment of a republican form of government. A State may be in the Government with a peculiar institution, and by the operation of rebellion lose that feature; but it was a State when it went into rebellion, and when it comes out without the institution it is still a state.

I hold it as a solemn obligation in any one of these States where the rebel armies have been beaten back or expelled—I care not how small the number of Union men, if enough to man the ship of State, I hold it, I say, a high duty to protect and secure to them a republican form of government. This is no new opinion. It is expressed in conformity with my understanding of the genius and theory of our Government. Then in adjusting and putting the Government upon its legs again, I think the progress of this work must pass into the hands of its friends. If a State is to be nursed until it again gets strength, it must be nursed by its friends, not smothered by its enemies.*

Now, permit me to remark, that while I have opposed dissolution and disintegration on the one

---

* On this and other points, President Johnson declared himself in his Nashville speech of June 9, 1864, from which these extracts are taken:

The question is, whether man is capable of self-government? I hold with Jefferson that government was made for the convenience of man, and not man for government. The laws and constitutions were designed as instruments to promote his welfare. And hence, from this principle, I conclude that governments can and ought to be changed and amended to conform to the wants, to the requirements and progress of the people, and the enlightened spirit of the age. Now, if any of your secessionists have lost faith in men's capability for self-government, and feel unfit for the exercise of this great right, go straight to rebeldom, take Jeff. Davis, Beauregard, and Bragg for your masters, and put their collars on your necks.

And let me say that now is the time to secure these fundamental principles, while the land is rent with anarchy and upheaves with the throes of a mighty revolution. While society is in this disordered state, and we are seeking security, let us fix the foundation of the Government on principles of eternal justice which will endure for all time. There is an element in our midst who are for perpetuating the institution of slavery. Let me say to you, Tennesseeans and men from the Northern States, that slavery is dead. It was not murdered by me. I told you long ago what the result would be if you endeavored to go out of the Union to save slavery; and that the result would be bloodshed, rapine, devastated fields, plundered villages and cities, and, therefore, I urged you to remain in the Union. In trying to save slavery, you killed it and lost your own freedom. Your slavery is dead, but I did not murder it. As Macbeth said to Banquo's bloody ghost:

> "'Never shake thy gory locks at me;
> Thou canst not say I did it.'"

Slavery is dead, and you must pardon me if I do not mourn over its dead body; you can bury it out of sight. In restoring the State, leave out that disturbing and dangerous element, and use only those parts of the machinery which will move in harmony.

But in calling a convention to restore the State, who shall restore and re-establish it? Shall the man who gave his influence and his means to destroy the Government? Is he to participate in the great work of reorganization? Shall he who brought this misery upon the State be permitted to control its destinies? If this be so, then all this precious blood of our brave soldiers and officers so freely poured out will have been wantonly spilled. All the glorious victories won by our noble armies will go for nought, and all the battle-fields which have been sown with dead heroes during the rebellion will have been made memorable in vain.

Why all this carnage and devastation? It was that treason might be put down and traitors punished. Therefore I say that traitors should take a back seat in the work of restoration. If there be but five thousand men in Tennessee loyal to the Constitution, loyal to freedom, loyal to justice, these true and faithful men should control the work of reorganization and reformation absolutely. I say that the traitor has ceased to be a citizen, and in joining the rebellion has become a public enemy. He forfeited his right to vote with loyal men when he renounced his citizenship and sought to destroy our Government. We say to the most honest and industrious foreigner who comes from England or Germany to dwell among us, and to add to the wealth of the country, "Before you can be a citizen you must stay here for five years." If we are so cautious about foreigners, who voluntarily renounce their homes to live with us, what should we say to the traitor, who, although born and reared among us, has raised a parricidal hand against the Government which always protected him? My judgment is that he should be subjected to a severe ordeal before he is restored to citizenship. A fellow who takes the oath merely to save his property, and denies the validity of the oath, is a perjured man, and not to be trusted. Before these repenting rebels can be trusted, let them bring forth the fruits of repentance. He who helped to make all these hand, on the other I am equally opposed to consolidation, or the centralization of power in the hands of a few. Sir, all this has been extorted from me by the remarks you have offered, and as I have already remarked, I might have adopted your speech as my own. I have detained you longer than I expected, but Governor Morton is responsible for that.

I scarcely know how to express my feeling in view of the kindness you have manifested on this occasion. Perhaps I ought not to add what I am about to say, but human nature is human nature. Indiana first named me for the Vice Presidency, though it was unsolicited by me. Indeed, there is not a man can say that I ever approached him on the subject. My eyes were turned to my own State. If I could restore her, the measure of my ambition was complete. I thank the State of Indiana for the confidence and regard she manifested toward me, which has resulted in what is now before me, placing me in the position I now occupy.

In conclusion, I will repeat that the vigor of my youth has been spent in advocating those great principles at the foundation of our Government, and, therefore, I have been by many denounced as a demagogue, I striving to please the people. I am free to say to you that my highest ambition was to please the people, for I believe that when I pleased them, I was pretty nearly right, and being in the right, I didn't care who assailed me. But I was going to say I have always advocated the principle, that government was made for man—not man for goverment; even as the good Book says that the Sabbath was made for man—not man for the Sabbath.

So far as in me lies, those principles shall be carried out; and, in conclusion, I tender you my profound and sincere thanks for your respect and support in the performance of the arduous duties now devolving upon me.

To Virginia Refugees.

April 24, 1865—A large number of Southern refugees had an interview, Hon. John C. Underwood making an address; to which the President replied:

It is hardly necessary for me on this occasion to say that my sympathies and impulses in connection with this nefarious rebellion beat in unison with yours. Those who have passed through this bitter ordeal, and who participated in it to a great extent, are more competent, as I think, to judge and determine the true policy which should be pursued. [Applause.]

I have but little to say on this question in response to what has been said. It enunciates and expresses my own feelings to the fullest extent, and in much better language than I can at the present moment summon to my aid.

The most that I can say is, that entering upon the duties that have devolved upon me under circumstances that are perilous and responsible, and being thrown into the position I now occupy unexpectedly, in consequence of the sad event—the heinous assassination which has taken place—in view of all that is before me, and the circumstances that surround me, I cannot but feel that your encouragement and kindness are peculiarly acceptable and appropriate.

I do not think you have been familiar with my course, if you who are from the South deem it necessary for me to make any professions as to the future on this occasion, or to express what my course will be upon questions that may arise. If my past life is no indication of what my future will be, my professions were both worthless and empty; and in returning you my sincere thanks for this encouragement and sympathy, I can only reiterate what I have said before, and, in part, what has just been read.

As far as clemency and mercy are concerned, and the proper exercise of the pardoning power, I think I understand the nature and character of the latter. In the exercise of clemency and mercy, that pardoning power should be exercised with caution. I do not give utterance to my opinions on this point in any spirit of revenge or unkind feelings. Mercy and clemency have been pretty large ingredients in my compound. Having been the executive of a State, and thereby placed in a position in which it was necessary to exercise clemency and mercy, I have been charged with going too far, being too lenient; and I have become satisfied that mercy without justice is a crime, and that when mercy and clemency are exercised by the executive it

---

widows and orphans, who draped the streets of Nashville in mourning, should suffer for his great crime. The work is in our own hands. We can destroy this rebellion. With Grant thundering on the Potomac before Richmond, and Sherman and Thomas on their march toward Atlanta, the day will ere long be ours. Will any madly persist in rebellion? Suppose that an equal number be slain in every battle, it is plain that the result must be the utter extermination of the rebels. Ah! these rebel leaders have a strong personal reason for holding out to save their necks from the halter; and these leaders must feel the power of the Government! Treason must be made odious, and traitors must be punished and impoverished. Their great plantations must be seized, and divided into small farms, and sold to honest, industrious men. The day for protecting the lands and negroes of these authors of the rebellion is past. It is high time it was. I have been most deeply pained at some things which have come under my observation. We get men in command who, under the influence of flattery, fawning, and caressing, grant protection to the rich traitor, while the poor Union man stands out in the cold, often unable to get a receipt or a voucher for his losses. [Cries of "That's so!" from all parts of the crowd.] The traitor can get lucrative contracts, while the loyal man is pushed aside, unable to obtain a recognition of his just stripes and shoulder-straps. I want them all to hear what I say. I have been on a gridiron for two years at the sight of these abuses. I blame not the Government for these things, which are the work of weak or faithless subordinates. Wrongs will be committed under every form of government and every administration. For myself, I mean to stand by the Government till the flag of the Union shall wave over every city, town, hill-top, and cross-roads, in its full power and majesty.

should always be done in view of justice, and in that manner alone is properly exercised that great prerogative.

The time has come, as you who have had to drink this bitter cup are fully aware, when the American people should be made to understand the true nature of crime. Of crime, generally, our people have a high understanding, as well as of the necessity for its punishment; but in the catalogue of crimes there is one—and that the highest known to the law and the Constitution—of which, since the days of Jefferson and Aaron Burr, they have become oblivious; that is TREASON. Indeed, one who has become distinguished in treason and in this rebellion said, that "when traitors become numerous enough, treason becomes respectable," and to become a traitor was to constitute a portion of the aristocracy of the country.

God protect the people against such an aristocracy.

Yes, the time has come when the people should be taught to understand the length and breath, the depth and height of treason. An individual occupying the highest position among us was lifted to that position by the free offering of the American people—the highest position on the habitable globe. This man we have seen, revered, and loved; one who, if he erred at all, erred ever on the side of clemency and mercy; that man we have seen treason strike through a fitting instrument; and we have beheld him fall like a bright star falling from its sphere.

Now, there is none but would say, if the question came up, what should be done with the individual who assassinated the chief magistrate of a nation—he is but a man, one man after all; but if asked what should be done with the assassin, what should be the penalty, the forfeit exacted, I know what response dwells in every bosom. It is, that he should pay the forfeit with his life. And hence we see that these are times when mercy and clemency without justice become a crime. The one should temper the other and bring about the proper mean. And if we would say this when the case was the simple murder of one man by his fellow man, what should we say when asked what shall be done with him, or them, or those who have raised impious hands to take away the life of a nation composed of thirty millions of people? What would be the reply to that question? But while in mercy we remember justice, in the language that has been uttered, I say justice toward the leaders, the conscious leaders; but I also say amnesty, conciliation, clemency, and mercy to the thousands of our countrymen who you and I know have been deceived or driven into this infernal rebellion.

And so I return to where I started from, and again repeat, that it is time our people were taught to know that treason is a crime—not a mere political difference, not a mere contest between two parties, in which one succeeded, and the other has simply failed. They must know it is treason, for if they had succeeded, the life of the nation would have been reft from it, the Union would have been destroyed.

Surely the Constitution sufficiently defines treason. It consists in levying war against the United States, and in giving their enemies aid and comfort. With this definition it requires the exercise of no great acumen to ascertain who are traitors. It requires no great perception to tell us who have levied war against the United States, nor does it require any great stretch of reasoning to ascertain who has given aid to the enemies of the United States. And when the Government of the United States does ascertain who are the conscious and intelligent traitors, the penalty and the forfeit should be paid.

I know how to appreciate the condition of being driven from one's home. I can sympathize with him whose all has been taken from him; with him who has been denied the place that gave his children birth; but let us, withal, in the restoration of true government, proceed temperately and dispassionately, and hope and pray that the time will come, as I believe, when we all can return and remain at our homes, and treason and traitors be driven from our land; [applause;] when again law and order shall reign, and the banner of our country be unfurled over every inch of territory within the area of the United States.

In conclusion, let me thank you most profoundly for this encouragement and manifestation of your regard and respect, and assure you that I can give no greater assurance regarding the settlement of this question than that I intend to discharge my duty, and in that way which shall in the earliest possible hour bring back peace to our distracted country, and hope the time is not far distant when our people can all return to their homes and firesides, and resume their various avocations.

Interview with George L. Stearns.

WASHINGTON, D. C., *Oct.* 3, 1865, 11½, A. M.

I have just returned from an interview with President Johnson, in which he talked for an hour on the process of reconstruction of rebel States. His manner was as cordial, and his conversation as free as in 1863, when I met him daily in Nashville.

His countenance is healthier, even more so than when I first knew him.

I remarked that the people of the North were anxious that the process of reconstruction should be thorough, and they wished to support him in the arduous work, but their ideas were confused by the conflicting reports constantly circulated, and especially by the present position of the Democratic party. It is industriously circulated in the Democratic clubs that he was going over to them. He laughingly replied, "Major, have you never known a man who for many years had differed from your views because you were in advance of him, claim them as his own when he came up to your standpoint?"

I replied, "I have, often." He said, "So have I," and went on: "The Democratic party finds its old position untenable, and is coming to ours; if it has come up to our position, I am glad of it. You and I need no preparation for this conversation; we can talk freely on this subject, for the thoughts are familiar to us; we can be perfectly frank with each other." He then commenced with saying that the States are in the Union, which is whole and indivisible.

Individuals tried to carry them out, but did not succeed, as a man may try to cut his throat and be prevented by the bystanders; and you cannot say he cut his throat because he tried to do it.

Individuals may commit treason and be punished, and a large number of individuals may constitute a rebellion, and be punished as traitors. Some States tried to get out of the Union, and we opposed it honestly, because we believed it to be wrong; and we have succeeded in putting down the rebellion. The power of those persons who made the attempt has been crushed, and now we want to reconstruct the State governments, and have the power to do it. The State institutions are prostrated, laid out on the ground, and they must be taken up and adapted to the progress of events; this cannot be done in a moment. We are making very rapid progress—so rapid I sometimes cannot realize it. It appears like a dream.

We must not be in too much of a hurry; it is better to let them reconstruct themselves than to force them to it; for if they go wrong the power is in our hands, and we can check them in any stage, to the end, and oblige them to correct their errors; we must be patient with them. I did not expect to keep out all who were excluded from the amnesty, or even a large number of them; but I intended they should sue for pardon, and so realize the enormity of the crime they had committed.

You could not have broached the subject of equal suffrage at the North seven years ago, and we must remember that the changes of the South have been more rapid, and they have been obliged to accept more unpalatable truth than the North has; we must give them time to digest a part, for we cannot expect such large affairs will be comprehended and digested at once. We must give them time to understand their new position.

I have nothing to conceal in these matters, and have no desire or willingness to take indirect courses to obtain what we want.

Our Government is a grand and lofty structure; in searching for its foundation we find it rests on the broad basis of popular rights. The elective franchise is not a natural right, but a political right. I am opposed to giving the States too much power, and also to a great consolidation of power in the central government.

If I interfered with the vote in the rebel States, to dictate that no negro shall vote, I might do the same for my own purposes in Pennsylvania. Our only safety lies in allowing each State to control the right of voting by its own laws, and we have the power to control the rebel States if they go wrong. If they rebel we have the army, and can control them by it, and, if necessary, by legislation also. If the General Government controls the right to vote in the States, it may establish such rules as will restrict the vote to a small number of persons, and thus create a central despotism.

My position here is different from what it would be if I was in Tennessee.

There I should try to introduce negro suffrage gradually; first those who had served in the army; those who could read and write; and perhaps a property qualification for others, say $200 or $250.

It would not do to let the negro have universal suffrage now; it would breed a war of races.

There was a time in the Southern States when the slaves of large owners looked down upon non-slaveowners because they did not own slaves; the larger the number of slaves the masters owned the prouder they were, and this has produced hostility between the mass of the whites and the negroes. The outrages are mostly from non-slaveholding whites against the negro, and from the negro upon the non-slaveholding whites.

The negro will vote with the late master, whom he does not hate, rather than with the non-slaveholding white, whom he does hate. Universal suffrage would create another war, not against us, but a war of races.

Another thing: This Government is the freest and best on earth, and I feel sure is destined to last; but to secure this we must elevate and purify the ballot. I for many years contended at the South that slavery was a political weakness; but others said it was political strength; they thought we gained three-fifths representation by it; I contended that we lost two-fifths.

If we had no slaves we should have had twelve Representatives more, according to the then ratio of representation. Congress apportions representation by States, not districts, and the State apportions by districts.

Many years ago I moved in the Legislature that the apportionment of Representatives to Congress in Tennessee should be by qualified voters.

The apportionment is now fixed until 1872; before that time we might change the basis of representation from population to qualified voters, North as well as South, and, in due course of time, the States, *without regard* to color, might extend the elective franchise to all who possessed certain mental, moral, or such other qualifications as might be determined by an enlightened public judgment.

BOSTON, *October* 18, 1865.

The above report was returned to me by President Johnson with the following endorsement. GEORGE L. STEARNS.

I have read the within communication and find it substantially correct.

I have made some verbal alterations.

A. J.

Address to the Colored Soldiers.

October 10, 1865—The first colored regiment of District of Columbia troops, recently returned from the South, marched to the Executive Mansion, and were addressed by the President, as follows:

MY FRIENDS: My object in presenting myself before you on this occasion is simply to thank you, members of one of the colored regiments which have been in tho service of the country to sustain and carry its banner and its laws triumphantly in every part of this broad land. I appear before you on the present occasion merely to tender you my thanks for the compliment you have paid me on your return home, to again be associated with your friends and your relations, and those you hold most sacred and dear. I have but little to say. It being unusual in this Government and in most of the other governments to have colored troops engaged in their cause, you have gone forth as events have shown, and served with patience and endurance in the cause of your country. This is your country as well as anybody else's country. This is the country in which you expect to live, and in which you should expect to do something by your example in civil life, as you have done in the field. This country is founded upon the principle of equality; and at the same time the standard by which persons are to be estimated is according to their merit and their worth. And you observe, no doubt, that for him who does his duty faithfully and honestly, there is always a just public judgment that will appreciate and measure out to him his proper reward.

I know that there is much well calculated in this Government, and since the late rebellion commenced, to excite the white against the black, and the black against the white man. These are things that you should all understand, and at the same time prepare yourselves for what is before you. Upon the return of peace and the surrender of the enemies of the country, it should be the duty of every patriot and every one who calls himself a Christian to remember that with a termination of the war his resentments should cease—that angry feelings should subside, and that every man should become calm and tranquil, and be prepared for what is before him.

This is another part of your mission. You have been engaged in the effort to sustain your country in the past, but the future is more important to you than the period in which you have just been engaged. One great question has been settled in this Government, and that is the question of slavery. The institution of slavery made war upon the United States, and the United States has lifted its strong arms in vindication of the Government and of free government, and in lifting the arm and appealing to the God of battles, it was decided that the institution of slavery must go down. This has been done, and the Goddess of Liberty, in bearing witness over many of our battle-fields since the struggle commenced, has made her loftiest flight and proclaimed that true liberty has been established upon a more permanent and enduring basis than heretofore. But this is not all; and as you have paid me the compliment to call upon me, I shall take the privilege of saying one or two words as I am before you.

Now, when the sword is returned to its scabbard, when your arms are reversed, and when the olive-branch of peace is extended, resentment and revenge should subside. Then what is to follow? You do understand, no doubt—and if you do not you cannot understand too soon—that simple liberty does not mean the privilege of going into the battle-field, or into the service of the country as a soldier. It means other things as well; and now when you have laid down your arms there are other objects of equal importance before you—now that the Government has triumphantly passed through this mighty rebellion, after the most gigantic battles the world ever saw.

The problem is before you, and it is best that you should understand it, and I therefore speak simply and plainly. Will you now, when you have retired from the army of the United States and taken the position of the citizen—when you have returned to the avocations of peace—will you give evidence to the world that you are capable and competent to govern yourselves? This is what you will have to do.

Liberty is not a mere idea, a mere vagary; when you come to examine this question of liberty you should not be mistaken in a mere idea for the reality. It does not consist in idleness. Liberty does not consist in being worthless. Liberty does not consist in doing in all things as we please; and there can be no liberty without law. In a government of freedom and liberty there must be law, and there must be obedience and submission to the law, without regard to color. Liberty—and may I not call you my countrymen?—liberty consists in the glorious privileges of freedom—consists in the glorious privileges of worth—of pursuing the ordinary avocations of peace with energy, with industry, and with economy; and that being done, all those who have been industrious and economical are permitted to appropriate and enjoy the products of their own labor. This is one of the great blessings of freedom; and hence we might ask the question and answer it by stating that liberty means freedom to work and enjoy the products of your own labor.

You will soon be mustered out of the ranks. It is for you to establish the great fact that you are fit and qualified to be free. Hence, freedom is not a mere idea, but it is something that exists in fact. Freedom is not simply the principle to live in idleness. Liberty does not mean simply to resort to the low saloons and other places of disreputable character. Freedom and liberty do not mean that the people ought to live in licentiousness, but liberty means simply to be industrious and to be virtuous, to be upright in all our dealings and relations with men; and to those now before me, members of the last regiment of colored volunteers from the District of Columbia, and the capital of the United States, I have to say, that a great deal depends upon yourselves; you must give evidence that you are competent for the rights that the government has guaranteed to you.

Hence, each and all of you must be measured according to his merit. If one man is more meritorious than the other, they cannot be equals, and he is the most exalted that is the most meritorious, without regard to color; and the idea of having a law passed in the morning that will make a white man black before night and a black man a white man before day is absurd. That is not the standard; it is your own conduct; it is your own merit; it is the development of your own talents and of your intellectual and moral qualities.

Let this, then, be your course; adopt systems of morality; abstain from all licentiousness; and let me say one thing here, for I am going to talk plainly. I have lived in a Southern State all my life, and know what has too often been the case. There is one thing you should esteem higher and more supreme than almost all others, and that is the solemn contract with all the penalties in the association of married life. Men and women should abstain from those qualities and habits that too frequently follow a war. Inculcate among your children and among your associates, notwithstanding you are just back from the army of the United States, that virtue, that merit, that intelligence are the standards to be observed, and those which you are determined to maintain during your future lives. He that is meritorious and virtuous, intellectual and well informed, must stand highest, without regard to color. It is the very basis upon which heaven itself rests—each individual takes his degree in the sublimer and more exalted regions in proportion to his merits and his virtue.

Then I shall say to you on this occasion, in returning to your homes and firesides, after feeling conscious and proud of having faithfully done your duty, return with the determination that you will perform your duty in the future as you have performed it in the past. Abstain from all those bickerings and jealousies and revengeful feelings which too often spring up between different races.

There is a great problem before us, and I may as well allude to it here in this connection, and that is, whether this race can be incorporated and mixed with the people of the United States—to be made a harmonious and permanent ingredient in the population. This is a problem not yet settled, but we are in the right line to do so. Slavery raised its head against the Government, and the Government raised its strong arm and struck it to the ground; hence, that part of the problem is settled. The institution of slavery is overthrown. But another part remains to be solved, and that is, can four millions of people, reared as they have been, with all their prejudices of the whites—can they take their places in the community, and be made to work harmoniously and congruously in our system? This is a problem to be considered. Are the digestive powers of the American Government sufficient to receive this element in a new shape, and digest it and make it work healthfully upon the system that has incorporated it?

This is the question to be determined. Let us make the experiment, and make it in good faith. If that cannot be done, there is another problem that is before us. If we have to become a separate and distinct people (although I trust that the system can be made to work harmoniously, and that the great problem will be settled without going any further)—if it should be so that the two races cannot agree and live in peace and prosperity, and the laws of Providence require that they should be separated—in that event, looking to the far distant future, and trusting in God that it may never come—if it should come, Providence, that works mysteriously, but unerringly and certainly, will point out the way, and the mode, and the manner by which these people are to be separated, and they are to be taken to their land of inheritance and promise, for such a one is before them. Hence we are making the experiment.

Hence, let me again impress upon you the importance of controlling your passions, developing your intellect, and of applying your physical powers to the industrial interests of the country; and that is the true process by which this question can be settled. Be patient, persevering, and forbearing, and you will help to solve this problem. Make for yourselves a reputation in this cause, as you have won for yourselves a reputation in the cause in which you have been engaged. In speaking to the members of this regiment, I want them to understand that, so far as I am concerned, I do not assume or pretend that I am stronger than the laws or course of nature, or that I am wiser than Providence itself. It is our duty to try and discover what these great laws are which are the foundation of all things, and, having discovered what they are, conform our action and conduct to them and to the will of God, who ruleth all things. He holds the destinies of nations in the palm of his hand, and He will solve the questions and rescue these people from the difficulties that have so long surrounded them. Then let us be patient, industrious, and persevering. Let us develop our intellectual and moral worth.

I trust what I have said may be understood and appreciated. Go to your homes and lead peaceful, prosperous, and happy lives, in peace with all men. Give utterance to no word that would cause dissensions, but do that which will be creditable to yourselves and to your country. To the officers who have led and so nobly commanded you in the field I also return my thanks, for the compliment you and they have conferred upon me.

Interview with Senator Dixon, of Connecticut.

January 28, 1866—The following is the substance of the conversation, as telegraphed that night over the country:

The President said he doubted the propriety at this time of making further amendments to the Constitution. One great amendment had already been made, by which slavery had forever been abolished within the limits of the United States, and a national guarantee thus given that the institution should never exist in the land. Propositions to amend the Constitution were becoming as numerous as preambles and resolutions at town meetings called to consider the most ordinary questions connected with the administration of local affairs. All this, in his opinion, had a tendency to diminish the dignity and prestige attached to the Constitution of the country, and to lessen the respect and confidence of the people in their great charter of freedom. If, however, amendments are to be made to the Constitution, changing the basis of representation and taxation, (and he did not deem them at all necessary at the present time,) he knew of none better than a simple proposition, embraced in a few lines, making in each State the number of qualified voters the basis of representation, and the value of property the basis of direct taxation. Such a proposition could be embraced in the following terms:

"Representatives shall be apportioned among the several States which may be included within this Union according to the number of qualified voters in each State.

"Direct taxes shall be apportioned among the several States which may be included within this Union according to the value of all taxable property in each State."

An amendment of this kind would, in his opinion, place the basis of representation and direct taxation upon correct principles. The qualified voters were, for the most part, men who were subject to draft and enlistment when it was necessary to repel invasion, suppress rebellion, and quell domestic violence and insurrection. They risk their lives, shed their blood and peril their all to uphold the Government, and give protection, security, and value to property. It seemed but just that property should compensate for the benefits thus conferred, by defraying the expenses incident to its protection and enjoyment.

Such an amendment, the President also suggested, would remove from Congress all issues in reference to the political equality of the races. It would leave the States to determine absolutely the qualifications of their own voters with regard to color; and thus the number of Representatives to which they would be entitled in Congress would depend upon the number upon whom they conferred the right of suffrage.

The President, in this connection, expressed the opinion that the agitation of the negro franchise question in the District of Columbia at this time was the mere entering-wedge to the agitation of the question throughout the States, and was ill-timed, uncalled-for, and calculated to do great harm. He believed that it would engender enmity, contention, and strife between the two races, and lead to a war between them, which would result in great injury to both, and the certain extermination of the negro population. Precedence, he thought, should be given to more important and urgent matters, legislation upon which was essential to the restoration of the Union, the peace of the country, and the prosperity of the people.

Interview with a Colored Delegation respecting Suffrage.

February 7, 1866—The delegation of colored representatives from different States of the country, now in Washington, to urge the interests of the colored people before the Government, had an interview with the President.

The President shook hands kindly with each member of the delegation.

ADDRESS OF GEORGE T. DOWNING.

Mr. GEORGE T. DOWNING then addressed the President as follows:

We present ourselves to your Excellency, to make known with pleasure the respect which we are glad to cherish for you—a respect which is your due, as our Chief Magistrate. It is our desire for you to know that we come feeling that we are friends meeting a friend. We should, however, have manifested our friendship by not coming to further tax your already much burdened and valuable time; but we have another object in calling. We are in a passage to equality before the law. God hath made it by opening a Red Sea. We would have your assistance through the same. We come to you in the name of the colored people of the United States. We are delegated to come by some who have unjustly worn iron manacles on their bodies—by some whose minds have been manacled by class legislation in States called free. The colored people of the States of Illinois, Wisconsin, Alabama, Mississippi, Florida, South Carolina, North Carolina, Virginia, Maryland, Pennsylvania, New York, New England States, and District of Columbia have specially delegated us to come.

Our coming is a marked circumstance, noting determined hope that we are not satisfied with an amendment prohibiting slavery, but that we wish it enforced with appropriate legislation. This is our desire. We ask for it intelligently, with the knowledge and conviction that the fathers of the Revolution intended freedom for every American; that they should be protected in their rights as citizens, and be equal before the law. We are Americans, native born Americans. We are citizens; we are glad to have it known to the world that you bear no doubtful record on this point. On this fact, and with confidence in the triumph of justice, we base our hope. We see no recognition of color or race in the organic law of the land. It knows no privileged class, and therefore we cherish the hope that we may be fully enfranchised, not only here in this District, but throughout the land. We respectfully submit that rendering anything less than this will be rendering to us less than our just due; that granting anything less than our full rights will be a disregard of our just rights and of due respect for our feelings. If the powers that be do so it will be used as a license, as it were, or an apology, for any community, or for individuals thus disposed, to outrage our rights and feelings. It has been shown in the present war that the Government may justly reach its strong arm into States, and demand from them, from those who owe it allegiance, their assistance and support. May it not reach out a like arm to secure and protect its subjects upon who it has a claim?

ADDRESS OF FRED. DOUGLASS.

Following upon Mr. Downing, Mr. Fred. Douglass advanced and addressed the President, saying:

Mr. President, we are not here to enlighten you, sir, as to your duties as the Chief Magistrate of this Republic, but to show our respect, and to present in brief the claims of our race to your favorable consideration. In the order of Divine Providence you are placed in a position where you have the power to save or destroy us, to bless or blast us—I mean our whole race. Your noble and humane predecessor placed in our hands the sword to assist in saving the nation, and we do hope that you, his able successor, will favorably regard the placing in our hands the ballot with which to save ourselves.

We shall submit no argument on that point. The fact that we are the subjects of Government, and subject to taxation, subject to volunteer in the service of the country, subject to being drafted, subject to bear the burdens of the State, makes it not improper that we should ask to share in the privileges of this condition.

I have no speech to make on this occasion. I simply submit these observations as a limited expression of the views and feelings of the delegation with which I have come.

RESPONSE OF THE PRESIDENT.

In reply to some of your inquiries, not to make a speech about this thing, for it is always best to talk plainly and distinctly about such matters, I will say that if I have not given evidence in my course that I am a friend of humanity, and to that portion of it which constitutes the colored population, I can give no evidence here. Everything that I have had, both as regards life and property, has been perilled in that cause, and I feel and think that I understand—not to be egotistic—what should be the true direction of this question, and what course of policy would result in the melioration and ultimate elevation, not only of the colored, but of the great mass of the people of the United States. I say that if I have not given evidence that I am a friend of humanity, and especially the friend of the colored man, in my past conduct, there is nothing that I can now do that would. I repeat, all that I possessed, life, liberty, and property, have been put up in connection with that question, when I had every inducement held out to take the other course, by adopting which I would have accomplished perhaps all that the most ambitious might have desired. If I know myself, and the feelings of my own heart, they have been for the colored man. I have owned slaves and bought slaves, but I never sold one. I might say, however, that practically, so far as my connection with slaves has gone, I have been their slave instead of their being mine. Some have even followed me here, while others are occupying and enjoying my property with my consent. For the colored race my means, my time, my all has been perilled; and now at this late day, after giving evidence that is tangible, that is practical, I am free to say to you that I do not like to be arraigned by some who can get up handsomely-rounded periods and deal in rhetoric, and talk about abstract ideas of liberty, who never perilled life, liberty, or property. This kind of theoretical, hollow, unpractical friendship amounts to but very little. While I say that I am a friend of the colored man, I do not want to adopt a policy that I believe will end in a contest between the races, which if persisted in will result in the extermination of one or the other. God forbid that I should be engaged in such a work!

Now, it is always best to talk about things practically and in a common sense way. Yes, I have said, and I repeat here, that if the colored man in the United States could find no other Moses, or any Moses that would be more able and efficient than myself, I would be his Moses to lead him from bondage to freedom; that I would pass him from a land where he had lived in slavery to a land (if it were in our reach) of freedom. Yes, I would be willing to pass with him through the Red sea to the Land of Promise, to the land of liberty; but I am not willing, under either circumstance, to adopt a policy which I believe will only result in the sacrifice of his life and the shedding of his blood. I think I know what I say. I feel what I say; and I feel well assured that if the policy urged by some be persisted in, it will result in great injury to the white as well as to the colored man. There is a great deal of talk about the sword in one hand accomplishing an end, and the ballot accomplishing another at the ballot-box.

These things all do very well, and sometimes have forcible application. We talk about justice; we talk about right; we say that the white man has been in the wrong in keeping the black man in slavery as long as he has. That is all true. Again, we talk about the Declaration of Independence and equality before the law. You understand all that, and know how to appreciate it. But, now, let us look each other in the face; let us go to the great mass of colored men throughout the slave States; let us take the condition in which they are at the present time—and it is bad enough, we all know—and suppose, by some magic touch you could say to every one, "you shall vote to-morrow;" how much would that ameliorate their condition at this time?

Now, let us get closer up to this subject, and talk about it. [The President here approached very near to Mr. Douglass.] What relation has the colored man and the white man heretofore occupied in the South? I opposed slavery upon two grounds. First, it was a great monopoly, enabling those who controlled and owned it to constitute an aristocracy, enabling the few to derive great profits and rule the many with an iron rod, as it were. And this is one great objection to it in a government, it being a monopoly. I was opposed to it secondly upon the abstract principle of slavery. Hence, in getting clear of a monopoly, we are getting clear of slavery at the same time. So you see there were two right ends accomplished in the accomplishment of the one.

Mr. Douglass. Mr. President, do you wish—

The President. I am not quite through yet.

Slavery has been abolished, A great national guarantee has been given, one that cannot be revoked. I was getting at the relation that subsisted between the white man and the colored men. A very small proportion of white persons compared with the whole number of such owned the colored people of the South. I might instance the State of Tennessee in illustration. There were there twenty-seven non-slaveholders to one slaveholder, and yet the slave power controlled the State. Let us talk about this matter as it is. Although the colored man was in slavery there, and owned as property in the sense and in the language of that locality and of that community, yet, in comparing his condition and his position there with the non-slaveholder, he usually estimated his importance just in proportion to the number of slaves that his master owned with the non-slaveholder.

Have you ever lived upon a plantation?

Mr. Douglass. I have, your excellency.

The President. When you would look over and see a man who had a large family, struggling hard upon a poor piece of land, you thought a great deal less of him than you did of your own master's negro, didn't you?

Mr. DOUGLASS. Not I!

The PRESIDENT. Well, I know such was the case with a large number of you in those sections. Where such is the case we know there is an enmity, we know there is a hate. The poor white man, on the other hand, was opposed to the slave and his master; for the colored man and his master combined kept him in slavery, by depriving him of a fair participation in the labor and productions of the rich land of the country.

Don't you know that a colored man, in going to hunt a master (as they call it) for the next year, preferred hiring to a man who owned slaves rather than to a man who did not? I know the fact, at all events. They did not consider it quite as respectable to hire to a man who did not own negroes as to one who did.

Mr. DOUGLASS. Because he wouldn't be treated as well.

The PRESIDENT. Then that is another argument in favor of what I am going to say. It shows that the colored man appreciated the slave owner more highly than he did the man who didn't own slaves. Hence the enmity between the colored man and the non-slaveholders. The white man was permitted to vote before—government was derived from him. He is a part and parcel of the political machinery.

Now, by the rebellion or revolution—and when you come back to the objects of this war, you find that the abolition of slavery was not one of the objects; Congress and the President himself declared that it was waged on our part in order to suppress the rebellion—the abolition of slavery has come as an incident to the suppression of a great rebellion—as an incident, and as an incident we should give it the proper direction.

The colored man went into this rebellion a slave; by the operation of the rebellion he came out a freedman—equal to a freeman in any other portion of the country. Then there is a great deal done for him on this point. The non-slaveholder who was forced into the rebellion, who was as loyal as those that lived beyond the limits of the State, but was carried into it, lost his property, and in a number of instances the lives of such were sacrificed, and he who has survived has come out of it with nothing gained, but a great deal lost.

Now, upon the principle of justice, should they be placed in a condition different from what they were before? On the one hand, one has gained a great deal; on the other hand, one has lost a great deal, and, in a political point of view, scarcely stands where he did before.

Now, we are talking about where we are going to begin. We have got at the hate that existed between the two races. The query comes up, whether these two races, situated as they were before, without preparation, without time for passion and excitement to be appeased, and without time for the slightest improvement, whether the one should be turned loose upon the other, and be thrown together at the ballot-box with this enmity and hate existing between them. The query comes up right there, whether we don't commence a war of races. I think I understand this thing, and especially is this the case when you force it upon a people without their consent.

You have spoken about government. Where is power derived from? We say it is derived from the people. Let us take it so, and refer to the District of Columbia by way of illustration. Suppose, for instance, here, in this political community, which, to a certain extent, must have government, must have laws, and putting it now upon the broadest basis you can put it—take into consideration the relation which the white has heretofore borne to the colored race—is it proper to force upon this community, without their consent, the elective franchise, without regard to color, making it universal?

Now, where do you begin? Government must have a controlling power—must have a lodgment. For instance, suppose Congress should pass a law authorizing an election to be held at which all over twenty-one years of age, without regard to color, should be allowed to vote, and a majority should decide at such election that the elective franchise should not be universal; what would you do about it? Who would settle it? Do you deny that first great principle of the right of the people to govern themselves? Will you resort to an arbitrary power, and say a majority of the people shall receive a state of things they are opposed to?

Mr. DOUGLASS. That was said before the war.

The PRESIDENT. I am now talking about a principle; not what somebody else said.

Mr. DOWNING. Apply what you have said, Mr. President, to South Carolina, for instance, where a majority of the inhabitants are colored.

The PRESIDENT. Suppose you go to South Carolina; suppose you go to Ohio. That doesn't change the principle at all. The query to which I have referred still comes up when government is undergoing a fundamental change. Government commenced upon this principle; it has existed upon it; and you propose now to incorporate into it an element that didn't exist before. I say the query comes up in undertaking this thing whether we have a right to make a change in regard to the elective franchise in Ohio, for instance: whether we shall not let the people in that State decide the matter for themselves.

Each community is better prepared to determine the depositary of its political power than anybody else, and it is for the Legislature, for the people of Ohio to say who shall vote, and not for the Congress of the United States. I might go down here to the ballot-box to-morrow and vote directly for universal suffrage; but if a great majority of the people said no, I should consider it would be tyrannical in me to attempt to force such upon them without their will. It is a fundamental tenet in my creed that the will of the people must be obeyed. Is there anything wrong or unfair in that?

Mr. DOUGLASS (smiling.) A great deal that is wrong, Mr. President, with all respect.

The PRESIDENT. It is the people of the States that must for themselves determine this thing. I do not want to be engaged in a work that will commence a war of races. I want to begin the work of preparation, and the States, or the people in each community, if a man demeans himself well, and shows evidence that this new state of affairs will operate, will protect him in all his rights, and give him every possible advantage when they become reconciled socially and politically to this state of things. Then will this new order of things work harmoniously; but forced upon the people before they are prepared for it, it will be resisted, and work inharmoniously. I feel a conviction that driving this matter upon the people, upon the community, will result in the injury of both races, and the ruin of one or the other. God knows I have no desire but the good of the whole human race. I would it were so that all you advocate could be done in the twinkling of an eye; but it is not in the nature of things, and I do not assume or pretend to be wiser than Providence, or stronger than the laws of nature.

Let us now seek to discover the laws governing this thing. There is a great law controlling it; let us endeavor to find out what that law is, and conform our actions to it. All the details will then properly adjust themselves and work out well in the end,

God knows that anything I can do I will do. In the mighty process by which the great end is to be reached, anything I can do to elevate the races, to soften and ameliorate their condition I will do, and to be able to do so is the sincere desire of my heart.

I am glad to have met you, and thank you for the compliment you have paid me.

Mr. Douglass. I have to return to you our thanks, Mr. President, for so kindly granting us this interview. We did not come here expecting to argue this question with your excellency, but simply to state what were our views and wishes in the premises. If we were disposed to argue the question, and you would grant us permission, of course we would endeavor to controvert some of the positions you have assumed.

Mr. Downing. Mr. Douglass, I take it that the President, by his kind expressions and his very full treatment of the subject, must have contemplated some reply to the views which he has advanced, and in which we certainly do not concur, and I say this with due respect.

The President. I thought you expected me to indicate to some extent what my views were on the subjects touched upon in your statement.

Mr. Downing. We are very happy, indeed, to have heard them.

Mr. Douglass. If the President will allow me, I would like to say one or two words in reply. You enfranchise your enemies and disfranchise your friends.

The President. All I have done is simply to indicate what my views are, as I supposed you expected me to, from your address.

Mr. Douglass. My own impression is that the very thing that your excellency would avoid in the southern States can only be avoided by the very measure that we propose, and I would state to my brother delegates that because I perceive the President has taken strong grounds in favor of a given policy, and distrusting my own ability to remove any of those impressions which he has expressed, I thought we had better end the interview with the expression of thanks. (Addressing the President.) But if your excellency will be pleased to hear, I would like to say a word or two in regard to that one matter of the enfranchisement of the blacks as a means of preventing the very thing which your excellency seems to apprehend—that is a conflict of races.

The President. I repeat, I merely wanted to indicate my views in reply to your address, and not to enter into any general controversy, as I could not well do so under the circumstances.

Your statement was a very frank one, and I thought it was due to you to meet it in the same spirit.

Mr. Douglass. Thank you, sir.

The President. I think you will find, so far as the South is concerned, that if you will all inculcate there the idea in connection with the one you urge, that the colored people can live and advance in civilization to better advantage elsewhere than crowded right down there in the South, it would be better for them.

Mr. Douglass. But the masters have the making of the laws, and we cannot get away from the plantation.

The President. What prevents you?

Mr. Douglass. We have not the single right of locomotion through the Southern States now.

The President. Why not; the government furnishes you with every facility.

Mr. Douglass. There are six days in the year that the negro is free in the South now, and his master then decides for him where he shall go, where he shall work, how much he shall work—in fact, he is divested of all political power. He is absolutely in the hands of those men.

The President. If the master now controls him or his action, would he not control him in his vote?

Mr. Douglass. Let the negro once understand that he has an organic right to vote, and he will raise up a party in the Southern States among the poor, who will rally with him. There is this conflict that you speak of between the wealthy slaveholder and the poor man.

The President. You touch right upon the point there. There is this conflict, and hence I suggest emigration. If he cannot get employment in the South, he has it in his power to go where he can get it.

In parting, the President said that they were both desirous of accomplishing the same ends, but proposed to do so by following different roads.

Mr. Douglass, on turning to leave, remarked to his fellow delegates: "The President sends us to the people, and we go to the people."

The President. Yes, sir; I have great faith in the people. I believe they will do what is right.

Reply of the Colored Delegation to the President.

To the Editor of the Chronicle:

Will you do us the favor to insert in your columns the following reply of the colored delegation to the President of the United States?

Geo. T. Downing,
In behalf of the Delegation.

Mr. President: In consideration of a delicate sense of propriety, as well as your own repeated intimations of indisposition to discuss or to listen to a reply to the views and opinions you were pleased to express to us in your elaborate speech to-day, the undersigned would respectfully take this method of replying thereto. Believing as we do that the views and opinions you expressed in that address are entirely unsound and prejudicial to the highest interests of our race as well as our country at large, we cannot do other than expose the same, and, as far as may be in our power, arrest their dangerous influence. It is not necessary at this time to call attention to more than two or three features of your remarkable address:

1. The first point to which we feel especially bound to take exception is your attempt to found a policy opposed to our enfranchisement, upon the alleged ground of an existing hostility on the part of the former slaves toward the poor white people of the South. We admit the existence of this hostility, and hold that it is entirely reciprocal. But you obviously commit an error by drawing an argument from an incident of a state of slavery, and making it a basis for a policy adapted to a state of freedom. The hostility between the whites and blacks of the South is easily explained. It has its root and sap in the relation of slavery, and was incited on both sides by the cunning of the slave masters. Those masters secured their ascendency over both the poor whites and the blacks by putting enmity between them.

They divided both to conquer each. There was no earthly reason why the blacks should not hate and dread the poor whites when in a state of slavery, for it was from this class that their masters received their slave-catchers, slave-drivers, and overseers. They were the men called in upon all occasions by the masters when any fiendish outrage was to be committed upon the slave. Now, sir, you cannot but perceive that, the cause of this hatred removed, the effect must be removed also. Slavery is abolished. The cause of antagonism is removed, and you must see that it is altogether illogical (and "putting new wine into old bottles," "mending new garments with old cloth") to legislate from slave-holding and slave-driving premises for a people whom you have repeatedly declared your purpose to maintain in freedom.

2. Besides, even if it were true, as you allege, that the hostility of the blacks toward the poor whites must necessarily project itself into a state of freedom, and that this enmity between the two races is even more intense in a state of freedom than in a state of slavery, in the name of Heaven, we reverently ask, how can you, in view of your professed desire to promote the welfare of the black man, deprive him of all means of defence, and clothe him whom you regard as his enemy in the panoply of political power? Can it be that you would recommend a policy which would arm the strong and cast down the defenceless? Can you, by any possibility of reasoning, regard this as just, fair, or wise? Experience proves that those are oftenest abused who can be abused with the greatest impunity. Men are whipped oftenest who are whipped easiest. Peace between races is not to be secured by degrading one race and exalting another, by giving power to one race and withholding it from another; but by maintaining a state of equal justice between all classes. First pure, then peaceable.

3. On the colonization theory you were pleased to broach, very much could be said. It is impossible to suppose, in view of the usefulness of the black man in time of peace as a laborer in the South, and in time of war as a soldier at the North, and the growing respect for his rights among the people, and his increasing adaptation to a high state of civilization in this his native land, there can ever come a time when he can be removed from this country without a terrible shock to its prosperity and peace. Besides, the worst enemy of the nation could not cast upon its fair name a greater infamy than to suppose that negroes could be tolerated among them in a state of the most degrading slavery and oppression, and must be cast away, driven into exile, for no other cause than having been freed from their chains.

GEORGE T. DOWNING,
JOHN JONES,
WILLIAM WHIPPER,
FREDERICK DOUGLASS,
LEWIS H. DOUGLASS,
and others.

WASHINGTON, *February* 7, 1866.

Remarks at an Interview with the Committee of the Legislature of Virginia.

February 10, 1866—A committee of the Senate and House of Delegates of Virginia called upon the President, for the purpose of presenting him with resolutions adopted by the General Assembly of Virginia. After some remarks by Mr. John B. Baldwin, chairman of the delegation, the President responded:

In reply, gentlemen, to the resolutions you have just presented to me, and the clear and forcible and concise remarks which you have made in explanation of the position of Virginia, I shall not attempt to make a formal speech, but simply to enter into a plain conversation in regard to the condition of things in which we stand.

As a premise to what I may say, permit me first to tender you my thanks for this visit, and next to express the gratification I feel in meeting so many intelligent, responsible, and respectable men of Virginia, bearing to me the sentiments which have been expressed in the resolutions of your Legislature and the remarks accompanying them.

They are, so far as they refer to the Constitution of the country, the sentiments and the principles embraced in the charter of the Government. The preservation of the Union has been, from my entrance into public life, one of my cardinal tenets. At the very incipiency of this rebellion I set my face against the dissolution of the Union of the States. I do not make this allusion for the purpose of bringing up anything which has transpired which may be regarded as of an unkind or unpleasant character, but I believed then, as I believe now, and as you have most unmistakably indicated, that the security and the protection of the rights of all the people were to be found in the Union; that we were certainly safer in the Union than we were out of it.

Upon this conviction I based my opposition to the efforts which were made to destroy the Union. I have continued those efforts, notwithstanding the perils through which I have passed, and you are not unaware that the trial has been a severe one. When opposition to the Government came from one section of the country, and that the section in which my life had been passed, and with which my interests were identified, I stood, as I stand now, contending for the Union, and asseverating that the best and surest way to obtain our rights and to protect our interests was to remain in the Union, under the protection of the Constitution.

The ordeal through which we have passed during the last four or five years demonstrates most conclusively that that opposition was right; and to-day, after the experiment has been made and has failed; after the demonstration has been most conclusively afforded that this Union cannot be dissolved, that it was not designed to be dissolved, it is extremely gratifying to me to meet gentlemen as intelligent and as responsible as yourselves, who are willing and anxious to accept and do accept the terms laid down in the Constitution and in obedience to the laws made in pursuance thereof.

We were at one period separated; the separation was to me painful in the extreme; but now, after having gone through a struggle in which the powers of the Government have been tried, when we have swung around to a point at which we meet to agree and are willing to unite our efforts for the preservation of the Government, which I believe is the best in the world, it is exceedingly gratifying to me to meet you to-day, standing upon common ground, rallying around the Constitution and the Union of these States, the preservation of which, as I conscientiously and honestly believe, will result in the promotion and the advancement of this people.

I repeat, I am gratified to meet you to-day, expressing the principles and announcing the sentiments to which you have given utterance, and I trust that the occasion will long be remembered. I have no doubt that your intention is to carry out and comply with every single principle laid down in the resolutions you have submitted. I know that some are distrustful; but I am of those who have confidence in the judgment, in the integrity, in the intelligence, in the virtue of the great mass of the American people; and having such confidence, I am willing to trust them, and I thank God that we have not yet reached that point where we have lost all confidence in each other.

The spirit of the Government can only be preserved, we can only become prosperous and great as a people, by mutual forbearance and confidence. Upon that faith and confidence alone can the Government be successfully carried on.

On the cardinal principle of representation to which you refer I will make a single remark. That principle is inherent; it constitutes one of the fundamental elements of this Government. The representatives of the States and of the people should have the qualifications prescribed by the Constitution of the United States, and *those qualifications most unquestionably imply loyalty*. He who comes as a representative, having the qualifications prescribed by the Constitution to fit him to take a seat in either of the deliberative bodies which constitute the national legislature, must necessarily, according to the intendment ofthe Constitution, *be a loyal man*, willing to abide by and devoted to the Union and the Constitution of the States. He cannot be for the Constitution, he cannot be for the Union, he cannot acknowledge obedience to all the laws, unless he is loyal. When the people send such men in good faith, they are entitled to represntation through them.

In going into the recent rebellion or insurrection against the Government of the United States we erred; and in returning and resuming our relations with the Federal Government, I am free to say that all the responsible positions and places ought to be confined distinctly and clearly to men who are loyal. If there were only five thousand loyal men in a State, or a less number, but sufficient to take charge of the political machinery of the State, those five thousand men, or the lesser number, are entitled to it, if all the rest should be otherwise inclined. I look upon it as being fundamental that the exercise of political power should be confined to loyal men; and I regard that as implied in the doctrines laid down in these resolutions and in the eloquent address by which they have been accompanied. I may say, furthermore, that after having passed through the great struggle in which we have been engaged, we should be placed upon much more acceptable ground in resuming all our relations to the General Government if we presented men unmistakably and unquestionably loyal to fill the places of power. This being done, I feel that the day is not far distant—I speak confidingly in reference to the great mass of the American people—when they will determine that this Union shall be made whole, and the great right of representation in the councils of the nation be acknowledged.

Gentlemen, that is a fundamental principle. "No taxation without representation" was one of the principles which carried us through the Revolution. This great principle will hold good yet; and if we but perform our duty, if we but comply with the spirit of the resolutions presented to me to-day, the American people will maintain and sustain the great doctrines upon which the Government was inaugurated. It can be done, and it will be done; and I think that if the effort be fairly and fully made, with forbearance and with prudence, and with discretion and wisdom, the end is not very far distant.

It seems to me apparent that from every consideration the best policy which could be adopted at present would be a restoration of these States and of the Government upon correct principles. We have some foreign difficulties, but the moment it can be announced that the Union of the States is again complete, that we have resumed our career of prosperity and greatness, at that very instant, almost, all our foreign difficulties will be settled; for there is no power upon the earth which will care to have a controversy or a rupture with the Government of the United States under such circumstances.

If these States be fully restored, the area for

the circulation of the national currency, which is thought by some to be inflated to a very great extent, will be enlarged, the number of persons through whose hands it is to pass will be increased, the quantity of commerce in which it is to be employed as a medium of exchange will be enlarged; and then it will begin to approximate what we all desire, a specie standard. If all the States were restored—if peace and order reigned throughout the land, and all the industrial pursuits—all the avocations of peace—were again resumed, the day would not be very far distant when we could put into the commerce of the world $250,000,000 or $300,000,000 worth of cotton and tobacco, and the various products of the Southern States, which would constitute, in part, a basis of this currency.

Then, instead of the cone being inverted, we should reverse the position, and put the base at the bottom, as it ought to be; and the currency of the country will rest on a sound and enduring basis; and surely that is a result which is calculated to promote the interests not only of one section, but of the whole country, from one extremity to the other. Indeed, I look upon the restoration of these States as being indispensable to all our greatness.

Gentlemen, I know nothing further that I could say in the expression of my feelings on this occasion—and they are not affected—more than to add, that I shall continue in the same line of policy which I have pursued from the commencement of the rebellion to the present period. My efforts have been to preserve the Union of the States. I never, for a single moment, entertained the opinion that a State could withdraw from the Union of its own will. That attempt was made. It has failed. I continue to pursue the same line of policy which has been my constant guide. I was against dissolution. Dissolution was attempted; it has failed; and now I cannot take the position that a State which attempted to secede is out of the Union, when I contended all the time that it could not go out, and that it never has been out. I cannot be forced into that position. Hence, when the States and their people shall have complied with the requirements of the Government, I shall be in favor of their resuming their former relations to this Government in all respects.

I do not intend to say anything personal, but you know as well as I do that at the beginning, and indeed before the beginning, of the recent gigantic struggle between the different sections of the country, there were extreme men South and there were extreme men North. I might make use of a homely figure—which is sometimes as good as any other, even in the illustrations of great and important questions—and say that it has been hammer at one end of the line and anvil at the other; and this great Government, the best the world ever saw, was kept upon the anvil and hammered before the rebellion, and it has been hammered since the rebellion; and there seems to be a disposition to continue the hammering until the Government shall be destroyed. I have opposed that system always, and I oppose it now.

The Government, in the assertion of its powers and in the maintenance of the principles of the constitution, has taken hold of one extreme, and with the strong arm of physical power has put down the rebellion. Now, as we swing around the circle of the Union, with a fixed and unalterable determination to stand by it, if we find the counterpart or the duplicate of the same spirit that played to this feeling and these persons in the South, this other extreme, which stands in the way must get out of it, and the Government must stand unshaken and unmoved on its basis. The Government must be preserved.

I will only say, in conclusion, that I hope all the people of this country, in good faith and in the fullness of their hearts, will, upon the principles which you have enunciated here to-day, of the maintenance of the Constitution and the preservation of the Union, lay aside every other feeling for the good of our common country, and with uplifted faces to heaven swear that our gods and our altars and all shall sink in the dust together rather than that this glorious Union shall not be preserved.

I am gratified to find the loyal sentiment of the country developing and manifesting itself in these expressions; and now that the attempt to destroy the government has failed at one end of the line, I trust we shall go on determined to preserve the Union in its original purity against all opposers.

I thank you, gentlemen, for the compliment you have paid me, and I respond most cordially to what has been said in your resolutions and address, and I trust in God that the time will soon come when we can meet under more favorable auspices than we do now.

Speech of the 22d February, 1866.

[*Report of National Intelligencer.*]

After returning his thanks to the committee which had waited upon him and presented him with the resolutions which had been adopted, the President said: The resolutions, as I understand them, are complimentary of the policy which has been adopted and pursued by the Administration since it came into power. I am free to say to you on this occasion that it is extremely gratifying to me to know that so large a portion of our fellow-citizens indorse the policy which has been adopted and which is intended to be carried out.

This policy has been one which was intended to restore the glorious Union—to bring those great States, now the subject of controversy, to their original relations to the Government of the United States. And this seems to be a day peculiarly appropriate for such a manifestation as this—the day that gave birth to him who founded the Government—that gave birth to the Father of our Country—that gave birth to him who stood at the portal when all these States entered into this glorious Confederacy. I say that the day is peculiarly appropriate to the indorsement of measures for the restoration of the Union that was founded by the Father of his Country. Washington, whose name this city bears, is embalmed in the hearts of all who love their Government. [A voice, "So is Andy Johnson."] Washington, in the language of his eulogists, was first in peace, first in war, and first in the hearts of his countrymen. No people can claim him—no nation can appropriate him. His eminence is acknowledged throughout the civilized world by all those who love free government. I have had the pleasure of a visit from the association which has been directing its efforts towards the completion of a monument erected to his name. I was prepared to meet them and give them my humble influence and countenance in aid of the work. Let the monument be erected to him who founded the Government, and that almost within the throw of a stone from the spot from which I now address you. Let it be completed. Let the pledges which all these States and corporations and associations have put in that monument be preserved as an earnest of our faith in and love of this Union, and let the monument be completed. And in connection with Washington, in speaking of the pledges that have been placed in that monument, let me refer to one from my own State—God bless her!—which has struggled for the preservation of this Union in the field and in the councils of the nation. Let me repeat, that she is now struggling in consequence of an innovation that has taken place in regard to her relation with the Federal Government growing out of the rebellion—she is now struggling to renew her relations with this Government and take the stand which she has occupied since 1796. Let me repeat the sentiment which that State inscribed upon her stone that is deposited within the monument of freedom and in commemoration of Washington; she is struggling to stand by the sentiment inscribed on that stone, and she is now willing to maintain that sentiment. And what is the sentiment? It is the sentiment which was enunciated by the immortal and the illustrious Jackson—"The Federal Union, it must be preserved."

Were it possible for that old man, who in statue is before me and in portrait behind me, to be called forth—were it possible to communicate with the illustrious dead, and he could be informed of the progress in the work of faction, and rebellion, and treason—that old man would turn over in his coffin, he would rise, shake off the habiliments of the tomb, and again extend that long arm and finger and reiterate the sentiment before enunciated, "the Federal Union, it must be preserved." But we witness what has transpired since his day. We remember what he said in 1833. When treason and treachery and infidelity to the Government and the Constitution of the United States stalked forth, it was his power and influence that went forth and crushed it in its incipiency. It was then stopped. But it was only stopped for a time, and the spirit continued. There were men disaffected towards the Government in both the North and South. There were peculiar institutions in the country to which some were adverse and others attached. We find that one portion of our countrymen advocated an institution in the South which others opposed in the North. This resulted in two extremes. That in the South reached a point at which the people there were disposed to dissolve the Government of the United States, and they sought to preserve their peculiar institutions. (What I say on this occasion I want to be understood.) There was a portion of our countrymen opposed to this, and they went to that extreme that they were willing to break up the Government to destroy this peculiar institution of the South.

I assume nothing here to-day but the citizen—one of you—who has been pleading for his country and the preservation of the Constitution. These two parties have been arrayed against each other, and I stand before you as I did in the Senate of the United States in 1860. I denounced there those who wanted to disrupt the Government, and I portrayed their true character. I told them that those who were engaged in the effort to break up the Government were traitors. I have not ceased to repeat that, and, as far as endeavor could accomplish it, to carry out the sentiment. I remarked, though, that there were two parties. One would destroy the Government to preserve slavery; the other would break up the Government to destroy slavery. The objects to be accomplished were different, it is true, so far as slavery was concerned; but they agreed in one thing—the destruction of the Government, precisely what I was always opposed to; and whether the disunionists came from the South or from the North, I stand now where I did then, vindicating the Union of these States and the Constitution of our country. The rebellion manifested itself in the South. I stood by the Government. I said I was for the Union with slavery. I said I was for the Union without slavery. In either alternative I was for the Government and the Constitution. The Government has stretched forth its strong arm, and with its physical power it has put down treason in the field. That is, the section of country that arrayed itself against the Government has been conquered by the force of the Government itself. Now, what had we said to those people? We said: "No compromise; we can settle this question with the South in eight and forty hours."

I have said it again and again, and I repeat it now, "disband your armies, acknowledge the supremacy of the Constitution of the United States, give obedience to the law, and the whole question is settled."

What has been done since? Their armies have been disbanded. They come now to meet us in a spirit of magnanimity and say, "We were mistaken; we made the effort to carry out the doctrine of secession and dissolve this Union, and having traced this thing to its logical and physical results, we now acknowledge the flag of our country, and promise obedience to the Constitution and the supremacy of the law."

I say, then, when you comply with the Constitution, when you yield to the law, when you acknowledge allegiance to the Government—I say let the door of the Union be opened, and the relation be restored to those that had erred and had strayed from the fold of our fathers.

Who has suffered more than I have? I ask the question. I shall not recount the wrongs and the sufferings inflicted upon me. It is not the course to deal with a whole people in a spirit of revenge. I know there has been a great deal said about the exercise of the pardon power, as regards the Executive; and there is no one who has labored harder than I to have the principals, the intelligent and conscious offenders, brought to justice and have the principle vindicated that "treason is a crime."

But, while conscious and intelligent traitors are to be punished, should whole communities and States be made to submit to the penalty of death? I have quite as much asperity, and perhaps as much resentment, as a man ought to have; but we must reason regarding man as he is, and must conform our action and our conduct to the example of Him who founded our holy religion.

I came into power under the Constitution of the country, and with the approbation of the people, and what did I find? I found eight millions of people who were convicted, condemned under the law, and the penalty was death; and, through revenge and resentment, were they all to be annihilated? Oh! may I not exclaim, how different would this be from the example set by the Founder of our holy religion, whose divine arch rests its extremities on the horizon while its span embraces the universe! Yes, He that founded this great scheme came into the world and saw men condemned under the law, and the sentence was death. What was his example? Instead of putting the world or a nation to death, He went forth on the cross and testified with His wounds that He would die and let the world live. Let them repent; let them acknowledge their rashness; let them become loyal, and let them be supporters of our glorious stripes and stars, and the Constitution of our country. I say let the leaders, the conscious, intelligent traitors, meet the penalties of the law. But as for the great mass, who have been forced into the rebellion—misled in other instances—let there be clemency and kindness, and a trust and a confidence in them. But, my countrymen, after having passed through this rebellion, and having given as much evidence of enmity to it as some who croak a great deal about the matter—when I look back over the battle-field and see many of those brave men in whose company I was, in localities of the rebellion where the contest was most difficult and doubtful, and who yet were patient; when I look back over these fields, and where the smoke has scarcely passed away; where the blood that has been shed has scarcely been absorbed—before their bodies have passed through the stages of decomposition—what do I find? The rebellion is put down by the strong arm of the Government in the field. But is this the only way in which we can have rebellions? This was a struggle against a change and a revolution of the Government, and before we fully get from the battle-fields—when our brave men have scarcely returned to their homes and renewed the ties of affection and love to their wives and their children—we are now almost inaugurated into another rebellion.

One rebellion was the effort of States to secede, and the war on the part of the Government was to prevent them from accomplishing that, and thereby changing the character of our Government and weakening its power. When the Government has succeeded, there is an attempt now to concentrate all power in the hands of a few at the federal head, and thereby bring about a consolidation of the Republic, which is equally objectionable with its dissolution. We find a power assumed and attempted to be exercised of a most extraordinary character. We see now that governments can be revolutionized without going into the battle-field; and sometimes the revolutions most distressing to a people are effected without the shedding of blood. That is, the substance of your Government may be taken away, while there is held out to you the form and the shadow. And now, what are the attempts, and what is being proposed? We find that by an irresponsible central directory nearly all the powers of Congress are assumed, without even consulting the legislative and executive departments of the Government. By a resolution reported by a committee, upon whom and in whom the legislative power of the Government has been lodged, that great principle in the Constitution which authorizes and empowers the legislative department, the Senate and House of Representatives, to be the judges of elections, returns, and qualifications of its own members, has been virtually taken away from the two respective branches of the national legislature, and conferred upon a committee, who must report before the body can act on the question of the admission of members to their seats. By this rule they assume a State is out of the Union, and to have its practical relations restored by that rule, before the House can judge of the qualifications of its own members. What position is that? You have been struggling for four years to put down a rebellion. You contended at the beginning of that struggle that a State had not a right to go out. You said it had neither the right nor the power, and it has been settled that the States had neither the right nor the power to go out of the Union. And when you determine by the executive, by the military, and by the public judgment, that these States cannot have any right to go out, this committee turns around and assumes that they are out, and that they shall not come in.

I am free to say to you, as your Executive, that I am not prepared to take any such position. I said in the Senate, in the very inception of this rebellion, that the States had no right to secede. That question has been settled. Thus determined, I cannot turn round and give the lie direct to all that I profess to have done during the last four years. I say that when the States that attempted to secede comply with the Constitution, and give sufficient evidence of loyalty, I shall extend to them the right hand of fellowship, and let peace and union be restored. I am opposed to the Davises, the Toombses, the Slidells, and the long list of such. But when I perceive, on the other hand, men—[A voice, "Call them off"]—I care not by what name you call them—still opposed to the Union, I am free to say to you that I am still with the people. I am still for the preservation of these States, for the preservation of this Union, and in favor of this great Government accomplishing its destiny.

[Here the President was called upon to give the names of three of the members of Congress to whom he had alluded as being opposed to the Union.]

The gentleman calls for three names. I am talking to my friends and fellow-citizens here. Suppose I should name to you those whom I look upon as being opposed to the fundamental principles of this Government, and as now laboring to destroy them. I say Thaddeus Stevens, of Pennsylvania; I say Charles Sumner, of Massachusetts; I say Wendell Phillips, of Massachusetts. [A voice, "Forney!"]

I do not waste my fire on dead ducks. I stand for the country, and though my enemies may traduce, slander, and vituperate, I may say, that has no force.

In addition to this, I do not intend to be governed by real or pretended friends, nor do I intend to be bullied by my enemies. An honest conviction is my sustenance, the Constitution my guide. I know, my countrymen, that it has been insinuated—nay, said directly, in high places—that if such a usurpation of power had been exercised two hundred years ago, in particular reigns, it would have cost an individual his head. What usurpation has Andrew Johnson been guilty of? [Cries of "None."] My only usurpation has been committed by standing between the people and the encroachments of power. And because I dared say in a conversation with a fellow-citizen and a Senator too, that I thought amendments to the constitution ought not to be so frequent, lest the instrument lose all its sanctity and dignity, and be wholly lost sight of in a short time, and because I happened to say in conversation that I thought that such and such an amendment was all that ought to be adopted, it was said that I had suggested such a usurpation of power as would have cost a king his head in a certain period! In connection with this subject, one has exclaimed that we are in the "midst of earthquakes and he trembled." Yes, there is an earthquake approaching, there is a groundswell coming, of popular judgment and indignation. The American people will speak, and by their instinct, if in no other way, know who are their friends, when and where and in whatever position I stand—and I have occupied many positions in the government, going through both branches of the legislature. Some gentleman here behind me says, "And was a tailor." Now, that don't affect me in the least. When I was a tailor I always made a close fit, and was always punctual to my customers, and did good work.

[A voice. No patchwork.]

The President. No, I did not want any patchwork. But we pass by this digression. Intimations have been thrown out—and when principles are involved and the existence of my country imperiled, I will, as on former occasions, speak what I think. Yes! Cost him his head! Usurpation! When and where have I been guilty of this? Where is the man in all the positions I have occupied, from that of alderman to the Vice Presidency, who can say that Andrew Johnson ever made a pledge that he did not redeem, or ever made a promise that he violated, or that he acted with falsity to the people!

They may talk about beheading; but when I am beheaded I want the American people to be the witness. I do not want by inuendoes of an indirect character in high places to have one say to a man who has assassination broiling in his heart, "there is a fit subject," and also exclaim that the "presidential obstacle" must be got out of the way, when possibly the intention was to institute assassination. Are those who want to destroy our institutions and change the character of the Government not satisfied with the blood that has been shed? Are they not satisfied with one martyr? Does not the blood of Lincoln appease the vengeance and wrath of the opponents of this Government? Is their thirst still unslaked? Do they want more blood? Have they not honor and courage enough to effect the removal of the presidential obstacle otherwise than through the hands of the assassin? I am not afraid of assassins; but if it must be, I would wish to be encountered where one brave man can oppose another. I hold him in dread only who strikes cowardly. But if they have courage enough to strike like men, (I know they are willing to wound, but they are afraid to strike;) if my blood is to be shed because I vindicate the Union and the preservation of this Government in its original purity and character, let it be so; but when it is done, let an altar of the Union be erected, and then, if necessary, lay me upon it, and the blood that now warms and animates my frame shall be poured out in a last libation as a tribute to the Union; and let the opponents of this Government remember that when it is poured out the blood of the martyr will be the seed of the church. The Union will grow. It will continue to increase in strength and power, though it may be cemented and cleansed with blood.

I have talked longer, my countrymen, than I intended. With many acknowledgments for the honor you have done me, I will say one word in reference to the amendments to the Constitution of the United States. Shortly after I reached Washington, for the purpose of being inaugurated Vice President, I had a conversation with Mr. Lincoln. We were talking about the condition of affairs, and in reference to matters in my own State. I said we had called a convention and demanded a constitution abolishing slavery in the State, which provision was not contained in the President's proclamation. This met with his approbation, and he gave me encouragement. In talking upon the subject of amendments to the Constitution, he said, "when the amendment to the Constitution now proposed is adopted by three-fourths of the States, I shall be pretty nearly or quite done as regards forming amendments to the Constitution if there should be one other adopted." I asked what that other amendment suggested was, and he replied, "I have labored to preserve this Union. I have toiled four years. I have been subjected to calumny and misrepresentation, and my great and sole desire has been to preserve these States intact under the Constitution, as they were before; and there should be an amendment to the Constitution which would *compel* the States to send their Senators and Representatives to the Congress of the United States." He saw, as part of the doctrine of secession, that the States could, if they were prepared, withdraw their Senators and Representatives; and he wished to remedy this evil by the adoption of the amendment suggested. Even that portion of the Constitution which differs from other organic law says that no State shall be deprived of its representation. We now find the position taken that States shall not be recognized; that we will impose taxation; and where taxes are to be imposed the Representatives elect from thence are met at the door, and told: "No; you must pay taxes, but you cannot participate in a Government which is to affect you for all time." Is this just? [Voices—"No! No!"] We see, then, where we are going. I repeat, that I am for the Union. I am for preserving all the States. They may have erred, but let us admit those into the counsels of the nation who are unmistakably loyal. Let the man who acknowledges allegiance to the Government, and swears to support the Constitution, (he cannot do this in good faith unless he is loyal; no amplification of the oath can make any difference; it is mere detail, which I care nothing about;) let him be unquestionably loyal to the Constitution of the United States and its Government, and willing to support it in its peril, and I am willing to trust him. I know that some do not attach so much importance to the principle as I do. One principle that carried us through the revolution was, that there should be no taxation without representation. I hold that that principle, which was laid down by our fathers for the country's good then, is important to its good now. If it was worth battling for then, it is worth battling for now. It is fundamental, and should be preserved so long as our Government lasts. I know it was said by some during the rebellion that the Constitution had been rolled up as a piece of parchment, and should be put away, and that in time of rebellion there was no constitution. But it is now unfolding; it must now be read and adjusted and understood by the American people.

I come here to-day to vindicate, in so far as I can in these remarks, the Constitution; to save it, as I believe; for it does seem that encroachment after encroachment is to be pressed; and as I resist encroachments on the Government, I stand to-day prepared to resist encroachments on the Constitution, and thereby preserve the Government. It is now peace, and let us have peace. Let us enforce the Constitution. Let us live under and by its provisions. Let it be published in blazoned characters, as though it were in the heavens, so that all may read and all may understand it. Let us consult that instrument, and, understanding its principles, let us apply them. I tell the opponents of this Government, and I care not from what quarter they come—East or West, North or South—"you that are engaged in the work of breaking up this Government are mistaken. The Constitution and the principles of free government are deeply rooted in the American heart." All the powers combined, I care not of what character they are, cannot destroy the image of freedom. They may succeed for a time, but their attempts will be futile. They may as well attempt to lock up the winds or chain the waves. Yes, they may as well attempt to repeal it, (as it would seem the Constitution can be;) by a concurrent resolution; but when it is submitted to the popular judgment, they will find it just as well to introduce a resolution repealing the law of gravitation; and the idea of preventing the restoration of the Union is as about as feasible as resistance to the great law of gravity which binds all to a common centre. This great law of gravitation will bring back those States to harmony and their relations to the Federal Government, and all machinations North and South cannot prevent it. All that is wanting is time, until the American people can understand what is going on, and be ready to accept the view just as it appears to me. I would to God that the whole American people could be assembled here to-day as you are. I could wish to have an amphitheatre large enough to contain the whole thirty millions, that they could be here and witness the great struggle to preserve the Constitution of our fathers. They could at once see what it is, and how it is, and what kind of spirit is manifested in the attempt to destroy the great principles of free government; and they could understand who is for them and who is against them, and who was for ameliorating their condition. Their opposers could be placed before them, and there might be a regular contest, and in the first tilt the enemies of the country would be crushed. I have detained you longer than I intended; but in this struggle I am your instrument. Where is the man or woman, in private or public life, that has not always received my attention and my time? Sometimes it is said, "that man Johnson is a lucky man." I will tell you what constitutes good fortune. Doing right and being for the people. The people in some particular or other, notwithstanding their sagacity and judgment, are frequently underrated or underestimated; but somehow or other the great mass of the people will find out who is for them and who is against them. You must indulge me in this allusion, when I say I can lay my hand on my bosom and say that in all the positions in which I have been placed—many of them as trying as any in which mortal man could be put—so far, thank God, I have not deserted the people, nor do I believe they will desert me. What sentiment have I swerved from? Can my calumniators put their finger on it? Can they dare indicate a discrepancy or a deviation from principle?

Have you heard them at any time quote my predecessor, who fell a martyr to his course, as coming in controversy with anything I advocated? An inscrutable Providence saw proper to remove him to, I trust, a better world than this, and I came into power. Where is there one principle in reference to this restoration that I have departed from? Then the war is not simply upon me, but it is upon my predecessor. I have tried to do my duty. I know some are jealous in view of the White House, and I say all that flummery has as little influence on me as it had heretofore. The conscious satisfaction of having performed my duty to my country, my children, and my God, is all the reward which I shall ask.

In conclusion of what I have to say, let me ask this vast concourse, this sea of upturned faces, to go with me—or I will go with you—and stand around the Constitution of our country; it is again unfolded, and the people are invited to read and understand it, and to maintain its provisions. Let us stand by the principles of our fathers, though the heavens fall; and then, though factions array their transient forces to give vituperation after vituperation in the most virulent manner, I intend to stand by the Constitution as the chief ark of our safety, as the palladium of our civil and religious liberty. Yes; let us cling to it as the mariner clings to the last plank when the night and the tempest close around him.

Accept my thanks, gentlemen, for the indulgence you have given me in my extemporaneous remarks. Let us go on, forgetting the past and looking only upon the future, and trusting in Him that can control all that is on high and here below, and hoping that hereafter our Union will be restored, and that we will have peace on earth and good will towards man.

Speech to the Colored People of the District of Columbia, Celebrating the Third Anniversary of their Emancipation.

April 19, 1866—I have nothing more to say to you on this occasion than to thank you for this compliment you have paid me in presenting yourselves before me on this your day of celebration. I come forward for the purpose of indicating my approbation and manifesting my appreciation of the respect thus offered or conferred.

I thank you for the compliment, and I mean what I say. And I will remark in this connection to this vast concourse that the time will come, and that, too, before a great while, when the colored population of the United States will find out who have selected them as a hobby and a pretence by which they can be successful in obtaining and maintaining power, and who have been their true friends, and wanted them to participate in and enjoy the blessings of freedom.

The time will come when it will be made known who contributed as much as any other man, and who, without being considered egotistic, I may say contributed more, in procuring the great national guarantee of the abolition of slavery in all the States, by the ratification of the amendment to the Constitution of the United States—giving a national guarantee that slavery shall no longer be permitted to exist or be re-established in any State or jurisdiction of the United States.

I know how easy it is to cater to prejudices, and how easy it is to excite feelings of prejudice and unkindness. I care not for that. I have been engaged in this work in which my all has been periled. I was not engaged in it as a hobby, nor did I ride the colored man for the sake of gaining power. What I did was for the purpose of establishing the great principles of freedom. And, thank God, I feel and know it to be so, that my efforts have contributed as much, if not more, in accomplishing this great national guarantee, than those of any other living man in the United States.

It is very easy for colored men to have pretended friends, ensconced in high places, and far removed from danger, whose eyes have only abstractly gazed on freedom; who have never exposed their limbs or property, and who never contributed a sixpence in furtherance of the great cause, while another periled his all, and put up everything sacred and dear to man, and those whom he raised and who lived with him now enjoy his property with his consent, and receive his aid and assistance; yet some who assume, and others who have done nothing, are considered the great defenders and protectors of the colored man.

I repeat, my colored friends, here to-day, the time will come, and that not far distant, when it will be proved who is practically your best friend.

My friendship, so far as it has gone, has not been for place or power, for I had these already. It has been a principle with me, and I thank God the great principle has been established, that wherever any individual, in the language of a distinguished orator and statesman, treads American soil, his soul swells within him beyond the power of chains to bind him, in appreciation of the great truth that he stands forth redeemed, regenerated, and disenthralled by the genius of universal emancipation!

Then let me mingle with you in celebration of the day which commenced your freedom. I do it in sincerity and truth, and trust in God the blessings which have been conferred may be enjoyed and appreciated by you, and that you may give them a proper direction.

There is something for all to do. You have high and solemn duties to perform, and you ought to remember that freedom is not a mere idea. It must be reduced to practical reality. Men in being free have to deny themselves many things which seem to be embraced in the idea of universal freedom.

It is with you to give evidence to the world and the people of the United States, whether you are going to appreciate this great boon as it should be, and that you are worthy of being freemen. Then let me thank you with sincerity for the compliment you have paid me by passing through here to-day and paying your respects to me. I repeat again, the time will come when you will know who has been your best friend, and who has not been your friend from mercenary considerations. Accept my thanks.

VI.

SPECIAL AND VETO MESSAGES OF PRESIDENT JOHNSON,

WITH THE

VOTES IN CONGRESS ON THE PASSAGE OF THE VETOED BILLS.

The Annual Message, December 4, 1865.

The following extracts relate to reconstruction:

I found the States suffering from the effects of a civil war. Resistance to the General Government appeared to have exhausted itself. The United States had recovered possession of their forts and arsenals, and their armies were in the occupation of every State which had attempted to secede. Whether the territory within the limits of those States should be held as conquered territory, under military authority emanating from the President as the head of the army, was the first question that presented itself for decision.

Now, military governments, established for an indefinite period, would have offered no security for the early suppression of discontent; would have divided the people into the vanquishers and the vanquished; and would have envenomed hatred, rather than have restored affection. Once established, no precise limit to their continuance was conceivable. They would have occasioned an incalculable and exhausting expense. Peaceful emigration to and from that portion of the country is one of the best means that can be thought of for the restoration of harmony, and that emigration would have been prevented; for what emigrant from abroad, what industrious citizen at home, would place himself willingly under military rule? The chief persons who have followed in the train of the army would have been dependents on the General Government, or men who expected profit from the miseries of their erring fellow-citizens. The powers of patronage and rule which would have been exercised, under the President, over a vast and populous and naturally wealthy region, are greater than, unless under extreme necessity, I should be willing to intrust to any one man; they are such as, for myself, I could never, unless on occasions of great emergency, consent to exercise. The wilful use of such powers, if continued through a period of years, would have endangered the purity of the general administration and the liberties of the States which remained loyal.

Besides, the policy of military rule over a conquered territory would have implied that the States whose inhabitants may have taken part in the rebellion had, by the act of those inhabitants, ceased to exist. But the true theory is, that all pretended acts of secession were, from the beginning, null and void. The States cannot commit treason, nor screen the individual citizens who may have committed treason, any more than they could make valid treaties or engage in lawful commerce with any foreign power. The States attempting to secede placed themselves in a condition where their vitality was impaired, but not extinguished—their functions suspended, but not destroyed.

But if any State neglects or refuses to perform its offices, there is the more need that the General Government should maintain all its authority, and, as soon as practicable, resume the exercise of all its functions. On this principle I have acted, and have gradually and quietly, and by almost imperceptible steps, sought to restore the rightful energy of the General Government and of the States. To that end, provisional governors have been appointed for the States, conventions called, governors elected, legislatures assembled, and Senators and Representatives chosen to the Congress of the United States. At the same time, the courts of the United States, as far as could be done, have been reopened, so that the laws of the United States may be enforced through their agency. The blockade has been removed and the custom-houses re-established in ports of entry, so that the revenue of the United States may be collected. The Post Office Department renews its ceaseless activity, and the General Government is thereby enabled to communicate promptly with its officers and agents. The courts bring security to persons and property; the opening of the ports invites the restoration of industry and commerce; the post office renews the facilities of social intercourse and of business. And is it not happy for us all, that the restoration of each one of these functions of the General Government brings with it a blessing to the States over which they are extended? Is it not a sure promise of harmony and renewed attachment to the Union that, after all that has happened, the return of the General Government is known only as a beneficence?

I know very well that this policy is attended with some risk; that for its success it requires at least the acquiescence of the States which it concerns; that it implies an invitation to those States, by renewing their allegiance to the United States, to resume their functions as States of the Union. But it is a risk that must be taken; in the choice of difficulties, it is the smallest risk; and to diminish, and, if possible, to remove all danger, I have felt it incumbent on me to assert one other power of the General Government—the power of pardon. As no State can throw a defence over the crime of treason, the power of pardon is exclusively vested in the executive government of the United States. In exercising that power, I have taken every precaution to connect it with the clearest recognition of the binding force of the laws of the United States, and an unqualified acknowledgment of the great social change of condition in regard to slavery which has grown out of the war.

The next step which I have taken to restore the constitutional relations of the States, has been an invitation to them to participate in the high office of amending the Constitution. Every patriot must wish for a general amnesty at the earliest epoch consistent with public safety. For this great end there is a need of a concurrence of all opinions, and the spirit of mutual conciliation. All parties in the late terrible conflict must work together in harmony. It is not too much to ask, in the name of the whole people, that, on the one side, the plan of restoration shall proceed in conformity with a willingness to cast the disorders of the past into oblivion; and that, on the other, the evidence of sincerity in the future maintenance of the Union shall be put beyond any doubt by the ratification of the proposed amendment to the Constitution, which provides for the abolition of slavery forever within the limits of our country. So long as the adoption of this amendment is delayed, so long will doubt and jealousy and uncertainty prevail. This is the measure which will efface the sad memory of the past; this is the measure which will most certainly call population and capital and security to those parts of the Union that need them most. Indeed, it is not too much to ask of the States which are now resuming their places in the family of the Union to give this pledge of perpetual loyalty and peace. Until it is done, the past, however much we may desire it, will not be forgotten. The adoption of the amendment reunites us beyond all power of disruption. It heals the wound that is imperfectly closed; it removes slavery, the element which has so long perplexed and divided the country; it makes of us once more a united people, renewed and strengthened, bound more than ever to mutual affection and support.

The amendment to the Constitution being adopted, it would remain for the States, whose powers have been so long in abeyance, to resume their places in the two branches of the national legislature, and thereby complete the work of restoration. Here it is for you, fellow-citizens of the Senate, and for you, fellow-citizens of the House of Representatives, to judge, each of you for yourselves, of the elections, returns, and qualifications of your own members.

The full assertion of the powers of the General Government requires the holding of circuit courts of the United States within the districts where their authority has been interrupted. In the present posture of our public affairs, strong objections have been urged to holding those courts in any of the States where the rebellion has existed; and it was ascertained, by inquiry, that the circuit court of the United States would not be held within the district of Virginia during the autumn or early winter, nor until Congress should have "an opportunity to consider and act on the whole subject." To your deliberations the restoration of this branch of the civil authority of the United States is therefore necessarily referred, with the hope that early provision will be made for the resumption of all its functions. It is manifest that treason, most flagrant in character, has been committed. Persons who are charged with its commission should have fair and impartial trials in the highest civil tribunals of the country, in order that the Constitution and the laws may be fully vindicated; the truth clearly established and affirmed that treason is a crime, that traitors should be punished and the offence made infamous; and, at the same time, that the question be judicially settled, finally and forever, that no State of its own will has the right to renounce its place in the Union.

The relations of the General Government towards the four millions of inhabitants whom the war has called into freedom have engaged my most serious consideration. On the propriety of attempting to make the freedmen electors by the proclamation of the Executive, I took for my counsel the Constitution itself, the interpretations of that instrument by its authors and their contemporaries, and recent legislation by Congress. When, at the first movement towards independence, the Congress of the United States instructed the several States to institute governments of their own, they left each State to decide for itself the conditions for the enjoyment of the elective franchise. During the period of the confederacy, there continued to exist a very great diversity in the qualifications of electors in the several States; and even within a State a distinction of qualification prevailed with regard to the officers who were to be chosen. The Constitution of the United States recognises the diversities when it enjoins that, in the choice of members of the House of Representatives of the United States, "the electors in each State shall have the qualifications requisite for electors of the most numerous branch of the State legislature." After the formation of the Constitution, it remained, as before, the uniform usage for each State to enlarge the body of its electors, according to its own judgment; and, under this system, one State after another has proceeded to increase the number of its electors, until now universal suffrage, or something very near it, is the general rule. So fixed was this reservation of power in the habits of the people, and so unquestioned has been the interpretation of the Constitution, that during the civil war the late President never harbored the purpose—certainly never avowed the purpose—of disregarding it; and in the acts of Congress, during that period, nothing can be found which during the continuance of hostilities, much less after their close, would have sanctioned any departure by the Executive from a policy which has so uniformly obtained. Moreover, a concession of the elective franchise to the freedmen, by act of the President of the United States, must have been extended to all colored men, wherever found, and so must have established a change of suffrage in the Northern, Middle, and Western States, not less than in the

Southern and Southwestern. Such an act would have created a new class of voters, and would have been an assumption of power by the President which nothing in the Constitution or laws of the United States would have warranted.

On the other hand, every danger of conflict is avoided when the settlement of the question is referred to the several States. They can, each for itself, decide on the measure, and whether it is to be adopted at once and absolutely, or introduced gradually and with conditions. In my judgment, the freedmen, if they show patience and manly virtues, will sooner obtain a participation in the elective franchise through the States than through the General Government, even if it had power to intervene. When the tumult of emotions that have been raised by the suddenness of the social change shall have subsided, it may prove that they will receive the kindliest usage from some of those on whom they have heretofore most closely depended.

But while I have no doubt that now, after the close of the war, it is not competent for the General Government to extend the elective franchise in the several States, it is equally clear that good faith requires the security of the freedmen in their liberty and in their property, their right to labor, and their right to claim the just return of their labor. I cannot too strongly urge a dispassionate treatment of this subject, which should be carefully kept aloof from all party strife. We must equally avoid hasty assumptions of any natural impossibility for the two races to live side by side, in a state of mutual benefit and good will. The experiment involves us in no inconsistency; let us, then, go on and make that experiment in good faith, and not be too easily disheartened. The country is in need of labor, and the freedmen are in need of employment, culture, and protection. While their right of voluntary migration and expatriation is not to be questioned, I would not advise their forced removal and colonization. Let us rather encourage them to honorable and useful industry, where it may be beneficial to themselves and to the country; and, instead of hasty anticipations of the certainty of failure, let there be nothing wanting to the fair trial of the experiment. The change in their condition is the substitution of labor by contract for the status of slavery. The freedman cannot fairly be accused of unwillingness to work, so long as a doubt remains about his freedom of choice in his pursuits, and the certainty of his recovering his stipulated wages. In this the interests of the employer and the employed coincide. The employer desires in his workmen spirit and alacrity, and these can be permanently secured in no other way. And if the one ought to be able to enforce the contract, so ought the other. The public interest will be best promoted if the several States will provide adequate protection and remedies for the freedmen. Until this is in some way accomplished, there is no chance for the advantageous use of their labor; and the blame of ill success will not rest on them.

I know that sincere philanthropy is earnest for the immediate realization of its remotest aims; but time is always an element in reform. It is one of the greatest acts on record to have brought four millions of people into freedom. The career of free industry must be fairly opened to them: and then their future prosperity and condition must, after all, rest mainly on themselves. If they fail, and so perish away, let us be careful that the failure shall not be attributable to any denial of justice. In all that relates to the destiny of the freedmen, we need not be too anxious to read the future; many incidents which, from a speculative point of view, might raise alarm, will quietly settle themselves.

Now that slavery is at an end or near its end, the greatness of its evil, in the point of view of public economy, becomes more and more apparent. Slavery was essentially a monopoly of labor, and as such locked the States where it prevailed against the incoming of free industry. Where labor was the property of the capitalist, the white man was excluded from employment, or had but the second best chance of finding it; and the foreign emigrant turned away from the region where his condition would be so precarious. With the destruction of the monopoly, free labor will hasten from all parts of the civilized world to assist in developing various and immeasurable resources which have hitherto lain dormant. The eight or nine States nearest the Gulf of Mexico have a soil of exuberant fertility, a climate friendly to long life, and can sustain a denser population than is found as yet in any part of our country. And the future influx of population to them will be mainly from the North, or from the most cultivated nations in Europe. From the sufferings that have attended them during our late struggle, let us look away to the future, which is sure to be laden for them with greater prosperity than has ever before been known. The removal of the monopoly of slave labor is a pledge that those regions will be peopled by a numerous and enterprising population, which will vie with any in the Union in compactness, inventive genius, wealth, and industry.

Message on the late Insurrectionary States.

To the Senate of the United States:

In reply to the resolution adopted by the Senate on the 12th instant, I have the honor to state that the rebellion waged by a portion of the people against the properly-constituted authorities of the Government of the United States has been suppressed; that the United States are in possession of every State in which the insurrection existed; and that, as far as could be done, the courts of the United States have been restored, post offices re-established, and steps taken to put into effective operation the revenue laws of the country.

As the result of the measures instituted by the Executive, with the view of inducing a resumption of the functions of the States comprehended in the inquiry of the Senate, the people in North Carolina, South Carolina, Georgia, Alabama, Mississippi, Louisiana, Arkansas, and Tennessee, have reorganized their respective State governments, and "are yielding obedience to the laws and Government of the United States" with more willingness and greater promptitude than under the circumstances could reasonably have been anticipated. The proposed amendment to the Constitution, providing for the abolition of slavery forever within the limits of the country, has been ratified by each one of those States, with the exception of Mississippi, from which no official information has yet been received; and in nearly all of them measures have been adopted or are now pending, to confer upon freedmen rights and privileges which are essential to their comfort, protection, and security. In Florida and Texas the people are making commendable progress in restoring their State governments, and no doubt is entertained that they will at an early period be in a condition to resume all of their practical relations to the Federal Government.

In "that portion of the Union lately in rebellion" the aspect of affairs is more promising than, in view of all the circumstances, could well have been expected. The people throughout the entire South evince a laudable desire to renew their allegiance to the Government, and to repair the devastations of war by a prompt and cheerful return to peaceful pursuits. An abiding faith is entertained that their actions will conform to their professions, and that, in acknowledging the supremacy of the Constitution and the laws of the United States, their loyalty will be unreservedly given to the Govment, whose leniency they cannot fail to appreciate, and whose fostering care will soon restore them to a condition of prosperity.

It is true that in some of the States the demoralizing effects of the war are to be seen in occasional disorders; but these are local in character, not frequent in occurrence, and are rapidly disappearing as the authority of civil law is extended and sustained. Perplexing questions were naturally to be expected from the great and sudden change in the relations between the two races; but systems are gradually developing themselves under which the freedman will receive the protection to which he is justly entitled, and by means of his labor make himself a useful and independent member of the community in which he has his home. From all the information in my possession, and from that which I have recently derived from the most reliable authority, I am induced to cherish the belief that sectional animosity is surely and rapidly merging itself into a spirit of nationality, and that representation, connected with a properly-adjusted system of taxation, will result in a harmonious restoration of the relations of the States to the national Union.

The report of Carl Schurz is herewith transmitted, as requested by the Senate. No reports from Hon. John Covode have been received by the President. The attention of the Senate is invited to the accompanying report of Lieutenant General Grant, who recently made a tour of inspection through several of the States whose inhabitants participated in the rebellion.

ANDREW JOHNSON.

WASHINGTON, D. C., *December* 18, 1865.

Accompanying Report of General Grant.

HEADQUARTERS ARMIES OF THE U. S.,
WASHINGTON, D. C., *December* 18, 1865.

SIR: In reply to your note of the 16th inst., requesting a report from me giving such information as I may be possessed of, coming within the scope of the inquiries made by the Senate of the United States in their resolution of the 12th instant, I have the honor to submit the following:

With your approval, and also that of the honorable Secretary of War, I left Washington city on the 27th of last month for the purpose of making a tour of inspection through some of the Southern States, or States lately in rebellion, and to see what changes were necessary to be made in the disposition of the military forces of the country; how these forces could be reduced and expenses curtailed, &c.; and to learn, as far as possible, the feelings and intentions of the citizens of those States toward the General Government.

The State of Virginia being so accessible to Washington city, and information from this quarter therefore being readily obtained, I hastened through the State without conversing or meeting with any of its citizens. In Raleigh, North Carolina, I spent one day; in Charleston, South Carolina, two days; Savannah and Augusta, Georgia, each one day. Both in traveling and while stopping, I saw much and conversed freely with the citizens of those States, as well as with officers of the army who have been stationed among them. The following are the conclusions come to by me:

I am satisfied that the mass of thinking men of the South accept the present situation of affairs in good faith. The questions which have heretofore divided the sentiments of the people of the two sections—slavery and States rights, or the right of a State to secede from the Union—they regard as having been settled forever by the highest tribunal—arms—that man can resort to. I was pleased to learn from the leading men whom I met, that they not only accepted the decision arrived at as final, but, now that the smoke of battle has cleared away and time has been given for reflection, that this decision has been a fortunate one for the whole country, they receiving like benefits from it with those who opposed them in the field and in council.

Four years of war, during which law was executed only at the point of the bayonet throughout the States in rebellion, have left the people possibly in a condition not to yield that ready obedience to civil authority the American people have generally been in the habit of yielding. This would render the presence of small garrisons throughout those States necessary until such time as labor returns to its proper channels, and civil authority is fully established. I did not meet any one, either those holding places under the Government or citizens of the Southern States, who think it practicable to withdraw the military from the South at present. The white and the black mutually require the protection of the General Government.

There is such universal acquiescence in the authority of the General Government throughout the portions of the country visited by me, that the mere presence of a military force, without regard to numbers, is sufficient to maintain order. The good of the country and economy require that the force kept in the interior, where there are many freedmen, (elsewhere in the Southern States than at forts upon the sea-coast no force is necessary,) should all be white troops. The reasons for this are obvious without mentioning many of them. The presence of black troops, lately slaves, demoralizes labor both by their advice and by furnishing in their camps a resort for the freedmen for long distances around. White troops generally excite no opposition, and therefore a small number of them can maintain order in a given district. Colored troops must be kept in bodies sufficient to defend themselves. It is not the thinking men who would use violence toward any class of troops sent among them by the General Government, but the ignorant in some cases might, and the late slave seems to be imbued with the idea that the property of his late master should by right belong to him, or at least should have no protection from the colored soldier. There is danger of collisions being brought on by such causes.

My observations lead me to the conclusion that the citizens of the Southern States are anxious to return to self-government within the Union as soon as possible; that while reconstructing, they want and require protection from the Government; that they are in earnest in wishing to do what they think is required by the Government, not humiliating to them as citizens, and that if such a course was pointed out they would pursue it in good faith. It is to be regretted that there cannot be a greater commingling at this time between the citizens of the two sections, and particularly of those intrusted with the law-making power.

I did not give the operations of the Freedmen's Bureau that attention I would have done if more time had been at my disposal. Conversations on the subject, however, with officers connected with the bureau lead me to think that in some of the States its affairs have not been conducted with good judgment or economy, and that the belief, widely spread among the freedmen of the Southern States, that the lands of their former owners will, at least in part, be divided among them, has come from the agents of this bureau. This belief is seriously interfering with the willingness of the freedmen to make contracts for the coming year. In some form the Freedmen's Bureau is an absolute necessity until civil law is established and enforced, securing to the freedmen their rights and full protection. At present, however, it is independent of the military establishment of the country, and seems to be operated by the different agents of the bureau according to their individual notions. Everywhere General Howard, the able head of the bureau, made friends by the just and fair instructions and advice he gave; but the complaint in South Carolina was, that when he left things went on as before. Many, perhaps the majority, of the agents of the Freedmen's Bureau advise the freedmen that by their own industry they must expect to live. To this end they endeavor to secure employment for them, and to see that both contracting parties comply with their engagements. In some instances, I am sorry to say, the freedman's mind does not seem to be disabused of the idea that a freedman has the right to live without care or provision for the future. The effect of the belief in division of lands is idleness and accumulation in camps, towns, and cities. In such cases I think it will be found that vice and disease will tend to the extermination, or great reduction of the colored race. It cannot be expected that the opinions held by men at the South for years can be changed in a day; and therefore the freedmen require for a few years not only laws to protect them, but the fostering care of those who will give them good counsel, and in whom they can rely.

The Freedmen's Bureau, being separated from the military establishment of the country, requires all the expense of a separate organization. One does not necessarily know what the other is doing, or what orders they are acting under. It seems to me this could be corrected by regarding every officer on duty with troops in the Southern States as agents of the Freedmen's Bureau, and then have all orders from the head of the bureau sent through department commanders. This would create a responsibility that would secure uniformity of action throughout all the South; would insure the orders and instructions from the head of the bureau being carried out; and would relieve from duty and pay a large number of employés of the Government.

I have the honor to be, very respectfully, your obedient servant, U. S. GRANT,
Lieutenant General.

His Excellency A. JOHNSON,
President of the United States.

Veto of the Freedmen's Bureau Bill, February 19, 1866.

To the Senate of the United States:

I have examined with care the bill which originated in the Senate, and has been passed by the two Houses of Congress, to amend an act entitled "An act to establish a Bureau for the relief of Freedmen and Refugees," and for other purposes. Having, with much regret, come to the conclusion that it would not be consistent with the public welfare to give my approval to the measure, I return the bill to the Senate with my objections to its becoming a law.

I might call to mind, in advance of these objections, that there is no immediate necessity for the proposed measure. The act to establish a bureau for the relief of freedmen and refugees, which was approved in the month of March last, has not yet expired. It was thought stringent and extensive enough for the purpose in view in time of war. Before it ceases to have effect, further experience may assist to guide us to a wise conclusion as to the policy to be adopted in time of peace.

I share with Congress the strongest desire to secure to the freedmen the full enjoyment of their freedom and property, and their entire independence and equality in making contracts for their labor; but the bill before me contains provisions which, in my opinion, are not warranted by the Constitution, and are not well suited to accomplish the end in view.

The bill proposes to establish, by authority of Congress, military jurisdiction over all parts of the United States containing refugees and freedmen. It would, by its very nature, apply with most force to those parts of the United States in which the freedmen most abound; and it expressly extends the existing temporary jurisdiction of the freedmen's bureau, with greatly enlarged powers, over those States "in which the ordinary course of judicial proceedings has been interrupted by the rebellion." The source from which this military jurisdiction is to emanate is none other than the President of the United States, acting through the War Department and the Commissioner of the Freedmen's Bureau. The agents to carry out this military jurisdiction are to be selected either from the army or from civil life; the country is to be divided into districts and sub-districts, and the number of salaried agents to be employed may be equal to the number of counties or parishes in all the United States where freedmen and refugees are to be found.

The subjects over which this military jurisdiction is to extend in every part of the United States include protection to "all employés, agents, and officers of this bureau in the exercise of the duties imposed" upon them by the bill. In eleven States it is further to extend over all cases affecting freedmen and refugees discriminated against "by local law, custom, or prejudice." In those eleven States, the bill subjects any white person who may be charged with depriving a freedman of "any civil rights or immunities belonging to white persons" to imprisonment or fine, or both, without, however, defining the "civil rights and immunities" which are thus to be secured to the freedmen by military law. This military jurisdiction also extends to all questions that may arise respecting contracts. The agent who is thus to exercise the office of a military judge may be a stranger, entirely ignorant of the laws of the place, and exposed to the errors of judgment to which all men are liable. The exercise of power, over which there is no legal supervision, by so vast a number of agents as is contemplated by the bill, must, by the very nature of man, be attended by acts of caprice, injustice, and passion.

The trials, having their origin under this bill, are to take place without the intervention of a jury, and without any fixed rules of law or evidence. The rules on which offences are to be "heard and determined" by the numerous agents are such rules and regulations as the President, through the War Department, shall prescribe. No previous presentment is required, nor any indictment charging the commission of a crime against the laws; but the trial must proceed on charges and specifications. The punishment will be—not what the law declares, but such as a court-martial may think proper; and from these arbitrary tribunals there lies no appeal, no writ of error to any of the courts in which the Constitution of the United States vests exclusively the judicial power of the country.

While the territory and the classes of actions and offences that are made subject to the measure are so extensive, the bill itself, should it become a law, will have no limitation in point of time, but will form a part of the permanent legislation of the country. I cannot reconcile a system of military jurisdiction of this kind with the words of the Constitution, which declare that "no person shall be held to answer for a capital or otherwise infamous crime unless upon a presentment or indictment of a grand jury, except in cases arising in the land and naval forces, or in the militia when in actual service in time of war or public danger;" and that "in all criminal prosecutions the accused shall enjoy the right to a speedy and public trial, by an impartial jury of the State or district wherein the crime shall have been committed." The safeguards which the experience and wisdom of ages taught our fathers to establish as securities for the protection of the innocent, the punishment of the guilty, and the equal administration of justice, are to be set aside, and, for the sake of a more vigorous interposition in behalf of justice, we are to take the risks of the many acts of injustice that would necessarily follow from an almost countless number of agents, established in every parish or county, in nearly a third of the States of the Union, over whose decisions there is to be no supervision or control by the federal courts. The power that would be thus placed in the hands of the President is such as in time of peace certainly ought never to be intrusted to any one man.

If it be asked whether the creation of such a tribunal within a State is warranted as a measure of war, the question immediately presents itself whether we are still engaged in war. Let us not unnecessarily disturb the commerce, and credit, and industry of the country, by declaring to the American people and to the world that the United States are still in a condition of civil war. At present there is no part of our country in which the authority of the United States is disputed. Offences that may be committed by individuals should not work a forfeiture of the rights of whole communities. The country has returned or is returning to a state of peace and industry, and the rebellion is, in fact, at an end. The measure, therefore, seems to be as inconsistent with the actual condition of the country as it is at variance with the Constitution of the United States.

If, passing from general considerations, we examine the bill in detail, it is open to weighty objections.

In time of war it was eminently proper that we should provide for those who were passing suddenly from a condition of bondage to a state of freedom.* But this bill proposes to make the

---

*I have obtained from an official source the following statement, not of the number of persons relieved, but of the number of rations issued by the Freedmen's Bureau, in each State, from June 1, 1865, to April 1, 1866—ten months:

	Refugees.	*Freedmen.*	*Total.*
Virginia	4,635	1,676,127	1,680,762
North Carolina	4,474	902,776	907,450
South Carolina and Georgia	24,974	861,653	886,627
Alabama	879,353	364,215	1,243,568
Louisiana	4,330	296,431	300,761
Texas	166	3,521	3,687
Mississippi	33,489	308,391	341,880
Arkansas	1,004,862	715,572	1,720,434
Kentucky and Tennessee	87,180	306,960	394,140
District of Columbia	3,834	440,626	444,460
	2,047,297	5,876,272	7,923,569

Total number of rations issued to freedmen for ten months	5,876,272
Total number of rations issued to refugees	2,047,297
Total number of rations issued to whites and blacks *for ten months*, from June 1, 1865, to April 1, 1866	7,923,519

Freedmen's Bureau, established by the act of 1865, as one of many great and extraordinary military measures to suppress a formidable rebellion, a permanent branch of the public administration, with its powers greatly enlarged. I have no reason to suppose, and I do not understand it to be alleged, that the act of March, 1865, has proved deficient for the purpose for which it was passed, although at that time, and for a considerable period thereafter, the Government of the United States remained unacknowledged in most of the States whose inhabitants had been involved in the rebellion. The institution of slavery, for the military destruction of which the Freedmen's Bureau was called into existence as an auxiliary, has been already effectually and finally abrogated throughout the whole country by an amendment of the Constitution of the United States, and practically its eradication has received the assent and concurrence of most of those States in which it at any time had an existence. I am not, therefore, able to discern in the condition of the country anything to justify an apprehension that the powers and agencies of the Freedmen's Bureau, which were effective for the protection of freedmen and refugees during the actual continuance of hostilities and of African servitude, will now, in a time of peace, and after the abolition of slavery, prove inadequate to the same proper ends. If I am correct in these views there can be no necessity for the enlargement of the powers of the bureau for which provision is made in the bill.

The third section of the bill authorizes a general and unlimited grant of support to the destitute and suffering refugees and freedmen, their wives and children. Succeeding sections make provision for the rent or purchase of landed estates for freedmen, and for the erection for their benefit of suitable buildings for asylums and schools—the expenses to be defrayed from the treasury of the whole people. The Congress of the United States has never heretofore thought itself empowered to establish asylums beyond the limits of the District of Columbia, except for the benefit of our disabled soldiers and sailors. It has never founded schools for any class of our own people; not even for the orphans of those who have fallen in the defence of the Union, but has left the care of education to the much more competent and efficient control of the States, of communities, of private associations, and of individuals. It has never deemed itself authorized to expend the public money for the rent or purchase of homes for the thousands, not to say millions, of the white race who are honestly toiling from day to day for their subsistence. A system for the support of indigent persons in the United States was never contemplated by the authors of the Constitution; nor can any good reason be advanced why, as a permanent establishment, it should be founded for one class or color of our people more than another. Pending the war many refugees and freedmen received support from the Government, but it was never intended that they should thenceforth be fed, clothed, educated, and sheltered by the United States. The idea on which the slaves were assisted to freedom was, that on becoming free they would be a self-sustaining population. Any legislation that shall imply that they are not expected to attain a self-sustaining condition must have a tendency injurious alike to their character and their prospects.

The appointment of an agent for every county and parish will create an immense patronage; and the expense of the numerous officers and their clerks, to be appointed by the President, will be great in the beginning, with a tendency steadily to increase. The appropriations asked by the Freedmen's Bureau, as now established for the year 1866, amount to $11,745,000. It may be safely estimated that the cost to be incurred under the pending bill will require double that amount—more than the entire sum expended in any one year under the administration of the second Adams. If the presence of agents in every parish and county is to be considered as a war measure, opposition, or even resistance, might be provoked; so that, to give effect to their jurisdiction, troops would have to be stationed within reach of every one of them, and thus a large standing force be rendered necessary. Large appropriations would, therefore, be required to sustain and enforce military jurisdiction in every county or parish from the Potomac to the Rio Grande. The condition of our fiscal affairs is encouraging; but, in order to sustain the present measure of public confidence, it is necessary that we practice, not merely customary economy, but, as far as possible, severe retrenchment.

In addition to the objections already stated, the fifth section of the bill proposes to take away land from its former owners without any legal proceedings being first had, contrary to that provision of the Constitution which declares that no person shall "be deprived of life, liberty, or property without due process of law." It does not appear that a part of the lands to which this section refers may not be owned by minors, or persons of unsound mind, or by those who have been faithful to all their obligations as citizens of the United States. If any portion of the land is held by such persons, it is not competent for any authority to deprive them of it. If, on the other hand, it be found that the property is liable to confiscation, even then it cannot be appropriated to public purposes until, by due process of law, it shall have been declared forfeited to the Government.

There is still further objection to the bill on grounds seriously affecting the class of persons to whom it is designed to bring relief. It will tend to keep the mind of the freedman in a state of uncertain expectation and restlessness, while to those among whom he lives it will be a source of constant and vague apprehension.

Undoubtedly the freedman should be protected, but he should be protected by the civil authorities, especially by the exercise of all the constitutional powers of the courts of the United States and of the States. His condition is not so exposed as may at first be imagined. He is in a portion of the country where his labor cannot well be spared. Competition for his services from planters, from those who are constructing or repairing railroads, and from capitalists in his vicinage, or from other States, will enable him to command almost his own terms. He also possesses a perfect right to change his place of abode; and if, therefore, he does not find in one community or State a mode of life suited to his desires, or proper remuneration for his labor, he can move to another, where that labor is more esteemed and better rewarded. In truth, however, each State, induced by its own wants and interests, will do what is necessary and proper to retain within its borders all the labor that is needed for the development of its resources. The laws that regulate supply and demand will maintain their force, and the wages of the laborer will be regulated thereby. There is no danger that the exceedingly great demand for labor will not operate in favor of the laborer.

Neither is sufficient consideration given to the ability of the freedmen to protect and take care of themselves. It is no more than justice to them to believe that as they have received their freedom with moderation and forbearance, so they will distinguish themselves by their industry and thrift, and soon show the world that in a condition of freedom they are self-sustaining, capable of selecting their own employment and their own places of abode, of insisting for themselves on a proper remuneration, and of establishing and maintaining their own asylums and schools. It is earnestly hoped that, instead of wasting away, they will, by their own efforts, establish for themselves a condition of respectability and prosperity. It is certain that they can attain to that condition only through their own merits and exertions.

In this connexion the query presents itself whether the system proposed by the bill will not, when put into complete operation, practically transfer the entire care, support, and control of four millions of emancipated slaves to agents, overseers, or task-masters, who, appointed at Washington, are to be located in every county and parish throughout the United States containing freedmen and refugees? Such a system would inevitably tend to a concentration of power in the Executive, which would enable him, if so disposed, to control the action of this numerous class, and use them for the attainment of his own political ends.

I cannot but add another very grave objection to this bill. The Constitution imperatively declares, in connection with taxation, that each State SHALL have at least one Representative, and fixes the rule for the number to which, in future times, each State shall be entitled. It also provides that the Senate of the United States SHALL be composed of two Senators from each State; and adds, with peculiar force, "that no State, without its consent, shall be deprived of its equal suffrage in the Senate." The original act was necessarily passed in the absence of the States chiefly to be affected, because their people were then contumaciously engaged in the rebellion. Now the case is changed, and some, at least, of those States are attending Congress by loyal representatives, soliciting the allowance of the constitutional right of representation. At the time, however, of the consideration and the passage of this bill, there was no Senator or Representative in Congress from the eleven States which are to be mainly affected by its provisions. The very fact that reports were and are made against the good disposition of the people of that portion of the country is an additional reason why they need, and should have, Representatives of their own in Congress, to explain their condition, reply to accusations, and assist, by their local knowledge, in the perfecting of measures immediately affecting themselves. While the liberty of deliberation would then be free, and Congress would have full power to decide according to its judgment, there could be no objection urged that the States most interested had not been permitted to be heard. The principle is firmly fixed in the minds of the American people, that there should be no taxation without representation. Great burdens have now to be borne by all the country, and we may best demand that they shall be borne without murmur when they are voted by a majority of the representatives of all the people. I would not interfere with the unquestionable right of Congress to judge, each house for itself, "of the elections, returns, and qualifications of its own members." But that authority cannot be construed as including the right to shut out, in time of peace, any State from the representation to which it is entitled by the Constitution. At present all the people of eleven States are excluded—those who were most faithful during the war not less than others. The State of Tennessee, for instance, whose authorities engaged in rebellion, was restored to all her constitutional relations to the Union by the patriotism and energy of her injured and betrayed people. Before the war was brought to a termination they had placed themselves in relations with the General Government, had established a State government of their own, and, as they were not included in the emancipation proclamation, they, by their own act, had amended their constitution so as to abolish slavery within the limits of their State. I know no reason why the State of Tennessee, for example, should not fully enjoy "all her constitutional relations to the United States."

The President of the United States stands towards the country in a somewhat different attitude from that of any member of Congress. Each member of Congress is chosen from a single district or State; the President is chosen by the people of all the States. As eleven States are not at this time represented in either branch of Congress, it would seem to be his duty, on all proper occasions, to present their just claims to Congress. There always will be differences of opinion in the community, and individuals may be guilty of transgressions of the law, but these do not constitute valid objections against the right of a State to representation. I would in nowise interfere with the discretion of Congress with regard to the qualifications of members; but I hold it my duty to recommend to you, in the interests of peace and in the interests of Union, the admission of every State to its share in public legislation, when, however insubordinate, insurgent, or rebellious its people may have been, it presents itself not only in an attitude of loyalty and harmony, but in the persons of representatives whose loyalty cannot be questioned under any existing constitutional or legal test. It is plain that an indefinite or permanent exclusion of any part of the country from representation must be attended by a spirit of disquiet and complaint. It is unwise and dangerous to pursue a course of measures which will unite a very large section of the country against another section of the country, however much the latter may preponderate. The course of emigration, the development of industry and business, and natural causes, will raise up at the South men as devoted to the Union as those of any other part of the land. But if they are all excluded from Congress; if, in a permanent statute, they are declared not to be in full constitutional relations to the country, they may think they have cause to become a unit in feeling and sentiment against the Government. Under the political education of the American people, the idea is inherent and ineradicable, that the consent of the majority of the whole people is necessary to secure a willing acquiescence in legislation.

The bill under consideration refers to certain of the States as though they had not "been fully restored in all their constitutional relations to the United States." If they have not, let us at once act together to secure that desirable end at the earliest possible moment. It is hardly necessary for me to inform Congress that, in my own judgment, most of those States, so far, at least, as depends upon their own action, have already been fully restored, and are to be deemed as entitled to enjoy their constitutional rights as members of the Union.* Reasoning from the Constitution itself, and from the actual situation of the country, I feel not only entitled, but bound to assume that, with the federal courts restored, and those of the several States in the full exercise of their functions, the rights and interests of all classes of the people will, with the aid of the military in cases of resistance to the laws, be essentially protected against unconstitutional infringement or violation. Should this expectation unhappily fail, which I do not anticipate, then the Executive is already fully armed with the powers conferred by the act of March, 1865, establishing the Freedmen's Bureau, and hereafter, as heretofore, he can employ the land and naval forces of the country to suppress insurrection or to overcome obstructions to the laws.

In accordance with the Constitution I return the bill to the Senate, in the earnest hope that a measure involving questions and interests so important to the country will not become a law, unless, upon deliberate consideration by the people, it shall receive the sanction of an enlightened public judgment. ANDREW JOHNSON.

WASHINGTON, *February* 19, 1866.

Copy of the Bill Vetoed.

AN ACT to amend an act entitled "An act to establish a Bureau for the relief of Freedmen and Refugees," and for other purposes.

Be it enacted, &c., That the act to establish a

---

*In response to this suggestion, this action took place in Congress:

When Representatives shall be Admitted from States declared in Insurrection.

IN HOUSE.

February 20, 1866—Mr. Stevens, from the Committee on Reconstruction, reported this concurrent resolution:

Resolved by the House of Representatives, (the Senate concurring,) That, in order to close agitation upon a question which seems likely to disturb the action of the Government, as well as to quiet the uncertainty which is agitating the minds of the people of the eleven States which have been declared to be in insurrection, no Senator or Representative shall be admitted into either branch of Congress from any of said States until Congress shall have declared such State entitled to such representation.

Which was agreed to—yeas 109, nays 40, as follow:

YEAS—Messrs. Allison, Anderson, James M. Ashley, Baker, Baldwin, Banks, Baxter, Beaman, Benjamin, Bidwell, Bingham, Blaine, Boutwell, Brandegee, Bromwell, Broomall, Buckland, Sidney Clarke, Cobb, Conkling, Cook, Cullom, Dawes, Defrees, Deming, Donnelly, Driggs, Eckley, Eggleston, Eliot, Farnsworth, Farquhar, Ferry, Garfield, Grinnell, Griswold, Abner C. Harding, Hart, Hayes, Henderson, Higby, Holmes, Hooper, Hotchkiss, Asahel W. Hubbard, Chester D. Hubbard, Demas Hubbard, jr., John H. Hubbard, James R. Hubbell, Hulburd, Ingersoll, Jenckes, Julian, Kelley, Kelso, Ketcham, Laflin, George V. Lawrence, William Lawrence, Loan, Longyear, Lynch, Marston, McClurg, McIndoe, McKee, McRuer, Mercur, Moorhead, Morrill, Morris, Moulton, Myers, O'Neill, Orth, Paine, Patterson, Perham, Pike, Plants, Pomeroy, Price, William H. Randall, John H. Rice, Sawyer, Schenck, Scofield, Shellabarger, Sloan, Spalding, Starr, Stevens, Thayer, John L. Thomas, jr., Trowbridge, Upson, Van Aernam, Burt Van Horn, Ward, Warner, Ellihu B. Washburne, William B. Washburn, Welker, Wentworth, Williams, James F. Wilson, Stephen F. Wilson, Windom, Woodbridge—109.

NAYS—Messrs. *Bergen*, *Boyer*, *Brooks*, *Chanler*, *Coffroth*, *Dawson*, *Eldridge*, *Finck*, *Glossbrenner*, *Goodyear*, *Grider*, Hale, *Aaron Harding*, *Hogan*, *Humphrey*, *Kerr*, Latham, *Marshall*, *McCullough*, Newell, *Niblack*, *Nicholson*, Phelps, *Radford*, *Samuel J. Randall*, Raymond, *Ritter*, *Rogers*, *Ross*, Rousseau, *Shanklin*, *Sitgreaves*, Smith, *Taber*, *Taylor*, *Thornton*, *Trimble*, *Voorhees*, Whaley, *Wright*—40.

February 21—A motion to reconsider the above vote having been entered, Mr. Stevens moved to lay it on the table; which was agreed to—yeas 108, nays 38, as follow:

YEAS—Messrs. Allison, Anderson, Delos R. Ashley, James M. Ashley, Baker, Baldwin, Banks, Barker, Baxter, Beaman, Benjamin, Bidwell, Bingham, Blaine, Boutwell, Brandegee, Bromwell, Broomall, Buckland, Reader W. Clarke, Cobb, Conkling, Cook, Cullom, Dawes, Defrees, Deming, Donnelly, Driggs, Dumont, Eckley, Eggleston, Eliot, Farquhar, Ferry, Garfield, Grinnell, Griswold, Abner C. Harding, Hart, Hayes, Henderson, Higby, Holmes, Hooper, Asahel W. Hubbard, Demas Hubbard, jr., John H. Hubbard, James R. Hubbell, Hulburd, Ingersoll, Jenckes, Julian, Kelley, Ketcham, Laflin, George V. Lawrence, William Lawrence, Loan, Longyear, Lynch, Marston, Marvin, McClurg, McIndoe, McRuer, Mercur, Moorhead, Morrill, Morris, Moulton, O'Neill, Orth, Paine, Perham, Pike, Plants, Pomeroy, Price, William H. Randall, Alexander H. Rice, John H. Rice, Rollins, Sawyer, Schenck, Scofield, Shellabarger, Sloan, Spalding, Starr, Stevens, Thayer, Francis Thomas, John L. Thomas, jr., Trowbridge, Upson, Van Aernam, Burt Van Horn, Ward, Warner, Ellihu B. Washburne, William B. Washburn, Welker, Wentworth, Williams, James F. Wilson, Stephen F. Wilson, Windom—108.

NAYS—Messrs. *Ancona*, *Bergen*, *Boyer*, *Brooks*, *Coffroth*, *Dawson*, Delano, *Denison*, *Eldridge*, *Finck*, *Glossbrenner*, *Goodyear*, *Grider*, Robert S. Hale, *Hogan*, *Edwin N. Hubbell*, *James M. Humphrey*, *Kerr*, Latham, *Marshall*, *McCullough*, Newell, *Niblack*, *Nicholson*, *Noell*, Phelps, *Radford*, *Ritter*, *Rogers*, *Ross*, Rousseau, *Shanklin*, *Sitgreaves*, *Strouse*, *Taber*, *Taylor*, *Trimble*, Whaley—38.

March 2—The SENATE passed the resolution—yeas 29, nays 18, as follow:

YEAS—Messrs. Anthony, Brown, Chandler, Clark, Conness, Cragin, Creswell, Fessenden, Foster, Grimes, Harris, Henderson, Howe, Kirkwood, Lane of Indiana, Morrill, Nye, Poland, Pomeroy, Ramsey, Sherman, Sprague, Sumner, Trumbull, Wade, Willey, Williams, Wilson, Yates—29.

NAYS—Messrs. *Buckalew*, Cowan, *Davis*, Dixon, Doolittle, *Guthrie*, *Hendricks*, *Johnson*, Lane of Kansas, *McDougall*, Morgan, *Nesmith*, Norton, *Riddle*, *Saulsbury*, Stewart, *Stockton*, Van Winkle—18.

bureau for the relief of freedmen and refugees, approved March three, eighteen hundred and sixty-five, shall continue in force until otherwise provided by law, and shall extend to refugees and freedmen in all parts of the United States; and the President may divide the section of country containing such refugees and freedmen into districts, each containing one or more States, not to exceed twelve in number, and, by and with the advice and consent of the Senate, appoint an assistant commissioner for each of said districts, who shall give like bond, receive the compensation, and perform the duties prescribed by this and the act to which this is an amendment; or said bureau may, in the discretion of the President, be placed under a commissioner and assistant commissioners, to be detailed from the army; in which event each officer so assigned to duty shall serve without increase of pay or allowances.

SEC. 2. That the commissioner, with the approval of the President, and when the same shall be necessary for the operations of the bureau, may divide each district into a number of sub-districts, not to exceed the number of counties or parishes in such district, and shall assign to each sub-district at least one agent, either a citizen, officer of the army, or enlisted man, who, if an officer, shall serve without additional compensation or allowance, and if a citizen or enlisted man, shall receive a salary of not less than five hundred dollars nor more than twelve hundred dollars annually, according to the services rendered, in full compensation for such services; and such agent shall, before entering on the duties of his office, take the oath prescribed in the first section of the act to which this is an amendment. And the commissioner may, when the same shall be necessary, assign to each assistant commissioner not exceeding three clerks, and to each of said agents one clerk, at an annual salary not exceeding one thousand dollars each, provided suitable clerks cannot be detailed from the army. And the President of the United States, through the War Department and the commissioner, shall extend military jurisdiction and protection over all employés, agents, and officers of this bureau in the exercise of the duties imposed or authorized by this act or the act to which this is additional.

SEC. 3. That the Secretary of War may direct such issues of provisions, clothing, fuel, and other supplies, including medical stores and transportation, and afford such aid, medical or otherwise, as he may deem needful for the immediate and temporary shelter and supply of destitute and suffering refugees and freedmen, their wives and children, under such rules and regulations as he may direct: *Provided*, That no person shall be deemed "destitute," "suffering," or "dependent upon the Government for support," within the meaning of this act, who, being able to find employment, could by proper industry and exertion avoid such destitution, suffering, or dependence.

SEC. 4. That the President is hereby authorized to reserve from sale, or from settlement, under the homestead or pre-emption laws, and to set apart for the use of freedmen and loyal refugees, male or female, unoccupied public lands in Florida, Mississippi, Alabama, Louisiana, and Arkansas, not exceeding in all three millions of acres of good land; and the commissioner, under the direction of the President, shall cause the same from time to time to be allotted and assigned, in parcels not exceeding forty acres each, to the loyal refugees and freedmen, who shall be protected in the use and enjoyment thereof for such term of time and at such annual rent as may be agreed on between the commissioner and such refugees or freedmen. The rental shall be based upon a valuation of the land, to be ascertained in such manner as the commissioner may, under the direction of the President, by regulation prescribe. At the end of such term, or sooner, if the commissioner shall assent thereto, the occupants of any parcels so assigned, their heirs and assigns, may purchase the land and receive a title thereto from the United States in fee, upon paying therefor the value of the land ascertained as aforesaid.

SEC. 5. That the occupants of land under Major General Sherman's special field order, dated at Savannah, January sixteen, eighteen hundred and sixty-five, are hereby confirmed in their possession for the period of three years from the date of said order; and no person shall be disturbed in or ousted from said possession during said three years, unless a settlement shall be made with said occupant, by the former owner, his heirs or assigns, satisfactory to the commissioner of the Freedmen's Bureau: *Provided*, That whenever the former owners of lands occupied under General Sherman's field order shall make application for restoration of said lands, the commissioner is hereby authorized, upon the agreement and with the written consent of said occupants, to procure other lands for them by rent or purchase, not exceeding forty acres for each occupant, upon the terms and conditions named in section four of this act, or to set apart for them, out of the public lands assigned for that purpose in section four of this act, forty acres each, upon the same terms and conditions.

SEC. 6. That the commissioner shall, under the direction of the President, procure in the name of the United States, by grant or purchase, such lands within the districts aforesaid as may be required for refugees and freedmen dependent on the Government for support; and he shall provide or cause to be erected suitable buildings for asylums and schools. But no such purchase shall be made, nor contract for the same entered into, nor other expense incurred, until after appropriations shall have been provided by Congress for such purposes. And no payment shall be made for lands purchased under this section, except for asylums and schools, from any moneys not specifically appropriated therefor. And the commissioner shall cause such lands from time to time to be valued, allotted, assigned, and sold in manner and form provided in the fourth section of this act, at a price not less than the cost thereof to the United States.

SEC. 7. That whenever in any State or district in which the ordinary course of judicial proceedings has been interrupted by the rebellion, and wherein, in consequence of any State or local law, ordinance, police or other regulation, custom, or prejudice, any of the civil rights or immunities belonging to white persons, including the right to make and enforce contracts, to sue, be parties, and give evidence, to inherit, purchase, lease, sell, hold and convey real and personal property, and to have full and equal benefit of all laws and proceedings for the security of person and estate, including the constitutional right of bearing arms, are refused or denied to negroes, mulattoes, freedmen, refugees, or any other persons, on account of race, color, or any previous condition of slavery or involuntary servitude, or wherein they or any of them are subjected to any other or different punishment, pains, or penalties, for the commission of any act or offence than are prescribed for white persons committing like acts or offences, it shall be the duty of the President of the United States, through the commissioner, to extend military protection and jurisdiction over all cases affecting such persons so discriminated against.

SEC. 8. That any person who, under color of any State or local law, ordinance, police, or other regulation or custom, shall, in any State or district in which the ordinary course of judicial proceedings has been interrupted by the rebellion, subject, or cause to be subjected, any negro, mulatto, freedman, refugee, or other person, on account of race or color, or any previous condition of slavery or involuntary servitude, or for any other cause, to the deprivation of any civil right secured to white persons, or to any other or different punishment than white persons are subject to for the commission of like acts or offences, shall be deemed guilty of a misdemeanor, and be punished by fine not exceeding one thousand dollars, or imprisonment not exceeding one year, or both; and it shall be the duty of the officers and agents of this bureau to take jurisdiction of, and hear and determine all offences committed against the provisions of this section, and also of all cases affecting negroes, mulattoes, freedmen, refugees, or other persons who are discriminated against in any of the particulars mentioned in the preceding section of this act, under such rules and regulations as the President of the United States, through the War Department, shall prescribe. The jurisdiction conferred by this and the preceding section on the officers and agents of this bureau shall cease and determine whenever the discrimination on account of which it is conferred ceases, and in no event to be exercised in any State in which the ordinary course of judicial proceedings has not been interrupted by the rebellion, nor in any such State after said State shall have been fully restored in all its constitutional relations to the United States, and the courts of the State and of the United States within the same are not disturbed or stopped in the peaceable course of justice.

SEC. 9. That all acts, or parts of acts, inconsistent with the provisions of this act, are hereby repealed.

The votes on passing this bill were:

IN SENATE.

1866, January 25—The bill passed—yeas 37, nays 10, as follow:

YEAS—Messrs. Anthony, Brown, Chandler, Clark, Conness, Cragin, Creswell, Dixon, Doolittle, Fessenden, Foot, Foster, Grimes, Harris, Henderson, Howard, Howe, Kirkwood, Lane of Indiana, Lane of Kansas, Morgan, Morrill, Norton, Nye, Poland, Pomeroy, Ramsey, Sherman, Sprague, Stewart, Sumner, Trumbull, Van Winkle, Wade, Williams, Wilson, Yates—37.

NAYS—Messrs. *Buckalew, Davis, Guthrie, Hendricks, Johnson, McDougall, Riddle, Saulsbury, Stockton, Wright*—10.

IN HOUSE.

February 6—The bill passed—yeas 137, nays 33, as follow:

YEAS—Messrs. Alley, Allison, Ames, Anderson, Delos R. Ashley, James M. Ashley, Baker, Baldwin, Banks, Barker, Baxter, Beaman, Benjamin, Bidwell, Bingham, Blaine, Blow, Boutwell, Brandegee, Bromwell, Broomall, Bundy, Reader W. Clarke, Sidney Clarke, Cobb, Conkling, Cook, Cullom, Darling, Davis, Dawes, Defrees, Delano, Deming, Dixon, Donnelly, Driggs, Dumont, Eckley, Eggleston, Eliot, Farnsworth, Farquhar, Ferry, Garfield, Grinnell, Griswold, Hale, Abner C. Harding, Hart, Hayes, Henderson, Higby, Hill, Holmes, Hooper, Hotchkiss, Asahel W. Hubbard, Chester D. Hubbard, Demas Hubbard, John H. Hubbard, James R. Hubbell, James Humphrey, Ingersoll, Jenckes, Julian, Kasson, Kelley, Kelso, Ketcham, Kuykendall, Laflin, Latham, George V. Lawrence, William Lawrence, Loan, Longyear, Lynch, Marston, Marvin, McClurg, McIndoe, McKee, McRuer, Mercur, Miller, Moorhead, Morrill, Morris, Moulton, Myers, Newell, O'Neill, Orth, Paine, Patterson, Perham, Phelps, Pike, Plants, Pomeroy, Price, William H. Randall, Raymond, Alexander H. Rice, John H. Rice, Rollins, Sawyer, Schenck, Scofield, Shellabarger, Sloan, Smith, Spalding, Starr, Stevens, Stilwell, Thayer, Francis Thomas, John L. Thomas, Trowbridge, Upson, Van Aernam, Burt Van Horn, Robert T. Van Horn, Ward, Warner, Ellihu B. Washburne, William B. Washburn, Welker, Wentworth, Whaley, Williams, James F. Wilson, Stephen F. Wilson, Windom, Woodbridge—137.

NAYS—Messrs. *Boyer, Brooks, Chanler, Dawson, Eldridge, Finck, Glossbrenner, Grider, Aaron Harding, Harris, Hogan, Edwin N. Hubbell, James M. Humphrey, Kerr, Le Blond, Marshall, McCullough, Niblack, Nicholson, Noell, Samuel J. Randall, Ritter, Rogers, Ross,* Rousseau, *Shanklin, Sitgreaves, Strouse, Taber, Taylor, Thornton, Trimble, Wright*—33.

February 21—In Senate, the vote on passing the bill, notwithstanding the objections of the President, was—yeas 30, nays 18, as follow:

YEAS—Messrs. Anthony, Brown, Chandler, Clark, Conness, Cragin, Creswell, Fessenden, Foster, Grimes, Harris, Henderson, Howard, Howe, Kirkwood, Lane of Indiana, Lane of Kansas, Morrill, Nye, Poland, Pomeroy, Ramsey, Sherman, Sprague, Sumner, Trumbull, Wade, Williams, Wilson, Yates—30.

NAYS—Messrs. *Buckalew*, Cowan, *Davis*, Dixon, Doolittle, *Guthrie, Hendricks, Johnson, McDougall*, Morgan, *Nesmith*, Norton, *Riddle, Saulsbury*, Stewart, *Stockton*, Van Winkle, Willey—18.

Two-thirds not having voted therefor, the bill failed.

Veto of the Civil Rights Bill, March 27, 1866.

To the Senate of the United States:

I regret that the bill which has passed both Houses of Congress, entitled "An act to protect all persons in the United States in their civil rights, and furnish the means of their vindication," contains provisions which I cannot approve, consistently with my sense of duty to the whole people, and my obligations to the Constitution of the United States. I am therefore constrained to return it to the Senate, the house in which it originated, with my objections to its becoming a law.

By the first section of the bill all persons born in the United States, and not subject to any foreign power, excluding Indians not taxed, are declared to be citizens of the United States. This provision comprehends the Chinese of the Pacific States, Indians subject to taxation, the people called Gipsies, as well as the entire race designated as blacks, people of color, negroes, mulattoes, and persons of African blood. Every individual of these races, born in the United

States, is by the bill made a citizen of the United States. It does not purport to declare or confer any other right of citizenship than federal citizenship. It does not purport to give these classes of persons any *status* as citizens of States, except that which may result from their *status* as citizens of the United States. The power to confer the right of State citizenship is just as exclusively with the several States as the power to confer the right of federal citizenship is with Congress.

The right of federal citizenship thus to be conferred on the several excepted races before mentioned, is now, for the first time, proposed to be given by law. If, as is claimed by many, all persons who are native-born already are, by virtue of the Constitution, citizens of the United States, the passage of the pending bill cannot be necessary to make them such. If, on the other hand, such persons are not citizens, as may be assumed from the proposed legislation to make them such, the grave question presents itself, whether, when eleven of the thirty-six States are unrepresented in Congress at the present time, it is sound policy to make our entire colored population and all other excepted classes citizens of the United States? Four millions of them have just emerged from slavery into freedom. Can it be reasonably supposed that they possess the requisite qualifications to entitle them to all the privileges and immunities of citizens of the United States? Have the people of the several States expressed such a conviction? It may also be asked whether it is necessary that they should be declared citizens, in order that they may be secured in the enjoyment of the civil rights proposed to be conferred by the bill? Those rights are, by federal as well as State laws, secured to all domiciled aliens and foreigners, even before the completion of the process of naturalization; and it may safely be assumed that the same enactments are sufficient to give like protection and benefits to those for whom this bill provides special legislation. Besides, the policy of the Government, from its origin to the present time, seems to have been that persons who are strangers to and unfamiliar with our institutions and our laws should pass through a certain probation, at the end of which, before attaining the coveted prize, they must give evidence of their fitness to receive and to exercise the rights of citizens, as contemplated by the Constitution of the United States. The bill, in effect, proposes a discrimination against large numbers of intelligent, worthy, and patriotic foreigners, and in favor of the negro, to whom, after long years of bondage, the avenues to freedom and intelligence have just now been suddenly opened. He must, of necessity, from his previous unfortunate condition of servitude, be less informed as to the nature and character of our institutions than he who, coming from abroad, has to some extent, at least, familiarized himself with the principles of a government to which he voluntarily intrusts "life, liberty, and the pursuit of happiness." Yet it is now proposed, by a single legislative enactment, to confer the rights of citizens upon all persons of African descent born within the extended limits of the United States, while persons of foreign birth, who make our land their home, must undergo a probation of five years, and can only then become citizens upon proof that they are "of good moral character, attached to the principles of the Constitution of the United States, and well disposed to the good order and happiness of the same."

The first section of the bill also contains an enumeration of the rights to be enjoyed by these classes, so made citizens, "in every State and Territory in the United States." These rights are, "to make and enforce contracts, to sue, be parties, and give evidence; to inherit, purchase, lease, sell, hold, and convey real and personal property;" and to have "full and equal benefit of all laws and proceedings for the security of person and property as is enjoyed by white citizens." So, too, they are made subject to the same punishments, pains, and penalties in common with white citizens, and to none other. Thus a perfect equality of the white and colored races is attempted to be fixed by federal law in every State of the Union, over the vast field of State jurisdiction covered by these enumerated rights. In no one of these can any State ever exercise any power of discrimination between the different races. In the exercise of State policy over matters exclusively affecting the people of each State, it has frequently been thought expedient to discriminate between the two races. By the statutes of some of the States, northern well as southren, it is enacted, for instance, that no white person shall intermarry with a negro or mulatto. Chancellor Kent says, speaking of the blacks, that "marriages between them and the whites are forbidden in some of the States where slavery does not exist, and they are prohibited in all the slaveholding States; and when not absolutely contrary to law, they are revolting, and regarded as an offence against public decorum."

I do not say that this bill repeals State laws on the subject of marriage between the two races; for, as the whites are forbidden to intermarry with the blacks, the blacks can only make such contracts as the whites themselves are allowed to make, and therefore connot, under this bill, enter into the marriage contract with the whites. I cite this discrimination, however, as an instance of the State policy as to discrimination, and to inquire whether, if Congress can abrogate all State laws of discrimination between the two races in the matter of real estate, of suits, and of contracts generally, Congress may not also repeal the State laws as to the contract of marriage between the two races? Hitherto every subject embraced in the enumeration of rights contained in this bill has been considered as exclusively belonging to the States. They all relate to the internal police and economy of the respective States. They are matters which in each State concern the domestic condition of its people, varying in each according to its own peculiar circumstances and the safety and well-being of its own citizens. I do not mean to say that upon all these subjects there are not federal restraints—as, for instance, in the State power of legislation over contracts, there is a federal limitation that no State shall pass a law impairing the obligations of contracts; and, as to crimes, that no State shall pass an *ex post facto* law; and, as to money, that no State shall make anything but gold and silver a legal tender. But where can we find a federal prohibition against the power of any State to discriminate, as do most of them, between aliens and citizens, between artificial persons called corporations and natural persons, in the right to hold real estate? If it be granted that Congress can repeal all State laws discriminating between whites and blacks in the subjects covered by this bill, why, it may be asked, may not Congress repeal, in the same way, all State laws discriminating between the two races on the subjects of suffrage and office? If Congress can declare by law who shall hold lands, who shall testify, who shall have capacity to make a contract in a State, then Congress can by law also declare who, without regard to color or race, shall have the right to sit as a juror or as a judge, to hold any office, and, finally, to vote, "in every State and Territory of the United States." As respects the Territories, they come within the power of Congress, for as to them the law-making power is the federal power; but as to the States no similar provision exists vesting in Congress the power "to make rules and regulations" for them.

The object of the second section of the bill is to afford discriminating protection to colored persons in the full enjoyment of all the rights secured to them by the preceding section. It declares "that any person who, under color of any law, statute, ordinance, regulation, or custom, shall subject, or cause to be subjected, any inhabitant of any State or Territory to the deprivation of any right secured or protected by this act, or to different punishment, pains, or penalties, on account of such person having at any time been held in a condition of slavery or involuntary servitude, except as a punishment for crime, whereof the party shall have been duly convicted, or by reason of his color or race, than is prescribed for the punishment of white persons, shall be deemed guilty of a misdemeanor, and, on conviction, shall be punished by a fine not exceeding one thousand dollars, or imprisonment not exceeding one year, or both, in the discretion of the court." This section seems to be designed to apply to some existing or future law of a State or Territory which may conflict with the provisions of the bill now under consideration. It provides for counteracting such forbidden legislation by imposing fine and imprisonment upon the legislators who may pass such conflicting laws, or upon the officers or agents who shall put or attempt to put them into execution. It means an official offence—not a common crime committed against law upon the persons or property of the black race. Such an act may deprive the black man of his property, but not of the right to hold property. It means a deprivation of the right itself, either by the State judiciary or the State legislature. It is therefore assumed that under this section members of State legislatures who should vote for laws conflicting with the provisions of the bill, that judges of the State courts who should render judgments in antagonism with its terms, and that marshals and sheriffs who should, as ministerial officers, execute processes sanctioned by State laws and issued by State judges in execution of their judgments, could be brought before other tribunals, and there subjected to fine and imprisonment for the performance of the duties which such State laws might impose. The legislation thus proposed invades the judicial power of the State. It says to every State court or judge, if you decide that this act is unconstitutional; if you refuse, under the prohibition of a State law, to allow a negro to testify; if you hold that over such a subject-matter the State law is paramount, and "under color" of a State law refuse the exercise of the right to the negro, your error of judgment, however conscientious, shall subject you to fine and imprisonment! I do not apprehend that the conflicting legislation which the bill seems to contemplate is so likely to occur as to render it necessary at this time to adopt a measure of such doubtful constitutionality.

In the next place, this provision of the bill seems to be unnecessary, as adequate judicial remedies could be adopted to secure the desired end, without invading the immunities of legislators, always important to be preserved in the interest of public liberty; without assailing the independence of the judiciary, always essential to the preservation of individual rights; and without impairing the efficiency of ministerial officers, always necessary for the maintenance of public peace and order. The remedy proposed by this section seems to be, in this respect, not only anomalous, but unconstitutional; for the Constitution guarantees nothing with certainty if it does not insure to the several States the right of making and executing laws in regard to all matters arising within their jurisdiction, subject only to the restriction that, in cases of conflict with the Constitution and constitutional laws of the United States, the latter should be held to be the supreme law of the land.

The third section gives the district courts of the United States exclusive "cognizance of all crimes and offences committed against the provisions of this act," and concurrent jurisdiction with the circuit courts of the United States of all civil and criminal cases "affecting persons who are denied, or cannot enforce in the courts or judicial tribunals of the State or locality where they may be, any of the rights secured to them by the first section." The construction which I have given to the second section is strengthened by this third section, for it makes clear what kind of denial or deprivation of the rights secured by the first section was in contemplation. It is a denial or deprivation of such rights "in the courts or judicial tribunals of the State." It stands, therefore, clear of doubt that the offence and the penalties provided in the second section are intended for the State judge, who, in the clear exercise of his functions as a judge, not acting ministerially but judicially, shall decide contrary to this federal law. In other words, when a State judge, acting upon a question involving a conflict between a State law and a federal law, and bound, according to his own judgment and responsibility, to give an impartial decision between the two, comes to the conclusion that the State law is valid and the federal law is invalid, he must not follow the dictates of his own judgment, at the peril of fine and imprisonment. The legislative department of the Government of the United States thus takes from the judicial department of the States the sacred and exclusive duty of judicial decision, and converts the State judge into a mere ministerial officer, bound to decide according to the will of Congress.

It is clear that, in States which deny to persons whose rights are secured by the first section of the bill any one of those rights, all criminal and civil cases affecting them will, by the provisions of the third section, come under the exclusive cognizance of the federal tribunals. It follows that if, in any State which denies to a colored person any one of all those rights, that person should commit a crime against the laws of a State—murder, arson, rape, or any other crime—all protection and punishment through the courts of the State are taken away, and he can only be tried and punished in the federal courts. How is the criminal to be tried? If the offence is provided for and punished by federal law, that law, and not the State law, is to govern. It is only when the offence does not happen to be within the purview of federal law that the federal courts are to try and punish him under any other law. Then resort is to be had to the "common law, as modified and changed" by State legislation, "so far as the same is not inconsistent with the Constitution and laws of the United States." So that over this vast domain of criminal jurisprudence provided by each State for the protection of its own citizens, and for the punishment of all persons who violate its criminal laws, federal law, whenever it can be made to apply, displaces State law. The question here naturally arises, from what source Congress derives the power to transfer to federal tribunals certain classes of cases embraced in this section? The Constitution expressly declares, that the judicial power of the United States "shall extend to all cases in law and equity arising under this Constitution, the laws of the United States, and treaties made, or which shall be made under their authority; to all cases affecting ambassadors, other public ministers and consuls; to all cases of admiralty and maritime jurisdiction; to controversies to which the United States shall be a party; to controversies between two or more States, between a State and citizens of another State, between citizens of different States, between citizens of the same State claiming land under grants of different States, and between a State, or the citizens thereof, and foreign States, citizens, or subjects," Here the judicial power of the United States is expressly set forth and defined; and the act of September 24, 1789, establishing the judicial courts of the United States, in conferring upon the federal courts jurisdiction over cases originating in State tribunals, is careful to confine them to the classes enumerated in the above-recited clause of the Constitution. This section of the bill undoubtedly comprehends cases and authorizes the exercise of powers that are not, by the Constitution, within the jurisdiction of the courts of the United States. To transfer them to those courts would be an exercise of authority well calculated to excite distrust and alarm on the part of all the States; for the bill applies alike to all of them—as well to those that have as to those that have not been engaged in rebellion.

It may be assumed that this authority is incident to the power granted to Congress by the Constitution, as recently amended, to enforce, by appropriate legislation, the article declaring that "neither slavery nor involuntary servitude, except as a punishment for crime whereof the party shall have been duly convicted, shall exist within the United States, or any place subject to their jurisdiction." It cannot, however, be justly claimed that, with a view to the enforcement of this article of the Constitution, there is at present any necessity for the exercise of all the powers which this bill confers. Slavery has been abolished, and at present nowhere exists within the jurisdiction of the United States; nor has there been, nor is it likely there will be, any attempt to revive it by the people or the States. If, however, any such attempt shall be made, it will then become the duty of the General Government to exercise any and all incidental powers necessary and proper to maintain inviolate this great constitutional law of freedom.

The fourth section of the bill provides that officers and agents of the Freedmen's Bureau shall be empowered to make arrests, and also that other officers may be specially commissioned for that purpose by the President of the United States. It also authorizes circuit courts of the United States and the superior courts of the Territories to appoint, without limitation, commissioners, who are to be charged with the performance of *quasi* judicial duties. The fifth section empowers the commissioners so to be selected by the courts to appoint in writing, under their hands, one or more suitable persons from time to time to execute warrants and other processes described by the bill. These numerous official agents are made to constitute a sort of police, in addition to the military, and are authorized to summon a *posse comitatus*, and even to call to their aid such portion of the land and naval forces of the United States, or of the militia, "as may be necessary to the performance of the duty with which they are charged." This extraordinary power is to be conferred upon agents irresponsible to the Government and to the people, to whose number the discretion of the commissioners is the only limit, and in whose hands such authority might be made a terrible engine of wrong, oppression, and fraud. The general statutes regulating the land and naval forces of the United States, the militia, and the execution of the laws, are believed to be adequate for every emergency which can occur in time of peace. If it should prove otherwise, Congress can at any time amend those laws in such a manner as, while subserving the public welfare, not to jeopard the rights, interests, and liberties of the people.

The seventh section provides that a fee of ten dollars shall be paid to each commissioner in every case brought before him, and a fee of five dollars to his deputy, or deputies, "for each person he or they may arrest and take before any such commissioner," "with such other fees as may be deemed reasonable by such commission," "in general for performing such other duties as may be required in the premises." All these fees are to be "paid out of the Treasury of the United States," whether there is a conviction or not; but in case of conviction they are to be recoverable from the defendant. It seems to me that under the influence of such temptations bad men might convert any law, however beneficent, into an instrument of persecution and fraud.

By the eighth section of the bill the United States courts, which sit only in one place for white citizens, must migrate, with the marshal and district attorney, (and necessarily with the clerk, although he is not mentioned,) to any part of the district upon the order of the President, and there hold a court "for the purpose of the more speedy arrest and trial of persons charged with a violation of this act;" and there the judge and officers of the court must remain, upon the order of the President, "for the time therein designated."

The ninth section authorizes the President, or such person as he may empower for that purpose, "to employ such part of the land or naval forces of the United States or of the militia as shall be necessary to prevent the violation and enforce to due execution of this act." This language seems to imply a permanent military force, that is to be always at hand, and whose only business is to be the enforcement of this measure over the vast region where it is intended to operate.

I do not propose to consider the policy of this bill. To me the details of the bill seem fraught with evil. The white race and the black race of the South have hitherto lived together under the relation of master and slave—capital owning labor. Now, suddenly, that relation is changed, and, as to ownership, capital and labor are divorced. They stand now each master of itself. In this new relation, one being necessary to the other, there will be a new adjustment, which both are deeply interested in making harmonious. Each has equal power in settling the terms, and, if left to the laws that regulate capital and labor, it is confidently believed that they will satisfactorily work out the problem. Capital, it is true, has more intelligence, but labor is never so ignorant as not to understand its own interests, not to know its own value, and not to see that capital must pay that value.

This bill frustrates this adjustment. It intervenes between capital and labor, and attempts to settle questions of political economy through the agency of numerous officials, whose interest it will be to foment discord between the two races; for as the breach widens their employment will continue, and when it is closed their occupation will terminate.

In all our history, in all our experience as a people, living under federal and State law, no such system as that contemplated by the details of this bill has ever before been proposed or adopted. They establish for the security of the colored race safeguards which go infinitely beyond any that the General Government has ever provided for the white race. In fact, the distinction of race and color is, by the bill, made to operate in favor of the colored and against the white race. They interfere with the municipal legislation of the States, with the relations existing exclusively between a State and its citizens, or between inhabitants of the same State—an absorption and assumption of power by the General Government which, if acquiesced in, must sap and destroy our federative system of limited powers, and break down the barriers which preserve the rights of the States. It is another step, or rather stride, towards centralization, and the concentration of all legislative powers in the national Government. The tendency of the bill must be to resuscitate the spirit of rebellion, and to arrest the progress of those influences which are more closely drawing around the States the bonds of union and peace.

My lamented predecessor, in his proclamation of the 1st of January, 1863, ordered and declared that all persons held as slaves within certain States and parts of States therein designated were, and thenceforward should be free, and, further, that the executive government of the United States, including the military and naval authorities thereof, would recognize and maintain the freedom of such persons. This guarantee has been rendered especially obligatory and sacred by the amendment of the Constitution abolishing slavery throughout the United States. I, therefore, fully recognize the obligation to protect and defend that class of our people, whenever and wherever it shall become necessary, and to the full extent compatible with the Constitution of the United States.

Entertaining these sentiments, it only remains for me to say, that I will cheerfully co-operate with Congress in any measure that may be necessary for the protection of the civil rights of the freedmen, as well as those of all other classes of persons throughout the United States, by judicial process, under equal and impartial laws, in conformity with the provisions of the Federal Constitution.

I now return the bill to the Senate, and regret that, in considering the bills and joint resolutions—forty-two in number—which have been thus far submitted for my approval, I am compelled to withhold my assent from a second measure that has received the sanction of both Houses of Congress.

ANDREW JOHNSON.

WASHINGTON, D. C., *March* 27, 1866.

Copy of the Bill Vetoed.

AN ACT to protect all persons in the United States in their civil rights, and furnish the means of their vindication.

Be it enacted, &c., That all persons born in the United States and not subject to any foreign power, excluding Indians, not taxed, are hereby declared to be citizens of the United States; and such citizens of every race and color, without regard to any previous condition of slavery or involuntary servitude, except as a punishment for crime whereof the party shall have been duly convicted, shall have the same right in every State and Territory in the United States to make and enforce contracts; to sue, be parties, and give evidence; to inherit, purchase, lease, sell, hold, and convey real and personal property; and to full and equal benefit of all laws and proceedings for the security of person and property as is enjoyed by white citizens, and shall be subject to like punishment, pains, and penalties, and to none other, any law, statute ordinance, regulation, or custom, to the contrary notwithstanding.

SEC. 2. That any person who, under color of any law, statute, ordinance, regulation, or custom, shall subject, or cause to be subjected, any inhabitant of any State or Territory to the deprivation of any right secured or protected by this act, or to different punishment, pains, or penalties on account of such person having at any time been held in a condition of slavery or involuntary servitude, except as a punishment for crime whereof the party shall have been duly convicted, or by reason of his color or race, than is prescribed for the punishment of white persons, shall be deemed guilty of a misdemeanor, and, on conviction, shall be punished by fine not exceeding one thousand dollars, or imprisonment not exceeding one year, or both, in the discretion of the court.

SEC. 3. That the district courts of the United States, within their respective districts, shall have, exclusively of the courts of the several States, cognizance of all crimes and offences committed against the provisions of this act, and also, concurrently with the circuit courts of the United States, of all causes, civil and criminal, affecting persons who are denied or cannot enforce in the courts or judicial tribunals of the State or locality where they may be any of the rights secured to them by the first section of this act; and if any suit or prosecution, civil or criminal, has been or shall be commenced in any State court against any such person, for any cause whatsoever, or against any officer, civil or military, or other person, for any arrest or imprisonment, trespasses, or wrongs done or committed by virtue or under color of authority derived from this act or the act establishing a bureau for the relief of freedmen and refugees, and all acts amendatory thereof, or for refusing to do any act upon the ground that it would be inconsistent with this act, such defendant shall have the right to remove such cause for trial to the proper district or circuit court in the manner prescribed by the "Act relating to *habeas corpus* and regulating judicial proceedings in certain cases," approved March three, eighteen hundred and sixty-three, and all acts amendatory thereof. The jurisdiction in civil and criminal matters hereby conferred on the district and circuit courts of the United States shall be exercised and enforced in conformity with the laws of the United States, so far as such laws are suitable to carry the same into effect; but in all cases where such laws are not adapted to the object, or are deficient in the provisions necessary to furnish suitable remedies and punish offences against law, the common law, as modified and changed by the constitution and statutes of the State wherein the court having jurisdiction of the cause, civil or criminal, is held, so far as the same is not inconsistent with the Constitution and laws of United States, shall be extended to and govern said courts in the trial and disposition of such cause, and, if of a criminal nature, in the infliction of punishment on the party found guilty.

SEC. 4. That the district attorneys, marshals, and deputy marshals of the United States, the commissioners appointed by the circuit court and territorial courts of the United States, with powers of arresting, imprisoning, or bailing offenders against the laws of the United States, the officers and agents of the Freedmen's Bureau, and every other officer who may be specially empowered by the President of the United States, shall be, and they are hereby, specially authorized and required, at the expense of the United States, to institute proceedings against all and every person who shall violate the provisions of this act, and cause him or them to be arrested and imprisoned, or bailed, as the case may be, for trial before such court of the United States or territorial court as by this act has cognizance of the offence. And with a view to affording reasonable protection to all persons in their constitutional rights of equality before the law, without distinction of race or color, or previous condition of slavery or involuntary servitude, except as a punishment for crime, whereof the party shall have been duly convicted, and to the prompt discharge of the duties of this act, it shall be the duty of the circuit courts of the United States and the superior courts of the Territories of the United States, from time to time, to increase the number of commissioners, so as to afford a speedy and convenient means for the arrest and examination of persons charged with a violation of this act. And such commissioners are hereby authorized and required to exercise and discharge all the powers and duties conferred on them by this act, and the same duties with regard to offences created by this act, as they are authorized by law to exercise with regard to other offences against the laws of the United States.

SEC. 5. That it shall be the duty of all marshals and deputy marshals to obey and execute all warrants and precepts issued under the provisions of this act, when to them directed; and should any marshal or deputy marshal refuse to receive such warrant or other process when tendered, or to use all proper means diligently to execute the same, he shall, on conviction thereof, be fined in the sum of one thousand dollars, to the use of the person upon whom the accused is alleged to have committed the offence. And the better to enable the said commissioners to execute their duties faithfully and efficiently, in conformity with the Constitution of the United States and the requirements of this act, they are hereby authorized and empowered, within their counties respectively, to appoint, in writing, under their hands, any one or more suitable persons, from time to time, to execute all such warrants and other process that may be issued by them in the lawful performance of their respective duties; and the persons so appointed to execute any warrant or process as aforesaid shall have authority to summon and call to their aid the bystanders or the *posse comitatus* of the proper county, or such portion of the land and naval forces of the United States, or of the militia, as may be necessary to the performance of the duty with which they are charged, and to insure a faithful observance of the clause of the Constitution which prohibits slavery, in conformity with the provisions of this act; and said warrants shall run and be executed by said officers anywhere in the State or Territory within which they are issued.

SEC. 6. That any person who shall knowingly

and wilfully obstruct, hinder or prevent any officer, or other person charged with the execution of any warrant or process issued under the provisions of this act, or any person or persons lawfully assisting him or them, from arresting any person for whose apprehension such warrant or process may have been issued, or shall rescue or attempt to rescue such person from the custody of the officer, other person or persons, or those lawfully assisting as aforesaid, when so arrested pursuant to the authority herein given and declared, or shall aid, abet, or assist any person so arrested as aforesaid, directly or indirectly, to escape from the custody of the officer or other person legally authorized as aforesaid, or shall harbor or conceal any person for whose arrest a warrant or process shall have been issued as aforesaid, so as to prevent his discovery and arrest after notice or knowledge of the fact that a warrant has been issued for the apprehension of such person, shall, for either of said offences, be subject to a fine not exceeding one thousand dollars, and imprisonment not exceeding six months, by indictment and conviction before the district court of the United States for the district in which said offence may have been committed, or before the proper court of criminal jurisdiction, if committed within any one of the organized Territories of the United States.

SEC. 7. That the district attorneys, the marshals, their deputies, and the clerks of the said district and territorial courts shall be paid for their services the like fees as may be allowed to them for similar services in other cases; and in all cases where the proceedings are before a commissioner, he shall be entitled to a fee of ten dollars in full for his services in each case, inclusive of all services incident to such arrest and examination. The person or persons authorized to execute the process to be issued by such commissioners for the arrest of offenders against the provisions of this act shall be entitled to a fee of five dollars for each person he or they may arrest and take before any such commissioner as aforesaid, with such other fees as may be deemed reasonable by such commissioner for such other additional services as may be necessarily performed by him or them, such as attending at the examination, keeping the prisoner in custody, and providing him with food and lodging during his detention, and until the final determination of such commissioner, and in general for performing such other duties as may be required in the premises; such fees to be made up in conformity with the fees usually charged by the officers of the courts of justice within the proper district or county, as near as may be practicable, and paid out of the treasury of the United States on the certificate of the judge of the district within which the arrest is made, and to be recoverable from the defendant as part of the judgment in case of conviction.

SEC. 8. That whenever the President of the United States shall have reason to believe that offences have been, or are likely to be committed against the provisions of this act within any judicial district, it shall be lawful for him, in his discretion, to direct the judge, marshal, and district attorney of such district to attend at such place within the district, and for such time as he may designate, for the purpose of the more speedy arrest and trial of persons charged with a violation of this act; and it shall be the duty of every judge or other officer, when any such requisition shall be received by him, to attend at the place and for the time therein designated.

SEC. 9. That it shall be lawful for the President of the United States, or such person as he may empower for that purpose, to employ such part of the land or naval forces of the United States, or of the militia, as shall be necessary to prevent the violation and enforce the due execution of this act.

SEC. 10. That upon all questions of law arising in any cause under the provisions of this act, a final appeal may be taken to the Supreme Court of the United States.

The votes on this bill were:

1866, February 2—The SENATE passed the bill—yeas 33, nays 12, as follow:

YEAS—Messrs. Anthony, Brown, Chandler, Clark, Conness, Cragin, Dixon, Fessenden, Foot, Foster, Harris, Henderson, Howard, Howe, Kirkwood, Lane of Indiana, Lane of Kansas, Morgan, Morrill, Nye, Poland, Pomeroy, Ramsey, Sherman, Sprague, Stewart, Sumner, Trumbull, Wade, Willey, Williams, Wilson, Yates—33.

NAYS—Messrs. *Buckalew*, Cowan, *Davis*, *Guthrie*, *Hendricks*, *McDougall*, *Nesmith*, Norton, *Riddle*, *Saulsbury*, *Stockton*, Van Winkle—12.

March 9—The bill being before the HOUSE,

Mr. ELDRIDGE moved that it lie on the table; which was disagreed to—yeas 32, nays 118, as follow:

YEAS—Messrs. *Ancona*, *Boyer*, *Brooks*, *Chanler*, *Coffroth*, *Dawson*, *Denison*, *Eldridge*, *Glossbrenner*, *Goodyear*, *Grider*, *Aaron Harding*, *Harris*, *Hogan*, *Edwin N. Hubbell*, *Kerr*, *Le Blond*, *Marshall*, *Niblack*, *Nicholson*, *Radford*, *Ritter*, *Rogers*, *Ross*, Rousseau, *Shanklin*, *Sitgreaves*, *Taber*, *Taylor*, *Thornton*, *Trimble*, *Winfield*.—32.

NAYS—Messrs. Alley, Allison, Ames, Anderson, D. R. Ashley, James M. Ashley, Baker, Baldwin, Banks, Baxter, Beaman, Bidwell, Bingham, Blaine, Blow, Boutwell, Bromwell, Broomall, Buckland, Bundy, Sidney Clarke, Cobb, Conkling, Cook, Cullom, Darling, Davis, Defrees, Delano, Deming, Dixon, Donnelly, Driggs, Dumont, Eliot, Farnsworth, Farquhar, Ferry, Grinnell, Abner C. Harding, Hart, Hayes, Henderson, Higby, Hill, Holmes, Hooper, Asahel W. Hubbard, Chester D. Hubbard, Demas Hubbard, jr., John H. Hubbard, Hulburd, James Humphrey, Ingersoll, Jenckes, Julian, Kelley, Kelso, Ketcham, Kuykendall, Latham, George V. Lawrence, William Lawrence, Loan, Longyear, Lynch, Marston, Marvin, McClurg, McKee, McRuer, Mercur, Miller, Moorhead, Morrill, Morris, Moulton, Myers, O'Neill, Orth, Paine, Perham, Phelps, Pike, Plants, Price, Raymond, Alexander H. Rice, John H. Rice, Sawyer, Schenck, Scofield, Shellabarger, Sloan, Spalding, Starr, Stevens, Thayer, Francis Thomas, John L. Thomas, jr., Trowbridge, Upson, Van Aernam, Burt Van Horn, Robert T. Van Horn, Ward, Warner, Ellihu B. Washburne, Henry D. Washburn, William B. Washburn, Welker, Wentworth, Whaley, Williams, James F. Wilson, Stephen F. Wilson, Windom, Woodbridge.—118.

March 13—The bill passed—yeas 111, nays 38, as follow:

YEAS—Messrs. Alley, Allison, Ames, Anderson, James M. Ashley, Baker, Baldwin, Banks, Baxter, Beaman, Bidwell, Blaine, Blow, Boutwell, Bromwell, Broomall, Buckland, Bundy, Sidney Clarke, Cobb, Conkling, Cook, Cullom, Darling, Davis, Dawes, Delano, Deming, Dixon, Donnelly, Driggs, Dumont, Eliot, Farnsworth, Farquhar, Ferry, Garfield, Grinnell, Abner C. Harding, Hart, Hayes, Higby, Hill, Holmes, Hooper, Asahel W. Hubbard, Chester D. Hubbard, Demas Hubbard, John H. Hubbard, Hulburd, James Humphrey, Ingersoll, Jenckes, Julian, Kelley, Kelso, Ketcham, Kuykendall, Laflin, George V. Lawrence, William Lawrence, Loan, Longyear, Lynch, Marston, Marvin, McClurg, McRuer, Mercur, Miller, Moorhead, Morrill, Morris, Moulton, Myers, Nowell, O'Neill, Orth, Paine, Perham, Pike, Plants, Price, Alexander H. Rice, Sawyer, Schenck, Scofield, Shellabarger, Sloan, Spalding, Starr, Stevens, Thayer, Francis Thomas, John L. Thomas, Trowbridge, Upson, Van Aernam, Burt Van Horn, Ward, Warner, Ellihu B. Washburne, William B. Washburn, Welker, Wentworth, Whaley, Williams, James F. Wilson, Stephen F. Wilson, Windom, Woodbridge—111.

NAYS—Messrs. *Ancona*, *Bergen*, Bingham, *Boyer*, *Conness*,

Coffroth, Dawson, Denison, Glossbrenner, Goodyear, Grider, Aaron Harding, Harris, Hogan, Edwin N. Hubbell, Jones, Kerr, Latham, *Le Blond, Marshall, McCullough, Nicholson*, Phelps, *Radford, Samuel J. Randall*, William H. Randall, *Ritter, Rogers, Ross*, Rousseau, *Shanklin, Sitgreaves*, Smith, *Taber, Taylor, Thornton, Trimble, Winfield*—38.

March 15—The Senate concurred in the House amendments.

March 27—The bill was vetoed.

April 6—The SENATE passed the bill, notwithstanding the objections of the President, by a vote of 33 yeas to 15 nays, as follow:

YEAS—Messrs. Anthony, Brown, Chandler, Clark, Conness, Cragin, Creswell, Edmunds, Fessenden, Foster, Grimes, Harris, Henderson, Howard, Howe, Kirkwood, Lane of Indiana, Morgan, Morrill, Nye, Poland, Pomeroy, Ramsey, Sherman, Sprague, Stewart, Sumner, Trumbull, Wade, Willey, Williams, Wilson, Yates—33.

NAYS—Messrs. *Buckalew*, Cowan, *Davis*, Doolittle, *Guthrie, Hendricks, Johnson*, Lane of Kansas, *McDougall, Nesmith*, Norton, *Riddle, Saulsbury*, Van Winkle, *Wright*—15.

April 9—The HOUSE OF REPRESENTATIVES again passed it—yeas 122, nays 41, as follow:

YEAS—Messrs. Alley, Allison, Delos R. Ashley, James M. Ashley, Baker, Baldwin, Banks, Barker, Baxter, Beaman, Benjamin, Bidwell, Boutwell, Brandegee, Bromwell, Broomall, Buckland, Bundy, Reader W. Clarke, Sidney Clarke, Cobb, Colfax, Conkling, Cook, Cullom, Darling, Davis, Dawes, Defrees, Delano, Deming, Dixon, Dodge, Donnelly, Eckley, Eggleston, Eliot, Farnsworth, Farquhar, Ferry, Garfield, Grinnell, Griswold, Hale, Abner C. Harding, Hart, Hayes, Henderson, Higby, Hill, Holmes, Hooper, Hotchkiss, Asahel W. Hubbard, Chester D. Hubbard, John H. Hubbard, James R. Hubbell, Hulburd, James Humphrey, Ingersoll, Jenckes, Kasson, Kelley, Kelso, Ketcham, Laflin, George V. Lawrence, William Lawrence, Loan, Longyear, Lynch, Marston, Marvin, McClurg, McIndoe, McKee, McRuer, Mercur, Miller, Moorhead, Morrill, Morris, Moulton, Myers, Newell, O'Neill, Orth, Paine, Patterson, Perham, Pike, Plants, Pomeroy, Price, Alexander H. Rice, John H. Rice, Rollins, Sawyer, Schenck, Scofield, Shellabarger, Spalding, Starr, Stevens, Thayer, Francis Thomas, John L. Thomas, jr., Trowbridge, Upson, Van Aernam, Burt Van Horn, Robert T. Van Horn, Ward, Ellihu B. Washburne, Henry D. Washburn, William B. Washburn, Welker, Wentworth, James F. Wilson, Stephen F. Wilson, Windom, Woodbridge.—122.

NAYS—Messrs. *Ancona, Bergen, Boyer, Coffroth, Dawson, Denison, Eldridge, Finck, Glossbrenner, Aaron Harding, Harris, Hogan, Edwin N. Hubbell, James M. Humphrey*, Latham, *Le Blond, Marshall, McCullough, Niblack, Nicholson, Noell*, Phelps, *Radford, Samuel J. Randall*, William H. Randall, Raymond, *Ritter, Rogers, Ross*, Rousseau, *Shanklin, Sitgreaves*, Smith, *Strouse, Taber, Taylor, Thornton, Trimble*, Whaley, *Winfield, Wright*.—41.

Whereupon the Speaker of the House declared the bill a law.

Veto of the Colorado Bill, May 15, 1866.

To the Senate of the United States:

I return to the Senate, in which house it originated, the bill which has passed both Houses of Congress, entitled "An act for the admission of the State of Colorado into the Union," with my objections to its becoming a law at this time.

First. From the best information which I have been able to obtain, I do not consider the establishment of a State government at present necessary for the welfare of the people of Colorado. Under the existing Territorial government all the rights, privileges, and interests of the citizens are protected and secured. The qualified voters choose their own legislators and their own local officers, and are represented in Congress by a delegate of their own selection. They make and execute their own municipal laws, subject only to revision by Congress—an authority not likely to be exercised, unless in extreme or extraordinary cases. The population is small, some estimating it so low as twenty-five thousand, while advocates of the bill reckon the number at from thirty-five thousand to forty thousand souls. The people are principally recent settlers, many of whom are understood to be ready for removal to other mining districts beyond the limits of the Territory, if circumstances shall render them more inviting. Such a population cannot but find relief from excessive taxation if the territorial system, which devolves the expenses of the executive, legislative, and judicial departments upon the United States, is for the present continued. They cannot but find the security of person and property increased by their reliance upon the national executive power for the maintenance of law and order against the disturbances necessarily incident to all newly organized communities.

Second. It is not satisfactorily established that a majority of the citizens of Colorado desire, or are prepared for an exchange of a territorial for a State government. In September, 1864, under the authority of Congress, an election was lawfully appointed and held, for the purpose of ascertaining the views of the people upon this particular question. 6,192 votes were cast, and of this number a majority of 3,152 was given against the proposed change. In September, 1865, without any legal authority, the question was again presented to the people of the Territory, with a view of obtaining a reconsideration of the result of the election held in compliance with the act of Congress approved March 21, 1864. At this second election 5,905 votes were polled, and a majority of 155 was given in favor of a State organization. It does not seem to me entirely safe to receive this, the last mentioned result, so irregularly obtained, as sufficient to outweigh the one which had been legally obtained in the first election. Regularity and conformity to law are essential to the preservation of order and stable government, and should, as far as practicable, always be observed in the formation of new States.

Third. The admission of Colorado, at this time, as a State into the federal Union, appears to me to be incompatible with the public interests of the country. While it is desirable that territories, when sufficiently matured, should be organized as States, yet the spirit of the Constitution seems to require that there should be an approximation towards equality among the several States comprising the Union. No State can have less or more than two Senators in Congress. The largest State has a population of four millions; several of the States have a population exceeding two millions; and many others have a population exceeding one million. A population of 127,000 is the ratio of apportionment of representatives among the several States.

If this bill should become a law, the people of Colorado, thirty thousand in number, would have in the House of Representatives one member, while New York, with a population of four millions, has but thirty-one; Colorado would have in the electoral college three votes, while New York has only thirty-three; Colorado would have in the Senate two votes, while New York has no more.

Inequalities of this character have already occurred, but it is believed that none have happened where the inequality was so great. When such inequality has been allowed, Congress is supposed to have permitted it on the ground of some high public necessity, and under circumstances which promised that it would rapidly disappear through the growth and development of the newly admitted State. Thus, in regard to the several States in what was formerly called the "northwest territory," lying east of the Mississippi, their rapid advancement in population rendered it certain that States admitted with only one or two representatives in Congress, would, in a very short period, be entitled to a great increase of representation. So, when California was admitted on the ground of commercial and political exigencies, it was well foreseen that that State was destined rapidly to become a great, prosperous, and important mining and commercial community. In the case of Colorado, I am not aware that any national exigency, either of a political or commercial nature, requires a departure from the law of equality, which has been so generally adhered to in our history.

If information submitted in connection with this bill is reliable, Colorado, instead of increasing, has declined in population. At an election for members of a territorial legislature held in 1861, 10,580 votes were cast. At the election before mentioned, in 1864, the number of votes cast was 6,192; while at the irregular election held in 1865, which is assumed as a basis for legislative action at this time, the aggregate of votes was 5,905. Sincerely anxious for the welfare and prosperity of every Territory and State, as well as for the prosperity and welfare of the whole Union, I regret this apparent decline of population in Colorado; but it is manifest that it is due to emigration which is going on from that Territory into other regions within the United States, which either are in fact, or are believed by the inhabitants of Colorado to be, richer in mineral wealth and agricultural resources. If, however, Colorado has not really declined in population, another census, or another election under the authority of Congress, would place the question beyond doubt, and cause but little delay in the ultimate admission of the Territory as a State, if desired by the people.

The tenor of these objections furnishes the reply which may be expected to an argument in favor of the measure derived from the enabling act which was passed by Congress on the 21st day of March, 1864. Although Congress then supposed that the condition of the Territory was such as to warrant its admission as a State, the result of two years' experience shows that every reason which existed for the institution of a territorial instead of a State government in Colorado, at its first organization, still continues in force.

The condition of the Union at the present moment is calculated to inspire caution in regard to the admission of new States. Eleven of the old States have been for some time, and still remain, unrepresented in Congress. It is a common interest of all the States, as well those represented as those unrepresented, that the integrity and harmony of the Union should be restored as completely as possible, so that all those who are expected to bear the burdens of the Federal Government shall be consulted concerning the admission of new States; and that in the mean time no new State shall be prematurely and unnecessarily admitted to a participation in the political power which the Federal Government wields, not for the benefit of any individual State or section, but for the common safety, welfare, and happiness of the whole country.

ANDREW JOHNSON.

WASHINGTON, D. C., *May* 15, 1866.

Copy of the Bill.

AN ACT for the admission of the State of Colorado into the Union.

Whereas, on the twenty-first day of March, anno Domini eighteen hundred and sixty-four, Congress passed an act to enable the people of Colorado to form a constitution and State government, and offered to admit said State, when so formed, into the Union upon compliance with certain conditions therein specified; and whereas it appears by a message of the President of the United States, dated January twelve, eighteen hundred and sixty-six, that the said people have adopted a constitution, which upon due examination is found to conform to the provisions and comply with the conditions of said act, and to be republican in its form of government, and that they now ask for admission into the Union:

Be it enacted, &c., That the constitution and State government which the people of Colorado have formed for themselves be, and the same is hereby, ratified, accepted, and confirmed, and that the said State of Colorado shall be, and is hereby, declared to be one of the United States of America, and is hereby admitted into the Union upon an equal footing with the original States, in all respects whatsoever.

SEC. 2. *And be it further enacted,* That the said State of Colorado shall be, and is hereby, declared to be entitled to all the rights, privileges, grants, and immunities, and to be subject to all the conditions and restrictions, of an act entitled "An act to enable the people of Colorado to form a constitution and a State government, and for the admission of such State into the Union on an equal footing with the original States," approved March twenty-first, eighteen hundred and sixty-four.

The votes on this bill were:

IN SENATE.

March 13—The bill was rejected—yeas 14, nays 21, as follow:

YEAS—Messrs. Chandler, Cragin, Kirkwood, Lane of Indiana, Lane of Kansas, *McDougall*, Nesmith, Norton, Pomeroy, Ramsey, Sherman, Stewart, Trumbull, Williams—14.

NAYS—Messrs. *Buckalew*, Conness, Creswell, *Davis*, Doolittle, Fessenden, Foster, Grimes, *Guthrie*, Harris, *Hendricks*, Morgan, Morrill, Poland, *Riddle*, Sprague, *Stockton*, Sumner, Van Winkle, Wade, Wilson—21.

Mr. Wilson entered a motion to reconsider the vote.

April 25—The Senate voted to reconsider; yeas 19, nays 13. (Same as below.)

The bill was then passed—yeas 19, nays 13, as follow:

YEAS—Messrs. Chandler, Clark, Conness, Cragin, Creswell, Howard, Howe, Kirkwood, Lane of Indiana, Nye, Pomeroy, Ramsey, Sherman, Sprague, Stewart, Trumbull, Van Winkle, Willey, Wilson—19.

NAYS—Messrs. *Buckalew*, *Davis*, Doolittle, Edmunds, Foster, Grimes, *Guthrie*, *Hendricks*, *McDougall*, Morgan, Poland, *Riddle*, Sumner—13.

IN HOUSE.

May 3—The bill was passed—yeas 81, nays 57, as follow:

YEAS—Messrs. Ames, Anderson, Delos R. Ashley, James M. Ashley, Baker, Banks, Barker, Beaman, Benjamin, Bidwell, Bingham, Blow, Brandegee, Bromwell, Buckland, Bundy, Reader W. Clarke, Sidney Clarke, Cobb, Conkling, Cullom, Defrees, Deming, Dixon, Dodge, Donnelly, Driggs, Dumont, Eckley, Farquhar, Ferry, Garfield, Grinnell, Abner C. Harding, Hart, Henderson, Holmes, Hotchkiss, Asahel W. Hubbard, Chester D. Hubbard, James R. Hubbell, Ingersoll, Jenckes, Kasson, Kelso, Ketcham, Laflin, Latham, George V. Lawrence, William Lawrence, Loan, Longyear, Marston, McClurg, McKee, Mercur, Miller, Moorhead, Moulton, Myers, O'Neill, Orth, Patterson, Plants, Alexander H. Rice, Rollins, Sawyer, Schenck, Shellabarger, Smith, Spalding, Francis Thomas, Trowbridge, Upson, Van Aernam, Burt Van Horn, Robert T. Van Horn, Warner, Welker, Whaley, Williams—81.

NAYS—Messrs. Allison, Alley, *Ancona*, Baxter, *Bergen*, Blaine, Boutwell, *Boyer*, Broomall, *Chanler*, *Coffroth*, Darling, *Dawson*, *Denison*, *Eldridge*, Eliot, *Finck*, *Glossbrenner*, *Grider*, Griswold, *Aaron Harding*, *Harris*, Higby, James Humphrey, Julian, Kelley, Kuykendall, *Le Blond*, Lynch, *Marshall*, *McCullough*, McRuer, Morrill, Morris, Newell, *Niblack*, Paine, Perham, Pike, Raymond, John H. Rice, *Ritter*, *Ross*, Rousseau, *Shanklin*, Stevens, Stilwell, *Strouse*, *Taylor*, *Thornton*, Ellihu B. Washburne, Henry D. Washburn, James F. Wilson, Windom, *Winfield*, Woodbridge, *Wright*—57.

Up to the time this page is put to press, no vote has been taken on the re-passage of the vetoed bill. When taken, it will be inserted in a subsequent page.

Message Respecting the Proposed Constitutional Amendment on Representation, &c., June 22, 1866.

To the Senate and House of Representatives:

I submit to Congress a report of the Secretary of State, to whom was referred the concurrent resolution of the 18th instant,* respecting a submission to the legislatures of the States of an additional article to the Constitution of the United States.

It will be seen from this report that the Secretary of State had, on the 16th instant, transmitted to the Governors of the several States certified copies of the joint resolution passed on the 13th instant, proposing an amendment to the Constitution.

Even in ordinary times any question of amending the Constitution must be justly regarded as of paramount importance. This importance is at the present time enhanced by the fact that the joint resolution was not submitted by the two Houses for the approval of the President, and that of the thirty-six States which constitute the Union eleven are excluded from representation in either House of Congress, although, with the single exception of Texas, they have been entirely restored to all their functions as States, in conformity with the organic law of the land, and have appeared at the national capital by Senators and Representatives, who have applied for and have been refused admission to the vacant seats.

Nor have the sovereign people of the nation been afforded an opportunity of expressing their views upon the important questions which the amendment involves. Grave doubts therefore may naturally and justly arise as to whether the action of Congress is in harmony with the sentiments of the people, and whether State legislatures, elected without reference to such an issue, should be called upon by Congress to decide respecting the ratification of the proposed amendment.

Waiving the question as to the constitutional validity of the proceedings of Congress upon the joint resolution proposing the amendment, or as to the merits of the article which it submits through the executive department to the legislatures of the States, I deem it proper to observe that the steps taken by the Secretary of State, as detailed in the accompanying report, are to be considered as purely ministerial, and in no sense whatever committing the Executive to an approval or a recommendation of the amendment to the State legislatures or to the people. On the contrary, a proper appreciation of the letter and spirit of the Constitution, as well as of the interests of national order, harmony, and union, and a due deference for an enlightened public judgment, may at this time well suggest a doubt whether any amendment to the Constitution ought to be proposed by Congress and pressed upon the legislatures of the several States for final decision until after the admission of such loyal Senators and Representatives of the now unrepresented States as have been, or may hereafter be, chosen in conformity with the Constitution and laws of the United States.

ANDREW JOHNSON.

WASHINGTON, D. C., *June* 22, 1866.

To the President:

The Secretary of State, to whom was referred the concurrent resolution of the two Houses of Congress of the 18th instant, in the following words: "That the President of the United States be requested to transmit forthwith to the executives of the several States of the United States copies of the article of amendment proposed by Congress to the State legislatures to amend the Constitution of the United States, passed June 13, 1866, respecting citizenship, the basis of representation, disqualification for office, and validity of the public debt of the United States, &c., to the end that the said States may proceed to act upon the said article of amendment, and that he request the executive of each State that may ratify said amendment to transmit to the Secretary of State a certified copy of such ratification," has the honor to submit the following report, namely: That on the 16th instant the Hon. Amasa Cobb, of the Committee of the House of Representatives on Enrolled Bills, brought to this Department and deposited therein an enrolled resolution of the two Houses of Congress, which was thereupon received by the Secretary of State and deposited among the rolls of the Department, a copy of which is hereunto an-

* This resolution passed the House under a suspension of the rules, which was agreed to, yeas 92, nays 25, (the latter all Democrats,) by a vote of yeas 87, nays 20, on a count by tellers. It passed the Senate same day without a division; and is a copy of a concurrent resolution passed in 1864, requesting President Lincoln to submit the anti-slavery amendment, changed only as to the phraseology descriptive of the amendment.

nexed. Thereupon the Secretary of State, upon the 16th instant, in conformity with the proceeding which was adopted by him in 1865, in regard to the then proposed and afterwards adopted congressional amendment of the Constitution of the United States concerning the prohibition of slavery, transmitted certified copies of the annexed resolution to the Governors of the several States, together with a certificate and circular letter. A copy of both of these communications are hereunto annexed.

Respectfully submitted,

WILLIAM H. SEWARD.

DEPARTMENT OF STATE, *June* 20, 1866.

[*Circular.*]

DEPARTMENT OF STATE, *June* 16, 1866.

To his Excellency ,

Governor of the State of

SIR: I have the honor to transmit an attested copy of a resolution of Congress, proposing to the legislatures of the several States a fourteenth article to the Constitution of the United States. The decisions of the several legislatures upon the subject are required by law to be communicated to this Department. An acknowledgment of the receipt of this communication is requested by

Your excellency's most obedient servant,

WILLIAM H. SEWARD.

VII.

MAJORITY AND MINORITY REPORTS

OF THE

JOINT COMMITTEE ON RECONSTRUCTION.

The Majority Report.

June 18, 1866—Mr. FESSENDEN in the Senate, and Mr. STEVENS in the House, submitted this

REPORT:

The Joint Committee of the two Houses of Congress, appointed under the concurrent resolution of December 13, 1865, *with direction to "inquire into the condition of the States which formed the so-called Confederate States of America, and report whether they or any of them are entitled to be represented in either House of Congress, with leave to report by bill or otherwise," ask leave to report:*

That they have attended to the duty assigned them as assiduously as other duties would permit, and now submit to Congress, as the result of their deliberations, a resolution proposing amendments to the Constitution, and two bills, of which they recommend the adoption.

Before proceeding to set forth in detail their reasons for the conclusion to which, after great deliberation, your committee have arrived, they beg leave to advert, briefly, to the course of proceedings they found it necessary to adopt, and to explain the reasons therefor.

The resolution under which your committee was appointed directed them to inquire into the condition of the Confederate States, and report whether they were entitled to representation in Congress. It is obvious that such an investigation, covering so large an extent of territory and involving so many important considerations, must necessarily require no trifling labor, and consume a very considerable amount of time. It must embrace the condition in which those States were left at the close of the war; the measures which have been taken towards the reorganization of civil government, and the disposition of the people towards the United States; in a word, their fitness to take an active part in the administration of national affairs.

As to their condition at the close of the rebellion, the evidence is open to all, and admits of no dispute. They were in a state of utter exhaustion. Having protracted their struggle against federal authority until all hope of successful resistance had ceased, and laid down their arms only because there was no longer any power to use them, the people of those States were left bankrupt in their public finances, and shorn of the private wealth which had before given them power and influence. They were also necessarily in a state of complete anarchy, without governments and without the power to frame governments except by the permission of those who had been successful in the war. The President of the United States, in the proclamations under which he appointed provisional governors, and in his various communications to them, has, in exact terms, recognized the fact that the people of those States were, when the rebellion was crushed, "deprived of all civil government," and must proceed to organize anew. In his conversation with Mr. Stearns, of Massachusetts, certified by himself, President Johnson said "the State institutions are prostrated, laid out on the ground, and they must be taken up and adapted to the progress of events." Finding the Southern States in this condition, and Congress having failed to provide for the contingency, his duty was obvious. As President of the United States he had no power, except to execute the laws of the land as Chief Magistrate. These laws gave him no authority over the subject of reorganization; but by the Constitution he was commander-in-chief of the army and navy of the United States. These Confederate States embraced a portion of the people of the Union who had been in a state of revolt, but had been reduced to obedience by force of arms. They were in an abnormal condition, without civil government, without commercial connections, without national or international relations, and subject only to martial law. By withdrawing their representatives in Congress, by renouncing the privilege of representation, by organizing a separate government, and by levying war against the United States, they destroyed their State constitutions in respect to the vital principle which connected their respective States with the Union and secured their federal relations; and nothing of those constitutions was left of which the United States were bound to take notice. For four years they had a *de facto* government, but it was usurped and illegal. They chose the tribunal of arms wherein to decide whether or not it should be legalized, and they were defeated. At the close of the rebellion, therefore, the people of the rebellious States were found, as the President expresses it, "deprived of all civil government."

Under this state of affairs it was plainly the duty of the President to enforce existing national laws, and to establish, as far as he could, such a system of government as might be provided for by existing national statutes. As commander-in-chief of a victorious army, it was his duty, under the law of nations and the army regulations, to restore order, to preserve property, and to protect the people against violence from any quarter until provision should be made by law for their government. He might, as President, assemble Congress and submit the whole matter to the law-making power; or he might continue military supervision and control until Congress should assemble on its regular appointed day. Selecting the latter alternative, he proceeded, by virtue of his power as commander-in-chief, to appoint provisional governors over the revolted States. These were regularly commissioned, and their compensation was paid, as the Secretary of War states, "from the appropriation for army contingencies, because the duties performed by the parties were regarded as of a temporary character; ancillary to the withdrawal of military force, the disbandment of armies, and the reduction of military expenditure; by provisional organizations for the protection of civil rights, the preservation of peace, and to take the place of armed force in the respective States." It cannot, we think, be contended that these governors possessed, or could exercise, any but military authority. They had no power to organize civil governments, nor to exercise any authority except that which inhered in their own persons under their commissions. Neither had the President, as commander-in-chief, any other than military power. But he was in exclusive possession of the military authority. It was for him to decide how far he would exercise it, how far he would relax it, when and on what terms he would withdraw it. He might properly permit the people to assemble, and to initiate local governments, and to execute such local laws as they might choose to frame not inconsistent with, nor in opposition to, the laws of the United States. And, if satisfied that they might safely be left to themselves, he might withdraw the military forces altogether, and leave the people of any or all of these States to govern themselves without his interference. In the language of the Secretary of State, in his telegram to the provisional governor of Georgia, dated October 28, 1865, he might "recognize the people of any State as having resumed the relations of loyalty to the Union," and act in his military capacity on this hypothesis. All this was within his own discretion, as military commander. But it was not for him to decide upon the nature or effect of any system of government which the people of these States might see fit to adopt. This power is lodged by the Constitution in the Congress of the United States, that branch of the government in which is vested the authority to fix the political relations of the States to the Union, whose duty is to guarantee to each State a republican form of government, and to protect each and all of them against foreign or domestic violence, and against each other. We cannot, therefore, regard the various acts of the President in relation to the formation of local governments in the insurrectionary States, and the conditions imposed by him upon their action, in any other light than as intimations to the people that, as commander-in-chief of the army, he would consent to withdraw military rule just in proportion as they should, by their acts, manifest a disposition to preserve order among themselves, establish governments denoting loyalty to the Union, and exhibit a settled determination to return to their allegiance, leaving with the law-making power to fix the terms of their final restoration to all their rights and privileges as States of the Union. That this was the view of his power taken by the President is evident from expressions to that effect in the communications of the Secretary of State to the various provisional governors, and the repeated declarations of the President himself. Any other supposition inconsistent with this would impute to the President designs of encroachment upon a co-ordinate branch of the government, which should not be lightly attributed to the Chief Magistrate of the nation.

When Congress assembled in December last the people of most of the States lately in rebellion had, under the advice of the President, organized local governments, and some of them had acceded to the terms proposed by him. In his annual message he stated, in general terms, what had been done, but he did not see fit to communicate the details for the information of Congress. While in this and in a subsequent message the President urged the speedy restoration of these States, and expressed the opinion that their condition was such as to justify their restoration, yet it is quite obvious that Congress must either have acted blindly on that opinion of the President, or proceeded to obtain the information requisite for intelligent action on the subject. The impropriety of proceeding wholly on the judgment of any one man, however exalted his station, in a matter involving the welfare of the republic in all future time, or of adopting any plan, coming from any source, without fully understanding all its bearings and comprehending its full effect, was apparent. The first step, therefore, was to obtain the required information. A call was accordingly made on the President for the information in his possession as to what had been done, in order that Congress might judge for itself as to the grounds of the belief expressed by him in the fitness of States recently in rebellion to participate fully in the conduct of national affairs. This information was not immediately communicated. When the response was finally made, some six weeks after your committee had been in actual session, it was found that the evidence upon which the President seemed to have based his suggestions was incomplete and unsatisfactory. Authenticated copies of the new constitutions and ordinances adopted by the conventions in three of the States had been submitted, extracts from newspapers furnished scanty information as to the action of one other State, and nothing appears to have been communicated as to the remainder. There was no evidence of the loyalty of those who had participated in these conventions, and in one State alone was any proposition made to submit the action of the conventions to the final judgment of the people.

Failing to obtain the desired information, and left to grope for light wherever it might be found, your committee did not deem it either advisable or safe to adopt, without further examination, the suggestions of the President, more especially as he had not deemed it expedient to remove the military force, to suspend martial law, or to restore the writ of *habeas corpus*, but still thought it necessary to exercise over the people of the rebellious States his military power and jurisdiction. This conclusion derived still greater force from the fact, undisputed, that in all these States, except Tennessee and perhaps Arkansas, the elections which were held for State officers and members of Congress had resulted, almost universally, in the defeat of candidates who had been true to the Union, and in the election of notorious and unpardoned rebels, men who could not take the prescribed oath of office, and who made no secret of their hostility to the Government and the people of the United States. Under these circumstances, anything like hasty action would have been as dangerous as it was obviously unwise. It appeared to your committee that but one course remained, viz: to investigate carefully and thoroughly the state of feeling and opinion existing among the people of these States; to ascertain how far their pretended loyalty could be relied upon, and thence to infer whether it would be safe to admit them at once to a full participation in the Government they had fought for four years to destroy. It was an equally important inquiry whether their restoration to their former relations with the United States should only be granted upon certain conditions and guarantees which would effectually secure the nation against a recurrence of evils so disastrous as those from which it had escaped at so enormous a sacrifice.

To obtain the necessary information recourse could only be had to the examination of witnesses whose position had given them the best means of forming an accurate judgment, who could state facts from their own observation, and whose character and standing afforded the best evidence of their truthfulness and impartiality. A work like this, covering so large an extent of territory, and embracing such complicated and extensive inquiries, necessarily required much time and labor. To shorten the time as much as possible, the work was divided and placed in the hands of four sub-committees, who have been diligently employed in its accomplishment. The results of their labors have been heretofore submitted, and the country will judge how far they sustain the President's views, and how far they justify the conclusions to which your committee have finally arrived.

A claim for the immediate admission of Senators and Representatives from the so-called Confederate States has been urged, which seems to your committee not to be founded either in reason or in law, and which cannot be passed without comment. Stated in a few words, it amounts to this: That inasmuch as the lately insurgent States had no legal right to separate themselves from the Union, they still retain their positions as States, and consequently the people thereof have a right to immediate representation in Congress without the imposition of any conditions whatever; and further, that until such admission Congress has no right to tax them for the support of the Government. It has even been contended that until such admission all legislation affecting their interests is, if not unconstitutional, at least unjustifiable and oppressive.

It is believed by your committee that all these propositions are not only wholly untenable, but, if admitted, would tend to the destruction of the Government.

It must not be forgotten that the people of these States, without justification or excuse, rose in insurrection against the United States. They deliberately abolished their State goverernments so far as the same connected them politically with the Union as members thereof under the Constitution. They deliberately renounced their allegiance to the Federal Government, and proceeded to establish an independent government for themselves. In the prosecution of this enterprise they seized the national forts, arsenals, dockyards, and other public property within their borders, drove out from among them those who remained true to the Union, and heaped every imaginable insult and injury upon the United States and its citizens. Finally they opened hostilities, and levied war against the Government.

They continued this war for four years with the most determined and malignant spirit, killing in battle and otherwise large numbers of loyal people, destroying the property of loyal citizens on the sea and on the land, and entailing on the Government an enormous debt, incurred to sustain its rightful authority. Whether legally and constitutionally or not, they did, in fact, withdraw from the Union and made themselves subjects of another government of their own creation. And they only yielded when, after a long, bloody, and wasting war, they were compelled by utter exhaustion to lay down their arms; and this they did not willingly, but declaring that they yielded because they could no longer resist, affording no evidence whatever of repentance for their crime, and expressing no regret, except that they had no longer the power to continue the desperate struggle.

It cannot, we think, be denied by any one, having a tolerable acquaintance with public law, that the war thus waged was a civil war of the greatest magnitude. The people waging it were necessarily subject to all the rules which, by the law of nations, control a contest of that character, and to all the legitimate consequences following it. One of those consequences was that, within the limits prescribed by humanity, the conquered rebels were at the mercy of the conquerors. That a government thus outraged had a most perfect right to exact indemnity for the injuries done and security against the recurrence of such outrages in the future would seem too clear for dispute. What the nature of that security should be, what proof should be required of a return to allegiance, what time should elapse before a people thus demoralized should be restored in full to the enjoyment of political rights and privileges, are questions for the law-making power to decide, and that decision must depend on grave considerations of the public safety and the general welfare.

It is moreover contended, and with apparent gravity, that, from the peculiar nature and character of our Government, no such right on the part of the conqueror can exist; that from the moment when rebellion lays down its arms and actual hostilities cease, all political rights of rebellious communities are at once restored; that, because the people of a State of the Union were once an organized community within the Union, they necessarily so remain, and their right to be represented in Congress at any and all times, and to participate in the government of the country under all circumstances, admits of neither question nor dispute. If this is indeed true, then is the Government of the United States powerless for its own protection, and flagrant rebellion, carried to the extreme of civil war, is a pastime which any State may play at, not only certain that it can lose nothing in any event, but may even be the gainer by defeat. If rebellion succeeds, it accomplishes its purpose and destroys the Government. If it fails, the war has been barren of results, and the battle may be still fought out in the legislative halls of the country. Treason, defeated in the field, has only to take possession of Congress and the cabinet.

Your committee does not deem it either necessary or proper to discuss the question whether the late Confederate States are still States of this Union, or can even be otherwise. Granting this profitless abstraction, about which so many words have been wasted, it by no means follows that the people of those States may not place themselves in a condition to abrogate the powers and privileges incident to a State of the Union, and deprive themselves of all pretence of right to exercise those powers and enjoy those privileges. A State within the Union has obligations to discharge as a member of the Union. It must submit to federal laws and uphold federal authority. It must have a government republican in form, under and by which it is connected with the General Government, and through which it can discharge its obligations. It is more than idle, it is a mockery, to contend that a people who have thrown off their allegiance, destroyed the local government which bound their States to the Union as members thereof, defied its authority, refused to execute its laws, and abrogated every provision which gave them political rights within the Union, still retain, through all, the perfect and entire right to resume, at their own will and pleasure, all their privileges within the Union, and especially to participate in its government, and to control the conduct of its affairs. To admit such a principle for one moment would be to declare that treason is always master and loyalty a blunder. Such a principle is void by its very nature and essence, because inconsistent with the theory of government, and fatal to its very existence.

On the contrary, we assert that no portion of the people of this country, whether in State or Territory, have the right, while remaining on its soil, to withdraw from or reject the authority of the United States. They must obey its laws as paramount, and acknowledge its jurisdiction. They have no right to secede; and while they can destroy their State governments, and place themselves beyond the pale of the Union, so far as the exercise of State privileges is concerned, they cannot escape the obligations imposed upon them by the Constitution and the laws, nor impair the exercise of national authority. The Constitution, it will be observed, does not act upon States, as such, but upon the people; while, therefore, the people cannot escape its authority, the States may, through the act of their people, cease to exist in an organized form, and thus dissolve their political relations with the United States.

That taxation should be only with the consent of the taxed, through their own representatives, is a cardinal principle of all free governments; but it is not true that taxation and representation must go together under all circumstances, and at every moment of time. The people of the District of Columbia and of the Territories are taxed, although not represented in Congress. If it is true that the people of the so-called Confederate States had no right to throw off the authority of the United States, it is equally true that they are bound at all times to share the burdens of government. They cannot, either legally or equitably, refuse to bear their just proportion of these burdens by voluntarily abdicating their rights and privileges as States of the Union, and refusing to be represented in the councils of the nation, much less by rebellion against national authority and levying war. To hold that by so doing they could escape taxation would be to offer a premium for insurrection, to reward instead of punishing for treason. To hold that as soon as government is restored to its full authority it can be allowed no time to secure itself against similar wrongs in the future, or else omit the ordinary exercise of its constitutional power to compel equal contribution from all towards the expenses of government, would be unreasonable in itself and unjust to the nation. It is sufficient to reply that the loss of representation by the people of the insurrectionary States was their own voluntary choice. They might abandon their privileges, but they could not escape their obligations; and surely they have no right to complain if, before resuming those privileges, and while the people of the United States are devising measures for the public safety, rendered necessary by the act of those who thus disfranchised themselves, they are compelled to contribute their just proportion of the general burden of taxation incurred by their wickedness and folly.

Equally absurd is the pretense that the legislative authority of the nation must be inoperative so far as they are concerned, while they, by their own act, have lost the right to take part in it. Such a proposition carries its own refutation on its face.

While thus exposing fallacies which, as your committee believe, are resorted to for the purpose of misleading the people and distracting their attention from the questions at issue, we freely admit that such a condition of things should be brought, if possible, to a speedy termination. It is most desirable that the Union of all the States should become perfect at the earliest moment consistent with the peace and welfare of the nation; that all these States should become fully represented in the national councils, and take their share in the legislation of the country. The possession and exercise of more than its just share of power by any section is injurious, as well to that section as to all others. Its tendency is distracting and demoralizing, and such a state of affairs is only to be tolerated on the ground of a necessary regard to the public safety. As soon as that safety is secured it should terminate.

Your committee came to the consideration of the subject referred to them with the most anxious desire to ascertain what was the condition of the people of the States recently in insurrection, and what, if anything, was necessary to be done before restoring them to the full enjoyment of all their original privileges. It was undeniable that the war into which they had plunged the country had materially changed their relations to the people of the loyal States. Slavery had been abolished by constitutional amendment. A large proportion of the population had become, instead of mere chattels, free men and citizens. Through all the past struggle these had remained true and loyal, and had, in large numbers, fought on the side of the Union. It was impossible to abandon them without securing them their rights as free men and citizens. The whole civilized world would have cried out against such base ingratitude, and the bare idea is offensive to all right-thinking men. Hence it became important to inquire what could be done to secure their rights, civil and political. It was evident to your committee that adequate security could only be found in appropriate constitutional provisions. By an original provision of the Constitution, representation is based on the whole number of free persons in each State, and three-fifths of all other persons. When all become free, representation for all necessarily follows. As a consequence the inevitable effect of the rebellion would be to increase the political power of the insurrectionary States, whenever they should be allowed to resume their positions as States of the Union. As representation is by the Constitution based upon population, your committee did not think it advisable to recommend a change of that basis. The increase of representation necessarily resulting from the abolition of slavery was considered the most important element in the questions arising out of the changed condition of affairs, and the necessity for some fundamental action in this regard seemed imperative. It appeared to your committee that the rights of these persons by whom the basis of representation had been thus increased should be recognized by the General Government. While slaves, they were not considered as having any rights, civil or political. It did not seem just or proper that all the political advantages derived from their becoming free should be confined to their former masters, who had fought against the Union, and withheld from themselves, who had always been loyal. Slavery, by building up a ruling and dominant class, had produced a spirit of oligarchy adverse to republican institutions, which finally inaugurated civil war. The tendency of continuing the domination of such a class, by leaving it in the exclusive possession of political power, would be to encourage the same spirit, and lead to a similar result. Doubts were entertained whether Congress had power, even under the amended Constitution, to prescribe the qualifications of voters in a State, or could act directly on the subject. It was doubtful, in the opinion of your committee, whether the States would consent to surrender a power they had always exercised, and to which they were attached. As the best, if not the only, method of surmounting the difficulty, and as eminently just and proper in itself, your committee came to the conclusion that political power should be possessed in all the States exactly in proportion as the right of suffrage should be granted, without distinction of color or race. This it was thought would leave the whole question with the people of each State, holding out to all the advantage of increased political power as an inducement to allow all to participate in its exercise. Such a provision would be in its nature gentle and persuasive, and would lead, it was hoped, at no distant day, to an equal participation of all, without distinction, in all the rights and privileges of citizenship, thus affording a full and adequate protection to all classes of citizens, since all would have, through the ballot-box, the power of self-protection.

Holding these views, your committee prepared an amendment to the Constitution to carry out this idea, and submitted the same to Congress. Unfortunately, as we think, it did not receive the necessary constitutional support in the Senate, and therefore could not be proposed for adoption by the States. The principle involved in that amendment is, however, believed to be sound, and your committee have again proposed it in another form, hoping that it may receive the approbation of Congress.

Your committee have been unable to find, in the evidence submitted to Congress by the President, under date of March 6, 1866, in compliance with the resolutions of January 5 and February 27, 1866, any satisfactory proof that either of the insurrectionary States, except, perhaps, the State of Tennessee, has placed itself in a condition to resume its political relations to the Union. The first step towards that end would necessarily be the establishment of a republican form of government by the people. It has been before remarked that the provisional governors, appointed by the President in the exercise of his military authority, could do nothing by virtue of the power thus conferred towards the establishment of a State government. They were acting under the War Department and paid out of its funds. They were simply bridging over the chasm between rebellion and restoration. And yet we find them calling conventions and convening legislatures. Not only this, but we find the conventions and legislatures thus convened acting under executive direction as to the provisions required to be adopted in their constitutions and ordinances as conditions precedent to their recognition by the President. The inducement held out by the President for compliance with the conditions imposed was, directly in one instance, and presumably, therefore, in others, the immediate admission of Senators and Representatives to Congress. The character of the conventions and legislatures thus assembled was not such as to inspire confidence in the good faith of their members. Governor Perry, of South Carolina, dissolved the convention assembled in that State before the suggestion had reached Columbia from Washington that the rebel war debt should be repudiated, and gave as his reason that it was a "revolutionary body." There is no evidence of the loyalty or disloyalty of the members of those conventions and legislatures except the fact of pardons being asked for on their account. Some of these States now claiming representation refused to adopt the conditions imposed. No reliable information is found in these papers as to the constitutional provisions of several of these States, while in not one of them is there the slightest evidence to show that these "amended constitutions," as they are called, have ever been submitted to the people for their adoption. In North Carolina alone an ordinance was passed to that effect, but it does not appear to have been acted on. Not one of them, therefore, has been ratified. Whether, with President Johnson, we adopt the theory that the old constitutions were abrogated and destroyed, and the people "deprived of all civil government," or whether we adopt the alternative doctrine that they were only suspended and were revived by the suppression of the rebellion, the new provisions must be considered as equally destitute of validity before adoption by the people. If the conventions were called for the sole purpose of putting the State government into operation, they had no power either to adopt a new constitution or to amend an old one without the consent of the people. Nor could either a convention or a legislature change the fundamental law without power previously conferred. In the view of your committee, it follows, therefore, that the people of a State where the constitution has been thus amended might feel themselves justified in repudiating altogether all such unauthorized assumptions of power, and might be expected to do so at pleasure.

So far as the disposition of the people of the insurrectionary States, and the probability of their adopting measures conforming to the changed condition of affairs, can be inferred from the papers submitted by the President as the basis of his action, the prospects are far from encouraging. It appears quite clear that the anti-slavery amendments, both to the State and Federal Constitutions, were adopted with reluctance by the bodies which did adopt them, while in some States they have been either passed by in silence or rejected. The language of all the provisions and ordinances of these States on the subject amounts to nothing more than an unwilling admission of an unwelcome truth. As to the ordinance of secession, it is, in some cases, declared "null and void," and in others simply "repealed;" and in no instance is a refutation of this deadly heresy considered worthy of a place in the new constitution.

If, as the President assumes, these insurrectionary States were, at the close of the war, wholly without State governments, it would seem that, before being admitted to participation in the direction of public affairs, such governments should be regularly organized. Long usage has established, and numerous statutes have pointed out, the mode in which this should be done. A convention to frame a form of government should be assembled under competent authority. Ordinarily, this authority emanates from Congress; but, under the peculiar circumstances, your committee is not disposed to criticise the President's action in assuming the power exercised by him in this regard. The convention, when assembled, should frame a constitution of government, which should be submitted to the people for adoption. If adopted, a legislature should be convened to pass the laws necessary to carry it into effect. When a State thus organized claims representation in Congress, the election of representatives should be provided for by law, in accordance with the laws of Congress regulating representation, and the proof that the action taken has been in conformity to law should be submitted to Congress.

In no case have these essential preliminary steps been taken. The conventions assembled seem to have assumed that the constitutions which had been repudiated and overthrown were still in existence, and operative to constitute the States members of the Union, and to have contented themselves with such amendments as they were informed were requisite in order to insure their return to an immediate participation in the Government of the United States. Not waiting to ascertain whether the people they represented would adopt even the proposed amendments, they at once ordered elections of representatives to Congress, in nearly all instances before an executive had been chosen to issue writs of election under the State laws, and such elections as were held were ordered by the conventions. In one instance, at least, the writs of election were signed by the provisional governor. Glaring irregularities and unwarranted assumptions of power are manifest in several cases, particularly in South Carolina, where the convention, although disbanded by the provisional governor on the ground that it was a revolutionary body, assumed to redistrict the State.

It is quite evident from all these facts, and indeed from the whole mass of testimony submitted by the President to the Senate, that in no instance was regard paid to any other consideration than obtaining immediate admission to Congress, under the barren form of an election in which no precautions were taken to secure regularity of proceedings or the assent of the people. No constitution has been legally adopted except, perhaps, in the State of Tennessee, and such elections as have been held were without authority of law. Your committee are accordingly forced to the conclusion that the States referred to have not placed themselves in a condition to claim representation in Congress, unless all the rules which have, since the foundation of the Government, been deemed essential in such cases should be disregarded.

It would undoubtedly be competent for Congress to waive all formalities and to admit these Confederate States to representation at once, trusting that time and experience would set all things right. Whether it would be advisable to do so, however, must depend upon other considerations of which it remains to treat. But it may well be observed, that the inducements to such a step should be of the very highest character. It seems to your committee not unreasonable to require satisfactory evidence that the ordinances and constitutional provisions which the President deemed essential in the first instance will be permanently adhered to by the people of the States seeking restoration, after being admitted to full participation in the government, and will not be repudiated when that object shall have been accomplished. And here the burden of proof rests upon the late insurgents who are seeking restoration to the rights and privileges which they willingly abandoned, and not upon the people of the United States who have never undertaken, directly or indirectly, to deprive them thereof. It should appear affirmatively that they are prepared and disposed in good faith to accept the results of the war, to abandon their hostility to the Government, and to live in peace and amity with the people of the loyal States, extending to all classes of citizens equal rights and privileges, and conforming to the republican idea of liberty and equality. They should exhibit in their acts something more than an unwilling submission to an unavoidable necessity—a feeling, if not cheerful, certainly not offensive and defiant. And they should evince an entire repudiation of all hostility to the General Government, by an acceptance of such just and reasonable conditions as that Government should think the public safety demands. Has this been done? Let us look at the facts shown by the evidence taken by the committee.

Hardly is the war closed before the people of these insurrectionary States come forward and haughtily claim, as a right, the privilege of participating at once in that Government which they had for four years been fighting to overthrow. Allowed and encouraged by the Executive to organize State governments, they at once placed in power leading rebels, unrepentant and unpardoned, excluding with contempt those who had manifested an attachment to the Union, and preferring, in many instances, those who had rendered themselves the most obnoxious. In the face of the law requiring an oath which would necessarily exclude all such men from federal offices, they elect, with very few exceptions, as Senators and Representatives in Congress men who had actively participated in the rebellion, insultingly denouncing the law as unconstitutional. It is only necessary to instance the election to the Senate of the late vice president of the Confederacy, a man who, against his own declared convictions, had lent all the weight of his acknowledged ability and of his influence as a most prominent public man to the cause of the rebellion, and who, unpardoned rebel as he is, with that oath staring him in the face, had the assurance to lay his credentials on the table of the Senate. Other rebels of scarcely less note or notoriety were selected from other quarters. Professing no repentance, glorying apparently in the crime they had committed, avowing still, as the uncontradicted testimony of Mr. Stephens and many others proves, an adherence to the pernicious doctrine of secession, and declaring that they yielded only to necessity, they insist, with unanimous voice, upon their rights as States, and proclaim that they will submit to no conditions whatever as preliminary to their resumption of power under that Constitution which they still claim the right to repudiate.

Examining the evidence taken by your committee still further, in connection with facts too notorious to be disputed, it appears that the southern press, with few exceptions, and those mostly of newspapers recently established by northern men, abound with weekly and daily abuse of the institutions and people of the loyal States; defends the men who led, and the principles which incited, the rebellion; denounces and reviles southern men who adhered to the Union; and strives, constantly and unscrupulously, by every means in its power, to keep alive the fire of hate and discord between the sections; calling upon the President to violate his oath of office, overturn the Government by force of arms, and drive the representatives of the people from their seats in Congress. The national banner is openly insulted, and the national airs scoffed at, not only by an ignorant populace, but at public meetings, and once, among other notable instances, at a dinner given in honor of a notorious rebel who had violated his oath and abandoned his flag. The same individual is elected to an important office in the leading city of his State, although an unpardoned rebel, and so offensive that the President refuses to allow him to enter upon his official duties. In another State the leading general of the rebel armies is openly nominated for governor by the speaker of the house of delegates, and the nomination is hailed by the people with shouts of satisfaction, and openly indorsed by the press.

Looking still further at the evidence taken

by your committee, it is found to be clearly shown, by witnesses of the highest character, and having the best means of observation, that the Freedmen's Bureau, instituted for the relief and protection of freedmen and refugees, is almost universally opposed by the mass of the population, and exists in an efficient condition only under military protection, while the Union men of the South are earnest in its defence, declaring with one voice that without its protection the colored people would not be permitted to labor at fair prices, and could hardly live in safety. They also testify that without the protection of United States troops Union men, whether of northern or southern origin, would be obliged to abandon their homes. The feeling in many portions of the country towards the emancipated slaves, especially among the uneducated and ignorant, is one of vindictive and malicious hatred. This deep-seated prejudice against color is assiduously cultivated by the public journals, and leads to acts of cruelty, oppression, and murder, which the local authorities are at no pains to prevent or punish. There is no general disposition to place the colored race, constituting at least two fifths of the population, upon terms even of civil equality. While many instances may be found where large planters and men of the better class accept the situation, and honestly strive to bring about a better order of things, by employing the freedmen at fair wages and treating them kindly, the general feeling and disposition among all classes are yet totally averse to the toleration of any class of people friendly to the Union, be they white or black; and this aversion is not unfrequently manifested in an insulting and offensive manner.

The witnesses examined as to the willingness of the people of the South to contribute, under existing laws, to the payment of the national debt, prove that the taxes levied by the United States will be paid only on compulsion and with great reluctance, while there prevails, to a considerable extent, an expectation that compensation will be made for slaves emancipated and property destroyed during the war. The testimony on this point comes from officers of the Union army, officers of the late rebel army, Union men of the Southern States, and avowed secessionists, almost all of whom state that, in their opinion, the people of the rebellious States would, if they should see a prospect of success, repudiate the national debt.

While there is scarcely any hope or desire among leading men to renew the attempt at secession at any future time, there is still, according to a large number of witnesses, including A. H. Stephens, who may be regarded as good authority on that point, a generally prevailing opinion which defends the legal right of secession, and upholds the doctrine that the first allegiance of the people is due to the States, and not to the United States. This belief evidently prevails among leading and prominent men as well as among the masses everywhere, except in some of the northern counties of Alabama and the eastern counties of Tennessee.

The evidence of an intense hostility to the Federal Union, and an equally intense love of the late Confederacy, nurtured by the war, is decisive. While it appears that nearly all are willing to submit, at least for the time being, to the federal authority, it is equally clear that the ruling motive is a desire to obtain the advantages which will be derived from a representation in Congress. Officers of the Union army on duty, and northern men who go South to engage in business, are generally detested and proscribed. Southern men who adhered to the Union are bitterly hated and relentlessly persecuted. In some localities prosecutions have been instituted in State courts against Union officers for acts done in the line of official duty, and similar prosecutions are threatened elsewhere as soon as the United States troops are removed. All such demonstrations show a state of feeling against which it is unmistakably necessary to guard.

The testimony is conclusive that after the collapse of the Confederacy the feeling of the people of the rebellious States was that of abject submission. Having appealed to the tribunal of arms, they had no hope except that by the magnanimity of their conquerors their lives, and possibly their property, might be preserved. Unfortunately, the general issue of pardons to persons who had been prominent in the rebellion, and the feeling of kindness and conciliation manifested by the Executive, and very generally indicated through the northern press, had the effect to render whole communities forgetful of the crime they had committed, defiant towards the Federal Government, and regardless of their duties as citizens. The conciliatory measures of the Government do not seem to have been met even half way. The bitterness and defiance exhibited toward the United States under such circumstances is without a parallel in the history of the world. In return for our leniency we receive only an insulting denial of our authority. In return for our kind desire for the resumption of fraternal relations we receive only an insolent assumption of rights and privileges long since forfeited. The crime we have punished is paraded as a virtue, and the principles of republican government which we have vindicated at so terrible cost are denounced as unjust and oppressive.

If we add to this evidence the fact that, although peace has been declared by the President, he has not, to this day, deemed it safe to restore the writ of *habeas corpus*, to relieve the insurrectionary States of martial law, nor to withdraw the troops from many localities, and that the commanding general deems an increase of the army indispensable to the preservation of order and the protection of loyal and well-disposed people in the South, the proof of a condition of feeling hostile to the Union and dangerous to the Government throughout the insurrectionary States would seem to be overwhelming.

With such evidence before them, it is the opinion of your committee—

I. That the States lately in rebellion were, at the close of the war, disorganized communities, without civil government, and without constitutions or other forms, by virtue of which political relations could legally exist between them and the Federal Government.

II. That Congress cannot be expected to recognize as valid the election of representatives from disorganized communities, which, from the very nature of the case, were unable to present their claim to representation under those established and recognized rules, the observance of which has been hitherto required.

III. That Congress would not be justified in admitting such communities to a participation in the government of the country without first providing such constitutional or other guarantees as will tend to secure the civil rights of all citizens of the Republic; a just equality of representation; protection against claims founded in rebellion and crime; a temporary restoration of the right of suffrage to those who have not actively participated in the efforts to destroy the Union and overthrow the Government; and the exclusion from positions of public trust of at least a portion of those whose crimes have proved them to be enemies to the Union, and unworthy of public confidence.

Your committee will, perhaps, hardly be deemed excusable for extending this report further; but inasmuch as immediate and unconditional representation of the States lately in rebellion is demanded as a matter of right, and delay, and even hesitation, is denounced as grossly oppressive and unjust, as well as unwise and impolitic, it may not be amiss again to call attention to a few undisputed and notorious facts, and the principles of public law applicable thereto, in order that the propriety of that claim may be fully considered and well understood.

The State of Tennessee occupies a position distinct from all the other insurrectionary States, and has been the subject of a separate report, which your committee have not thought it expedient to disturb. Whether Congress shall see fit to make that State the subject of separate action, or to include it in the same category with all others, so far as concerns the imposition of preliminary conditions, it is not within the province of this committee either to determine or advise.

To ascertain whether any of the so-called Confederate States "are entitled to be represented in either House of Congress," the essential inquiry is, whether there is, in any one of them, a constituency qualified to be represented in Congress. The question how far persons claiming seats in either House possess the credentials necessary to enable them to represent a duly qualified constituency is one for the consideration of each House separately, after the preliminary question shall have been finally determined.

We now propose to re-state, as briefly as possible, the general facts and principles applicable to all the States recently in rebellion.

First. The seats of the senators and representatives from the so-called Confederate States became vacant in the year 1861, during the second session of the Thirty-sixth Congress, by the voluntary withdrawal of their incumbents, with the sanction and by direction of the legislatures or conventions of their respective States. This was done as a hostile act against the Constitution and Government of the United States, with a declared intent to overthrow the same by forming a southern confederation. This act of declared hostility was speedily followed by an organization of the same States into a confederacy, which levied and waged war, by sea and land, against the United States. This war continued more than four years, within which period the rebel armies besieged the national capital, invaded the loyal States, burned their towns and cities, robbed their citizens, destroyed more than 250,000 loyal soldiers, and imposed an increased national burden of not less than $3,500,000,000, of which seven or eight hundred millions have already been met and paid. From the time these confederated States thus withdrew their representation in Congress and levied war against the United States, the great mass of their people became and were insurgents, rebels, traitors, and all of them assumed and occupied the political, legal, and practical relation of enemies of the United States. This position is established by acts of Congress and judicial decisions, and is recognized repeatedly by the President in public proclamations, documents, and speeches.

Second. The States thus confederated prosecuted their war against the United States to final arbitrament, and did not cease until all their armies were captured, their military power destroyed, their civil officers, State and confederate, taken prisoners or put to flight, every vestige of State and confederate government obliterated, their territory overrun and occupied by the federal armies, and their people reduced to the condition of enemies conquered in war, entitled only by public law to such rights, privileges, and conditions as might be vouchsafed by the conqueror. This position is also established by judicial decisions, and is recognized by the President in public proclamations, documents, and speeches.

Third. Having voluntarily deprived themselves of representation in Congress, for the criminal purpose of destroying the Federal Union, and having reduced themselves, by the act of levying war, to the condition of public enemies, they have no right to complain of temporary exclusion from Congress; but on the contrary, having voluntarily renounced the right to representation, and disqualified themselves by crime from participating in the Government, the burden now rests upon them, before claiming to be reinstated in their former condition, to show that they are qualified to resume federal relations. In order to do this, they must prove that they have established, with the consent of the people, republican forms of government in harmony with the Constitution and laws of the United States, that all hostile purposes have ceased, and should give adequate guarantees against future treason and rebellion—guarantees which shall prove satisfactory to the Government against which they rebelled, and by whose arms they were subdued.

Fourth. Having, by this treasonable withdrawal from Congress, and by flagrant rebellion and war, forfeited all civil and political rights and privileges under the Constitution, they can only be restored thereto by the permission and authority of that constitutional power against which they rebelled and by which they were subdued.

Fifth. These rebellious enemies were conquered by the people of the United States, acting through all the co-ordinate branches of the Government, and not by the executive department alone. The powers of conqueror are not so vested in the President that he can fix and regulate the terms of settlement and confer congressional representation on conquered rebels and traitors. Nor can he, in any way, qualify enemies of the Government to exercise its law-making power. The authority to restore rebels to political power in the Federal Government can be exercised only with the concurrence of all the departments in which political power is vested; and hence the several proclamations of the President to the people of the Confederate States cannot be considered as extending beyond the purposes declared, and can only be regarded as provisional permission by the commander-in-chief of the army to do certain acts, the effect and validity whereof is to be determined by the constitutional government, and not solely by the executive power.

Sixth. The question before Congress is, then, whether conquered enemies have the right, and shall be permitted at their own pleasure and on their own terms, to participate in making laws for their conquerors; whether conquered rebels may change their theatre of operations from the battle-field, where they were defeated and overthrown, to the halls of Congress, and, through their representatives, seize upon the Government which they fought to destroy; whether the national treasury, the army of the nation, its navy, its forts and arsenals, its whole civil administration, its credit, its pensioners, the widows an orphans of those who perished in the war, the public honor, peace and safety, shall all be turned over to the keeping of its recent enemies without delay, and without imposing such conditions as, in the opinion of Congress, the security of the country and its institutions may demand.

Seventh. The history of mankind exhibits no example of such madness and folly. The instinct of self-preservation protests against it. The surrender by Grant to Lee, and by Sherman to Johnston, would have been disasters of less magnitude, for new armies could have been raised, new battles fought, and the Government saved. The anti-coercive policy, which, under pretext of avoiding bloodshed, allowed the rebellion to take form and gather force, would be surpassed in infamy by the matchless wickedness that would now surrender the halls of Congress to those so recently in rebellion, until proper precautions shall have been taken to secure the national faith and the national safety.

Eighth. As has been shown in this report, and in the evidence submitted, no proof has been afforded by Congress of a constituency in any one of the so-called Confederate States, unless we except the State of Tennessee, qualified to elect Senators and Representatives in Congress. No State constitution, or amendment to a State constitution, has had the sanction of the people. All the so-called legislation of State conventions and legislatures has been had under military dictation. If the President may, at his will, and under his own authority, whether as military commander or chief executive, qualify persons to appoint Senators and elect Representatives, and empower others to appoint and elect them, he thereby practically controls the organization of the legislative department. The constitutional form of government is thereby practically destroyed, and its powers absorbed in the Executive. And while your committee do not for a moment impute to the President any such design, but cheerfully concede to him the most patriotic motives, they cannot but look with alarm upon a precedent so fraught with danger to the Republic.

Ninth. The necessity of providing adequate safeguards for the future, before restoring the insurrectionary States to a participation in the direction of public affairs, is apparent from the bitter hostility to the Government and people of the United States yet existing throughout the conquered territory, as proved incontestably by the testimony of many witnesses and by undisputed facts.

Tenth. The conclusion of your committee therefore is, that the so-called Confederate States are not at present entitled to representation in the Congress of the United States; that, before allowing such representation, adequate security for future peace and safety should be required; that this can only be found in such changes of the organic law as shall determine the civil rights and privileges of all citizens in all parts of the Republic, shall place representation on an equitable basis, shall fix a stigma upon treason, and protect the loyal people against future claims for the expenses incurred in support of rebellion and for manumitted slaves, together with an express grant of power in Congress to enforce those provisions. To this end they offer a joint resolution for amending the Constitution of the United States, and the two several bills designed to carry the same into effect, before referred to.

Before closing this report, your committee beg leave to state that the specific recommendations submitted by them are the result of mutual concession, after a long and careful comparison of conflicting opinions. Upon a question of such magnitude, infinitely important as it is to the future of the Republic, it was not to be expected that all should think alike. Sensible of the imperfections of the scheme, your committee submit it to Congress as the best they could agree upon, in the hope that its imperfections may be cured, and its deficiencies supplied, by legislative wisdom; and that, when finally adopted, it may tend to restore peace and harmony to the whole country, and to place our republican institutions on a more stable foundation.

W. P. Fessenden,
James W. Grimes,
Ira Harris,
J. M. Howard,
George H. Williams,
Thaddeus Stevens,
Ellihu B. Washburne,
Justin S. Morrill,
Jno. A. Bingham,
Roscoe Conkling,
George S. Boutwell.

Minority Report.

June 22—Mr. Johnson in the Senate, and Mr. Rogers in the House, submitted this

REPORT:

The undersigned, a minority of the joint committee of the Senate and House of Representatives, constituted under the concurrent resolution of the 13th of December, 1865, making it their duty to "inquire into the condition of the States which formed the so-called Confederate States of America, and to report whether they or any of them are entitled to be represented in either House of Congress, with leave to report by bill or otherwise," not being able to concur in the measures recommended by the majority, or in the grounds upon which they base them, beg leave to report:

In order to obtain a correct apprehension of the subject, and as having a direct bearing upon it, the undersigned think it all important clearly to ascertain what was the effect of the late insurrection upon the relations of the States where it prevailed to the General Government, and of the people collectively and individually of such States. To this inquiry they therefore first address themselves.

First, as to the States. Did the insurrection at its commencement, or at any subsequent time, legally dissolve the connection between those States and the General Government? In our judgment, so far from this being a "profitless abstraction," it is a vital inquiry. For if that connection was not disturbed, such States during the entire rebellion were as completely component States of the United States as they were before the rebellion, and were bound by all the obligations which the Constitution imposes, and entitled to all its privileges. Was not this their condition?

The opposite view alone can justify the denial of such rights and privileges. That a State of the Union can exist without possessing them is inconsistent with the very nature of the Government and terms of the Constitution. In its nature the Government is formed of and by States possessing equal rights and powers. States unequal are not known to the Constitution. In its original formation perfect equality was secured. They were granted the same representation in the Senate, and the same right to be represented in the House of Representatives; the difference in the latter being regulated only by a difference in population. But every State, however small its population, was secured one Representative in that branch. Each State was given the right, and the same right, to participate in the election of President and Vice President, and all alike were secured the benefit of the judicial department. The Constitution, too, was submitted to the people of each State separately, and adopted by them in that capacity. The convention which framed it considered, as they were bound to do, each as a separate sovereignty, that could not be subjected to the Constitution except by its own consent. That consent was consequently asked and given. The equality, therefore, of rights was the condition of the original thirteen States before the Government was formed, and such equality was not only not interfered with, but guaranteed to them as well in regard to the powers conferred upon the General Government, as to those reserved to the States or to the people of the States.

The same equality is secured to the States which have been admitted into the Union since the Constitution was adopted. In each instance the State admitted has been "declared to be one of the United States, on an *equal footing with the original States in all respects whatever*."

The Constitution, too, so far as most of the powers it contains are concerned, operates directly upon the people in their individual and aggregate capacity, and on all alike. Each citizen, therefore, of every State owes the same allegiance to the General Government, and is entitled to the same protection. The obligation of this allegiance it is not within the legal power of his State or of himself to annul or evade. It is made paramount and perpetual, and for that very reason it is equally the paramount duty of the General Government to allow to the citizens of each State, and to the State, the rights secured to both, and the protection necessary to their full enjoyment. A citizen may, no doubt, forfeit such rights by committing a crime against the United States upon conviction of the same, where such forfeiture by law antecedently passed is made a part of the punishment. But a State cannot in its corporate capacity be made liable to such a forfeiture, for a State, as such, under the Constitution, cannot commit or be indicted for a crime. No legal proceeding, criminal or civil, can be instituted to deprive a State of the benefits of the Constitution, by forfeiting as against her any of the rights it secures. Her citizens, be they few or many, may be proceeded against under the law and convicted, but the State remains a State of the Union. To concede that, by the illegal conduct of her own citizens, she can be withdrawn from the Union, is virtually to concede the right of secession. For what difference does it make as regards the result whether a State can rightfully secede, (a doctrine, by-the-by, heretofore maintained by statesmen North as well as South,) or whether by the illegal conduct of her citizens she ceases to be a State of the Union? In either case the end is the same. The only difference is that by the one theory she ceases by law to be such a State, and by the other by crime, without and against law. But the doctrine is wholly erroneous. A State once in the Union must abide in it forever. She can never withdraw from or be expelled from it. A different principle would subject the Union to dissolution at any moment. It is, therefore, alike perilous and unsound.

Nor do we see that it has any support in the measures recommended by the majority of the committee. The insurrectionary States are by these measures conceded to be States of the Union. The proposed constitutional amendment is to be submitted to them as well as to the other States. In this respect each is placed on the same ground. To consult a State not in the Union on the propriety of adopting a constitutional amendment to the government of the Union, and which is necessarily to affect those States only composing the Union, would be an absurdity; and to allow an amendment, which States in the Union might desire, to be defeated by the votes of States not in the Union, would be alike nonsensical and unjust. The very measure, therefore, of submitting to all the States forming the Union before the insurrection a constitutional amendment, makes the inquiry, whether all at this time are in or out of the Union, a vital one. If they are not, all should not be consulted; if they are, they should be, and should be only because they are. The very fact, therefore, of such a submission concedes that the Southern States are, and never ceased to be, States of the Union.

Tested, therefore, either by the nature of our Government or by the terms of the Constitution, the insurrection, now happily and utterly suppressed, has in no respect changed the relations of the States, where it prevailed, to the General Government. On the contrary, they are to all intents and purposes as completely States of the Union as they ever were. In further support of this proposition, if it needed any, we may confidently appeal to the fact just stated, that the very measure recommended, a constitutional amendment to be submitted to such States, furnishes such support; for, looking to and regarding the rights of the other States, such a submission has no warrant or foundation except upon the hypothesis that they are as absolutely States of the Union as any of the other States. It can never be under any circumstances a "profitless abstraction" whether under the Constitution a State is or is not a State of the Union. It can never be such an abstraction whether the people of a State once in the Union can voluntarily or by compulsion escape or be freed from the obligations it enjoins, or be deprived of the rights it confers or the protection it affords.

A different doctrine necessarily leads to a dissolution of the Union. The Constitution supposes that insurrections may exist in a State, and provides for their suppression by giving Congress the power to "call forth the militia" for the purpose. The power is not to subjugate the State within whose limits the insurrection may prevail, and to extinguish it as a State, but to preserve it as such by subduing the rebellion, by acting on the individual persons engaged in it, and not on the State at all. The power is altogether conservative; it is to protect a State, not to destroy it; to prevent her being taken out of the Union by individual crime, not, in any contingency, to put her out or keep her out. The continuance of the Union of all the States is necessary to the intended existence of the Government. The Government is formed by a constitutional association of States, and its integrity depends on the continuance of the entire association. If one State is withdrawn from it by any cause, to that extent is the Union dissolved. Those that remain may exist as a government, but it is not the very government the Constitution designs. That consists of all; and its character is changed and its power is diminished by the absence of any one.

A different principle leads to a disintegration that must sooner or later result in the separation of all, and the consequent destruction of the Government. To suppose that a power to preserve may, at the option of the body to which it is given, be used to destroy, is a proposition repugnant to common sense; and yet, as the late insurrection was put down by means of that power, that being the only one conferred upon Congress to that end, that proposition is the one on which alone it can be pretended that the Southern States are not in the Union now as well as at first.

The idea that the war power, as such, has been used, or could have been used, to extinguish the rebellion, is, in the judgment of the undersigned, utterly without foundation. That power was given for a different contingency—for the contingency of a conflict with other governments, an international conflict. If it had been thought that that power was to be resorted to to suppress a domestic strife, the words "appropriate to that object" would have been used. But so far from this having been done, in the same section that confers it, an express provision is inserted to meet the exigency of a domestic strife or insurrection. To subdue that, authority is given to call out the militia. Whether, in the progress of the effort to suppress an insurrection, the rights incident to war as between the United States and foreign nations may not arise, is a question which in no way changes the character of the contest as between the Government and the insurrectionists. The exercise of such rights may be found convenient, or become necessary for the suppression of the rebellion, but the character of the conflict is in no way changed by a resort to them. That remains, as at first, and must from its very nature during its continuance remain, a mere contest in which the Government seeks, and can only seek, to put an end to the rebellion. That achieved, the original condition of things is at once restored. Two judicial decisions have been made, by judges of eminent and unquestioned ability, which fully sustain our view. In one, that of Amy Warwick, before the United States district court of Massachusetts, Judge Sprague, referring to the supposed effect of the belligerent rights which it was conceded belonged to the Government during the rebellion, by giving it, when suppressed, the rights of conquest, declared:

"It has been supposed that if the Government have the right of a belligerent, then, after the rebellion is suppressed, it will have the rights of conquest; that a State and its inhabitants may be permanently divested of all political advantages, and treated as foreign territory conquered by arms. This is an error, a grave and dangerous error. Belligerent rights cannot be exercised where there are no belligerents. Conquest of a foreign country gives absolute, unlimited sovereign rights, but no nation ever makes such a conquest of its own territory. If a hostile power, either from without or within, takes and holds possession and dominion over any portion of its territory, and the nation, by force of arms, expel or overthrow the enemy, and suppresses hostilities, it acquires no new title, and merely regains the possession of that of which it has been temporarily deprived. The nation acquires no new sovereignty, but merely maintains its previous rights.

"When the United States take possession of a rebel district, they merely vindicate their preexisting title. Under despotic governments confiscation may be unlimited, but under our Government *the right of sovereignty over any portion of a State is given and limited by the Constitution*, and will be the same after the war as it was before."

In the other, an application for *habeas corpus* to Mr. Justice Nelson, one of the judges of the

Supreme Court of the United States, by James Egan, to be discharged from an imprisonment to which he had been sentenced by a military commission in South Carolina, for the offence of murder alleged to have been committed in that State, and the discharge was ordered, and, in an opinion evidently carefully prepared, among other things, said:

"For all that appears, the civil local courts of the State of South Carolina were in the full exercise of their judicial functions at the time of this trial, as restored by the suppression of the rebellion, some seven months previously, and by the revival of the laws and the reorganization of the State in obedience to, and in conformity with, its constitutional duties to the Union. Indeed, long previous to this the provisional government had been appointed by the President, who is commander-in-chief of the army and navy of the United States, (and whose will under martial law constituted the only rule of action,) for the special purpose of changing the existing state of things, and restoring the civil government over the people. In operation of this appointment, a new constitution had been formed, a governor and legislature elected under it, *and the State placed in the full enjoyment, or entitled to the full enjoyment, of all her constitutional rights and privileges.* The constitutional laws of the Union were thereby enjoyed and obeyed, and were as authoritative and binding over the people of the State as in any other portion of the country. Indeed, the moment the rebellion was suppressed, and the government growing out of it subverted, *the ancient laws resumed their accustomed sway, subject only to the new reorganization by the appointment of the proper officer to give them operation and effect.* This organization and appointment of the public functionaries, which was under the superintendence and direction of the President, the commander-in-chief of the army and navy of the country, and who, as such, had previously governed the State, from imperative necessity, by the force of martial law, had already taken place, and the necessity no longer existed."

This opinion is the more authoritative than it might possibly be esteemed otherwise, from its being the first elaborate statement of the reasons which governed the majority of the Supreme Court at the last term in their judgment in the case of Milligan and others, that military commissions for the trial of civilians are not constitutional. Mr. Justice Nelson was one of that majority, and of course was advised of the grounds of their decision. We submit that nothing could be more conclusive in favor of the doctrine for which they are cited than these judgments. In the one, the proposition of conquest of a State as a right under the war to suppress the insurrection is not only repudiated by Judge Sprague, but, because of the nature of our Government, is considered to be legally impossible. "The right of sovereignty over any portion of a State will," he tells us, "only be the same after the war as it was before." In the other, we are told "that the suppression of the rebellion restores the courts of the State," and that when her government is reorganized she at once is "in the full enjoyment, or entitled to the full enjoyment, of all her constitutional rights and privileges."

Again, a contrary doctrine is inconsistent with the obligation which the Government is under to each citizen of a State. Protection to each is a part of that obligation—protection not only as against a foreign, but a domestic foe. To hold that it is in the power of any part of the people of a State, whether they constitute a majority or minority, by engaging in insurrection and adopting any measure in its prosecution to make citizens who are not engaged in it, but opposed to it, enemies of the United States, having no right to the protection which the Constitution affords to citizens who are true to their allegiance, is as illegal as it would be flagrantly unjust. During the conflict the exigency of the strife may justify a denial of such protection, and subject the unoffending citizen to inconvenience or loss; but the conflict over, the exigency ceases, and the obligation to afford him all the immunities and advantages of the Constitution, one of which is the right to be represented in Congress, becomes absolute and imperative. A different rule would enable the Government to escape a clear duty, and to commit a gross violation of the Constitution. It has been said that the Supreme Court have entertained a different doctrine in the prize cases. This, in the judgment of the undersigned, is a clear misapprehension. One of the questions in those cases was, whether in such a contest as was being waged for the extinguishment of the insurrection, belligerent rights, as *between the United States and other nations,* belonged to the former. The Court properly held that they did; but the parties engaged in the rebellion were designated as traitors, and liable to be tried as traitors when the rebellion should terminate. If the Confederate States, by force of insurrection, became foreign States and lost their character as States of the Union, then the contest was an international one, and treason was no more committed by citizens of the former against the latter, than by those of the latter against the former. Treason necessarily assumes allegiance to the government, and allegiance necessarily assumes a continuing obligation to the government. Neither predicament was true, except upon the hypothesis that the old state of things continued. In other words, that the States, notwithstanding the insurrection, were continuously, and are now, States of the United States, and their citizens responsible to the Constitution and the laws. Second: what is there, then, in the present political condition of such States that justifies their exclusion from representation in Congress? Is it because they are without organized governments, or without governments republican in point of form? In fact, we know that they have governments completely organized with legislative, executive, and judicial functions. We know that they are now in successful operation; no one within their limits questions their legality, or is denied their protection. How they were formed, under what auspices they were formed, are inquiries with which Congress has no concern. The right of the people of a State to form a government for themselves has never been questioned. In the absence of any restriction that right would be absolute; any form could be adopted that they might determine upon. The Constitution imposes but a single restriction—that the government adopted shall be "of a republican form," and this is done in the obligation to guarantee every State such a form. It gives no power to frame a constitution for a State. It operates alone upon one already formed by the State. In the words of the Federalist, (No. 44,) "it supposes a pre-existing government of the form which is to be guaranteed." It is not pretended that the existing governments of the States in question are not of the required form. The objection is that they were not legally established. But it is confidently submitted that that is a matter with which Congress has nothing to do. The power to establish or modify a State government belongs exclusively to the people of the State. When they shall exercise it, how they shall exercise it, what provisions it shall contain, it is their exclusive right to decide, and when decided, their decision is obligatory upon everybody, and independent of all congressional control, if such government be *republican*. To convert an obligation of guarantee into an authority to interfere in any way in the formation of the government to be guaranteed is to do violence to language. If it be said that the President did illegally interfere in the organization of such governments, the answers are obvious: First. If it was true, if the people of such States not only have not, but do not, complain of it, but, on the contrary, have pursued his advice, and are satisfied with and are living under the governments they have adopted, and those governments are republican in form, what right has Congress to interfere or deny their legal existence? Second. Conceding, for argument's sake, that the President's alleged interference was unauthorized, does it not, and for the same reason, follow that any like interference by Congress would be equally unauthorized? A different view is not to be maintained because of the difference in the nature of the powers conferred upon Congress and the President, the one being legislative and the other executive; for it is equally, and upon the same ground, beyond the scope of either to form a government for a people of a State once in the Union, or to expel such a State from the Union, or to deny, temporarily or permanently, the rights which belong to a State and her people under the Constitution.

Congress may admit new States, but a State once admitted ceases to be within its control, and can never again be brought within it. What changes her people may at any time think proper to make in her constitution is a matter with which neither Congress nor any department of the General Government can interfere, unless such changes make the State government anti-republican, and then it can only be done under the obligation to guarantee that it be republican. Whatever may be the extent of the power conferred upon Congress in the 3d section, article 4, of the Constitution, to admit new States—in what manner and to what extent they can, under that power, interfere in the formation and character of the Constitution of such States preliminary to admission into the Union, no one has ever pretended that when that is had, the State can again be brought within its influence. The power is exhausted when once executed, the subject forthwith passing out of its reach. The State admitted, like the original thirteen States, becomes at once and forever independent of congressional control. A different view would change the entire character of the Government as its framers and their contemporaries designed and understood it to be. They never intended to make the State governments subordinate to the General Government. Each was to move supreme within its own orbit; but as each would not alone have met the exigencies of a government adequate to all the wants of the people, the two, in the language of Mr. Jefferson, constituted "co-ordinate departments of one single and integral whole;" the one having the power of legislation and administration "in affairs which concerned their own citizens only;" the other, "whatever concerned foreigners, or citizens of other States." Within their respective limits each is paramount. The States, as to all powers not delegated to the General Government, are as independent of that government as the latter, in regard to all powers that are delegated to it, is independent of the governments of the States. The proposition, then, that Congress can, by force or otherwise, under the war or insurrectionary or any other power, expel a State from the Union, or reduce it to a territorial condition and govern it as such, is utterly without foundation. The undersigned deem it unnecessary to examine the question further. They leave it upon the observations submitted, considering it perfectly clear that States, notwithstanding occurring insurrections, continue to be States of the Union.

Thirdly. If this is so, it necessarily follows that the rights of States under the Constitution, as originally possessed and enjoyed by them, are still theirs, and those they are now enjoying, as far as they depend upon the executive and judicial departments of the government. By each of these departments they are recognized as States. By the one, all officers of the government required by law to be appointed in such States have been appointed, and are discharging, without question, their respective functions. By the other they are, as States, enjoying the benefit, and subjected to the powers of that department; a fact conclusive to show that, in the estimation of the judiciary, they are, as they were at first, States of the Union, bound by the laws of the Union, and entitled to all the rights incident to that relation. And yet, so far they are denied that right which the Constitution properly esteems as the security of all the others—that right, without which government is anything but a republic—is indeed but a tyranny—the right of having a voice in the legislative department, whose laws bind them in person and in property;—this, it is submitted, is a state of things without example in a representative republican government; and Congress, as long as it denies this right, is a mere despotism. Citizens may be made to submit to it by force, or dread of force, but a fraternal spirit and good feeling toward those who impose it, so important to the peace and prosperity of the country, are not to be hoped for, but rather unhappiness, dissatisfaction, and enmity. There is but one ground on which such conduct can find any excuse—a supposed public necessity; the peril of destruction to which the government would be subjected, if the right was allowed. But for such a supposition there is not, in the opinion of the undersigned, even a shadow of foundation.

The representatives of the States in which there was no insurrection, if the others were represented, would in the House, under the present apportionment, exceed the latter by a majority of seventy-two votes, and have a decided preponderance in the Senate. What danger to the Government, then, can possibly arise from southern representation? Are the present Senators and Representatives fearful of themselves? Are they apprehensive that they might be led to the destruction of our institutions by the persuasion, or any other influence, of southern members? How disparaging to themselves is such an apprehension. Are they apprehensive that those who may succeed them from their respective States may be so fatally led astray? How disparaging is that supposition to the patriotism and wisdom of their constituents. Whatever effect on mere party success in the future such a representation may have we shall not stop to inquire. The idea that the country is to be kept in turmoil, States to be reduced to bondage, and their rights under the Constitution denied, and their citizens degraded, with a view to the continuance in power of a mere political party, cannot for a moment be entertained without imputing gross dishonesty of purpose and gross dereliction of duty to those who may entertain it. Nor do we deem it necessary to refer particularly to the evidence taken by the committee to show that there is nothing in the present condition of the people of the southern States that even excuses on that ground a denial of representation to them. We content ourselves with saying that in our opinion the evidence most to be relied upon, whether regarding the character of the witnesses or their means of information, shows that representatives from the southern States would prove perfectly loyal. We specially refer for this only to the testimony of Lieutenant General Grant. His loyalty and his intelligence no one can doubt. In his letter to the President of the 18th of December, 1865, after he had recently visited South Carolina, North Carolina, and Georgia, he says:

"*Both in travelling and while stopping, I saw much and conversed freely with the citizens of those States, as well as with officers of the army who have been among them.* The following are the conclusions come to by me:

"I am satisfied that *the mass of thinking men of the South accept the present situation of affairs in good faith.* The questions which have heretofore divided the sentiments of the people of the two sections—slavery and State rights, or the right of a State to secede from the Union—they regard as having been settled forever by the highest tribunal, arms, that man can resort to. *I was pleased to learn from the leading men whom I met that they not only accepted the decision arrived at as final, but that now, the smoke of battle has cleared away and time has been given for reflection, that this decision has been a fortunate one for the whole country,* they receiving the like benefits from it with those who opposed them in the field and in the cause. * *

"My observations lead me to the conclusion that the citizens of the southern States *are anxious to return to self-government within the Union* as soon as possible; that while reconstructing, they *want and require protection from the Government; that they are in earnest in wishing to do what they think is required by the Government, not humiliating to them as citizens;* and that if such a course was pointed out, they would pursue it in good faith. *It is to be regretted that there cannot be a greater commingling at this time between the citizens of the two sections, and particularly of those intrusted with the law-making power.*"

Secession, as a practical doctrine ever hereafter to be resorted to, is almost utterly abandoned. It was submitted to and failed before the ordeal of battle. Nor can the undersigned imagine why, if its revival is anticipated as possible, the committee have not recommended an amendment to the Constitution guarding against it in terms. Such an amendment, it cannot be doubted, the southern as well as northern States would cheerfully adopt. The omission of such a recommendation is pregnant evidence that secession, as a constitutional right, is thought by the majority of the committee to be, practically, a mere thing of the past, as all the proof taken by them shows it to be, in the opinion of all the leading southern men who hitherto entertained it. The desolation around them, the hecatombs of their own slain, the stern patriotism of the men of the other States, exhibited by unlimited expenditure of treasure and of blood, and their love of the Union so sincere and deep-seated that it is seen they will hazard all to maintain it, have convinced the South that, as a practical doctrine, secession is extinguished forever. State secession, then, abandoned, and slavery abolished by the southern States themselves, or with their consent, upon what statesmanlike ground can such States be denied all the rights which the Constitution secures to States of the Union? All admit that to do so at the earliest period is demanded by every consideration of duty and policy, and none deny that the actual interest of the country is to a great extent involved in such admission. The staple productions of the Southern States are as important to the other States as to themselves. Those staples largely enter into the wants of all alike, and they are also most important to the financial credit of the Government. Those staples will never be produced as in the past until real peace, resting, as it can alone rest, on the equal and uniform operation of the Constitution and laws on all, is attained. To suppose that a brave and sensitive people will give an undivided attention to the increase of mere material wealth while retained in a state of political inferiority and degradation is mere folly. They desire to be again in the Union, to enjoy the benefits of the Constitution, and they invoke you to receive them. They have adopted constitutions free from any intrinsic objection, and have agreed to every stipulation thought by the President to be necessary for the protection and benefit of all, and in the opinion of the undersigned they are amply sufficient. Why exact, as a preliminary condition to representation, more? What more are supposed to be necessary? First, the repudiation of the rebel debt; second, the denial of all obligation to pay for manumitted slaves; third, the inviolability of our own debt. If these provisions are deemed necessary, they cannot be defeated, if the South were disposed to defeat them, by the admission into Congress of their representatives. Nothing is more probable, in the opinion of the undersigned, than that many of the southern States would adopt them all; but those measures the committee connect with others which we think the people of the South will never adopt. They are asked to disfranchise a numerous class of their citizens, and also to agree to diminish their representation in Congress, and of course in the electoral college, or to admit to the right of suffrage their colored males of twenty-one years of age and upwards, (a class now in a condition of almost utter ignorance,) thus placing them on the same political footing with white citizens of that age. For reasons so obvious that the dullest may discover them, the right is not directly asserted of granting suffrage to the negro. That would be obnoxious to most of the Northern and Western States, so much so that their consent was not to be anticipated; but as the plan adopted, because of the limited number of negroes in such States, will have no effect on their representation, it is thought it may be adopted, while in the southern States it will materially lessen their number. That these latter States will assent to the measure can hardly be expected. The effect, then, if not the purpose, of the measure is forever to deny representatives to such States, or, if they consent to the condition, to weaken their representative power, and thus, probably, secure a continuance of such a party in power as now control the legislation of the Government. The measure, in its terms and its effect, whether designed or not, is to degrade the southern States. To consent to it will be to consent to their own dishonor.

The manner, too, of presenting the proposed constitutional amendment, in the opinion of the undersigned, is impolitic and without precedent. The several amendments suggested have no connection with each other; each, if adopted, would have its appropriate effect if the others were rejected; and each, therefore, should be submitted as a separate article, without subjecting it to the contingency of rejection if the States should refuse to ratify the rest. Each by itself, if an advisable measure, should be submitted to the people, and not in such a connection with those which they may think unnecessary or dangerous as to force them to reject all. The repudiation of the rebel debt, and all obligation to compensate for the loss of slave property, and the inviolability of the debts of the Government, no matter how contracted, provided for by some of the sections of the amendment, we repeat, we believe would meet the approval of many of the southern States; but these no State can sanction without sanctioning others, which we think will not be done by them or by some of the northern States. To force negro suffrage upon any State by means of a penalty of a loss of part of its representation, will not only be to impose a disparaging condition, but virtually to interfere with the clear right of each State to regulate suffrage for itself, without the control of the Government of the United States. Whether that control be exerted directly or indirectly, it will be considered, as it is, a fatal blow to the right which every State in the past has held vital, the right to regulate her franchise.

To punish a State for not regulating it in a particular way, so as to give to all classes of the people the privilege of suffrage, is but seeking to accomplish incidentally what, if it should be done at all, should be done directly. No reason, in the view of the undersigned, can be suggested for the course adopted, other than a belief that such a direct interference would not be sanctioned by the northern and western States, while, as regards such States, the actual recommendation, because of the small proportion of negroes within their limits, will not in the least lessen their representative power in Congress or their influence in the presidential election, and they may therefore sanction it. This very inequality in its operation upon the States renders the measure, in our opinion, most unjust, and, looking to the peace and quiet of the country, most impolitic. But the mode advised is also not only without but against all precedent. When the Constitution was adopted it was thought to be defective in not sufficiently protecting certain rights of the States and the people. With the view of supplying a remedy for this defect, on the 4th March, 1789, various amendments by a resolution constitutionally passed by Congress were submitted for ratification to the States. They were twelve in number. Several of them were even less independent of each other than are those recommended by the committee. But it did not occur to the men of that day that it was right to force the States to adopt or reject all. Each was, therefore, presented as a separate article. The language of the resolution was, "that the following articles be proposed to the legislatures of the several States as amendments of the Constitution of the United States, ALL OR ANY OF WHICH ARTICLES, when ratified by three-fourths of the said legislatures, to be valid to all intents and purposes as parts of the Constitution. The Congress of that day was willing to obtain either of the submitted amendments—to get a part, if not able to procure the whole. They thought (and in that we submit they but conformed to the letter and spirit of the amendatory clause of the Constitution,) that the people have the right to pass severally on any proposed amendments. This course of our fathers is now departed from, and the result will probably be that no one of the suggested amendments, though some may be approved, will be ratified. This will certainly be the result, unless the States are willing practically to relinquish the right they have always enjoyed, never before questioned by any recognized statesman, and all-important to their interest and security—the right to regulate the franchise in all their elections.

There are, too, some general considerations

that bear on the subject, to which we will now refer.

First. One of the resolutions of the Chicago convention, by which Mr. Lincoln was first nominated for the presidency, says, "that the maintenance inviolate of *the rights of the States* is essential to the balance of power on which the prosperity and endurance of our political fabric depend." In his inaugural address of 4th March, 1861, which received the almost universal approval of the people, among other things he said, "*no State of its own mere motion can lawfully get out of the Union*;" and that "in view of the Constitution and the laws, the Union is unbroken, and to the extent of my ability I shall take care, as the Constitution itself expressly enjoins upon me, that the laws of the Union be faithfully executed in all the States."

Second. Actual conflict soon afterwards ensued. The South, it was believed, misapprehended the purpose of the Government in carrying it on, and Congress deemed it imporant to dispel that misapprehension by declaring what the purpose was. This was done in July, 1861, by their passing the following resolution, offered by Mr. Crittenden: "That in this national emergency, Congress, banishing all feeling of mere passion or resentment, will recollect only its duty to the whole country; that this war is not waged, upon our part, in any spirit of oppression, nor for any purpose of conquest or subjugation, nor purpose of overthrowing or interfering with the rights or established institutions of those States, but to defend and maintain the supremacy of the Constitution, and to preserve the Union, with all the dignity, equality, and rights of the several States unimpaired; that as soon as these objects are accomplished, the war ought to cease." The vote in the House was 119 for and 2 against it, and in the Senate 30 for and 5 against it. The design to conquer or subjugate, or to curtail or interfere in any way with the rights of the States, is in the strongest terms thus disclaimed, and the only avowed object asserted to be "to defend and maintain the spirit of the Constitution, and to preserve the Union, AND THE DIGNITY, EQUALITY, AND RIGHTS OF THE SEVERAL STATES UNIMPAIRED." Congress, too, by the act of 13th July, 1861, empowered the President to declare, by proclamation, "that the inhabitants of such State or States where the insurrection existed are in a state of insurrection against the United States," and thereupon to declare that "all commercial intercourse by and between the same, by the citizens thereof and the citizens of the United States, shall cease and be unlawful *so long as such condition of hostility shall continue*." Here, also, Congress evidently deals with the States as being in the Union and to remain in the Union. It seeks to keep them in by forbidding commercial intercourse between their citizens and the citizens of the other States so long, and so long *only*, as *insurrectionary hostility shall continue*. That ended, they are to be, as at first, entitled to the same intercourse with citizens of other States that they enjoyed before the insurrection. In other words, in this act, as in the resolution of the same month, the dignity, equality, and rights of such States (the insurrection ended) were not to be held in any respect impaired. The several proclamations of amnesty issued by Mr. Lincoln and his successor under the authority of Congress are also inconsistent with the idea that the parties included within them are not to be held, in the future, restored to all rights belonging to them as citizens of their respective States. A power to pardon is a power to restore the offender to the condition in which he was before the date of the offence pardoned.

It is now settled that a pardon removes not only the punishment, but *all* the legal disabilities consequent on the crime. (7 Bac. Ab. Tit. Par.) Bishop on Criminal Law (vol. 1, p. 713) states the same doctrine. The amnesties so declared would be but false pretences if they were, as now held, to leave the parties who have availed themselves of them in almost every particular in the condition they would have been in if they had rejected them. Such a result, it is submitted, would be a foul blot on the good name of the nation. Upon the whole, therefore, in the present state of the country, the excitement which exists, and which may mislead legislatures already elected, we think that the matured sense of the people is not likely to be ascertained on the subject of the proposed amendment by its submission to existing State legislatures. If it should be done at all, the submission should either be to legislatures hereafter to be elected, or to conventions of the people chosen for the purpose. Congress may select either mode, but they have selected neither. It may be submitted to legislatures already in existence, whose members were heretofore elected with no view to the consideration of such a measure; and it may consequently be adopted, though a majority of the people of the States disapprove of it. In this respect, if there were no other objections to it, we think it most objectionable.

Whether regard be had to the nature or the terms of the Constitution, or to the legislation of Congress during the insurrection, or to the course of the judicial department, or to the conduct of the executive, the undersigned confidently submit that the southern States are States in the Union, and entitled to every right and privilege belonging to the other States. If any portion of their citizens be disloyal, or are not able to take any oath of office that has been or may be constitutionally prescribed, is a question irrespective of the right of the States to be represented. Against the danger, whatever that may be, of the admission of disloyal or disqualified members into the Senate or House, it is in the power of each branch to provide against by refusing such admission. Each by the Constitution is made the judge of the election returns and qualifications of its own members. No other department can interfere with it. Its decision concludes all others. The only corrective, when error is committed, consists in the responsibility of the members to the people. But it is believed by the undersigned to be the clear duty of each house to admit any Senator or Representative who has been elected according to the constitutional laws of the State, and who is able and willing to subscribe the oath required by constitutional law.

It is conceded by the majority that "it would

undoubtedly be competent for Congress to waive all formalities, and to admit those Confederate States at once, trusting that time and experience would set all things right." It is not, therefore, owing to a want of constitutional power that it is not done. It is not because such States are not States with republican forms of government. The exclusion must therefore rest on considerations of safety or of expediency alone. The first, that of safety, we have already considered, and, as we think, proved it to be without foundation. Is there any ground for the latter expediency? We think not. On the contrary, in our judgment, their admission is called for by the clearest expediency. Those States include a territorial area of 850,000 square miles, an area larger than that of five of the leading nations of Europe. They have a coast line of 3,000 miles, with an internal water line, including the Mississippi, of about 36,000 miles. Their agricultural products in 1850 were about $560,000,000 in value, and their population 9,664,656. Their staple productions are of immense and growing importance and are almost peculiar to that region. That the North is deeply interested in having such a country and people restored to all the rights and privileges that the Constitution affords no sane man, not blinded by mere party considerations, or not a victim of disordering prejudice, can for a moment doubt. Such a restoration is also necessary to the peace of the country. It is not only important but vital to the potential wealth of which that section of our country is capable, that cannot otherwise be fully developed. Every hour of illegal political restraint, every hour the possession of the rights the Constitution gives is denied, is not only in a political but a material sense of great injury to the North as well as to the South. The southern planter works for his northern brethren as well as for himself. His labors heretofore inured as much if not more to their advantage than to his. Whilst harmony in the past between the sections gave to the whole a prosperity, a power, and a renown of which every citizen had reason to be proud, the restoration of such harmony will immeasurably increase them all. Can it, will it be restored as long as the South is kept in political and dishonoring bondage? and can it not, will it not be restored by an opposite policy? By admitting her to all the rights of the Constitution, and by dealing with her citizens as equals and as brothers, not as inferiors and enemies, such a course as this will, we are certain, soon be seen to bind them heart and soul to the Union, and inspire them with confidence in its government, by making them feel that all enmity is forgotten, and that justice is being done to them. The result of such a policy, we believe, will at once make us in very truth one people, as happy, as prosperous, and as powerful as ever existed in the tide of time; while its opposite cannot fail to keep us divided, injuriously affect the particular and general welfare of citizen and Government, and, if long persisted in, result in danger to the nation. In the words of an eminent British whig statesman, now no more, "A free constitution and large exclusions from its benefit cannot subsist together; the constitution will destroy them, or they will destroy the constitution." It is hoped that, heeding the warning, we will guard against the peril by removing its cause.

The undersigned have not thought it necessary to examine into the legality of the measures adopted, either by the late or the present President, for the restoration of the southern States. It is sufficient for their purpose to say that, if those of President Johnson were not justified by the Constitution, the same may at least be said of those of his predecessor. We deem such an examination to be unnecessary, because, however it might result, the people of the several States who possessed, as we have before said, the exclusive right to decide for themselves what constitutions they should adopt, have adopted those under which they respectively live. The motives of neither President, however, whether the measures were legal or not, are liable to censure. The sole object of each was to effect a complete and early union of all the States; to make the General Government, as it did at first, embrace all, and to extend its authority and secure its privileges and blessings to all alike. The purity of motive of President Johnson in this particular, as was to have been expected, is admitted by the majority of the committee to be beyond doubt; for, whatever was their opinion of the unconstitutionality of his course, and its tendency to enlarge the executive power, they tell us that they "do not for a moment impute to him any such design, but cheerfully concede to him the most patriotic motives." And we cannot forbear to say, in conclusion, upon that point, that he sins against light, and closes his eyes to the course of the President during the rebellion, from its inception to its close, who ventures to impeach his patriotism. Surrounded by insurrectionists, he stood firm. His life was almost constantly in peril, and he clung to the Union, and discharged all the obligations it imposed upon him, even the closer because of the peril. And now that he has escaped unharmed, and by the confidence of the people has had devolved upon him the executive functions of the Government, to charge him with disloyalty is either a folly or a slander: folly in the fool who believes it; slander in the man of sense, if any such there be, who utters it.

REVERDY JOHNSON,
A. J. ROGERS,
HENRY GRIDER.

VIII.

VOTES ON PROPOSED CONSTITUTIONAL AMENDMENTS.

The Constitutional Amendment, as Finally Adopted and Submitted to the Legislatures of the States.

IN SENATE.

1866, June 8—The Amendment in these words, as finally amended, was brought to a vote:

Joint resolution proposing an amendment to the Constitution of the United States.

Resolved by the Senate and House of Representatives of the United States of America in Congress assembled, (two-thirds of both Houses concurring,) That the following article be proposed to the legislatures of the several States as an amendment to the Constitution of the United States, which, when ratified by three-fourths of said legislatures, shall be valid as part of the Constitution, namely:

ARTICLE 14.

SECTION 1. All persons born or naturalized in the United States, and subject to the jurisdiction thereof, are citizens of the United States and of the State wherein they reside. No State shall make or enforce any law which shall abridge the privileges or immunities of citizens of the United States; nor shall any State deprive any person of life, liberty, or property, without due process of law, nor deny to any person within its jurisdiction the equal protection of the laws.

SEC. 2. Representatives shall be apportioned among the several States according to their respective numbers, counting the whole number of persons in each State, excluding Indians not taxed. But when the right to vote at any election for the choice of electors for President and Vice-President of the United States, representatives in Congress, the executive and judicial officers of a State, or the members of the legislature thereof, is denied to any of the male inhabitants of such State, being twenty-one years of age, and citizens of the United States, or in any way abridged, except for participation in rebellion or other crime, the basis of representation therein shall be reduced in the proportion which the number of such male citizens shall bear to the whole number of male citizens twenty-one years of age in such State.

SEC. 3. No person shall be a senator or representative in Congress, or elector of President and Vice-President, or hold any office, civil or military, under the United States, or under any State, who, having previously taken an oath, as a member of Congress, or as an officer of the United States, or as a member of any State legislature, or as an executive or judicial officer of any State, to support the Constitution of the United States, shall have engaged in insurrection or rebellion against the same, or given aid or comfort to the enemies thereof. But Congress may, by a vote of two-thirds of each house, remove such disability.

SEC. 4. The validity of the public debt of the United States, authorized by law, including debts incurred for payment of pensions and bounties for services in suppressing insurrection or rebellion, shall not be questioned. But neither the United States nor any State shall assume or pay any debt or obligation incurred in aid of insurrection or rebellion against the United States, or any claim for the loss or emancipation of any slave; but all such debts, obligations and claims shall be held illegal and void.

SEC. 5. The Congress shall have power to enforce, by appropriate legislation, the provisions of this article.

It passed—yeas 33, nays 11, as follow:

YEAS—Messrs. Anthony, Chandler, Clark, Conness, Cragin, Creswell, Edmunds, Fessenden, Foster, Grimes, Harris, Henderson, Howard, Howe, Kirkwood, Lane of Kansas, Lane of Indiana, Morgan, Morrill, Nye, Poland, Pomeroy, Ramsey, Sherman, Sprague, Stewart, Sumner, Trumbull, Wade, Willey, Williams, Wilson, Yates—33.

NAYS—Messrs. Cowan, *Davis*, Doolittle, *Guthrie*, *Hendricks*, *Johnson*, *McDougall*, Norton, *Riddle*, *Saulsbury*, Van Winkle—11.

ABSENT—Messrs. Brown, *Buckalew*, Dixon, *Nesmith*, *Wright*—5.

IN HOUSE.

June 13—The Amendment passed—yeas 138, nays 36, as follow:

YEAS—Messrs. Alley, Allison, Ames, Anderson, Delos R. Ashley, James M. Ashley, Baker, Baldwin, Banks, Barker, Baxter, Beaman, Benjamin, Bidwell, Bingham, Blaine, Blow, Boutwell, Brandegee, Bromwell, Broomall, Buckland, Bundy, Reader W. Clarke, Sidney Clarke, Cobb, Conkling, Cook, Cullom, Darling, Davis, Dawes, Defrees, Delano, Deming, Dixon, Dodge, Donnelly, Driggs, Dumont, Eckley, Eggleston, Eliot, Farnsworth, Farquhar, Ferry, Garfield, Grinnell, Griswold, Hale, Abner C. Harding, Hart, Hayes, Henderson, Higby, Holmes, Hooper, Hotchkiss, Asahel W. Hubbard, Chester D. Hubbard, Demas Hubbard, jr., John H. Hubbard, James R. Hubbell, Hulburd, Ingersoll, Jenckes, Julian, Kasson, Kelley, Kelso, Ketcham, Kuykendall, Laflin, Latham, George V. Lawrence, William Lawrence, Loan, Longyear, Lynch, Marston, Marvin, McClurg, McKee, McRuer, Mercur, Miller, Moorhead, Morrill, Morris, Moulton, Myers, Newell, O'Neill, Orth, Paine, Patterson, Perham, Phelps, Pike, Plants, Pomeroy, Price, William H. Randall, Raymond, Alexander H. Rice, John H. Rice, Rollins, Sawyer, Schenck, Scofield, Shellabarger, Sloan, Smith, Spalding, Stevens, Stillwell, Thayer, Francis Thomas, John L. Thomas, Trowbridge, Upson, Van Aernam, Burt Van Horn, Robert T. Van Horn, Ward, Warner, Ellihu B. Washburne, Henry D. Washburn, William B. Washburn, Welker, Wentworth, Whaley, Williams, James F. Wilson, Stephen F. Wilson, Windom, Woodbridge, the Speaker—138.

NAYS—Messrs. *Ancona*, *Bergen*, *Boyer*, *Chanler*, *Coffroth*, *Dawson*, *Denison*, *Eldridge*, *Finck*, *Glossbrenner*, *Grider*, *Aaron Harding*, *Hogan*, *Edwin N. Hubbell*, *James M. Humphrey*, *Johnson*, *Kerr*, *Le Blond*, *Marshall*, *McCullough*, *Niblack*, *Nicholson*, *Radford*, *Samuel J. Randall*, *Ritter*, *Rogers*, *Ross*, *Shanklin*, *Sitgreaves*, *Strouse*, *Taber*, *Taylor*, *Thornton*, *Trimble*, *Winfield*, *Wright*—36.

NOT VOTING—Messrs. Culver, *Goodyear*, *Harris*, Hill, James Humphrey, *Jones*, McIndoe, *Noell*, Rousseau, Starr—10.

Preliminary Proceedings.

Prior to the adoption of the joint resolution in the form above stated, these reports were made from the Joint Committee, and these votes were taken in the two Houses:

IN HOUSE.

April 30—Mr. Stevens, from the Joint Select Committee on Reconstruction reported a joint resolution, as follows:

A joint resolution proposing an amendment to the Constitution of the United States.

Be it resolved, &c., (two-thirds of both Houses concurring,) That the following article be proposed to the legislatures of the several States as an amendment to the Constitution of the United States, which, when ratified by three-fourths of said legislatures, shall be valid as part of the Constitution, namely:

ARTICLE —.

SEC. 1. No State shall make or enforce any law which shall abridge the privileges or immunities of citizens of the United States; nor shall any State deprive any person of life, liberty, or property without due process of law, nor deny to any person within its jurisdiction the equal protection of the laws.

SEC. 2. Representatives shall be apportioned among the several States which may be included within this Union, according to their respective numbers, counting the whole number of persons in each State, excluding Indians not taxed. But whenever in any State the elective franchise shall be denied to any portion of its male citizens not less than twenty-one years of age, or in any way abridged, except for participation in rebellion or other crime, the basis of representation in such State shall be reduced in the proportion which the number of such male citizens shall bear to the whole number of male citizens not less than twenty-one years of age.

SEC. 3. Until the 4th day of July, in the year 1870, all persons who voluntarily adhered to the late insurrection, giving it aid and comfort, shall be excluded from the right to vote for representatives in Congress and for electors for President and Vice-President of the United States.

SEC. 4. Neither the United States nor any State shall assume or pay any debt or obligation already incurred, or which may hereafter be incurred, in aid of insurrection or of war against the United States, or any claim for compensation for loss of involuntary service or labor.

SEC. 5. The Congress shall have power to enforce, by appropriate legislation, the provisions of this article.

Objection having been made to its being a special order for Tuesday, May 8, and every day thereafter until disposed of, Mr. Stevens moved a suspension of the rules to enable him to make that motion; which was agreed to—yeas 107, nays 20.

The NAYS were: Messrs. *Ancona, Bergen, Boyer, Coffroth, Dawson, Eldridge, Finck, Grider, Aaron Harding, James M. Humphrey*, Latham, *Marshall, Niblack, Nicholson, Ritter, Ross, Strouse, Taylor, Thornton, Winfield*—20.

May 10—Mr. Stevens demanded the previous question; which was seconded, on a count, 85 to 57; and the main question was ordered—yeas 84, nays 79, as follow:

YEAS—Messrs. Allison, Ames, Anderson, Banks, Baxter, Bidwell, Boutwell, Bromwell, Broomall, *Chanler*, Reader W. Clarke, Sidney Clarke, Cobb, Conkling, Cook, Defrees, Dixon, Driggs, Dumont, Eckley, Eggleston, *Eldridge*, Eliot, *Grider*, Grinnell, *Aaron Harding*, Abner C. Harding, *Harris*, Hart, Higby, Holmes, Hooper, Hotchkiss, Asahel W. Hubbard, Demas Hubbard, Ingersoll, Julian, Kelley, Kelso, *Kerr*, William Lawrence, *Le Blond*, Loan, Lynch, Marston, McClurg, *McCullough*, McIndoe, Mercur, Morrill, Moulton, *Niblack*, O'Neill, Orth, Paine, Patterson, Perham, Pike, Price, John H. Rice, *Ritter, Rogers*, Rollins, *Ross*, Rousseau, Sawyer, Schenck, Scofield, *Shanklin*, Shellabarger, Spalding, Stevens, Francis Thomas, John L. Thomas, *Thornton*, Trowbridge, Upson, Ward, Elihu B. Washburne, Welker, James F. Wilson, Stephen F. Wilson, Windom, Woodbridge—84.

NAYS—Messrs. Alley, *Ancona*, Delos R. Ashley, James M. Ashley, Baker, Baldwin, Barker, Beaman, Benjamin, *Bergen*, Bingham, Blaine, Blow, *Boyer*, Buckland, Bundy, *Coffroth*, Cullom, Darling, Davis, Dawes, *Dawson*, Delano, Deming, Dodge, Donnelly, Farnsworth, Ferry, Finck, Garfield, *Glossbrenner*, Goodyear, Griswold, Hayes, Henderson, Chester D. Hubbard, James R. Hubbell, Hulburd, James Humphrey, Jenckes, Kasson, Ketcham, Kuykendall, Laflin, Latham, George V. Lawrence, Longyear, *Marshall*, McKee, McRuer, Miller, Moorhead, Morris, Myers, Newell, Phelps, Plants, *Radford, Samuel J. Randall*, William H. Randall, Raymond, Alexander H. Rice, *Sitgreaves*, Smith, Stillwell, *Strouse, Taber, Taylor*, Thayer, *Trimble*, Burt Van Horn, Robert T. Van Horn, Warner, Henry D. Washburn, William B. Washburn, Whaley, Williams, *Winfield, Wright*—79.

The joint resolution, as above printed, then passed—yeas 128, nays 37, as follow:

YEAS—Messrs. Alley, Allison, Ames, Anderson, Delos R. Ashley, James M. Ashley, Baker, Baldwin, Banks, Barker, Baxter, Beaman, Benjamin, Bidwell, Bingham, Blaine, Blow, Boutwell, Bromwell, Broomall, Buckland, Bundy, Reader W. Clarke, Sidney Clarke, Cobb, Conkling, Cook, Cullom, Darling, Davis, Dawes, Defrees, Delano, Deming, Dixon, Dodge, Donnelly, Driggs, Dumont, Eckley, Eggleston, Eliot, Farnsworth, Ferry, Garfield, Grinnell, Griswold, Abner C. Harding, Hart, Hayes, Henderson, Higby, Holmes, Hooper, Hotchkiss, Asahel W. Hubbard, Chester D. Hubbard, Demas Hubbard, James R. Hubbell, Hulburd, James Humphrey, Ingersoll, Jenckes, Julian, Kasson, Kelley, Kelso, Ketcham, Kuykendall, Laflin, George V. Lawrence, William Lawrence, Loan, Longyear, Lynch, Marston, McClurg, McIndoe, McKee, McRuer, Mercur, Miller, Moorhead, Morrill, Morris, Moulton, Myers, Newell, O'Neill, Orth, Paine, Patterson, Perham, Pike, Plants, Price, William H. Randall, Raymond, Alexander H. Rice, John H. Rice, Rollins, Sawyer, Schenck, Scofield, Shellabarger, Spalding, Stevens, Stillwell, Thayer, Francis Thomas, John L. Thomas, Trowbridge, Upson, Van Aernam, Burt Van Horn, Robert T. Van Horn, Ward, Warner, Elihu B. Washburne, Henry D. Washburn, William B. Washburn, Welker, Williams, James F. Wilson, Stephen F. Wilson, Windom, Woodbridge, the Speaker—128.

NAYS—Messrs. *Ancona, Bergen, Boyer, Chanler, Coffroth, Dawson, Eldridge, Finck, Glossbrenner, Goodyear, Grider, Aaron Harding, Harris, Kerr*, Latham, *Le Blond, Marshall, McCullough, Niblack*, Phelps, *Radford, Samuel J. Randall, Ritter, Rogers, Ross*, Rousseau, *Shanklin, Sitgreaves*, Smith, *Strouse, Taber, Taylor, Thornton, Trimble*, Whaley, *Winfield, Wright*—37.

The amendments of the Senate were made to this proposition, when it was finally adopted by each House, in the form first stated.

The Accompanying Bills.

April 30—Mr. Stevens, from the same committee, also reported this bill:

A Bill to provide for restoring the States lately in insurrection to their full political rights.

Whereas it is expedient that the States lately in insurrection should, at the earliest day consistent with the future peace and safety of the Union, be restored to full participation in all political rights; and whereas the Congress did, by joint resolution, propose for ratification to the legislatures of the several States, as an amendment to the Constitution of the United States, an article in the following words, to wit:

[For article, see page 102.]

Now, therefore,

Be it enacted, &c., That whenever the above-recited amendment shall have become part of the

Constitution of the United States, and any State lately in insurrection shall have ratified the same, and shall have modified its constitution and laws in conformity therewith, the Senators and Representatives from such State, if found duly elected and qualified, may, after having taken the required oaths of office, be admitted into Congress as such.

SEC. 2. *And be it further enacted*, That when any State lately in insurrection shall have ratified the foregoing amendment to the Constitution, any part of the direct tax under the act of August 5, 1861, which may remain due and unpaid in such State may be assumed and paid by such State; and the payment thereof, upon proper assurances from such State to be given to the Secretary of the Treasury of the United States, may be postponed for a period not exceeding ten years from and after the passage of this act.

April 30—Mr. Stevens, from the same committee, also reported this bill:

A Bill declaring certain persons ineligible to office under the Government of the United States.

Be it enacted, &c., That no person shall be eligible to any office under the Government of the United States who is included in any of the following classes, namely:

1. The president and vice president of the confederate States of America, so called, and the heads of departments thereof.

2. Those who in other countries acted as agents of the confederate States of America, so called.

3. Heads of Departments of the United States, officers of the army and navy of the United States, and all persons educated at the Military or Naval Academy of the United States, judges of the courts of the United States, and members of either House of the Thirty-Sixth Congress of the United States who gave aid or comfort to the late rebellion.

4. Those who acted as officers of the confederate States of America, so called, above the grade of colonel in the army or master in the navy, and any one who, as Governor of either of the so-called confederate States, gave aid or comfort to the rebellion.

5. Those who have treated officers or soldiers or sailors of the army or navy of the United States, captured during the late war, otherwise than lawfully as prisoners of war.

Neither of these bills has been voted on up to the time this page goes to press.

The Negatived Amendment on Representation and Direct Taxes.

IN HOUSE.

January 22, 1866—Mr. Stevens reported this proposition from the Joint Select Committee:

Resolved, &c., (two-thirds of both Houses concurring,) That the following article be proposed to the legislatures of the several States as an amendment to the Constitution of the United States; which, when ratified by three-fourths of the said legislatures, shall be valid as part of said Constitution, namely:

ARTICLE —. Representatives and direct taxes shall be apportioned among the several States which may be included within this Union, according to their respective numbers, counting the whole number of persons in each State, excluding Indians not taxed: *Provided*, That whenever the elective franchise shall be denied or abridged in any State on account of race or color, all persons of such race or color shall be excluded from the basis of representation.

Mr. Stevens moved to insert the word "therein" after the word "persons" where it last occurs.

Sundry propositions of amendment were offered, and

January 30—The report was recommitted, without instructions—the motion of Mr. Le Blond to commit it to the Committee of the Whole having been lost, yeas 37, nays 133. (Messrs. McRuer and Rousseau and 35 Democrats made up the affirmative vote.)

The Negatived Constitutional Amendment on Representation.

IN HOUSE.

January 31, 1866—Mr. Stevens reported from the Committee on Reconstruction this joint resolution:

Joint Resolution proposing to amend the Constitution of the United States.

Resolved, &c., (two-thirds of both Houses concurring,) That the following article be proposed to the legislatures of the several States as an amendment to the Constitution of the United States, which, when ratified by three-fourths of said legislatures, shall be valid as part of said Constitution, namely:

ARTICLE —.

Representatives shall be apportioned among the several States which may be included within this Union according to their respective numbers, counting the whole number of persons in each State, excluding Indians not taxed: *Provided*, That whenever the elective franchise shall be denied or abridged in any State on account of race or color, all persons therein of such race or color shall be excluded from the basis of representation.

Mr. Schenck submitted this as a substitute for the "Article:"

Representatives shall be apportioned among the several States which may be included within this Union according to the number of male citizens of the United States over twenty-one years of age having the qualifications requisite for electors of the most numerous branch of the State legislature. The Congress, at their first session after the ratification of this amendment by the required number of States, shall provide by law for the actual enumeration of such voters; and such actual enumeration shall be separately made in a general census of the population of all the States within every subsequent term of ten years, in such manner as the Congress may by law direct. The number of Representatives shall not exceed one for every one hundred and twenty-five thousand of actual population, but each State shall have at least one Representative.

Mr. Schenck's substitute was disagreed to—yeas 29, nays 131, as follow:

YEAS—Messrs. Anderson, Bromwell, Bundy, Reader W. Clarke, Sidney Clarke, Darling, Davis, Defrees, Farnsworth, Abner C. Harding, Hayes, Hill, Chester D. Hubbard, James R. Hubbell, Jas. Humphrey, Ingersoll, Kuykendall, William Lawrence, *Marshall*, *McCullough*, Miller, Orth, Pike, *Ross*, Schenck, Shellabarger, Sloan, *Thornton*, Van Horn—29.

NAYS—Messrs. Alley, Allison, Ames, James M. Ashley, Baker, Banks, Barker, Baxter, Beaman, Benjamin, *Bergen*, Bidwell, Bingham, Blaine, Blow, Boutwell, *Boyer*, Brandegee, *Brooks*, Broomall, Buckland, *Chanler*, Cobb, Conkling, Cook, Cullom, Dawes, *Dawson*, Delano, Deming, *Denison*, Dixon, Donnelly, Eckley, Eggleston, *Eldridge*, Eliot, Farquhar, Ferry, *Finck*, Garfield, *Grider*, Grinnell, Griswold, Hale, *Aaron Harding*, *Harris*, Hart, *Hogan*, Holmes, Hooper, Hotchkiss, Asahel W. Hubbard, Demas Hubbard, jr., John H. Hubbard, *Edwin N. Hubbell*, Hulburd, *James M. Humphrey*, Jenckes, *Johnson*, Julian, Kasson, Kelley, Kelso, *Kerr*, Ketcham, Laflin, Latham, George V. Lawrence, *Le Blond*, Longyear, Lynch, Marston, Marvin, McClurg, McIndoe, McKee, Mercur, Moorhead, Morrill, Morris, Moulton, Myers, *Niblack*, *Nicholson*, *Noell*, O'Neill, Paine, Patterson, Perham, Phelps, Plants, Pomeroy, Price, *Samuel J. Randall*, William H. Randall, Alexander H. Rice, John H. Rice, *Ritter*, *Rogers*, Rollins, Sawyer, Scofield, *Shanklin*, Smith, Spalding, Starr, Stevens, *Strouse*, *Taber*, *Taylor*, Thayer, Francis Thomas, John L. Thomas, jr., *Trimble*, Upson, Van Aernam, Burt Van Horn, *Voorhees*, Ward, Warner, Ellihu B. Washburne, William B. Washburn, Welker, Wentworth, Whaley, Williams, James F. Wilson, Stephen F. Wilson, Windom, *Wright*—131.

The joint resolution, as reported, was then agreed to—yeas 120, nays 46, as follow:

YEAS—Messrs. Alley, Allison, Ames, Anderson, James M. Ashley, Baker, Banks, Barker, Baxter, Beaman, Benjamin, Bidwell, Bingham, Blaine, Blow, Boutwell, Brandegee, Bromwell, Broomall, Buckland, Bundy, Reader W. Clarke, Sidney Clarke, Cobb, Conkling, Cook, Cullom, Darling, Davis, Dawes, Defrees, Delano, Deming, Dixon, Donnelly, Eckley, Eggleston, Farnsworth, Farquhar, Ferry, Garfield, Grinnell, Griswold, Abner C. Harding, Hart, Hayes, Hill, Holmes, Hooper, Hotchkiss, Asahel W. Hubbard, Chester D. Hubbard, Demas Hubbard, jr., John H. Hubbard, James R. Hubbell, Hulburd, Jas. Humphrey, Ingersoll, Julian, Kasson, Kelley, Kelso, Ketcham, Kuykendall, Laflin, George V. Lawrence, William Lawrence, Longyear, Lynch, Marston, Marvin, McClurg, McIndoe, McKee, Mercur, Miller, Moorhead, Morrill, Morris, Moulton, Myers, O'Neill, Orth, Paine, Patterson, Perham, Pike, Plants, Pomeroy, Price, Alexander H. Rice, John H. Rice, Rollins, Sawyer, Schenck, Scofield, Shellabarger, Sloan, Spalding, Starr, Stevens, Stillwell, Thayer, Francis Thomas, John L. Thomas, jr., Upson, Van Aernam, Burt Van Horn, Robert T. Van Horn, Ward, Warner, Ellihu B. Washburne, William B. Washburn, Welker, Wentworth, Williams, James F. Wilson, Stephen F. Wilson, Windom, Woodbridge—120.

NAYS—Messrs. Baldwin, *Bergen*, *Boyer*, *Brooks*, *Chanler*, *Dawson*, *Denison*, *Eldridge*, Eliot, *Finck*, *Grider*, Hale, *Aaron Harding*, *Harris*, *Hogan*, *Edwin N. Hubbell*, *James M. Humphrey*, Jenckes, *Johnson*, *Kerr*, Latham, *Le Blond*, *Marshall*, *McCullough*, *Niblack*, *Nicholson*, *Noell*, Phelps, *Samuel J. Randall*, William H. Randall, Raymond, *Ritter*, *Rogers*, *Ross*, Rousseau, *Shanklin*, *Sitgreaves*, Smith, *Strouse*, *Taber*, *Taylor*, *Thornton*, *Trimble*, *Voorhees*, Whaley, *Wright*, —46.

[Messrs. Driggs and Newell, February 1, stated they would have voted aye, if present.]

IN SENATE.

March 9, 1866—The resolution of the House was rejected—yeas 25, nays 22, as follow, (two-thirds being necessary:)

YEAS—Messrs. Anthony, Chandler, Clark, Conness, Cragin, Creswell, Fessenden, Foster, Grimes, Harris, Howe, Kirkwood, Lane of Indiana, McDougall, Morgan, Morrill, Nye, Poland, Ramsey, Sherman, Sprague, Trumbull, Wade, Williams, Wilson—25.

NAYS—Messrs. Brown, *Buckalew*, Cowan, *Davis*, Dixon, Doolittle, *Guthrie*, Henderson, *Hendricks*, *Johnson*, Lane of Kansas, *Nesmith*, Norton, Pomeroy, *Riddle*, *Saulsbury*, Stewart, *Stockton*, Sumner, Van Winkle, Willey, Yates—22.

Report on Privileges and Immunities of Citizens.

IN HOUSE.

February 13, 1866—Mr. Bingham reported from the Joint Reconstruction Committee, this joint resolution, which was re-committed and ordered to be printed:

Joint Resolution proposing an amendment to the Constitution of the United States.

Resolved, &c., (two-thirds of both Houses concurring,) That the following article be proposed to the legislatures of the several States as an amendment to the Constitution of the United States, which, when ratified by three-fourths of the said legislatures, shall be valid as part of said Constitution, viz:

ARTICLE —.

The Congress shall have power to make all laws which shall be necessary and proper to secure to the citizens of each State all privileges and immunities of citizens in the several States, and to all persons in the several States equal protection in the rights of life, liberty, and property.

February 26—Mr. Bingham reported it back, without amendment.

February 28—Mr. Eldridge moved that it lie on the table; which was disagreed to—yeas 41, nays 110, as follow:

YEAS—Messrs. *Ancona*, *Bergen*, *Brooks*, *Chanler*, *Coffroth*, Davis, *Dawson*, *Denison*, *Eldridge*, *Finck*, *Glossbrenner*, *Goodyear*, *Grider*, Griswold, Hale, *A. Harding*, *Hogan*, *E. N. Hubbell*, *Kerr*, Kuykendall, *Marshall*, Marvin, *McCullough*, *Niblack*, *Nicholson*, *Noell*, Phelps, *S. J. Randall*, *Ritter*, *Rogers*, *Ross*, Rousseau, *Shanklin*, *Sitgreaves*, *Strouse*, *Taber*, *Taylor*, *Thornton*, *Trimble*, *Winfield*, *Wright*—41.

NAYS—Messrs. Alley, Allison, Ames, Anderson, Delos R. Ashley, James M. Ashley, Baker, Baldwin, Banks, Barker, Baxter, Benjamin, Bidwell, Bingham, Blaine, Blow, Boutwell, Brandegee, Broomall, Buckland, Bundy, Reader W. Clarke, Sidney Clarke, Cobb, Conkling, Cook, Cullom, Darling, Defrees, Delano, Deming, Donnelly, Dumont, Eckley, Eggleston, Eliot, Farnsworth, Farquhar, Ferry, Garfield, Grinnell, Abner C. Harding, Hart, Hayes, Higby, Holmes, Hooper, Hotchkiss, Demas Hubbard, jr., John H. Hubbard, James R. Hubbell, Hulburd, James Humphrey, Ingersoll, Jenckes, Julian, Kelley, Kelso, Ketcham, Laflin, Latham, George V. Lawrence, William Lawrence, Loan, Longyear, Lynch, Marston, McClurg, McKee, McRuer, Mercur, Moorhead, Morrill, Morris, Moulton, Myers, Newell, O'Neill, Orth, Paine, Patterson, Perham, Pike, Price, Raymond, Alexander H. Rice, John H. Rice, Sawyer, Schenck, Shellabarger, Sloan, Spalding, Stevens, Thayer, Francis Thomas, John L. Thomas, jr., Trowbridge, Van Aernam, Burt Van Horn, Warner, Ellihu B. Washburne, Henry D. Washburn, Wm. B. Washburn, Welker, Wentworth, Williams, James F. Wilson, Stephen F. Wilson, Windom, Woodbridge—110.

And on motion of Mr. Conkling, its further consideration was postponed until the second Tuesday in April.

There was no further vote on it.

IN SENATE.

February 13—Mr. Fessenden reported the same resolution, which was laid over, and not again considered.

Report Concerning Tennessee.

IN HOUSE.

March 5, 1866—Mr. Bingham reported from the Select Joint Committee on Reconstruction this

Joint Resolution concerning the State of Tennessee.

Resolved, &c., That whereas the people of Tennessee have made known to the Congress of the United States their desire that the constitutional relations heretofore existing between them and the United States may be fully established, and did, on the twenty-second day of February, eighteen hundred and sixty-five, by a large popular vote, adopt and ratify a constitution of government, republican in form and not inconsistent with the Constitution and laws of the United States, and a State government has been organized under the provisions thereof, which said provisions and the laws passed in pursuance thereof proclaim and denote loyalty to the Union; and whereas the people of Tennessee are found to be in a condition to exercise the functions of a State within this Union, and can only exercise the same by the consent of the law-making power of the United States: Therefore, the State of Tennessee is hereby declared to be one of the United States of America, on an equal footing with the other States, upon the express condition that the people of Tennessee will maintain and enforce, in good faith, their existing constitution and laws, excluding those who have been engaged in rebellion against the United States from the exercise of the elective franchise, for the respective periods of time therein provided for, and shall exclude the same persons for the like respective periods of time from eligibility to office; and the State of Tennessee shall never assume or pay any debt or obligation contracted or incurred in aid of the late rebellion; nor shall said State ever in any manner claim from the United States or make any allowance or compensation for slaves emancipated or liberated in any way whatever; which conditions shall be ratified by the Legislature of Tennessee, or the people thereof, as the Legislature may direct, before this act shall take effect.

The resolution was ordered to be printed, and was recommitted to the committee, and has not been voted on, up to the time this page goes to press.

Payment of Rebel Debt.

December 19, 1865—Mr. James F. Wilson reported from the Committee on the Judiciary the following joint resolution to amend the Constitution of the United States:

Be it resolved by the Senate and House of Representatives of the United States in Congress assembled, (two-thirds of both Houses concurring,) That the following article be proposed to the legislatures of the several States as an amendment to the Constitution of the United States, which, when ratified by three-fourths of said legislatures, shall be valid to all intents and purposes as a part of said Constitution, namely:

ARTICLE —. No tax, duty, or impost shall be laid, nor shall any appropriation of money be made, by either the United States, or any one of the States thereof, for the purpose of paying, either in whole or in part, any debt, contract, or liability whatsoever, incurred, made, or suffered by any one or more of the States, or the people thereof, for the purpose of aiding rebellion against the Constitution and laws of the United States.

Which was passed—yeas 151, nays 11, as follow:

YEAS—Messrs. Alley, Allison, Ames, Anderson, James M. Ashley, Baker, Baldwin, Banks, Barker, Baxter, Beaman, Benjamin, *Bergen*, Bidwell, Bingham, Blow, Boutwell, *Boyer*, Brandegee, Bromwell, Broomall, Buckland, Bundy, *Chanler*, Reader W. Clarke, Sidney Clarke, Cobb, Conkling, Cook, Cullom, Darling, Dawes, Defrees, Delano, Deming, Dixon, Donnelly, Driggs, Dumont, Eckley, Eggleston, Eliot, Farnsworth, Farquhar, Ferry, *Finck*, Garfield, Grinnell, Griswold, Hale, Abner C. Harding, Hart, Hayes, Henderson, Higby, Hill, *Hogan*, Holmes, Hooper, Hotchkiss, Asahel W. Hubbard, Chester D. Hubbard, Demas Hubbard, jr., John H. Hubbard, James R. Hubbell, Hulburd, Ingersoll, Jenckes, *Johnson*, Julian, Kasson, Kelley, Kelso, *Kerr*, Ketcham, Kuykendall, Laflin, Latham, George V. Lawrence, William Lawrence, Loan, Longyear, Lynch, *Marshall*, Marston, Marvin, McClurg, McKee, McRuer, Mercur, Miller, Morrill, Moulton, Myers, Newell, *Niblack*, *Noell*, O'Neill, Orth, Paine, Patterson, Perham, Phelps, Pike, Plants, Price, *Radford*, *Samuel J. Randall*, William H. Randall, Raymond, Alexander H. Rice, John H. Rice, Rollins, *Ross*, Rousseau, Sawyer, Schenck, Scofield, Shellabarger, *Sitgreaves*, Sloan, Smith, Spalding, Starr, Stevens, Stillwell, *Strouse*, *Taber*, *Taylor*, Thayer, Francis Thomas, John L. Thomas, *Thornton*, Trowbridge, Upson, Van Aernam, Burt Van Horn, Robert T. Van Horn, *Voorhees*, Ward, Warner, Ellihu B. Washburne, William B. Washburn, Welker, Wentworth, Whaley, Williams, James F. Wilson, Stephen F. Wilson, Windom, *Wright*—151.

NAYS—Messrs. *Brooks*, *Denison*, *Eldridge*, *Grider*, *Aaron Harding*, *McCullough*, *Nicholson*, *Ritter*, *Rogers*, *Shanklin*, *Trimble*—11.

It was not acted on in the Senate; but the substance of it is included in the amendment as finally adopted.

IX.

MEMBERS OF THE CABINET OF PRESIDENT JOHNSON,

AND OF THE

THIRTY-NINTH CONGRESS,

WITH

NAMES OF CLAIMANTS FROM THE INSURRECTIONARY STATES.

PRESIDENT JOHNSON'S CABINET.

Secretary of State—WILLIAM H. SEWARD, of New York.
Secretary of Treasury—HUGH MCCULLOCH, of Indiana.
Secretary of War—EDWIN M. STANTON, of Ohio.
Secretary of Navy—GIDEON WELLES, of Connecticut.
Postmaster General—WILLIAM DENNISON, of Ohio.
Secretary of Interior—JAMES HARLAN, of Iowa.
Attorney General—JAMES SPEED, of Kentucky.

THIRTY-NINTH CONGRESS.

Senate.

LAFAYETTE S. FOSTER, of Connecticut, *President of the Senate, and Acting Vice President.*
John W. Forney, of Pennsylvania, *Secretary.*
Maine—William Pitt Fessenden, Lot M. Morrill.
New Hampshire—Daniel Clark, Aaron H. Cragin.
Vermont—Solomon Foot,* Luke P. Poland.
Massachusetts—Charles Sumner, Henry Wilson.
Rhode Island—Henry B. Anthony, William Sprague.
Connecticut—James Dixon, Lafayette S. Foster.
New York—Ira Harris, Edwin D. Morgan.
New Jersey—William Wright, John P. Stockton.†
Pennsylvania—Charles R. Buckalew, Edgar Cowan.
Delaware—George Read Riddle, Willard Saulsbury.
Maryland—John A. J. Creswell, Reverdy Johnson.
Ohio—John Sherman, Benjamin F. Wade.
Kentucky—James Guthrie, Garrett Davis.
Indiana—Henry S. Lane, Thomas A. Hendricks.
Illinois—Lyman Trumbull, Richard Yates.

*Died March 28, 1866. His successor, George F. Edmunds, qualified April 5, 1866.

† Voted—yeas 22, nays 21—not entitled to a seat in the Senate, March 27, 1866. The vote on the amendment declaring him not entitled was as follow:

YEAS—Messrs. Brown, Chandler, Clark, Conness, Cragin, Creswell, Fessenden, Grimes, Howard, Howe, Kirkwood, Lane of Indiana, Nye, Pomeroy, Ramsey, Sherman, Sprague, Sumner, Wade, Williams, Wilson, Yates—22.

NAYS—Messrs. Anthony, *Buckalew*, Cowan, *Davis*, Doolittle, *Guthrie*, Harris, Henderson, *Hendricks*, *Johnson*, Lane of Kansas, *McDougall*, Morgan, *Nesmith*, Norton, Poland, *Riddle*, *Saulsbury*, Trumbull, Van Winkle, Willey—21.

Missouri—B. Gratz Brown, John B. Henderson.
Michigan—Zachariah Chandler, Jacob M. Howard.
Iowa—James W. Grimes, Samuel J. Kirkwood.*
Wisconsin—James R. Doolittle, Timothy O. Howe.
California—John Conness, James A. McDougall.
Minnesota—Daniel S. Norton, Alexander Ramsey.
Oregon—James W. Nesmith, George H. Williams.
Kansas—Samuel C. Pomeroy, James H. Lane.
West Virginia—Peter G. Van Winkle, Waitman T. Willey.
Nevada—James W. Nye, William M. Stewart.

Senators Chosen from the late Insurrectionary States.

Alabama—Lewis E. Parsons, George S. Houston.
Arkansas—Elisha Baxter, William D. Snow.
Florida—William Marvin, Wilkerson Call.
Georgia—Alexander H. Stephens, Herschel V. Johnson.
Louisiana—Randall Hunt, Henry Boyce. (R. King Cutler and Michael Hahn also claim under a former election in October, 1864.)
Mississippi—William L. Sharkey, James L. Alcorn.
North Carolina—William A. Graham, John Pool.
South Carolina—Benjamin F. Perry, John L. Manning.
Tennessee—David T. Patterson, Joseph S. Fowler.
Texas—
Virginia—John C. Underwood, Joseph Segar.

MEMORANDUM.

Mr. A. H. Stephens was a delegate from Georgia to the convention which framed the "Confederate" constitution, and was Vice President of the "Confederacy" until its downfall. Mr. H. V. Johnson was a senator in the rebel congress in the first and second congresses, as was Mr. Graham, from North Carolina. Mr. Pool was a senator in the Legislature of North Carolina. Mr. Perry was a "Confederate States" judge. Mr. Manning was a volunteer aid to

*Credentials presented January 20, 1866, and he took his seat January 24, 1866.

General Beauregard at Fort Sumter and Manassas. Mr. Alcorn was in the Mississippi militia.

House of Representatives.

SCHUYLER COLFAX, of Indiana, *Speaker*.
Edward McPherson, of Pennsylvania, *Clerk*.

Maine—John Lynch, Sidney Perham, James G. Blaine, John H. Rice, Frederick A. Pike.

New Hampshire—Gilman Marston, Edward H. Rollins, James W. Patterson.

Vermont—Frederick E. Woodbridge, Justin S. Morrill, Portus Baxter.

Massachusetts—Thomas D. Eliot, Oakes Ames, Alexander H. Rice, Samuel Hooper, John B. Alley, Nathaniel P. Banks, George S. Boutwell, John D. Baldwin, William B. Washburn, Henry L. Dawes.

Rhode Island—Thomas A. Jenckes, Nathan F. Dixon.

Connecticut—Henry C. Deming, Samuel L. Warner, Augustus Brandegee, John H. Hubbard.

New York—Stephen Taber, Teunis G. Bergen, James Humphrey*, Morgan Jones, Nelson Taylor, Henry J. Raymond, John W. Chanler, James Brooks†, William A. Darling, William Radford, Charles H. Winfield, John H. Ketcham, Edwin N. Hubbell, Charles Goodyear, John A. Griswold, Robert S. Hale, Calvin T. Hulburd, James M. Marvin, Demas Hubbard, Jr., Addison H. Laflin, Roscoe Conkling, Sidney T. Holmes, Thomas T. Davis, Theodore M. Pomeroy, Daniel Morris, Giles W. Hotchkiss, Hamilton Ward, Roswell Hart, Burt Van Horn, James M. Humphrey, Henry Van Aernam.

New Jersey—John F. Starr, William A. Newell, Charles Sitgreaves, Andrew J. Rogers, Edwin R. V. Wright.

Pennsylvania—Samuel J. Randall, Charles O'Neill, Leonard Myers, William D. Kelley, M. Russell Thayer, Benjamin M. Boyer, John M. Broomall, Sydenham E. Ancona, Thaddeus Stevens, Myer Strouse, Philip Johnson, Charles Denison, Ulysses Mercur, George F. Miller, Adam J. Glossbrenner, Alexander H. Coffroth‡, Abraham A. Barker, Stephen F. Wilson, Glenni W. Scofield, Charles V. Culver, John L. Dawson, James K. Moorhead, Thomas Williams, George V. Lawrence.

Delaware—John A. Nicholson.

Maryland—Hiram McCullough, John L. Thomas, Jr., Charles E. Phelps, Francis Thomas, Benjamin G. Harris.

Ohio—Benjamin Eggleston, Rutherford B. Hayes, Robert C. Schenck, William Lawrence, Francis C. Le Blond, Reader W. Clarke, Samuel Shellabarger, James R. Hubbell, Ralph P. Buckland, James M. Ashley, Hezekiah S. Bundy, William E. Finck, Columbus Delano, Martin Welker, Tobias A. Plants, John A. Bingham, Ephraim R. Eckley, Rufus P. Spalding, James A. Garfield.

Kentucky—Lawrence S. Trimble, Burwell C. Ritter, Henry Grider, Aaron Harding, Lovell H. Rousseau, Green Clay Smith, George S. Shanklin, William H. Randall, Samuel McKee.

*Died June 16, 1866.
† Unseated April 6, 1866, and William E. Dodge qualified as his successor.
‡ Admitted to a seat on *prima facie* case February 19, 1866. July 9.—Committee reported in favor of Wm. H. Koontz, contestant.

Indiana—William E. Niblack, Michael C. Kerr, Ralph Hill, John H. Farquhar, George W. Julian, Ebenezer Dumont, Daniel W. Voorhees,* Godlove S. Orth, Schuyler Colfax, Joseph H. Defrees, Thomas N. Stillwell.

Illinois—John Wentworth, John F. Farnsworth, Ellihu B. Washburne, Abner C. Harding, Ebon C. Ingersoll, Burton C. Cook, Henry P. H. Bromwell, Shelby M. Cullom, Lewis W. Ross, Anthony Thornton, Samuel S. Marshall, Jehu Baker, Andrew J. Kuykendall, Samuel W. Moulton.

Missouri—John Hogan, Henry T. Blow, Thomas E. Noell, John R. Kelso, Joseph W. McClurg, Robert T. Van Horn, Benjamin F. Loan, John F. Benjamin, George W. Anderson.

Michigan—Fernando C. Beaman, Charles Upson, John W. Longyear, Thomas W. Ferry, Rowland E. Trowbridge, John F. Driggs.

Iowa—James F. Wilson, Hiram Price, William B. Allison, Josiah B. Grinnell, John A. Kasson, Asahel W. Hubbard.

Wisconsin—Halbert E. Paine, Ithamar C. Sloan, Amasa Cobb, Charles A. Eldridge, Philetus Sawyer, Walter D. McIndoe.

California—Donald C. McRuer, William Higby, John Bidwell.

Minnesota—William Windom, Ignatius Donnelly.

Oregon—James H. D. Henderson.

Kansas—Sidney Clarke.

West Virginia—Chester D. Hubbard, George R. Latham, Kellian V. Whaley.

Nevada—Delos R. Ashley.

Members chosen in the late Insurrectionary States.

Alabama—C. C. Langdon, George C. Freeman, Gen. Cullen A. Battle, Joseph W. Taylor, B. T. Pope, Thomas J. Foster.

Arkansas—William Byers, George H. Kyle, James M. Johnson.

Florida—F. McLeod.

Georgia—Solomon Cohen, Gen. Philip Cook, Hugh Buchanan, E. G. Cabiness, J. D. Matthews, J. H. Christy, Gen. W. T. Wofford.

Louisiana—Louis St. Martin, Jacob Barker, Robert C. Wickliffe, John E. King, John S. Ray. (Henry C. Warmoth claims seat as *delegate*, under universal suffrage election.)

Mississippi—Col. Arthur E. Reynolds, Col. Richard A. Pinson, James T. Harrison, A. M. West, E. G. Peyton.

North Carolina—Jesse R. Stubbs, Charles C. Clark, Thomas C. Fuller, Col. Josiah Turner, Jr., Bedford Brown, S. H. Walkup, Alex. H. Jones.

South Carolina—Col. John D. Kennedy, William Aiken, Gen. Samuel McGowan, James Farrow.

Tennessee—Nathaniel G. Taylor, Horace Maynard, William B. Stokes, Edmund Cooper, William B. Campbell, Samuel M. Arnell, Isaac R. Hawkins, John W. Leftwich.

Texas—

Virginia—W. H. B. Custis, Lucius H. Chandler, B. Johnson Barbour, Robert Ridgway, Beverly A. Davis, Alex. H. H. Stuart, Robert Y. Conrad, Daniel H. Hoge.

* Unseated February 23, 1866, and Henry D. Washburn qualified as his successor.

MEMORANDUM.

Of the *Alabama* delegation, Mr. Battle was a general in the rebel army, and Mr. Foster a representative in the first and second rebel congresses.

Of the *Georgia* delegation, Messrs. Cook and Wofford were generals in the rebel service.

Of the *Mississippi* delegation, Messrs. Reynolds and Pinson were colonels in the rebel service; Mr. Harrison was a member of the rebel provisional congress.

Of the *North Carolina* delegation, Mr. Fuller was a representative in the first rebel congress, and Mr. Turner was a colonel in the rebel army, and a representative in the second rebel congress; Mr. Brown was a member of the State convention which passed the secession ordinance in 1861, and voted for it.

Of the *South Carolina* delegation, Mr. Kennedy was colonel and Mr. McGowan brigadier general in the rebel army; Mr. Farrow was a representative in the first and second rebel congresses.

Of the *Virginia* delegation, Messrs. Stuart and Conrad were members of the secession convention of Virginia, in 1861, and continued to participate after the passage of the ordinance and the beginning of hostilities.

X.

VOTES IN THE HOUSE OF REPRESENTATIVES

ON VARIOUS POLITICAL DECLARATORY RESOLUTIONS.

Payment of the Public Debt.

December 5, 1865—Mr. Samuel J. Randall offered this resolution:

Resolved, That, as the sense of this House, the public debt created during the late rebellion was contracted upon the faith and honor of the nation; that it is sacred and inviolate, and must and ought to be paid, principal and interest; that any attempt to repudiate or in any manner to impair or scale the said debt shall be universally discountenanced, and promptly rejected by Congress if proposed.

Which was agreed to—yeas 162, nays 1, as follow:

YEAS—Messrs. Alley, Allison, Ames, *Ancona*, Anderson, James M. Ashley, Baker, Baldwin, Banks, Barker, Baxter, Beaman, Benjamin, *Bergen*, Bidwell, Bingham, Blaine, Blow, Boutwell, *Boyer*, Brandegee, Bromwell, Broomall, Buckland, Bundy, *Chanler*, Reader W. Clarke, Sidney Clarke, Cobb, Conkling, Cook, Cullom, Culver, Darling, Davis, Dawes, *Dawson*, Defrees, Delano, Deming, *Denison*, Dixon, Donnelly, Driggs, Dumont, Eckley, Eggleston, Eliot, Farnsworth, Farquhar, Ferry, *Finck*, Garfield, *Glossbrenner*, *Goodyear*, Grinnell, Griswold, Hale, Abner C. Harding, Hart, Hayes, Henderson, Higby, Hill, *Hogan*, Holmes, Hooper, Hotchkiss, Asahel W. Hubbard, Chester D. Hubbard, Demas Hubbard, jr., John H. Hubbard, *Edwin N. Hubbell*, James R. Hubbell, Hulburd, James Humphrey, *James M. Humphrey*, Ingersoll, Jenckes, *Johnson*, Julian, Kasson, Kelley, Kelso, *Kerr*, Ketcham, Kuykendall, Laflin, Latham, George V. Lawrence, William Lawrence, Loan, Longyear, Marston, Marvin, McClurg, *McCullough*, McIndoe, McKee, McRuer, Mercur, Miller, Moorhead, Morrill, Morris, Moulton, Myers, Newell, *Niblack*, *Nicholson*, *Noell*, O'Neill, Orth, Paine, Patterson, Perham, Phelps, Pike, Plants, Pomeroy, Price, *Radford*, *Samuel J. Randall*, William H. Randall, Raymond, Alexander H. Rice, *Rogers*, Rollins, *Ross*, Sawyer, Schenck, Scofield, *Shanklin*, Shellabarger, *Sitgreaves*, Sloan, Smith, Spalding, Starr, Stevens, Stillwell, *Strouse*, *Taber*, Thayer, Francis Thomas, John L. Thomas, jr., *Thornton*, Trowbridge, Upson, Burt Van Horn, Ward, Warner, Ellihu B. Washburne, William B. Washburn, Welker, Wentworth, Whaley, Williams, Wilson, Windom, *Winfield*, *Wright*—162.

NAY—Mr. *Trimble*.

NOT VOTING—Messrs. *Brooks*, *Eldridge*, *Grider*, *Aaron Harding*, *Le Blond*, Lynch, *Marshall*, John H. Rice, *Ritter*, *Taylor*, Van Aernam, R. T. Van Horn, S. F. Wilson, F. E. Woodbridge—14.

"Treason Ought to be Punished."

December 14, 1865—Mr. Henderson, of Oregon, submitted the following resolution:

Resolved, That treason against the United States Government is a crime that ought to be punished.

Mr. Hale moved it be laid on the table which was disagreed to; and, under the previous question, it was then passed—yeas 153, nays none, as follow:

YEAS—Messrs. Alley, Ames, *Ancona*, Anderson, James M. Ashley, Baker, Baldwin, Banks, Barker, Beaman, Benjamin, *Bergen*, Bidwell, Bingham, Blaine, Blow, Boutwell, *Boyer*, Bromwell, *Brooks*, Broomall, Buckland, Bundy, Reader W. Clarke, Sidney Clarke, Cobb, Conkling, Cook, Cullom, Darling, Davis, Dawes, *Dawson*, Defrees, Deming, *Denison*, Dixon, Donnelly, Driggs, Eckley, Eggleston, *Eldridge*, Eliot, Farquhar, Ferry, *Finck*, *Glossbrenner*, *Grider*, Grinnell, Griswold, Hale, *Aaron Harding*, Abner C. Harding, Hart, Hayes, Henderson, Higby, *Hogan*, Holmes, Hooper, Hotchkiss, Asahel W. Hubbard, Chester D. Hubbard, Demas Hubbard, jr., John H. Hubbard, *Edwin N. Hubbell*, James R. Hubbell, Hulburd, James Humphrey, *James M. Humphrey*, Ingersoll, Jenckes, *Johnson*, Julian, Kasson, Kelley, Kelso, *Kerr*, Ketcham, Kuykendall, George V. Lawrence, William Lawrence, *Le Blond*, Loan, Longyear, Lynch, *Marshall*, Marston, Marvin, McClurg, *McCullough*, McIndoe, McKee, McRuer, Mercur, Moorhead, Morrill, Morris, Myers, *Nicholson*, *Noell*, O'Neill, Orth, Paine, Perham, Pike, Plants, Price, *Radford*, *Samuel J. Randall*, William H. Randall, Alexander H. Rice, John H. Rice, *Ritter*, *Rogers*, Rollins, *Ross*, Rousseau, Sawyer, Scofield, *Shanklin*, Shellabarger, *Sitgreaves*, Sloan, Smith, Spalding, Starr, Stevens, *Strouse*, *Taber*, *Taylor*, Thayer, John L. Thomas, jr., *Thornton*, *Trimble*, Trowbridge, Upson, Van Aernam, Burt Van Horn, *Voorhees*, Ward, Warner, Ellihu B. Washburne, William B. Washburn, Welker, Wentworth, Whaley, Williams, James F. Wilson, Stephen F. Wilson, Windom, *Winfield*, Woodbridge—153.

NAYS—None.

Representation of the late so-called Confederate States.

December 14, 1865—Mr. James F. Wilson submitted this resolution:

Resolved, That all papers which may be offered relative to the representation of the late so-called Confederate States of America, or either of them, shall be referred to the joint committee of fifteen without debate, and no members shall be admitted from either of said so-called States, until Congress shall declare such States or either of them entitled to representation.

Which was passed—yeas 107, nays 56, as follow:

YEAS—Messrs. Alley, Allison, Ames, Anderson, James M. Ashley, Baker, Baldwin, Banks, Barker, Baxter, Beaman, Benjamin, Bidwell, Bingham, Blaine, Boutwell, Brandegee, Bromwell, Broomall, Buckland, Bundy, Reader W. Clarke, Sidney Clarke, Cobb, Conkling, Cook, Cullom, Defrees, Deming, Dixon, Donnelly, Driggs, Eckley, Eliot, Ferry, Grinnell, Abner C. Harding, Hart, Hayes, Henderson, Higby, Holmes, Hooper, Hotchkiss, Asahel W. Hubbard, Chester D. Hubbard, Demas Hubbard, jr., John H. Hubbard, Hulburd, Ingersoll, Jenckes, Julian, Kelley, Kelso, Ketcham, Kuykendall, Laflin, George V. Lawrence, William Lawrence, Loan, Longyear, Marston, Marvin, McClurg, McIndoe, McKee, McRuer, Mercur, Moorhead, Morrill, Morris, Moulton, Myers, Newell, O'Neill, Orth, Paine, Patterson, Perham, Pike, Plants, Price, Alexander H. Rice, John H. Rice, Rollins, Sawyer, Scofield, Shellabarger, Sloan, Spalding, Starr, Stevens, Thayer, Trowbridge, Upson, Van Aernam, Burt Van Horn, Ward, Warner, Ellihu B. Washburne, William B. Washburn, Welker, Wentworth, Williams, James F. Wilson, Stephen F. Wilson, Windom—107.

NAYS—Messrs. *Ancona*, *Bergen*, Blow, *Boyer*, *Brooks*, Darling, Davis, *Dawson*, *Denison*, *Eldridge*, Farquhar, *Finck*, *Glossbrenner*, *Grider*, Griswold, Hale, *Harding*, Hill, *Hogan*, *Edwin N. Hubbell*, James R. Hubbell, James Humphrey, *James M. Humphrey*, *Johnson*, Kasson, *Kerr*, Latham, *Le Blond*, *Marshall*, *Niblack*, *Nicholson*, *Noell*, Phelps, *Radford*, *Samuel J. Randall*, William H. Randall, Raymond, *Ritter*, *Rogers*, *Ross*, Rousseau, *Shanklin*, *Sitgreaves*, Smith, Stillwell, *Strouse*, *Taber*, *Taylor*, Francis Thomas, John L. Thomas, jr., *Thornton*, *Trimble*, *Voorhees*, Whaley, *Winfield*, *Wright*—56.

Elective Franchise in the States.

December 18, 1865—Mr. Thornton submitted this resolution:

Whereas, at the first movement toward independence, the Congress of the United States instructed the several States to institute governments of their own, and left each State to decide for itself the conditions for the enjoyment of the elective franchise; and whereas during the period of the confederacy there continued to exist a very great diversity in the qualifications of electors in the several States; and whereas the Constitution of the United States recognizes these diversities when it enjoins that in the choice of members of the House of Representatives the electors in each State shall have the qualifications requisite for the electors of the most numerous branch of the State legislatures; and whereas, after the formation of the Constitution, it remained, as before, the uniform usage of each State to enlarge the body of its electors according to its own judgment; and whereas so fixed was the reservation in the habits of the people, and so unquestioned has been the interpretation of the Constitution, that during the civil war the late President never harbored the purpose, certainly never avowed the purpose, of disregarding it: Therefore,

Resolved, That any extension of the elective franchise to persons in the States, either by act of the President or of Congress, would be an assumption of power which nothing in the Constitution of the United States would warrant, and that, to avoid every danger of conflict, the settlement of this question should be referred to the several States.

Mr. Ellihu B. Washburne moved that it be laid on the table; which was agreed to—yeas 111, nays 46, as follow:

YEAS—Messrs. Alley, Allison, Ames, Anderson, James M. Ashley, Baker, Baldwin, Banks, Barker, Baxter, Beaman, Benjamin, Bidwell, Bingham, Blow, Boutwell, Brandegee, Broomall, Buckland, Bundy, Reader W. Clarke, Sidney Clarke, Conkling, Cook, Darling, Dawes, Defrees, Delano, Deming, Dixon, Driggs, Dumont, Eckley, Eggleston, Eliot, Farnsworth, Garfield, Grinnell, Hale, Abner C. Harding, Hart, Hayes, Henderson, Higby, Holmes, Hooper, Hotchkiss, Asahel W. Hubbard, Demas Hubbard, jr., John H. Hubbard, James R. Hubbell, Hulburd, James Humphrey, Jenckes, Julian, Kelley, Kelso, Ketcham, Laflin, Latham, George V. Lawrence, William Lawrence, Loan, Longyear, Lynch, Marston, Marvin, McClurg, McIndoe, McKee, McRuer, Mercur, Miller, Moorhead, Morrill, Moulton, Myers, Newell, O'Neill, Paine, Patterson, Perham, Pike, Plants, Price, Raymond, Alexander H. Rice, John H. Rice, Rollins, Sawyer, Schenck, Scofield, Shellabarger, Spalding, Starr, Stevens, Thayer, Trowbridge, Upson, Van Aernam, Burt Van Horn, Robert T. Van Horn, Ward, Warner, Ellihu B. Washburne, William B. Washburn, Welker, Wentworth, Williams, James F. Wilson, Stephen F. Wilson—111.

NAYS—Messrs. *Ancona*, *Bergen*, *Boyer*, Bromwell, *Brooks*, *Chanler*, *Dawson*, *Denison*, *Eldridge*, Farquhar, *Finck*, *Goodyear*, *Grider*, *Aaron Harding*, Hill, *Hogan*, Chester D. Hubbard, *Edwin D. Hubbell*, Ingersoll, *Johnson*, *Kerr*, Kuykendall, *Marshall*, *McCullough*, *Niblack*, *Nicholson*, *Noell*, Orth, *Radford*, *Samuel J. Randall*, William H. Randall, *Ritter*, *Rogers*, *Ross*, Rousseau, *Shanklin*, *Sitgreaves*, Smith, Stillwell, *Strouse*, *Taber*, *Taylor*, *Thornton*, *Trimble*, Whaley, *Wright*—46.

February 26, 1866—Mr. Defrees offered this resolution, which was laid over:

Resolved, That it is the opinion of this House that Congress has no constitutional right to fix the qualification of electors in the several States.

May 21—It was referred to the Committee on the Judiciary—yeas 86, nays 30. The nays were:

Messrs. *Ancona*, *Dawson*, Defrees, *Denison*, *Eldridge*, *Glossbrenner*, *Goodyear*, *Grider*, *Aaron Harding*, *Hogan*, *Edwin N. Hubbell*, *James M. Humphrey*, *Kerr*, Kuykendall, George V. Lawrence, *Le Blond*, *McCullough*, *Niblack*, *Nicholson*, *Samuel J. Randall*, *Ritter*, *Rogers*, *Ross*, *Sitgreaves*, Stillwell, *Taber*, *Taylor*, Henry D. Washburn, *Winfield*, *Wright*—30.

Test Oath.

December 18, 1865—Mr. Hill submitted this resolution:

Resolved, That the act of July 2, 1862, prescribing an oath to be taken and subscribed by persons elected or appointed to office under the Government of the United States before entering upon the duties of such office, is of binding force and effect on all departments of the public service, and should in no instance be dispensed with.

Mr. Finck moved that it be tabled; which was disagreed to—yeas 32, nays 126, as follow:

YEAS—Messrs. *Ancona*, *Bergen*, *Boyer*, *Brooks*, *Chanler*, *Dawson*, *Denison*, *Eldridge*, *Finck*, *Grider*, *Aaron Harding*, *Harris*, *Hogan*, *Edwin N. Hubbell*, *Johnson*, *Kerr*, Latham, *Marshall*, *McCullough*, *Niblack*, *Nicholson*, *Noell*, *Samuel J. Randall*, *Ritter*, *Rogers*, *Ross*, *Shanklin*, *Sitgreaves*, *Strouse*, *Taber*, *Thornton*, *Trimble*—32.

NAYS—Messrs. Alley, Allison, Ames, Anderson, James M. Ashley, Baker, Baldwin, Banks, Barker, Baxter, Beaman, Benjamin, Bidwell, Bingham, Blow, Boutwell, Brandegee, Bromwell, Broomall, Buckland, Bundy, Reader W. Clarke, Sidney Clarke, Conkling, Cook, Cullom, Darling, Davis, Dawes, Defrees, Delano, Deming, Dixon, Driggs, Dumont, Eggleston, Eliot, Farnsworth, Farquhar, Ferry, Garfield, Grinnell, Hale, Abner C. Harding, Hart, Hayes, Henderson, Higby, Hill, Holmes, Hooper, Hotchkiss, Asahel W. Hubbard, Demas Hubbard, jr., John H. Hubbard, James R. Hubbell, Hulburd, James Humphrey, Ingersoll, Jenckes, Julian, Kasson, Kelley, Kelso, Ketcham, Kuykendall, Laflin, George V. Lawrence, William Lawrence, Loan, Longyear, Lynch, Marston, Marvin, McClurg, McIndoe, McKee, McRuer, Mercur, Miller, Moorhead, Morrill, Myers, Newell, O'Neill, Orth, Paine, Patterson, Perham, Phelps, Pike, Plants, Price, William H. Randall, Raymond, Alexander H. Rice, John H. Rice, Rollins, Rousseau, Sawyer, Schenck, Scofield, Shellabarger, Smith, Spalding, Starr, Stevens, Stillwell, Thayer, John L. Thomas, Trowbridge, Upson, Van

Aernam, Burt Van Horn, Robert T. Van Horn, Ward, Warner, Ellihu B. Washburne, William B. Washburn, Welker, Wentworth, Whaley, Williams, James F. Wilson, Stephen F. Wilson—125.

It then passed.

Test Oath for Lawyers.

January 15, 1866—Mr. Stevens offered this resolution:

Resolved, That the Committee on the Judiciary be instructed to inquire into the expediency of so amending the act of January 24, 1865, relative to the test oath, as to allow attorneys-at-law to practice their profession without taking said oath, on an equal footing with the members of all other professions.

Which was agreed to—yeas 82, nays, 77, as follow:

YEAS—Messrs. Alley, Ames, *Ancona*, *Bergen*, Blow, *Boyer*, *Brooks*, Buckland, Bundy, *Chanler*, Cobb, Cook, Darling, Davis, *Dawson*, *Denison*, Driggs, *Eldridge*, Farquhar, Ferry, *Finck*, *Glossbrenner*, *Goodyear*, *Grider*, Griswold, Hale, *Aaron Harding*, Abner C. Harding, Higby, Hill, *Hogan*, Hooper, John H. Hubbard, *Edwin N. Hubbell*, James R. Hubbell, James Humphrey, *James M. Humphrey*, Ingersoll, *Johnson*, Kasson, *Kerr*, Kuykendall, Latham, George V. Lawrence, *Le Blond*, *Marshall*, Marston, Marvin, *McCullough*, McRuer, Miller, Moorhead, *Niblack*, *Nicholson*, *Noell*, Orth, Phelps, Pike, Plants, Pomeroy, Price, *Radford*, *Samuel J. Randall*, Raymond, *Ritter*, *Rogers*, *Ross*, Sawyer, *Shanklin*, *Sitgreaves*, Smith, Stevens, Stillwell, *Strouse*, *Taber*, *Taylor*, Thayer, Francis Thomas, *Thornton*, *Trimble*, Trowbridge, *Winfield*—82.

NAYS—Messrs. Allison, Anderson, Delos R. Ashley, James M. Ashley, Baker, Banks, Barker, Baxter, Beaman, Benjamin, Bidwell, Bingham, Blaine, Boutwell, Brandegee, Bromwell, Reader W. Clarke, Sidney Clarke, Conkling, Dawes, Defrees, Delano, Deming, Dixon, Donnelly, Eckley, Eggleston, Eliot, Farnsworth, Grinnell, Hart, Hayes, Henderson, Holmes, Asahel W. Hubbard, Demas Hubbard, jr., Hulburd, Jenckes, Julian, Kelley, Kelso, Laflin, William Lawrence, Loan, Longyear, Lynch, McClurg, McKee, Mercur, Morrill, Morris, Moulton, O'Neill, Paine, Perham, Randall, Alexander H. Rice, John H. Rice, Rollins, Schenck, Scofield, Shellabarger, Sloan, Spalding, Starr, John L. Thomas, jr., Upson, Van Aernam, Burt Van Horn, Ward, Ellihu B. Washburne, William B. Washburn, Welker, Williams, James F. Wilson, Windom, Woodbridge—77.

Endorsement of the President's Policy.

December 21, 1865—Mr. Voorhees submitted these resolutions, which were postponed till January 9, 1866:

Resolved, That the message of the President of the United States, delivered at the present Congress, is regarded by this body as an able and patriotic State paper.

2. That the principles therein advocated for the restoration of the Union are the safest and most practicable that can now be applied to our disordered domestic affairs.

3. That no State, or any number of States confederated together, can in any manner sunder their connection with the Federal Union, except by a total subversion of our present system of government; and that the President in enunciating this doctrine in his late message has but given expression to the sentiments of all those who deny the right or power of a State to secede.

4. That the President is entitled to the thanks of Congress and the country for his faithful, wise, and successful efforts to restore civil government, law, and order to those States whose citizens were lately in insurrection against the federal authority; and we hereby pledge ourselves to aid, assist, and uphold him in the policy which he has adopted to give harmony, peace, and union to the country.

January 9—Mr. Bingham offered this substitute:

Resolved, That this House has an abiding confidence in the President, and that in the future, as in the past, he will co-operate with Congress in restoring to equal position and rights with the other States in the Union all the States lately in insurrection.

Mr. Bingham moved to refer the resolutions and the substitute to the Committee on Reconstruction; which was agreed to—yeas 107, nays 42, as follow:

YEAS—Messrs. Allison, Ames, Anderson, James M. Ashley, Baker, Baldwin, Banks, Baxter, Beaman, Benjamin, Bidwell, Bingham, Blaine, Boutwell, Brandegee, Bromwell, Broomall, Buckland, Bundy, Reader W. Clarke, Sidney Clarke, Cobb, Conkling, Cook, Cullom, Davis, Dawes, Defrees, Deming, Donnelly, Driggs, Eggleston, Eliot, Ferry, Garfield, Grinnell, Hale, A. C. Harding, Hart, Hayes, Henderson, Higby, Hill, Holmes, Hooper, Asahel W. Hubbard, Chester D. Hubbard, John H. Hubbard, James R. Hubbell, Hulburd, Ingersoll, Jenckes, Julian, Kelley, Kelso, Ketcham, Kuykendall, Laflin, Latham, William Lawrence, Loan, Longyear, Lynch, Marvin, McClurg, McKee, McRuer, Mercur, Miller, Moorhead, Morrill, Morris, Moulton, Myers, Newell, O'Neill, Orth, Paine, Patterson, Perham, Phelps, Pike, Plants, Price, Alexander H. Rice, John H. Rice, Rollins, Sawyer, Scofield, Shellabarger, Smith, Spalding, Stevens, Stillwell, Thayer, John L. Thomas, jr., Trowbridge, Upson, Van Aernam, Burt Van Horn, Warner, Ellihu B. Washburne, William B. Washburn, Welker, Williams, S. F. Wilson, Windom—107.

NAYS—Messrs. *Ancona*, *Bergen*, *Boyer*, *Brooks*, *Chanler*, Darling, *Dawson*, *Denison*, *Eldridge*, *Glossbrenner*, *Grider*, *Aaron Harding*, *Hogan*, *J. M. Humphrey*, *Kerr*, *Le Blond*, *Marshall*, *Niblack*, *Nicholson*, *Noell*, *Radford*, *Samuel J. Randall*, Raymond, *Ritter*, *Rogers*, *Ross*, *Strouse*, *Taber*, *Taylor*, *Voorhees*, *Winfield*, *Wright*—42.

Withdrawal of Military Force.

January 8, 1866—Mr. Thos. Williams submitted this resolution:

Resolved, That in order to the maintenance of the national authority and the protection of the loyal citizens of the seceding States, it is the sense of this House that the military forces of the Government should not be withdrawn from those States until the two Houses of Congress shall have ascertained and declared their further presence there no longer necessary.

Which was passed—yeas 94, nays 37, as follow:

YEAS—Messrs. Ames, Anderson, Delos R. Ashley, Baker, Banks, Baxter, Beaman, Benjamin, Bidwell, Bingham, Blaine, Boutwell, Brandegee, Bromwell, Broomall, Bundy, Reader W. Clarke, Sidney Clarke, Cobb, Conkling, Cook, Cullom, Defrees, Deming, Donnelly, Driggs, Eggleston, Eliot, Farnsworth, Farquhar, Ferry, Garfield, Grinnell, Abner C. Harding, Hart, Hayes, Henderson, Higby, Hill, Holmes, Hooper, Hubbard, Chester D. Hubbard, John H. Hubbard, James R. Hubbell, Hulburd, Jenckes, Julian, Kelley, Kelso, Ketcham, Kuykendall, Laflin, William Lawrence, Loan, Longyear, Lynch, Marvin, McClurg, McKee, McRuer, Mercur, Miller, Moorhead, Morrill, Morris, Moulton, Myers, O'Neill, Orth, Paine, Patterson, Plants, Price, Alexander H. Rice, Rollins, Sawyer, Scofield, Shellabarger, Spalding, Stevens, Thayer, Trowbridge, Upson, Van Aerman, Burt Van Horn, Robert T. Van Horn, Ward, Warner, Ellihu B. Washburne, Welker, Williams, Stephen F. Wilson, Windom—94.

NAYS—Messrs. *Ancona*, *Bergen*, *Boyer*, *Brooks*, *Chanler*, Davis, *Dawson*, Delano, *Denison*, *Eldridge*, *Glossbrenner*, *Grider*, *A. Harding*, *Hogan*, *Edwin N. Hubbell*, *James M. Humphrey*, *Kerr*, Latham, *Le Blond*, *Marshall*, *Niblack*, *Nicholson*, *Noell*, *Samuel J. Randall*, Raymond, *Ritter*, *Rogers*, *Ross*, Smith, Stillwell, *Strouse*, *Taber*, *Taylor*, *Voorhees*, *Winfield*, Woodbridge, *Wright*—37.

The Legal Effect of Rebellion—the Duty of Congress—the Writ of Habeas Corpus, and Thanks to the President.

February 19, 1866—Mr. Longyear submitted these resolutions:

Resolved, That in the language of the proclamation of the President of May 29, 1865, "the rebellion which was waged by a portion of the people of the United States against the properly constituted authorities of the Government thereof in the most violent and revolting form, but whose organized and armed forces have now been almost entirely overcome, has in its revolutionary progress deprived the people" of the States in which it was organized "of all civil government."

2. That whenever the people of any State are thus "deprived of all civil government," it becomes the duty of Congress, by appropriate legislation, to enable them to organize a State government, and in the language of the Constitution "to guarantee to such State a republican form of government."

3. That it is the deliberate sense of this House that the condition of the rebel States fully justifies the President in maintaining the suspension of the writ of *habeas corpus* in those States.

4. That it is the deliberate sense of this House that the condition of the rebel States fully justifies the President in maintaining military possession and control thereof, and that the President is entitled to the thanks of the nation for employing the war power for the protection of Union citizens and the freedmen in those States.

Mr. Finck moved they be laid on the table; which was disagreed to—yeas 29, nays 119, as follow:

YEAS—Messrs. *Ancona, Bergen, Brooks, Chanler, Dawson, Eldridge, Finck, Glossbrenner, Goodyear, Grider, Aaron Harding, Hogan, James M. Humphrey, Kerr, Le Blond, Marshall, McCullough, Niblack, Nicholson, Radford, Samuel J. Randall, Ritter, Rogers, Ross, Shanklin, Taber, Thornton, Trimble, Voorhees*—29.

NAYS—Messrs. Allison, Anderson, Delos R. Ashley, James M. Ashley, Baker, Baldwin, Banks, Baxter, Beaman, Benjamin, Bidwell, Bingham, Blaine, Boutwell, Bromwell, Broomall, Reader W. Clarke, Sidney Clarke, Cobb, Conkling, Cook, Cullom, Dawes, Deming, Donnelly, Driggs, Eckley, Eggleston, Eliot, Farnsworth, Farquhar, Ferry, Garfield, Grinnell, Griswold, Hale, Abner C. Harding, Hayes, Henderson, Higby, Holmes, Hooper, Asahel W. Hubbard, Chester D. Hubbard, Demas Hubbard, John H. Hubbard, James R. Hubbell, Hulburd, James Humphrey, Ingersoll, Jenckes, Julian, Kasson, Kelley, Kelso, Ketcham, Kuykendall, Laflin, Latham, George V. Lawrence, William Lawrence, Loan, Longyear, Lynch, Marvin, McClurg, McIndoe, McKee, McRuer, Mercur, Moorhead, Morrill, Morris, Moulton, Myers, O'Neill, Orth, Paine, Patterson, Perham, Phelps, Pike, Plants, Pomeroy, Price, William H. Randall, Raymond, Alexander H. Rice, John H. Rice, Rollins, Rousseau, Sawyer, Schenck, Scofield, Shellabarger, Sloan, Smith, Spalding, Starr, Stevens, Thayer, John L. Thomas, Trowbridge, Upson, Van Aernam, Burt Van Horn, Robert T. Van Horn, Ward, Warner, Ellihu B. Washburne, William B. Washburn, Welker, Wentworth, Whaley, Williams, James F. Wilson, Stephen F. Wilson, Windom, Woodbridge—119.

A division of the question having been demanded, the *first* resolution was agreed to—yeas 102, nays 36, as follow:

YEAS—Messrs. Allison, Anderson, Delos R. Ashley, James M. Ashley, Baker, Baldwin, Banks, Baxter, Beaman, Benjamin, Bidwell, Bingham, Blaine, Boutwell, Brandegee, Bromwell, Broomall, Reader W. Clarke, Sidney Clarke, Cobb, Conkling, Cook, Defrees, Deming, Donnelly, Driggs, Eckley, Eggleston, Eliot, Farnsworth, Ferry, Garfield, Grinnell, Abner C. Harding, Hayes, Henderson, Higby, Holmes, Hooper, Asahel W. Hubbard, Demas Hubbard, John H. Hubbard, James R. Hubbell, Hulburd, Ingersoll, Jenckes, Julian, Kasson, Kelley, Kelso, Ketcham, Kuykendall, Laflin, William Lawrence, Loan, Longyear, Lynch, Marston, Marvin, McClurg, McIndoe, McKee, McRuer, Moorhead, Morrill, Morris, Moulton, Myers, O'Neill, Orth, Paine, Perham, Pike, Plants, Pomeroy, Price, William H. Randall, Alexander H. Rice, John H. Rice, Rollins, Schenck, Scofield, Shellabarger, Sloan, Spalding, Starr, Stevens, Thayer, Trowbridge, Upson, Van Aernam, Ward, Warner, Ellihu B. Washburne, William B. Washburn, Welker, Wentworth, Williams, James F. Wilson, Stephen F. Wilson, Windom, Woodbridge—102.

NAYS.—Messrs. *Ancona, Bergen, Boyer, Brooks, Chanler, Dawson, Eldridge, Finck, Glossbrenner, Goodyear, Grider,* Hale, *Aaron Harding, Hogan,* Chester D. Hubbard, *Kerr,* Latham, *McCullough,* Mercur, *Niblack, Nicholson,* Phelps, *Radford, Samuel J. Randall,* Raymond, *Ritter, Rogers, Ross,* Rousseau, *Shanklin,* Smith, *Taber,* John L. Thomas, *Thornton, Trimble,* Whaley—36.

The *second* resolution was agreed to—yeas 104, nays 33, as follow:

YEAS—Messrs. Anderson, Delos R. Ashley, James M. Ashley, Baker, Baldwin, Banks, Baxter, Beaman, Benjamin, Bidwell, Bingham, Boutwell, Brandegee, Bromwell, Broomall, Reader W. Clarke, Cobb, Conkling, Cook, Cullom, Defrees, Deming, Donnelly, Driggs, Eckley, Eggleston, Eliot, Farnsworth, Ferry, Garfield, Grinnell, Griswold, Hale, Abner C. Harding, Hayes, Henderson, Higby, Holmes, Hooper, Hotchkiss, Asahel W. Hubbard, Chester D. Hubbard, Demas Hubbard, John H. Hubbard, James R. Hubbell, Hulburd, Ingersoll, Jenckes, Julian, Kelley, Kelso, Ketcham, Laflin, William Lawrence, Loan, Longyear, Lynch, Marvin, McClurg, McIndoe, McKee, McRuer, Mercur, Moorhead, Morrill, Morris, Moulton, Myers, O'Neill, Orth, Paine, Perham, Pike, Plants, Pomeroy, Price, William H. Randall, Alexander H. Rice, John H. Rice, Rollins, Sawyer, Schenck, Scofield, Shellabarger, Sloan, Spalding, Starr, Stevens, Thayer, John L. Thomas, Trowbridge, Upson, Van Aernam, Burt Van Horn, Ward, Ellihu B. Washburne, William B. Washburn, Welker, Wentworth, Williams, James F. Wilson, Stephen F. Wilson, Windom, Woodbridge—104.

NAYS—Messrs. *Ancona, Bergen, Boyer, Brooks, Chanler, Dawson, Eldridge, Finck, Glossbrenner, Goodyear, Grider, Aaron Harding, Hogan,* Kasson, *Kerr,* Latham, *Le Blond, McCullough, Niblack, Nicholson,* Phelps, *Radford, Samuel J. Randall,* Raymond, *Ritter, Rogers, Ross, Shanklin,* Smith, *Taber, Thornton, Trimble,* Whaley—33.

The *third* resolution was agreed to—yeas 120, nays 26, as follow:

YEAS—Messrs. Allison, Anderson, James M. Ashley, Baker, Baldwin, Banks, Baxter, Beaman, Benjamin, Bidwell, Bingham, Blaine, Boutwell, Brandegee, Bromwell, Broomall, Reader W. Clarke, Sidney Clarke, Cobb, Conkling, Cook, Cullom, Dawes, Defrees, Deming, Donnelly, Driggs, Eckley, Eggleston, Eliot, Farnsworth, Farquhar, Ferry, Garfield, Grinnell, Griswold, Hale, Abner C. Harding, Hayes, Henderson, Higby, Holmes, Hooper, Hotchkiss, Chester D. Hubbard, Demas Hubbard, John H. Hubbard, James R. Hubbell, Hulburd, James Humphrey, Ingersoll, Jenckes, Julian, Kasson, Kelley, Kelso, Ketcham, Kuykendall, Laflin, Latham, George V. Lawrence, William Lawrence, Loan, Longyear, Lynch, Marston, Marvin, McClurg, McIndoe, McKee, McRuer, Mercur, Moorhead, Morrill, Morris, Moulton, Myers, O'Neill, Orth, Paine, Patterson, Perham, Phelps, Pike, Plants, Pomeroy, Price, William H. Randall, Raymond, Alexander H. Rice, John H. Rice, Rollins, Sawyer, Schenck, Scofield, Shellabarger, Sloan, Smith, Spalding, Starr, Stevens, Thayer, John L. Thomas, Trowbridge, Upson, Van Aernam, Burt Van Horn, Robert T. Van Horn, Ward, Warner, Ellihu B. Washburne, William B. Washburn, Welker, Wentworth, Whaley, Williams, James F. Wilson, Stephen F. Wilson, Windom, Woodbridge—120.

NAYS—Messrs. *Ancona, Bergen, Boyer, Brooks, Chanler, Dawson, Eldridge, Finck, Glossbrenner, Goodyear, Grider, Aaron Harding, James M. Humphrey, Kerr, Le Blond, McCullough,* Newell, *Niblack, Radford, Ritter, Rogers, Ross, Shanklin, Taber, Thornton, Trimble*—26.

The first clause of the *fourth* resolution was agreed to—yeas 118, nays 23, as follow:

YEAS—Messrs. Allison, Delos R. Ashley, James M. Ashley, Baker, Baldwin, Banks, Baxter, Beaman, Benjamin, Bidwell, Bingham, Blaine, Boutwell, Brandegee, Bromwell, Broomall, Reader W. Clarke, Sidney Clarke, Cobb, Conkling, Cook, Cullom, Dawes, Defrees, Deming, Driggs, Eckley, Eggleston, Eliot, Farnsworth, Farquhar, Ferry, Garfield, Grinnell, Griswold, Hale, Abner C. Harding, Hayes, Henderson, Higby, Holmes, Hooper, Hotchkiss, Chester D. Hubbard, Demas Hubbard, jr., John H. Hubbard, James R. Hubbell, Hulburd, James Humphrey, Ingersoll, Jenckes, Julian, Kasson, Kelley, Kelso, Ketcham, Kuykendall, Laflin, Latham, George V. Lawrence, William Lawrence, Loan, Longyear, Lynch, Marston, Marvin, McClurg, McIndoe, McKee, McRuer, Mercur, Moorhead, Morris, Moulton, Myers, O'Neill, Orth, Paine, Patterson, Perham, Phelps, Plants, Pomeroy, Price, William H. Randall, Raymond, Alexander H. Rice, John H. Rice, Rollins, Rousseau, Sawyer, Schenck, Scofield, Shellabarger, Sloan, Smith, Starr, Stevens, Thayer, Francis Thomas, John L. Thomas, jr., Trowbridge, Upson, Van Aernam, Burt Van Horn, Robert T. Van Horn, Ward,

Warner, Elihu B. Washburne, William B. Washburn, Welker, Wentworth, Whaley, Williams, James F. Wilson, Stephen F. Wilson, Windom, Woodbridge—118.

NAYS—Messrs. *Ancona, Bergen, Boyer, Brooks, Dawson, Eldridge, Finck, Glossbrenner, Goodyear, Aaron Harding, James M. Humphrey, McCullough, Niblack, Nicholson, Radford, Samuel J. Randall, Ritter, Rogers, Ross, Shanklin, Taber, Thornton, Trimble*—23.

The second clause of the *fourth* resolution was agreed to—yeas 135, nays 8, as follow:

YEAS—Messrs. Allison, *Ancona*, Anderson, James M. Ashley, Baker, Baldwin, Banks, Baxter, Beaman, Benjamin, *Bergen*, Bidwell, Bingham, Blaine, Boutwell, *Boyer*, Brandegee, Bromwell, *Brooks*, Broomall, Reader W. Clarke, Sidney Clarke, Cobb, Conkling, Cook, Cullom, *Dawson*, Defrees, Deming, Donnelly, Driggs, Eckley, Eggleston, *Eldridge*, Eliot, Farnsworth, Farquhar, Ferry, *Finck*, Garfield, *Glossbrenner*, *Goodyear*, Griswold, Hale, Abner C. Harding, Hayes, Higby, Holmes, Hooper, Hotchkiss, Chester D. Hubbard, Demas Hubbard, John H. Hubbard, James R. Hubbell, Hulburd, James Humphrey, *James M. Humphrey*, Ingersoll, Jenckes, *Johnson*, Julian, Kasson, Kelley, Kelso, *Kerr*, Ketcham, Kuykendall, Laflin, Latham, George V. Lawrence, William Lawrence, *Le Blond*, Loan, Longyear, Lynch, Marston, Marvin, McClurg, McIndoe, McKee, Mercur, Moorhead, Morrill, Morris, Moulton, Myers, O'Neill, Orth, Paine, Patterson, Perham, Phelps, Pike, Plants, Pomeroy, Price, *Radford, Samuel J. Randall*, William H. Randall, Raymond, Alexander H. Rice, John H. Rice, Rollins, Rousseau, Sawyer, Schenck, Scofield, Shellabarger, Sloan, Smith, Spalding, Starr, Stevens, *Taber*, Thayer, Francis Thomas, John L. Thomas, *Thornton*, Trowbridge, Upson, Van Aernam, Burt Van Horn, Robert T. Van Horn, Ward, Warner, Elihu B. Washburne, William B. Washburn, Welker, Wentworth, Whaley, Williams, James F. Wilson, Stephen F. Wilson, Windom, Woodbridge—135.

NAYS—Messrs. *Grider, Aaron Harding, McCullough, Nicholson, Ritter, Rogers, Shanklin, Trimble*—8.

Recognition of State government of North Carolina.

March 5, 1866—The SPEAKER having proposed to lay before the House a communication signed Jonathan Worth, Governor of North Carolina, Mr. Stevens objected to its reception; and on the question, will the House receive the same, the yeas were 38, nays 100, as follow:

YEAS—Messrs. Delos R. Ashley, *Bergen, Brooks, Chanler*, Davis, *Dennison, Eldridge, Finck, Goodyear, Grider*, Hale, *Aaron Harding, Hogan*, Edwin N. Hubbell, James Humphrey, *Kerr*, Kuykendall, Latham, *Marshall*, McRuer, Newell, *Niblack, Nicholson*, *Noell*, Phelps, *Radford*, Raymond, *Ritter, Rogers, Ross*, Rousseau, *Shanklin, Taber, Taylor, Thornton, Trimble*, Whaley, *Winfield*.—38.

NAYS—Messrs. Alley, Allison, Ames, Anderson, James M. Ashley, Baker, Banks, Barker, Baxter, Beaman, Benjamin, Bidwell, Bingham, Blaine, Boutwell, Brandegee, Bromwell, Broomall, Buckland, Bundy, Sidney Clarke, Cobb, Cook, Cullom, Defrees, Deming, Donnelly, Driggs, Dumont, Eckley, Eliot, Farnsworth, Farquhar, Ferry, Grinnell, Abner C. Harding, Hayes, Henderson, Higby, Hill, Holmes, Hooper, Hotchkiss, Asahel W. Hubbard, Demas Hubbard, jr., John H. Hubbard, James R. Hubbell, Hulburd, Ingersoll, Jenckes, Julian, Kelley, Kelso, Ketcham, William Lawrence, Lynch, Marston, McClurg, McKee, Miller, Morris, Moulton, Myers, O'Neill, Orth, Paine, Patterson, Perham, Pike, Price, William H. Randall, Alexander H. Rice, John H. Rice, Rollins, Sawyer, Schenck, Scofield, Shellabarger, Sloan, Spalding, Stevens, Stillwell, Thayer, Francis Thomas, John L. Thomas, jr., Trowbridge, Upson, Van Aernam, Burt Van Horn, Robert T. Van Horn, Warner, Elihu B. Washburne, Henry D. Washburn, Welker, Wentworth, Williams, James F. Wilson, Stephen F. Wilson, Windom, Woodbridge.—100.

Trial of Jefferson Davis.

June 11, 1866—Mr. Boutwell offered this resolution:

Whereas it is notorious that Jefferson Davis was the leader of the late rebellion, and is guilty of treason under the laws of the United States; and whereas by the proclamation of the President of May, 1865, the said Davis was charged with complicity in the assassination of President Lincoln, and said proclamation has not been revoked nor annulled: Therefore,

Be it resolved, As the opinion of the House of Representatives, that said Davis should be held in custody as a prisoner, and subjected to a trial according to the laws of the land.

Which was agreed to—yeas 105, nays 19, as follow:

YEAS—Messrs. Alley, Allison, James M. Ashley, Baker, Baldwin, Banks, Baxter, Beaman, Bidwell, Bingham, Blaine, Boutwell, Bromwell, Buckland, Bundy, Reader W. Clarke, Sidney Clarke, Cobb, Conkling, Cook, Cullom, Darling, Davis, Dawes, Defrees, Donnelly, Eckley, Eliot, Farnsworth, Farquhar, Ferry, Garfield, Grinnell, Griswold, Hale, Abner C. Harding, Hart, Hayes, Henderson, Higby, Holmes, Hooper, Hotchkiss, Chester D. Hubbard, John H. Hubbard, James R. Hubbell, Julian, Kelso, Ketcham, Kuykendall, Laflin, Latham, George V. Lawrence, William Lawrence, Loan, Longyear, Lynch, *Marshall*, Marvin, McClurg, McKee, McRuer, Mercur, Miller, Moorhead, Morrill, Morris, Moulton, Myers, O'Neill, Orth, Paine, Perham, Phelps, Pike, Plants, Pomeroy, Price, William H. Randall, Raymond, Alexander H. Rice, Sawyer, Schenck, Scofield, Shellabarger, Sloan, Smith, Spalding, Thayer, John L. Thomas, *Thornton*, Trowbridge, Upson, Van Aernam, Ward, Warner, Henry D. Washburn, Welker, Whaley, Williams, James F. Wilson, Stephen F. Wilson, Windom, Winfield, Woodbridge—105.

NAYS—Messrs. *Ancona, Boyer, Coffroth, Eldridge, Finck, Glossbrenner, Grider, Harris, Hogan, Johnson, McCullough, Niblack, Samuel J. Randall, Ritter, Rogers, Sitgreaves, Taber, Trimble, Wright*—19.

Neutrality—The Fenians.

June 11, 1866—Mr. Ancona offered this resolution:

Whereas the Irish people and their brothers and friends in this country are moved by a patriotic purpose to assert the independence and re-establish the nationality of Ireland; and whereas the active sympathies of the people of the United States are naturally with all men who struggle to achieve such ends, more especially when those engaged therein are the acknowledged friends of our Government, as are the Irish race, they having shed their blood in defense of our flag in every battle of every war in which the republic has been engaged; and whereas the British Government, against whom they are struggling, is entitled to no other or greater consideration from us as a nation than that demanded by the strict letter of international law, for the reason that during our late civil war she did in effect, by her conduct, repeal her neutrality laws; and whereas when reparation is demanded for damages to our commerce, resulting from her willful neglect to enforce the same, she arrogantly denies all responsibility, and claims to be the judge in her own case; and whereas the existence of our neutrality law of 1818 compels the executive department of this Government to discriminate most harshly against those who have ever been and are now our friends, and in favor of those who have been faithless, not only to the general principles of comity which should exist between friendly States, but also to the written law of their own nation upon this subject: Therefore,

Be it resolved, That the Committee on Foreign Affairs be, and they are hereby, instructed to report a bill repealing an act approved April 20, 1818, entitled "An act in addition to an act for the punishment of certain crimes against the United States," and to repeal the act therein mentioned, it being the neutrality law, under the terms of which the President's proclamation against the Fenians was issued.

Mr. Davis, of New York, moved to lay it on

the table, which was lost—yeas 5, (Messrs. Cobb, Davis, Grinnell, Hale, Trowbridge,) nays 112.

Mr. Schenck moved this as a substitute:

Resolved, That the President of the United States, in the opinion of this House, should reconsider the policy which has been adopted by him as between the British Government and that portion of the Irish people who, under the name of Fenians, are struggling for their independent nationality; and that he be requested to adopt as nearly as practicable that exact course of procedure which was pursued by the Government of Great Britain on the occasion of the late civil war in this country between the United States and rebels in revolt, recognizing both parties as lawful belligerents, and observing between them a strict neutrality.

Mr. Hale moved to table it; which was lost—yeas 8, (Messrs. Cobb, Davis, Dawes, Dodge, Griswold, Hale, Sloan, Trowbridge,) nays 113.

Mr. Banks moved to refer to the Committee on Foreign Affairs, stating that if referred the committee would report upon it. The motion was agreed to—yeas 87, nays 35, as follow:

YEAS—Messrs. Alley, Allison, Delos R. Ashley, James M. Ashley, Baker, Baldwin, Banks, Baxter, Beaman, Bidwell, Bingham, Blaine, Boutwell, Bromwell, Buckland, Bundy, Reader W. Clarke, Sidney Clarke, Cobb, Cook, Cullom, Dawes, Defrees, Delano, Dodge, Driggs, Eckley, Farnsworth, Farquhar, Grinnell, Harris, Hart, Hayes, Holmes, Demas Hubbard, Edwin N. Hubbell, Jenckes, *Jones*, Kasson, Kelley, Kuykendall, Laflin, Latham, George V. Lawrence, William Lawrence, Longyear, Marvin, McClurg, McKee, McRuer, Mercur, Miller, Morrill, Morris, Moulton, Myers, O'Neill, Orth, Paine, Perham, Phelps, Pike, Plants, Price, William H. Randall, Raymond, Alexander H. Rice, John H. Rice, Ross, Rousseau, Sawyer, Schenck, Scofield, Shellabarger, Sloan, Spalding, Thayer, Trowbridge, Upson, Ward, Welker, Whaley, Williams, James F. Wilson, Stephen F. Wilson, Windom, Woodbridge—87.

NAYS—Messrs. *Ancona*, *Bergen*, *Boyer*, *Chanler*, *Coffroth*, Darling, Davis, Dumont, *Eldridge*, *Finck*, *Glossbrenner*, *Grider*, Hale, *Aaron Harding*, *Hogan*, *James M. Humphrey*, *Johnson*, *Kerr*, Ketcham, *McCullough*, *Niblack*, Pomeroy, *Samuel J. Randall*, *Ritter*, *Rogers*, *Sitgreaves* Smith, Stillwell, *Strouse*, *Taber*, *Taylor*, *Thornton*, *Trimble*, *Winfield*, *Wright*—35.

XI.

VOTES ON SUFFRAGE IN THE DISTRICT OF COLUMBIA

AND OTHER POLITICAL BILLS.

Suffrage in District of Columbia.

IN HOUSE.

January 10, 1866—Pending this bill, offered by Mr. Kelley, December 5, 1865, and reported from the Judiciary Committee by Mr. James F. Wilson, December 18, and then postponed till this day:

A Bill extending the right of suffrage in the District of Columbia.

Be it enacted, &c., That from all laws and parts of laws prescribing the qualifications of electors for any office in the District of Columbia the word "white" be, and the same is hereby, stricken out, and that from and after the passage of this act no person shall be disqualified from voting at any election held in the said District on account of color.

SEC. 2. That all acts of Congress and all laws of the State of Maryland in force in said District and all ordinances of the cities of Washington and Georgetown inconsistent with the provisions of this act are hereby repealed and annulled.

After debate, Mr. Wilson moved its recommitment.

Mr. Hale moved to amend by adding these words: with instructions to amend the bill so as to extend the right of suffrage in the District of Columbia to all persons coming within either of the following classes, irrespective of caste or color, but subject only to existing provisions and qualifications other than those founded on caste or color, to wit:

First. Those who can read the Constitution of the United States.

Second. Those who are assessed for and pay taxes on real or personal property within the District.

Third. Those who have served in and been honorably discharged from the military or naval service of the United States, and to restrict such right of suffrage to the classes above named, and to include proper provisions excluding from the right of suffrage those who have borne arms against the United States during the late rebellion, or given aid or comfort to said rebellion.

January 17, 1866—Mr. Wilson accepted Mr. Hale's amendment as part of his.

January 18—Mr. Darling moved to postpone the bill till April 3.

Mr. Niblack moved to lay the bill on the table, which was disagreed to—yeas 47, nays 123, as follow:

YEAS—Messrs. *Ancona*, Delos R. Ashley, *Bergen*, *Boyer*, *Brooks*, *Chanler*, *Dawson*, *Denison*, *Eldridge*, *Finck*, *Glossbrenner*, *Goodyear*, *Grider*, *Aaron Harding*, *Hogan*, Chester D. Hubbard, *Edwin N. Hubbell*, *James M. Humphrey*, *Johnson*, *Jones*, *Kerr*, Kuykendall, Latham, *Le Blond*, *Marshall*, *McCullough*, *Niblack*, *Nicholson*, *Noell*, Phelps, *Radford*, *Samuel J. Randall*, William H. Randall, *Ritter*, *Rogers*, *Ross*, *Shanklin*, *Sitgreaves*, Smith, *Strouse*, *Taber*, *Taylor*, John L. Thomas, jr., *Thornton*, *Trimble*, *Voorhees*, *Winfield*—47.

NAYS—Messrs. Alley, Allison, Ames, Anderson, James M. Ashley, Baker, Baldwin, Banks, Barker, Baxter, Beaman,

Bidwell, Bingham, Blaine, Blow, Boutwell, Brandegee, Bromwell, Broomall, Buckland, Bundy, Reader W. Clarke, Sidney Clarke, Cobb, Conkling, Cook, Cullom, Darling, Davis, Dawes, Defrees, Delano, Deming, Dixon, Donnelly, Driggs, Eckley, Eggleston, Eliot, Farnsworth, Farquhar, Ferry, Garfield, Grinnell, Griswold, Hale, Abner C. Harding, Hart, Hayes, Henderson, Higby, Hill, Holmes, Hooper, Asahel W. Hubbard, Demas Hubbard, jr., John H. Hubbard, Hulburd, James Humphrey, Ingersoll, Jenckes, Julian, Kasson, Kelley, Kelso, Ketcham, Laflin, George V. Lawrence, William Lawrence, Loan, Longyear, Lynch, Marston, Marvin, McClurg, McKee, Mercur, Miller, Moorhead, Morrill, Morris, Moulton, Myers, O'Neill, Orth, Paine, Patterson, Perham, Pike, Plants, Pomeroy, Price, Raymond, Alexander H. Rice, John H. Rice, Rollins, Sawyer, Schenck, Scofield, Shellabarger, Sloan, Spalding, Starr, Stevens, Stillwell, Thayer, Francis Thomas, Trowbridge, Upson, Van Aernam, Burt Van Horn, Robert T. Van Horn, Ward, Warner, Ellihu B. Washburne, William B. Washburn, Welker, Wentworth, Williams, James F. Wilson, Stephen F. Wilson, Windom, Woodbridge—123.

Mr. Darling modified his motion so as to postpone until the first Tuesday in March, which was disagreed to—yeas 34, nays 138, as follow:

YEAS—Messrs. Anderson, Banks, Conkling, Darling, Davis, Defrees, Eggleston, Farquhar, Ferry, Griswold, Hale, Hart, Henderson, Hill, *Hogan*, Jas. Humphrey, Kasson, Ketcham, Kuykendall, Laflin, Latham, George V. Lawrence, Marvin, Mercur, Miller, Orth, Phelps, William H. Randall, Raymond, Smith, Stillwell, John L. Thomas, jr., *Trimble*, Robert T. Van Horn—34.

NAYS—Messrs. Alley, Allison, Ames, *Ancona*, Delos R. Ashley, James M. Ashley, Baker, Baldwin, Barker, Baxter, Beaman, Benjamin, *Bergen*, Bidwell, Bingham, Blaine, Blow, Boutwell, *Boyer*, Brandegee, Bromwell, *Brooks*, Broomall, Bundy, *Chanler*, Reader W. Clarke, Sidney Clarke, Cobb, Cook, Cullom, Dawes, *Dawson*, Deming, *Denison*, Dixon, Donnelly, Driggs, Eckley, *Eldridge*, Eliot, Farnsworth, *Finck*, Garfield, *Glossbrenner*, *Goodyear*, *Grider*, Grinnell, *Aaron Harding*, Abner C. Harding, Hayes, Higby, Holmes, Hooper, A. W. Hubbard, Chester D. Hubbard, Demas Hubbard, jr., John H. Hubbard, *Edwin N. Hubbell*, Hulburd, *James M. Humphrey*, Ingersoll, Jenckes, *Johnson*, *Jones*, Julian, Kelley, Kelso, *Kerr*, William Lawrence, *Le Blond*, Loan, Longyear, Lynch, *Marshall*, Marston, McClurg, *McCullough*, McKee, Moorhead, Morrill, Morris, Moulton, Myers, *Niblack*, *Nicholson*, *Noell*, O'Neill, Paine, Patterson, Perham, Pike, Plants, Pomeroy, Price, *Radford*, *Samuel J. Randall*, Alexander H. Rice, John H. Rice, *Ritter*, *Rogers*, Rollins, *Ross*, Sawyer, Schenck, Scofield, *Shanklin*, Shellabarger, *Sitgreaves*, Sloan, Spalding, Starr, Stevens, *Strouse*, *Taber*, *Taylor*, Thayer, Francis Thomas, *Thornton*, Trowbridge, Upson, Van Aernam, Burt Van Horn, *Voorhees*, Ward, Warner, Ellihu B. Washburne, William B. Washburn, Welker, Wentworth, Williams, James F. Wilson, Stephen F. Wilson, Windom, *Winfield*, Woodbridge—135.

The question recurring on Mr. Wilson's motion to commit with instructions, Mr. Schenck moved to strike from the proposed instructions these words: "Those who are assessed for and pay taxes on real or personal property within the district;" which was agreed to.

The motion to recommit as amended, was then disagreed to—yeas 53, nays, 117, as follow:

YEAS—Messrs. Anderson, Banks, Blow, Brandegee, Bromwell, Buckland, Reader W. Clarke, Conkling, Darling, Davis, Dawes, Defrees, Delano, Deming, Dixon, Driggs, Eckley, Eggleston, Ferry, Griswold, Hale, Hart, Hayes, Henderson, Hooper, Hulburd, James Humphrey, Jenckes, Kasson, Ketcham, Kuykendall, Laflin, Latham, George V. Lawrence, William Lawrence, Longyear, Marvin, Miller, Moorhead, Morris, Myers, O'Neill, Plants, Raymond, Alexander H. Rice, Schenck, Stillwell, Trowbridge, Burt Van Horn, Robert T. Van Horn, Warner, William B. Washburn, Woodbridge—53.

NAYS—Messrs. Alley, Allison, Ames, *Ancona*, Delos R. Ashley, James M. Ashley, Baker, Baldwin, Barker, Baxter, Beaman, Benjamin, *Bergen*, Bidwell, Bingham, Blaine, Boutwell, *Boyer*, *Brooks*, Broomall, Bundy, *Chanler*, Clarke, Cobb, Cook, Cullom, *Dawson*, *Denison*, Donnelly, *Eldridge*, Eliot, Farnsworth, Farquhar, *Finck*, Garfield, *Glossbrenner*, *Goodyear*, *Grider*, Grinnell, *Aaron Harding*, Abner C. Harding, Higby, Hill, *Hogan*, Holmes, Asahel W. Hubbard, Chester D. Hubbard, Demas Hubbard, jr., John H. Hubbard, *Edwin N. Hubbell*, *James M. Humphrey*, Ingersoll, *Johnson*, *Jones*, Julian, Kelley, Kelso, *Kerr*, *Le Blond*, Loan, Lynch, *Marshall*, Marston, McClurg, *McCullough*, McKee, Mercur, Morrill, Moulton, *Niblack*, *Nicholson*, *Noell*, Orth, Paine, Patterson, Perham, Phelps, Pomeroy, Price, *Radford*, *Samuel J. Randall*, William H. Randall, John H. Rice, *Ritter*, *Rogers*, Rollins, *Ross*, Sawyer, Scofield, *Shanklin*, Shellabarger, *Sitgreaves*, Sloan, Smith, Spalding, Starr, Stevens, *Strouse*, *Taber*, *Taylor*, Thayer, Francis Thomas, John L. Thomas, jr., *Thornton*, *Trimble*, Upson, Van Aernam, *Voorhees*, Ward, Ellihu B. Washburne, Welker, Wentworth, Williams, James F. Wilson, Stephen F. Wilson, Windom, Winfield—117.

The bill was then passed—yeas 116, nays 54, as follow:

YEAS—Messrs. Alley, Allison, Ames, James M. Ashley, Baker, Baldwin, Banks, Barker, Baxter, Beaman, Bidwell, Bingham, Blaine, Blow, Boutwell, Brandegee, Bromwell, Broomall, Buckland, Bundy, Reader W. Clarke, Sidney Clarke, Cobb, Conkling, Cook, Cullom, Darling, Davis, Dawes, Defrees, Delano, Deming, Dixon, Donnelly, Driggs, Eckley, Eggleston, Eliot, Farnsworth, Ferry, Garfield, Grinnell, Griswold, Hale, Abner C. Harding, Hart, Hayes, Higby, Holmes, Hooper, Asahel W. Hubbard, Demas Hubbard, jr., John H. Hubbard, Hulburd, James Humphrey, Ingersoll, Jenckes, Julian, Kasson, Kelley, Kelso, Ketcham, Laflin, George V. Lawrence, William Lawrence, Loan, Longyear, Lynch, Marston, Marvin, McClurg, Mercur, Miller, Moorhead, Morrill, Morris, Moulton, Myers, O'Neill, Orth, Paine, Patterson, Perham, Pike, Plants, Pomeroy, Price, Raymond, Alexander H. Rice, John H. Rice, Rollins, Sawyer, Schenck, Scofield, Shellabarger, Sloan, Spalding, Starr, Stevens, Thayer, Francis Thomas, Trowbridge, Upson, Van Aernam, Burt Van Horn, Ward, Warner, Ellihu B. Washburne, William B. Washburn, Welker, Wentworth, Williams, James F. Wilson, Stephen F. Wilson, Windom, Woodbridge—116.

NAYS—Messrs. *Ancona*, Anderson, Delos R. Ashley, Benjamin, *Bergen*, *Boyer*, *Brooks*, *Chanler*, *Dawson*, *Denison*, *Eldridge*, Farquhar, *Finck*, *Glossbrenner*, *Goodyear*, *Grider*, *Harding*, Henderson, Hill, *Hogan*, Chester D. Hubbard, *Edwin N. Hubbell*, *James M. Humphrey*, *Johnson*, *Jones*, *Kerr*, Kuykendall, Latham, *Le Blond*, *Marshall*, *McCullough*, McKee, *Niblack*, *Nicholson*, *Noell*, Phelps, *Radford*, *Samuel J. Randall*, William H. Randall, *Ritter*, *Rogers*, *Ross*, *Shanklin*, *Sitgreaves*, Smith, Stillwell, *Strouse*, *Taber*, *Taylor*, *Thornton*, *Trimble*, Robert T. Van Horn, *Voorhees*, *Winfield*—54.

IN SENATE.

June 27, 1866—The bill, as reported to the Senate from its committee amended, was considered, the pending question being Mr. Morrill's motion to insert in the first section the words in brackets, below:

That from and after the passage of this act, each and every male person, excepting paupers and persons under guardianship, of the age of twenty-one years and upwards, who has not been convicted of any infamous crime, or offence, and who is a citizen of the United States, and who shall have resided in the said district for the period of six months previous to any election therein, [and excepting persons who may have voluntarily left the District of Columbia to give aid and comfort to the rebels in the late rebellion,] shall be entitled to the elective franchise, and shall be deemed an elector and entitled to vote at any election in said District, without any distinction on account of color or race.

Mr. Morrill moved further to amend by inserting, also, after "therein," the words "and who can read the Constitution of the United States in the English language, and write his name;" which was disagreed to—yeas 15, nays 19, as follow:

YEAS—Messrs. Anthony, Cragin, Edmunds, Fessenden, Foster, Harris, Kirkwood, Morrill, Poland, Pomeroy, Sherman, Trumbull, Wade, Willey, Williams—15.

NAYS—Messrs. Brown, *Buckalew*, Conness, *Davis*, Grimes, *Guthrie*, *Hendricks*, Howard, Howe, Morgan, Norton, Nye, Ramsey, Sprague, Stewart, Sumner, Van Winkle, Wilson, Yates—19.

Mr. Willey offered this substitute for the bill:

In all elections to be held hereafter in the District of Columbia, the following described persons, and those only, shall have the right to vote, namely: first, all those persons who were actually residents of said District and qualified to vote therein at the elections held therein in the year 1865, under the statutes then in force; second, all persons residents of said District who have been duly mustered into the military or naval service of the United States during the late rebellion, and have been or shall hereafter be honorably discharged therefrom; third, male citizens of the United States who shall have attained the age of twenty-one years, (excepting paupers, persons *non compotes mentis*, or convicted of an infamous offence,) and who, being residents of the ward or district in which they shall offer to vote, shall have resided in said District for the period of one year next preceding any election, and who shall have paid the taxes assessed against them, and who can read, and who can write their names.

No further vote has been taken up to date of putting this page to press.

West Virginia Bill.

February 6, 1866—The HOUSE passed a joint resolution giving the consent of Congress to the transfer of Berkeley and Jefferson counties to West Virginia—yeas 112, nays 24; (the latter all Democrats except Mr. Baker.) The SENATE passed it, March 6—yeas 32, nays 5.—Mr. *Johnson*, of Maryland, voted aye; the other Democrats, voting, voted nay.

Extending the Homestead Act.

IN HOUSE.

February 7, 1866—A bill providing that all the public lands in Alabama, Mississippi, Louisiana, Arkansas, and Florida, shall be disposed of according to the stipulations of the homestead law of 1862, no entry to be made for more than eighty acres, and no discrimination to be made on account of race or color, and the mineral lands to be reserved, was considered.

Mr. Taber moved to add this proviso:

And provided, also, That nothing in this act shall be so construed as to preclude such persons as have been or shall be pardoned by the President of the United States for their participation in the recent rebellion from the benefit of this act.

Which was disagreed to—yeas 37, nays 104, as follow:

YEAS—Messrs. Delos R. Ashley, *Bergen, Boyer, Brooks*, Buckland, *Chanler, Eldridge, Finck, Glossbrenner, Grider, Aaron Harding, Hogan*, Chester D. Hubbard, *Edwin N. Hubbell, James M. Humphrey, Kerr*, Latham, *Le Blond, Marshall, McCullough*, McRuer, *Niblack, Nicholson, Noell*, Phelps, *Ritter, Rogers, Ross, Shanklin, Sitgreaves, Strouse, Taber, Taylor*, Thayer, *Thornton, Trimble, Voorhees*—37.

NAYS—Messrs. Alley, Allison, Ames, James M. Ashley, Baker, Baldwin, Banks, Barker, Baxter, Beaman, Benjamin, Bidwell, Bingham, Blaine, Blow, Boutwell, Brandegee, Bromwell, Broomall, Bundy, Reader W. Clarke, Sidney Clarke, Cobb, Conkling, Cook, Cullom, Darling, Davis, Dawes, Defrees, Deming, Donnelly, Driggs, Eckley, Eggleston, Eliot, Farnsworth, Farquhar, Ferry, Garfield, Hale, Abner C. Harding, Hart, Hayes, Higby, Hill, Hooper, Hotchkiss, Demas Hubbard, jr., John H. Hubbard, Ingersoll, Jenckes, Julian, Kasson, Kelley, Kelso, Kuykendall, Laflin, George V. Lawrence, William Lawrence, Longyear, Lynch, Marston, Marvin, McClurg, McIndoe, Mercur, Miller, Moorhead, Morris, Moulton, Myers, Newell, O'Neill, Orth, Paine, Patterson, Perham, Price, William H. Randall, Alexander H. Rice, John H. Rice, Rollins, Sawyer, Schenck, Sloan, Smith, Spalding, Starr, Stevens, Trowbridge, Upson, Van Aernam, Burt Van Horn, Ward, Warner, Elihu B Washburne, William B. Washburn, Welker, Wentworth, James F. Wilson, Stephen F. Wilson, Windom, Woodbridge—104.

February 8—The bill passed—yeas 112, nays 29; the latter all Democrats, except Messrs. Driggs and Latham.

The bill as finally passed provided that until January 1, 1867, any person applying for the benefit of the act shall swear "that he has not borne arms against the United States, or given aid and comfort to its enemies."

Habeas Corpus.

IN HOUSE.

March 20—The bill to amend an act entitled "An act relating to *habeas corpus*, and regulating judicial proceedings in certain cases," approved March 3, 1863, was passed—yeas 113, nays 31, as follow:

YEAS—Messrs. Alley, Allison, Ames, Anderson, Delos R. Ashley, James M. Ashley, Baker, Baldwin, Banks, Barker, Baxter, Beaman, Bidwell, Bingham, Blaine, Blow, Boutwell, Bromwell, Broomall, Buckland, Bundy, Reader W. Clarke, Conkling, Cook, Cullom, Delano, Deming, Dixon, Driggs, Dumont, Eggleston, Eliot, Farnsworth, Farquhar, Ferry, Garfield, Grinnell, Abner C. Harding, Hart, Hayes, Henderson, Hill, Holmes, Hooper, Asahel W. Hubbard, Chester D. Hubbard, Demas Hubbard, jr., John H. Hubbard, James R. Hubbell, Hulburd, Ingersoll, Jenckes, Kasson, Kelley, Kelso, Ketcham, Kuykendall, Laflin, Latham, George V. Lawrence, William Lawrence, Loan, Lynch, Marston, Marvin, McClurg, McKee, McRuer, Miller, Moorhead, Morrill, Morris, Moulton, Myers, Newell, Noell, O'Neill, Orth, Paine, Perham, Phelps, Pike, Plants, Price, William H. Randall, Raymond, John H. Rice, Rollins, Rousseau, Sawyer, Scofield, Shellabarger, Sloan, Smith, Stevens, Stillwell, Thayer, Trowbridge, Upson, Van Aernam, Burt Van Horn, Robert T. Van Horn, Ward, Warner, Elihu B. Washburne, William B. Washburn, Welker, Wentworth, Whaley, Williams, James F. Wilson, Windom, Woodbridge—113.

NAYS—Messrs. *Ancona, Bergen, Boyer, Brooks, Chanler, Coffroth, Dawson, Eldridge, Glossbrenner, Grider*, Hale, *Aaron Harding, Hogan, Edwin N. Hubbell, James M. Humphrey, Jones, Kerr, Le Blond, Marshall, McCullough, Nicholson, Samuel J. Randall, Ritter, Rogers, Ross, Sitgreaves, Strouse, Taber, Thornton, Trimble, Winfield*—31.

IN SENATE.

April 20—The bill passed—yeas 30, nays 4, as follow:

YEAS—Messrs. Anthony, Chandler, Clark, Conness, Cragin, Doolittle, Edmunds, Foster, Henderson, Howard, Howe, *Johnson*, Kirkwood, Lane of Indiana, Morgan, Norton, Nye, Poland, Pomeroy, Ramsey, Sprague, Stewart, Sumner, Trumbull, Van Winkle, Wade, Willey, Williams, Wilson, Yates—30.

NAYS—Messrs *Buckalew, Guthrie, Hendricks, Saulsbury*—4.

No Denial of the Elective Franchise on Account of Color.

IN HOUSE.

1866, May 15—Pending the bill to amend the organic acts of the territories of Nebraska, Colorado, Dakota, Montana, Washington, Idaho, Arizona, Utah, and New Mexico, of which this is the ninth section:

"That within the territories aforesaid there shall be no denial of the elective franchise to citizens of the United States because of race or color, and all persons shall be equal before the law. And all acts or parts of acts, either of Congress or the legislative assemblies of the territories aforesaid, inconsistent with the provisions of this act, are hereby declared null and void."

Mr. Le Blond moved to strike it out, which was disagreed to—yeas 36, nays 76, as follow:

YEAS—Messrs. *Ancona*, Delos R. Ashley, *Bergen*, *Boyer*, *Chanler*, *Dawson*, *Denison*, *Eldridge*, *Finck*, *Glossbrenner*, *Goodyear*, *Grider*, *Aaron Harding*, Chester D. Hubbard, *Edwin N. Hubbell*, *Kerr*, Kuykendall, Latham, *Le Blond*, *Marshall*, *Niblack*, *Nicholson*, Phelps, William H. Randall, *Ritter*, *Rogers*, *Ross*, Rousseau, *Shanklin*, *Sitgreaves*, *Strouse*, *Taber*, *Taylor*, *Trimble*, Whaley, *Wright*—36.

NAYS—Messrs. Allison, Ames, Anderson, James M. Ashley, Baker, Baldwin, Banks, Baxter, Blaine, Blow, Boutwell, Brandegee, Broomall, Sidney Clarke, Cook, Cullom, Darling, Davis, Dawes, Deming, Donnelly, Dumont, Eggleston, Farnsworth, Ferry, Garfield, Griswold, Hart, Hayes, Higby, Holmes, Hooper, Hotchkiss, Asahel W. Hubbard, Demas Hubbard, John H. Hubbard, Hulburd, Ingersoll, Jenckes, Julian, Kelley, Kelso, William Lawrence, Loan, Longyear, Lynch, Marston, McClurg, McRuer, Mercur, Miller, Moorhead, Morrill, Orth, Paine, Patterson, Perham, Pike, Plants, Price, Rollins, Sawyer, Spalding, Thayer, Francis Thomas, Van Aernam, Burt Van Horn, Ward, arner, Ellihu B. Washburne, William B. Washburn, Welker, Williams, James F. Wilson, Stephen F. Wilson, Windom—76.

The bill then passed—yeas 79, nays 43.

IN SENATE.

June 29—The bill was considered but **not** voted on.

XII.

POLITICAL AND MILITARY MISCELLANEOUS.

Union National Platform, June, 1864.

Resolved, That it is the highest duty of every American citizen to maintain against all their enemies the integrity of the Union and the paramount authority of the Constitution and laws of the United States; and that, laying aside all differences of political opinions, we pledge ourselves, as Union men, animated by a common sentiment and aiming at a common object, to do everything in our power to aid the Government in quelling by force of arms the Rebellion now raging against its authority, and in bringing to the punishment due to their crimes the Rebels and traitors arrayed against it.

Resolved, That we approve the determination of the Government of the United States not to compromise with Rebels, or to offer them any terms of peace, except such as may be based upon an unconditional surrender of their hostility and a return to their just allegiance to the Constitution and laws of the United States, and that we call upon the Government to maintain this position, and to prosecute the war with the utmost possible vigor to the complete suppression of the Rebellion, in full reliance upon the self-sacrificing patriotism, the heroic valor, and the undying devotion of the American people to the country and its free institutions.

Resolved, That as Slavery was the cause, and now constitutes the strength of this Rebellion, and as it must be, always and everywhere, hostile to the principles of Republican Government, justice, and the National safety demand its utter and complete extirpation from the soil of the Republic; and that, while we uphold and maintain the acts and proclamations by which the Government, in its own defence, has aimed a death-blow at this gigantic evil, we are in favor, furthermore, of such an amendment to the Constitution, to be made by the people in conformity with its provisions, as shall terminate and forever prohibit the existence of Slavery within the limits or the jurisdiction of the United States.

Resolved, That the thanks of the American people are due to the soldiers and sailors of the Army and Navy, who have periled their lives in defence of their country and in vindication of the honor of its flag; that the nation owes to them some permanent recognition of their patriotism and their valor, and ample and permanent provision for those of their survivors who have received disabling and honorable wounds in the service of the country; and that the memories of those who have fallen in its defence shall be held in grateful and everlasting remembrance.

Resolved, That we approve and applaud the practical wisdom, the unselfish patriotism, and the unswerving fidelity to the Constitution and the principles of American Liberty, with which Abraham Lincoln has discharged, under circumstances of unparalleled difficulty, the great duties and responsibilities of the Presidential office; that we approve and endorse, as demanded by the emergency and essential to the preservation of the nation and as within the provisions of the Constitution, the measures and acts which he has adopted to defend the nation against its open and secret foes; that we approve, especially, the Proclamation of Emancipation, and the employment as Union soldiers of men heretofore held in slavery; and that we have full confidence in his determination to carry these and all other Constitutional measures essential to the salvation of the country into full and complete effect.

Resolved, That we deem it essential to the general welfare that harmony should prevail in the National Councils, and we regard as worthy of public confidence and official trust those only who cordially endorse the principles proclaimed in these resolutions, and which should characterize the administration of the Government.

Resolved, That the Government owes to all men employed in its armies, without regard to distinction of color, the full protection of the laws of war; and that any violation of these laws, or of the usages of civilized nations in time of war, by the Rebels now in arms, should be made the subject of prompt and full redress.

Resolved, That foreign immigration, which in the past has added so much to the wealth, development of resources, and increase of power to this nation—the asylum of the oppressed of all nations—should be fostered and encouraged by a liberal and just policy.

Resolved, That we are in favor of the speedy construction of the Railroad to the Pacific coast.

Resolved, That the National faith, pledged for the redemption of the public debt, must be kept inviolate, and that for this purpose we recommend economy and rigid responsibility in the public expenditures, and a vigorous and just system of taxation; and that it is the duty of every loyal State to sustain the credit and promote the use of the National currency.

Resolved, That we approve the position taken by the Government that the people of the United States can never regard with indifference the attempt of any European Power to overthrow by force or to supplant by fraud the institutions of any Republican Government on the Western Continent; and that they will view with extreme jealousy, as menacing to the peace and independence of their own country, the efforts of any such power to obtain new footholds for Monarchical Governments, sustained by foreign military force, in near proximity to the United States.

Democratic National Platform, August, 1864.

Resolved, That in the future, as in the past, we will adhere with unswerving fidelity to the Union under the Constitution as the only solid foundation of our strength, security and happiness as a people, and as a framework of government equally conducive to the welfare and prosperity of all the States, both northern and southern.

Resolved, That this convention does explicitly declare, as the sense of the American people, that after four years of failure to restore the Union by the experiment of war, during which, under the pretence of a military necessity, or war power higher than the Contitution, the Constitution itself has been disregarded in every part, and public liberty and private right alike trodden down and the material prosperity of the country essentially impaired—justice, humanity, liberty and the public welfare demand that immediate efforts be made for a cessation of hostilities, with a view to an ultimate convention of the States, or other peaceable means, to the end that at the earliest practicable moment peace may be restored on the basis of the Federal Union of the States.

Resolved, That the direct interference of the military authorities of the United States in the recent elections held in Kentucky, Maryland, Missouri, and Delaware, was a shameful violation of the Constitution; and a repetition of such acts in the approaching election will be held as revolutionary, and resisted with all the means and power under our control.

Resolved, That the aim and object of the Democratic party is to preserve the Federal Union and the rights of the States unimpaired; and they hereby declare that they consider that the administrative usurpation of extraordinary and dangerous powers not granted by the constitution; the subversion of the civil by military law in States not in insurrection; the arbitrary military arrest, imprisonment, trial and sentence of American citizens in States where civil law exists in full force; the suppression of freedom of speech and of the press; the denial of the right of asylum; the open and avowed disregard of State rights; the employment of unusual test-oaths, and the interference with and denial of the right of the people to bear arms in their defence, is calculated to prevent a restoration of the Union and the perpetuation of a government deriving its just powers from the consent of the governed.

Resolved, That the shameful disregard of the Administration to its duty in respect to our fellow-citizens who now are, and long have been, prisoners of war in a suffering condition, deserves the severest reprobation, on the score alike of public policy and common humanity.

Resolved, That the sympathy of the Democratic party is heartily and earnestly extended to the soldiery of our army and sailors of our navy, who are, and have been in the field and on the sea, under the flag of their country; and, in the event of its attaining power, they will receive all the care, protection, and regard that the brave soldiers and sailors of the Republic have so nobly earned.

Call for a National Union Convention, 1866.

A National Union Convention, of at least two delegates from each congressional district of all the States, two from each Territory, two from the District of Columbia, and four delegates at large from each State, will be held at the city of Philadelphia, on the second Tuesday (14th) of August next.

Such delegates will be chosen by the electors of the several States who sustain the Administration in maintaining unbroken the Union of the States under the Constitution which our fathers established, and who agree in the following propositions, viz:

The Union of the States is, in every case, indissoluble, and is perpetual; and the Constitution of the United States, and the laws passed by Congress in pursuance thereof, supreme, and constant, and universal in their obligation;

The rights, the dignity, and the equality of the States in the Union, including the right of representation in Congress, are solemnly guaranteed by that Constitution, to save which from overthrow so much blood and treasure were expended in the late civil war;

There is no right anywhere to dissolve the Union or to separate States from the Union, either by voluntary withdrawal, by force of arms, or by Congressional action; neither by the secession of the States, nor by the exclusion of their loyal and qualified representatives, nor by the National Government in any other form;

Slavery is abolished, and neither can, nor ought to be, re-established in any State or Territory within our jurisdiction;

Each State has the undoubted right to prescribe the qualifications of its own electors, and no external power rightfully can, or ought to, dictate, control, or influence the free and voluntary action of the States in the exercise of that right;

The maintenence inviolate of the rights of the States, and especially of the right of each State to order and control its own domestic concerns, according to its own judgment exclusively, subject only to the Constitution of the United States, is essential to that balance of power on which the perfection and endurance of our political fabric depend, and the overthrow of that system by the usurpation and centralization of power in Congress would be a revolution, dangerous to republican government and destructive of liberty;

Each House of Congress is made by the Constitution the sole judge of the elections, returns, and qualifications of its members; but the exclusion of loyal Senators and Representatives, properly chosen and qualified under the Constitution and laws, is unjust and revolutionary;

Every patriot should frown upon all those acts and proceedings everywhere, which can serve no other purpose than to rekindle the animosities of war, and the effect of which upon our moral, social, and material interests at home, and upon our standing abroad, differing only in degree, is injurious like war itself;

The purpose of the war having been to preserve the Union and the Constitution by putting down the rebellion, and the rebellion having been suppressed, all resistance to the authority of the General Government being at an end, and the war having ceased, war measures should also cease, and should be followed by measures of peaceful administration, so that union, harmony, and concord may be encouraged, and industry, commerce, and the arts of peace revived and promoted; and the early restoration of all the States to the exercise of their constitutional powers in the national Government is indispensably necessary to the strength and the defence of the Republic, and to the maintenance of the public credit;

All such electors in the thirty-six States and nine Territories of the United States, and in the District of Columbia, who, in a spirit of patriotism and love for the Union, can rise above personal and sectional considerations, and who desire to see a truly National Union Convention, which shall represent all the States and Territories of the Union, assemble, as friends and brothers, under the national flag, to hold counsel together upon the state of the Union, and to take measures to avert possible danger from the same, are specially requested to take part in the choice of such delegates.

But no delegate will take a seat in such convention who does not loyally accept the national situation and cordially endorse the principles above set forth, and who is not attached, in true allegiance, to the Constitution, the Union, and the Government of the United States.

WASHINGTON, June 25, 1866.

A. W. RANDALL,
President.
J. R. DOOLITTLE,
O. H. BROWNING,
EDGAR COWAN,
CHARLES KNAP,
SAMUEL FOWLER,
Executive Committee National Union Club.

We recommend the holding of the above convention, and endorse the call therefor.

DANIEL S. NORTON, JAMES DIXON,
J. W. NESMITH, T. A. HENDRICKS,

Address of Democratic Congressmen, 1866.

To the People of the United States:

Dangers threaten. The Constitution—the citadel of our liberties—is directly assailed. The future is dark, unless the people will come to the rescue.

In this hour of peril National Union should be the watchword of every true man.

As essential to National Union we must maintain unimpaired the rights, the dignity, and the equality of the States, including the right of representation in Congress, and the exclusive right of each State to control its own domestic concerns, subject only to the Constitution of the United States.

After a uniform construction of the Constitution for more than half a century, the assumption of new and arbitrary powers in the Federal Government is subversive of our system and destructive of liberty.

A free interchange of opinion and kind feeling between the citizens of all the States is necessary to the perpetuity of the Union. At present eleven States are excluded from the national council. For seven long months the present Congress has persistently denied any right of representation to the people of these States. Laws, affecting their highest and dearest interests, have been passed without their consent, and in disregard of the fundamental principle of free government. This denial of representation has been made to all the members from a State, although the State, in the language of the President, "presents itself, not only in an attitude of loyalty and harmony, but in the persons of representatives whose loyalty cannot be questioned under any existing constitutional or legal test."

The representatives of nearly one-third of the States have not been consulted with reference to the great questions of the day. There has been no nationality surrounding the present Congress. There has been no intercourse between the representatives of the two sections, producing mutual confidence and respect. In the language of the distinguished lieutenant general,

"It is to be regretted that, at this time, there cannot be a greater commingling between the citizens of the two sections, and particularly of those intrusted with the law-making power."

This state of things should be removed at once and forever.

Therefore, to preserve the National Union, to vindicate the sufficiency of our admirable Constitution, to guard the States from covert attempts to deprive them of their true position in the Union, and to bring together those who are unnaturally severed, and for these great national purposes only, we cordially approve the call for a National Union Convention, to be held at the city of Philadelphia, on the second Tuesday (14th) of August next, and endorse the principles therein set forth.

We, therefore, respectfully, but earnestly, urge upon our fellow-citizens in each State and Territory and congressional district in the United States, in the interest of Union and in a spirit of harmony, and with direct reference to the principles contained in said call, to act promptly in the selection of wise, moderate, and conservative men to represent them in said Convention, to the end that *all* the States shall at once be restored to their practical relations to the Union, the Constitution be maintained, and peace bless the whole country.

W. E. Niblack,	Reverdy Johnson,
Anthony Thornton,	Thos. A. Hendricks,
Michael C. Kerr,	Wm. Wright,
G. S. Shanklin,	James Guthrie,
Garrett Davis,	J. A. McDougall,
H. Grider,	Wm. Radford,
Thomas E. Noell,	S. S. Marshall,
Samuel J. Randall,	Myer Strouse,
Lewis W. Ross,	Chas. Sitgreaves,
Stephen Taber,	S. E Ancona,
J. M. Humphrey,	E. N. Hubbell,
John Hogan,	B. C. Ritter,
B. M. Boyer,	A. Harding.
Teunis G. Bergen,	A. J. Glossbrenner,
Chas. Goodyear,	E. R. V. Wright,
Chas. H. Winfield,	A. J. Rogers,
A. H. Coffroth,	H. McCullough,
Lovell H. Rousseau,	F. C. Le Blond,
Philip Johnson,	W. E. Finck,
Chas. A. Eldridge,	L. S. Trimble,

John L. Dawson.

WASHINGTON, *July* 4, 1866.

The Elections of 1866.

NEW HAMPSHIRE—Smyth, Union, 35,018; Sinclair, Democrat, 30,176.

CONNECTICUT—Hawley, Union, 43,974; English, Democrat, 43,433.

RHODE ISLAND—Burnside, Union, 8,197; Pierce, Democrat, 2,816.

OREGON—Wood, Union, 327 majority.

At the special election in CONNECTICUT, in the fall of 1865, on suffrage, the vote stood:

For colored suffrage, 27,217; against, 33,489. majority against, 6,272.

In WEST VIRGINIA, a vote was taken in May, on ratifying this constitutional amendment:

"No person who, since the 1st day of June, 1861, has given or shall give voluntary aid or assistance to the rebellion against the United States, shall be a citizen of this State, or be allowed to vote at any election held therein, unless he has volunteered into the military or naval service of the United States, and has been or shall be honorably discharged therefrom."

The majority in its favor is 6,922.

In the Territory of NEBRASKA, a vote was taken, with this result: For the proposed State constitution, 3,938; against it, 3,838. *Congress*—Marquette, Union, 4,110; Brooke, Democrat, 3,974. *Governor*—Butler, Union, 4,093; Morton, Democrat, 3,948.

Correspondence between General Grant and General Lee.

APRIL 7, 1865.

Gen. R. E. LEE, *Commanding C. S. A.:*

GENERAL: The result of the last week must convince you of the hopelessness of further resistance on the part of the Army of Northern Virginia in this struggle. I feel that it is so, and regard it as my duty to shift from myself the responsibility of any further effusion of blood, by asking of you the surrender of that portion of the Confederate States army known as the Army of Northern Virginia.

Very respectfully, your obedient servant,
U. S. GRANT, *Lieut. Gen.*,
Commanding Armies of the United States.

APRIL 7, 1865.

GENERAL: I have received your note of this date. Though not entirely of the opinion you express of the hopelessness of the further resistance on the part of the Army of Northern Virginia, I reciprocate your desire to avoid a useless effusion of blood, and therefore before considering your proposition I ask the terms you will offer on condition of its surrender.

R. E. LEE, *General.*

To Lieut. Gen. GRANT, *Commanding Armies of the United States.*

APRIL 8, 1865.

General R. E. LEE, *Commanding C. S. A.:*

GENERAL: Your note of last evening, in reply to mine of same date, asking conditions on which I will accept the surrender of the Army of Northern Virginia, is just received.

In reply I would say that peace being my first desire, there is but one condition I insist upon, viz: That the men surrendered shall be disqualified for taking up arms again against the Government of the United States, until properly exchanged. I will meet you, or designate officers to meet any officers you may name, for the same purpose, at any point agreeable to you, for the purpose of arranging definitely the terms upon which the surrender of the Army of Northern Virginia will be received.

Very respectfully, your obedient servant,
U. S. GRANT, *Lieut. Gen.*,
Commanding Armies of the United States.

APRIL 8, 1865.

GENERAL: I received, at a late hour, your note of to-day, in answer to mine of yesterday. I did not intend to propose the surrender of the Army of Northern Virginia, but to ask the terms of your proposition. To be frank, I do not think the emergency has arisen to call for the surrender of this army; but as the restoration of peace should be the sole object of all, I desire to know whether your proposal would tend to that end. I cannot, therefore, meet you with a view to surrender the Army of Northern Virginia; but as far as your proposition may affect the Confederate States forces under my command, and tend to the restoration of peace, I should be pleased to meet you at 10 A. M. to-morrow, on the old stage road to Richmond, between the picket lines of the two armies.

Very respectfully, your obedient servant,
R. E. LEE, *General, C. S. A.*

To Lieut. Gen. U. S. GRANT, *Commanding Armies U. S. A.*

APRIL 9.

General R. E. LEE, *Commanding C. S. A.:*

GENERAL: Your note of yesterday is received. As I have no authority to treat on the subject of peace, the meeting proposed for 10 A. M. to-day could lead to no good. I will state, however, General, that I am equally anxious for peace with yourself, and the whole North entertain the same feeling.

The terms upon which peace can be had are well understood. By the South laying down their arms they will hasten that most desirable event, save thousands of human lives, and hundreds of millions of property not yet destroyed. Sincerely hoping that all our difficulties may be settled without the loss of another life, I subscribe myself, very respectfully, your obedient servant,

U. S. GRANT, *Lieut. Gen. U. S. A.*

APRIL 9, 1865.

GENERAL: I received your note of this morning on the picket line, whither I had come to meet you and ascertain definitely what terms were embraced in your proposition of yesterday with reference to the surrender of this army. I now request an interview in accordance with the offer contained in your letter of yesterday for that purpose.

Very respectfully, your obedient servant,

R. E. LEE, *General.*

To Lieut. Gen. GRANT, *Com'g U. S. Armies.*

APRIL 9.

General R. E. LEE, *Commanding C. S. A.:*

Your note of this date is but this moment (11.50 A. M.) received, in consequence of my having passed from the Lynchburg road to the Farmville and Lynchburg road. I am at this writing about four miles west of Walter's Church, and will push forward to the front for the purpose of meeting you.

Notice sent to me on this road where you wish the interview to take place, will meet me.

Very respectfully, your obedient servant,

U. S. GRANT, *Lieut. Gen.,*
Commanding Armies of United States.

APPOMATTOX C. H., *April* 9, 1865.

General R. E. LEE, *Commanding C. S. A.:*

In accordance with the substance of my letter to you of the 8th instant, I propose to receive the surrender of the Army of Northern Virginia on the following terms, to wit:

Rolls of all the officers and men to be made in duplicate, one copy to be given to an officer designated by me, the other to be retained by such officer or officers as you may designate.

The officers to give their individual paroles not to take arms against the Government of the United States until properly exchanged, and each company or regimental commander sign a like parole for the men of their commands. The arms, artillery, and public property to be parked and stacked, and turned over to the officers appointed by me to receive them. This will not embrace the side-arms of officers, nor their private horses or baggage.

This done, each officer and man will be allowed to return to their homes, not to be disturbed by United States authority so long as they observe their parole and the laws in force where they may reside.

Very respectfully,

U. S. GRANT, *Lieut. Gen.*

HEADQ'RS ARMY OF NORTHERN VIRGINIA,
April 9, 1865.

Lieut. Gen. U. S. GRANT, *Com'g U. S. Armies:*

GENERAL: I have received your letter of this date containing the terms of surrender of the Army of Northern Virginia, as proposed by you. As they are substantially the same as those expressed in your letter of the 8th instant, they are accepted. I will proceed to designate the proper officer to carry the stipulations into effect.

Very respectfully, your obedient servant,

R. E. LEE, *General.*

The other Rebel armies subsequently surrendered on substantially the same terms.

Agreement between Generals Sherman and Johnston.

Memorandum, or Basis of Agreement, made this 18th day of April, A. D. 1865, near Durham's Station, in the State of North Carolina, by and between General Joseph E. Johnston, commanding Confederate army, and Major General William T. Sherman, commanding Army of the United States, both being present:

1. The contending armies now in the field to maintain the *status quo*, until notice is given by the commanding general of any one to its opponent, and reasonable time, say forty-eight hours, allowed.

2. The Confederate armies now in existence to be disbanded and conducted to their several State capitals, therein to deposit their arms and public property in the State arsenal, and each officer and man to execute and file an agreement to cease from acts of war, and to abide the action of both State and Federal authorities. The number of arms and munitions of war to be reported to the Chief of Ordnance at Washington city, subject to the future action of the Congress of the United States, and in the meantime to be used solely to maintain peace and order within the borders of the States respectively.

3. The recognition by the Executive of the United States of the several State governments, on their officers and legislatures taking the oath prescribed by the Constitution of the United States; and where conflicting State governments have resulted from the war, the legitimacy of all shall be submitted to the Supreme Court of the United States.

4. The re-establishment of the Federal Courts in the several States, with powers as defined by the Constitution and laws of Congress.

5. The people and inhabitants of all these States to be guaranteed, so far as the Executive can, their political rights and franchise, as well as their rights of person and property, as defined by the Constitution of the United States, and of the States respectively.

6. The Executive authority of the Government of the United States not to disturb any of the people by reason of the late war, so long as they live in peace and quiet, and abstain from acts of armed hostility, and obey the laws in existence at the place of their residence.

7. In general terms, the war to cease, a general amnesty, so far as the Executive of the United States can command, on the condition of the disbandment of the Confederate armies, dis-

tribution of arms; and the resumption of peaceable pursuits by the officers and men hitherto composing such armies. Not being fully empowered by our respective principals to fulfil these terms, we individually and officially pledge ourselves to promptly obtain an answer thereto, and to carry out the above programme.

W. T. SHERMAN,
Maj. Gen., Commanding Army U. S. in N. C.
J. E. JOHNSTON,
General, Commanding C. S. A. in N. C.

The following official dispatch to the Associated Press gives the particulars of its disapproval, and the supposed reasons therefor:

WASHINGTON, April 22.—Yesterday evening a bearer of despatches arrived from General Sherman. An agreement for a suspension of hostilities, and a memorandum of what is called a basis for peace, had been entered into on the 18th inst., by General Sherman with the rebel General Johnston, the rebel General Breckinridge being present at the conference.

A Cabinet meeting was held at 8 o'clock in the evening, at which the action of General Sherman was disapproved by the President, the Secretary of War, by General Grant, and by every member of the Cabinet.

General Sherman was ordered to resume hostilities immediately, and he was directed that the instructions given by the late President, in the following telegram, which was penned by Mr. Lincoln himself, at the Capitol, on the night of the 3d of March, were approved by President Andrew Johnson, and were reiterated to govern the action of military commanders.

On the night of the 3d of March, while President Lincoln and his Cabinet were at the Capitol, a telegram from General Grant was brought to the Secretary of War, informing him that General Lee had requested an interview or conference to make an arrangement for terms of peace. The letter of General Lee was published in a message of Davis to the rebel Congress.

General Grant's telegram was submitted to Mr. Lincoln, who, after pondering a few minutes, took up his pen and wrote with his own hand the following reply, which he submitted to the Secretary of State and Secretary of War. It was then dated, addressed, and signed by the Secretary of War, and telegraphed to General Grant:

WASHINGTON, March 3, 1866, 12 P. M.—*Lieutenant General Grant:* The President directs me to say to you that he wishes you to have no conference with General Lee, unless it be for the capitulation of General Lee's army, or on some minor and purely military matter. He instructs me to say that you are not to decide, discuss, or confer upon any political question. Such questions the President holds in his own hands, and will submit them to no military conferences or conventions. Meantime, you are to press to the utmost your military advantages.

EDWIN M. STANTON,
Secretary of War.

After the Cabinet meeting last night, General Grant started for North Carolina to direct operations against Johnston's army.

EDWIN M. STANTON,
Secretary of War.

It is reported that this proceeding of General Sherman was disapproved for the following, among other, reasons:

1. It was an exercise of authority not vested in General Sherman, and on its face shows that both he and Johnston knew that General Sherman had no authority to enter into any such arrangement.

2. It was a practical acknowledgment of the rebel government.

3. It undertook to re-establish the rebel State governments that had been overthrown at the sacrifice of many thousand loyal lives and immense treasure, and placed the arms and munitions of war in the hands of the rebels at their respective capitals, which might be used as soon as the armies of the United States were disbanded, and used to conquer and subdue the loyal States.

4. By the restoration of rebel authority in their respective States they would be enabled to re-establish slavery.

5. It might furnish a ground of responsibility by the Federal Government to pay the rebel debt, and certainly subjects the loyal citizens of rebel States to debt contracted by rebels in the State.

6. It would put in dispute the existence of loyal State governments, and the new State of West Virginia, which had been recognized by every department of the United States Government.

7. It practically abolished the confiscation laws, and relieved the rebels, of every degree, who had slaughtered our people, from all pains and penalties for their crimes.

8. It gave terms that had been deliberately, repeatedly, and solemnly rejected by President Lincoln, and better terms than the rebels had ever asked in their most prosperous condition.

9. It formed no basis of true and lasting peace, but relieved the rebels from the pressure of our victories, and left them in condition to renew their efforts to overthrow the United States Government and subdue the loyal States whenever their strength was recruited and any opportunity should offer.

General Grant's Orders.

[General Orders, No. 3.]

WAR DEPARTMENT,
ADJUTANT GENERAL'S OFFICE,
WASHINGTON, *January* 12, 1866.

TO PROTECT PERSONS AGAINST IMPROPER CIVIL SUITS AND PENALTIES IN LATE REBELLIOUS STATES.

Military division and department commanders, whose commands embrace or are composed of any of the late rebellious States, and who have not already done so, will at once issue and enforce orders protecting from prosecution or suits in the State, or municipal courts of such State, all officers and soldiers of the armies of the United States, and all persons thereto attached, or in anywise thereto belonging, subject to military authority, charged with offences for acts done in their military capacity, or pursuant to orders from proper military authority; and to protect from suit or prosecution all loyal citizens, or persons charged with offences done against the rebel forces, directly or indirectly, during the existence of the rebellion; and all persons, their agents and employés, charged with the occupancy of abandoned lands or plantations, or the possession or custody of any kind of property whatever, who occupied, used, possessed, or controlled the same pursuant to the order of the President, or any of the civil or military departments of the Government, and to protect them from any penalties or damages that may have been or may be pronounced or adjudged in said courts in any of such cases; and also protecting colored persons from prosecutions in any of said States charged with offences for which white persons are not prosecuted or punished in the same manner and degree.

By command of Lieutenant General Grant:

E. D. Townsend,
Assistant Adjutant General.

SUPPRESSION OF DISLOYAL NEWSPAPERS.

Headquarters Armies of United States,
Washington, *Feb.* 17, 1866.

You will please send to these headquarters as soon as practicable, and from time to time thereafter, such copies of newspapers published in your department as contain sentiments of disloyalty and hostility to the Government in any of its branches, and state whether such paper is habitual in its utterance of such sentiments. The persistent publication of articles calculated to keep up a hostility of feeling between the people of different sections of the country cannot be tolerated. This information is called for with a view to their suppression, which will be done from these headquarters only.

By order of Lieutenant General Grant:

T. S. Bowers,
Assistant Adjutant General.

Democratic Convention of Penn., March 5, 1866.

The Democracy of Pennsylvania, in Convention met, recognizing a crisis in the affairs of the Republic, and esteeming the immediate restoration of the Union paramount to all other issues, do resolve:

1. That the States, whereof the people were lately in rebellion, are integral parts of the Union and are entitled to representation in Congress by men duly elected who bear true faith to the Constitution and laws, and in order to vindicate the maxim that taxation without representation is tyranny, such representatives should be forthwith admitted.

2. That the faith of the Republic is pledged to the payment of the national debt, and Congress should pass all laws necessary for that purpose.

3. That we owe obedience to the Constitution of the United States, (including the amendment prohibiting slavery), and under its provisions will accord to those emancipated all their rights of person and property.

4. That each State has the exclusive right to regulate the qualifications of its own electors.

5. That the white race alone is entitled to the control of the Government of the Republic, and we are unwilling to grant the negroes the right to vote.

6. That the bold enunciation of the principles of the Constitution and the policy of restoration contained in the recent annual message and Freedmen's Bureau veto message of President Johnson entitle him to the confidence and support of all who respect the Constitution and love their country.

7. That the nation owes to the brave men of our armies and navy a debt of lasting gratitude for their heroic services in defence of the Constitution and the Union; and that while we cherish with a tender affection the memories of the fallen, we pledge to their widows and orphans the nation's care and protection.

8. That we urge upon Congress the duty of equalizing the bounties of our soldiers and sailors.

The following was also adopted:

Resolved, That the thanks of the Democracy of Pennsylvania be tendered to the Hon. Charles R. Buckalew and Hon. Edgar Cowan, for their patriotic support of the President's restoration policy; and that such thanks are due to all the democratic members of Congress for their advocacy of the restoration policy of President Johnson.

Union Convention of Pennsylvania, March 7.

2. That the most imperative duty of the present is to gather the legitimate fruits of the war, in order that our Constitution may come out of the rebellion purified, our institutions strengthened, and our national life prolonged.

3. That failure in these grave duties would be scarcely less criminal than would have been an acquiescence in secession and in the treasonable machinations of the conspirators, and would be an insult to every soldier who took up arms to save the country.

4. That filled with admiration at the patriotic devotion and fearless courage with which Andrew Johnson resisted and denounced the efforts of the rebels to overthrow the National Government, Pennsylvania rejoiced to express her entire confidence in his character and principles, and appreciation of his noble conduct, by bestowing her suffrage upon him for the second position in honor and dignity in the country. His bold and outspoken denunciation of the crime of treason, his firm demands for the punishment of the guilty offenders, and his expressions of thorough sympathy with the friends of the Union, secured for him the warmest attachment of her people, who, remembering his great services and sacrifices, while traitors and their sympathizers alike denounced his patriotic action, appeal to him to stand firmly by the side, and to repose upon the support of the loyal masses, whose votes formed the foundation of his promotion, and who pledge to him their unswerving support in all measures by which treason shall be stigmatized, loyalty recognized, and the freedom, stability, and unity of the National Union restored.

5. That the work of restoring the late insurrectionary States to their proper relations to the Union necessarily devolves upon the law-making power, and that until such action shall be taken no State lately in insurrection is entitled to representation in either branch of Congress; that, as preliminary to such action, it is the right of Congress to investigate for itself the condition of the legislation of those States, to inquire respecting their loyalty, and to prescribe the terms of restoration, and that to deny this necessary constitutional power is to deny and imperil one of the dearest rights belonging to our representative form of government, and that we cordially approve of the action of the Union representatives in Congress from Pennsylvania on this subject.

6. That no man who has voluntarily engaged in the late rebellion, or has held office under the rebel organization, should be allowed to sit in the Congress of the Union, and that the law known as the test oath should not be repealed, but should be enforced against all claimants for seats in Congress.

7. That the national faith is sacredly pledged to the payment of the national debt incurred in the war to save the country and to suppress rebellion, and that the people will not suffer this faith to be violated or impaired; but all debts incurred to support the rebellion were unlawful, void, and of no obligation, and shall never be assumed by the United States, nor shall any State be permitted to pay any evidences of so vile and wicked engagements.

15. That in this crisis of public affairs, full of grateful recollections of his marvellous and memorable services on the field of battle, we turn to the example of unfaltering and uncompromising loyalty of Lieutenant General Grant with a confidence not less significant and unshaken, because at no period of our great struggle has his proud name been associated with a doubtful patriotism, or used for sinister purposes by the enemies of our common country.

17. That the Hon. Edgar Cowan, Senator from Pennsylvania, by his course in the Senate of the United States, has disappointed the hopes and forfeited the confidence of those to whom he owes his place, and that he is hereby most earnestly requested to resign.

The following resolution was offered as a substitute for the fourth resolution, but after some discussion was withdrawn:

That, relying on the well-tried loyalty and devotion of Andrew Johnson to the cause of the Union in the dark days of treason and rebellion, and remembering his patriotic conduct, services, and sufferings, which in times past endeared his name to the Union party; and now reposing full confidence in his ability, integrity, and patriotism, we express the hope and confidence that the policy of his Administration will be so shaped and conducted as to save the nation from the perils which still surround it.

The fourth resolution was then adopted—yeas 109, nays 21.

General Grant's Order for the Protection of Citizens.

HEADQUARTERS OF THE ARMY,
ADJUTANT GENERAL'S OFFICE,
WASHINGTON, *July* 6, 1866.

[General Orders, No. 44.]

Department, district, and post commanders in the States lately in rebellion are hereby directed to arrest all persons who have been or may hereafter be charged with the commission of crimes and offences against officers, agents, citizens, and inhabitants of the United States, irrespective of color, in cases where the civil authorities have failed, neglected, or are unable to arrest and bring such parties to trial, and to detain them in military confinement until such time as a proper judicial tribunal may be ready and willing to try them.

A strict and prompt enforcement of this order is required.

By command of Lieutenant General Grant:

E. D. TOWNSEND,
Assistant Adjutant General.

Unconditional Union Convention of Maryland, June 6, 1866.

Resolved, That the registered loyal voters of Maryland will listen to no propositions to repeal or modify the registry law, which was enacted in conformity with the provisions of the constitution, and must remain in full force until such time as the registered voters of the State shall decree that the organic law shall be changed.

2. That the loyal people of the State are "the legitimate guardians and depositaries of its power," and that the disloyal "have no just right to complain of the hardships of a law which they have themselves deliberately provoked."

3. That it is the opinion of this convention, that if disloyal persons should be registered, it will be the duty of judges of election to administer the oath prescribed by the constitution to all whose loyalty may be challenged, and, in the language of the constitution, to "*carefully exclude from voting*" all that are disqualified.

4. That we cordially endorse the reconstruction policy of Congress, which excludes the leaders of the rebellion from all offices of profit or trust under the National Government, and places the basis of representation on the only just and honest principle, and that a white man in Virginia or South Carolina should have just as much representative power, and no more, than a white man in Pennsylvania or Ohio.

5. That the question of negro suffrage is not an issue in the State of Maryland, but is raised by the enemies of the Union party for the purpose of dividing and distracting it, and by this means to ultimately enable rebels to vote.

6. That we are pledged to the maintenance of the present constitution of Maryland, which expressly and emphatically prohibits both rebel suffrage and negro suffrage, and we are equally determined to uphold the registry law, which disfranchises rebels and excludes negroes from voting, and have no desire or intention of rescinding or abolishing either the constitution or the registry law.

7. That we warn the Union men of Maryland "that no Union man, high or low, should court the favor of traitors, as they can never win it—from the first they have held him as their enemy, and to the last they will be his; and that they should eschew petty rivalries, frivolous jealousies, and self-seeking cabals; so shall they save themselves falling one by one, an unpitied sacrifice, in a contemptible struggle."

The vote upon the adoption of each resolution was unanimous, with the exception of the sixth resolution, upon which a division was called, and the result showed 54 yeas to 14 nays.

The resolutions were then read as a whole, and adopted unanimously as the utterance of the Convention.

Convention of Southern Unionists.

TO THE LOYAL UNIONISTS OF THE SOUTH:

The great issue is upon us! The majority in Congress, and its supporters, firmly declare that "the rights of the citizen enumerated in the Constitution, and established by the supreme law, must be maintained inviolate."

Rebels and rebel sympathizers assert that "the rights of the citizen must be left to the States alone, and under such regulations as the respective States choose voluntarily to prescribe."

We have seen this doctrine of State sovereignty carried out in its practical results until all authority in Congress was denied, the Union temporarily destroyed, the constitutional rights of the citizen of the South nearly annihilated, and the land desolated by civil war.

The time has come when the restructure of Southern State government must be laid on constitutional principles, or the despotism, grown up under an atrocious leadership, be permitted to remain. We know of no other plan than that Congress, under its constitutional powers, shall now exercise its authority to establish the principle whereby protection is made coextensive with citizenship.

We maintain that no State, either by its organic law or legislation can make transgression on the rights of the citizen legitimate. We demand and ask you to concur in demanding protection to every citizen of the great Republic on the basis of equality before the law; and further, that no State government should be recognized as legitimate under the Constitution in so far as it does not by its organic law make impartial protection full and complete.

Under the doctrine of "State sovereignty," with rebels in the foreground, controlling Southern legislatures, and embittered by disappointment in their schemes to destroy the Union, there will be no safety for the loyal element of the South. Our reliance for protection is now on Congress, and the great Union party that has stood and is standing by our nationality, by the constitutional rights of the citizen, and by the beneficent principles of the government.

For the purpose of bringing the loyal Unionists of the South into conjunctive action with the true friends of republican government in the North, we invite you to send delegates in goodly numbers from all the Southern States, including Missouri, Kentucky, West Virginia, Maryland, and Delaware, to meet at Independence Hall, in the city of Philadelphia, on the first Monday of September next. It is proposed that we should meet at that time to recommend measures for the establishment of such government in the South as accords with and protects the rights of all citizens. We trust this call will be responded to by numerous delegations of such as represent the true loyalty of the South. That kind of government which gives full protection to all rights of the citizen, such as our fathers intended, we claim as our birthright. Either the lovers of constitutional liberty must rule the nation or rebels and their sympathizers be permitted to misrule it. Shall loyalty or disloyalty have the keeping of the destinies of the nation? Let the responses to this call which is now in circulation for signatures, and is being numerously signed, answer. Notice is given that gentlemen at a distance can have their names attached to it by sending a request by letter directed to D. W. Bingham, Esq., of Washington, D. C.

Tennessee..............W. B. STOKES,
JOS. S. FOWLER,
JAMES GETTYS.
Texas......................A. J. HAMILTON,
GEO. W. PASCHAL,
LORENZO SHERWOOD,
C. B. SABIN.
Georgia..................G. W. ASHBURN,
HENRY G. COLE.
Missouri..................J. W. McCLURG,
JOHN R. KELSO,
J. F. BENJAMIN,
GEO. W. ANDERSON.
Virginia...................JOHN B. TROTH,
J. M. STEWART,
WM. N. BERKLEY,
ALLEN C. HARMON,
LEWIS McKENZIE,
J. W. HUNNICUTT,
JOHN C. UNDERWOOD,
BURNHAM WARDWELL,
ALEX. M. DAVIS.
North Carolina........BYRON LAFLIN,
DANIEL R. GOODLOE.
Alabama..................GEORGE REESE,
D. H. BINGHAM,
M. R. SAFFOLD,
J. H. LARCOMBE,

WASHINGTON, *July* 4, 1866.

XIII.—*Interesting Figures chiefly from the Census of 1860, bearing on Representation.*

STATES.*	White Population.	Free Colored.	Slaves.	Aggregate Population.	Representative Population.	White Males over 20.	Colored Males over 20.	Vote of 1860.	Apportionment under Census of 1860.	Based on three fifths Slave Population.	According to whole populat'n, including Colored.	According to White Suffrage.
California	†358,110	4,086	....	379,994	362,196	206,442	2,339	108,840	3	....	3	7
Connecticut	451,504	8.627	....	460,147	460,147	127.996	2,091	77,246	4	....	4	4
Illinois	1,704,291	7,628	....	1,711,951	1.711,951	4_9,503	1,753	339,693	14	....	13	15
Indiana	1,338,710	11,428	....	1,350.428	1,350,428	316,804	2,565	272,143	11	....	10	11
Iowa	673,779	1,069	....	674,913	674.913	164,535	290	12 ,331	6	....	5	6
Kansas	106,390	625	2	107,206	107,206	31.037	149	....	1	....	1	1
Maine	62 ,947	1,327	....	628,279	628,279	167.724	362	97,918	5	....	5	6
Massachusetts	1,221,432	9,002	....	1,231,066	1,231,066	339,086	2,512	169,175	10	....	9	12
Michigan	736,142	6,799	....	749,113	749.113	200,474	1,918	154.747	6	....	6	7
Minnesota	169,395	259	....	172,023	172.023	48,186	65	34,799	2	....	2	2
New Hampshire	325,579	494	....	326.073	326,073	91,954	149	65,953	3	....	3	3
New Jersey	646,699	25,318	18	672,035	672,027	167,441	6,291	121,125	5	....	5	6
New York	3.831,590	49.C0	....	3,880.735	3,880,735	1,027,344	12.989	675.156	31	....	29	35
Ohio	2,302,808	36,673	....	2,339,511	2,339,511	562,901	8,770	442,441	19	....	18	19
Oregon	52.160	128	....	52,465	52.465	17.736	53	14,410	1	....	1	1
Pennsylvania	2,849,529	56,949	....	2,9_6.215	2,906,215	702,316	13,631	476,442	24	....	22	24
Rhode Island	170.649	3,952	....	174,620	174.620	46,417	1.023	19,951	2	....	2	2
Vermont	314.369	709	....	315,098	315.098	87,462	194	42,844	3	....	3	3
Wisconsin	773,693	1,171	....	775,881	775,881	198,914	353	152,170	6	....	6	7
	18,653,776	225,849	20	18,907.753	18,880 947	4.944.272	57.497	3,393.392	156		147	171
Alabama	526,271	2,690	435.080	964,201	790,169	118.589	96,458	90,357	6	1	7	4
Arkansas	324,143	144	111,115	435,450	391,004	73,963	25.044	54,053	3	1	3	3
Delaware	90.589	19,829	1.798	112,216	111,496	22,429	4,679	16.0 9	1	....	1	1
Florida	77,747	932	61,745	140,424	115.726	18,687	14,315	14 347	1	....	1	1
Georgia	591.550	3.500	462,198	1,057,286	872,406	132,479	97,170	106,365	7	2	8	5
Kentucky	919,484	10,684	225,483	1,15_,_84	1,065,490	217.885	50,442	146,216	9	1	9	8
Louisiana	357,456	18,647	331,726	708,002	575,311	101,499	101,814	50.510	5	2	6	4
Maryland	515,918	83,942	87,189	687,049	652,173	123,371	38,039	92.502	5	....	5	5
Mississippi	353,899	773	436,631	791,305	616,652	[illegible]5.838	113,828	69.120	5	2	6	3
Missouri	1,063,489	3,572	114,931	1,182,012	1,136,039	268.262	21,872	165,518	9	1	9	9
North Carolina	629,942	30,403	331,059	992,622	860,197	143,443	74.356	47.601	7	2	8	5
South Carolina	291.300	9,914	402.406	703,708	542,745	68,154	87.781	‡35,000	4	2	5	2
Tennessee	826,722	7,300	275.719	1,109,801	999 513	189.470	56,770	145,333	8	1	9	7
Texas	420,891	355	182 566	604.215	531.188	109 625	38,704	62,986	4	1	5	4
Virginia*	1,047,299	58,042	490.865	1,596.318	1,390,972	245.683	123 613	167,223	11	2	12	9
	8.036,700	250.787	3,950.511	12,240.293	10.660 081	1.924,375	944 885	1.263,200	85	18	94	70
Grand Total	26,690,476	476.636	3.950.531	31.148.046	29,550 028	6.868.647	1 002,382	4.656,652	241	18	241	241
Representative Ratio	....	....	....	....	....	....	....	....	127,000	....	133,700	29,300

* Nevada admitted since, with one Representative—making whole number, at present, 242. West Virginia created since, with three Representatives—leaving Virginia 8, instead of 11 allowed in 1860.
† Including Asiatics. ‡ Estimated.

Votes in the U. S. House of Representatives on the Various Tariffs.

STATES.	Tariff of 1816.		Tariff of 1824.		Tariff of 1828.		Tariff of 1832.		Tariff of 1842.		Tariff of 1846.		Tariff of 1857.		Tariff of 1861.		Tariff of 1864.		Tariff Bill of 1866.*	
	Yeas.	Nays.	Yeas.	Nays.	Yeas.	Nays.	Yeas.	Nays.	Yeas.	Nays.	Yeas.	Nays.	Yeas.	Nays.	Yeas.	Nays.	Yeas.	Nays.	Yeas.	Nays.
NEW ENGLAND STATES.																				
Maine	......	......	1	6	0	7	6	1	3	3	7	1	6	0	5	0	3	0	3	0
New Hampshire	1	3	1	5	4	2	5	0	0	4	4	0	1	1	3	0	2	1	3	0
Vermont	4	1	5	0	4	1	0	3	5	0	0	3	0	3	3	0	3	0	3	0
Massachusetts	7	4	1	11	2	11	4	8	10	1	0	9	9	0	9	0	8	0	10	0
Connecticut	2	2	5	1	4	2	2	3	6	0	0	4	4	0	4	0	1	0	2	0
Rhode Island	2	0	2	0	1	1	0	2	2	0	0	1	1	1	2	0	1	0	2	0
	16	10	15	23	15	21	17	17	26	8	11	18	21	5	26	0	18	1	23	0
MIDDLE STATES.																				
New York	20	2	26	8	27	6	27	2	23	9	14	16	16	12	18	2	14	2	16	4
New Jersey	5	0	6	0	5	0	3	3	6	0	0	5	2	1	4	0	1	1	1	3
Pennsylvania	17	3	24	1	23	0	14	12	19	0	2	23	3	15	22	0	15	0	19	1
Delaware	......	......	1	0	1	0	0	1	1	0	0	1	0	1	1	0	1	0	0	1
Maryland	2	5	3	6	1	5	8	0	4	3	1	2	4	1	2	2	1	0	1	4
	44	10	60	15	57	11	52	18	53	12	17	47	25	30	47	4	32	3	37	13
SOUTHERN STATES.																				
Virginia	7	13	1	21	3	15	11	8	3	17	14	1	13	0	......	......	......	......	......	......
West Virginia	......	......	......	......	......	......	......	......	......	......	......	......	......	......	......	......	......	......	3	0
North Carolina	0	11	0	13	0	13	8	4	0	11	5	3	6	0	0	4	......	......	......	......
South Carolina	4	3	0	9	0	8	3	6	0	6	7	0	4	0	0	4	......	......	......	......
Georgia	3	3	0	7	0	7	1	6	0	8	5	2	4	0	0	6	......	......	......	......
Florida	......	......	......	......	......	......	......	......	......	......	1	0	1	0	0	0	......	......	......	......
Alabama	......	......	0	3	0	3	2	1	0	4	7	0	7	0	0	8	......	......	......	......
Mississippi	......	......	0	1	0	1	1	0	0	2	4	0	4	0	0	3	......	......	......	......
Louisiana	0	1	0	3	0	3	1	2	2	1	3	1	4	0	0	2	......	......	......	......
Texas	......	......	......	......	......	......	......	......	......	......	2	0	1	0	0	1	......	......	......	......
	14	31	1	57	3	50	27	27	5	49	48	7	44	0	0	37	......	......	3	0
WESTERN STATES.																				
Kentucky	6	1	11	0	12	0	9	3	4	8	3	7	6	2	4	4	0	4	1	7
Tennessee	3	2	2	7	0	9	9	0	1	13	6	6	7	0	1	3	......	......	......	......
Ohio	5	0	14	0	13	0	13	0	9	6	12	8	5	14	13	5	4	10	15	3
Indiana	......	......	2	0	3	0	3	0	3	3	6	2	3	8	2	4	2	4	0	7
Illinois	......	......	1	0	1	0	1	0	1	2	4	0	4	4	4	2	3	4	0	12
Missouri	......	......	1	0	0	1	1	0	1	1	4	0	0	3	0	4	5	0	2	4
Arkansas	......	......	......	......	......	......	......	......	0	1	......	......	2	0	0	0	......	......	......	......
Iowa	......	......	......	......	......	......	......	......	......	......	......	......	1	1	1	0	6	0	2	3
Michigan	......	......	......	......	......	......	......	......	1	0	3	0	1	3	3	0	4	0	4	0
Minnesota	......	......	......	......	......	......	......	......	......	......	......	......	......	......	2	0	1	0	0	2
Wisconsin	......	......	......	......	......	......	......	......	......	......	......	......	1	2	2	0	2	2	2	2
Kansas	......	......	......	......	......	......	......	......	......	......	......	......	......	......	......	......	1	0	1	0
	14	3	31	7	29	10	36	3	24	34	38	23	30	37	32	22	28	24	27	40
PACIFIC STATES.																				
California	......	......	......	......	......	......	......	......	......	......	......	......	2	0	0	1	3	0	2	0
Oregon	......	......	......	......	......	......	......	......	......	......	......	......	......	......	......	......	......	......	1	0
Nevada	......	......	......	......	......	......	......	......	......	......	......	......	......	......	......	......	......	......	1	0
	......	......	......	......	......	......	......	......	......	......	......	......	2	0	0	1	3	0	4	0
Grand Total	88	54	107	102	105	94	132	65	104	103	114	95	122	72	105	64	81	28	94	53

Statement of the Public Debt of the United States on the 1st of June, 1866.

Debt bearing Coin Interest		$1,195,825,191 80
Debt bearing Currency Interest		1,147,223,226 28
Matured Debt not presented for payment		4,900,429 64
Debt bearing no Interest.—U. S. Notes	$402,128,318 00	
Fractional Currency	27,334,965 04	
Gold Certificates of Deposit	22,568,320 00	
		452,031,603 04
Total Debt		2,799,979,450 76
Amount in Treasury, Coin	50,679,957 72	
" " Currency	79,011,125 52	
		129,691,083 24
Amount of Debt, less Cash in Treasury		$2,670,288,367 52

* July 12—In SENATE, postponed till December next—yeas 23, nays 17, as follow:

YEAS—Messrs. Brown, *Davis*, Doolittle, Foster, Grimes, *Guthrie*, Harris, Henderson, *Hendricks*, *Johnson*, Kirkwood, Lane, Morgan, *Nesmith*, Norton, Pomeroy, *Riddle*, *Sauls bury*, Sumner, Trumbull, Willey, Williams, Wilson—23.

NAYS—Messrs. Anthony, Chandler, Clark, Conness, Cowan, Cragin, Edmunds, Fessenden, Howard, Howe, Poland, Ramsey, Sherman, Sprague, Stewart, Van Winkle, Wade—17.

INDEX.

Alabama, reconstruction facts, 12, 21–34; claimants in Congress, 107, 108; resolutions of legislature, 22; laws on freedmen, 33, 34.

Amendment of Constitution, President Johnson's message, and Secretary Seward's report upon, 83, 84; votes adopting, 102; preliminary votes and propositions, 103–106.

Amnesty, President Johnson's proclamation of, 9; Mr. Seward's circular, 10.

Ancona, Sydenham E., resolution on Fenians, 113.

Anti-slavery Amendment, announcement of ratification of, 6; action of insurrectionary States, 19–24; President Johnson's telegrams respecting, 22, 23, 25.

Appointments to office, President Johnson's order respecting, 17.

Arkansas, President Johnson's telegram to Gov. Murphy, 28; claimants in Congress, 107, 108.

Arrest of Davis, Clay, &c., order for, 7; release of Clay, *note*, 8; resolution on trial of Davis, 113.

Assassins of Abraham Lincoln, President Johnson's orders for trial and punishment of, 7.

Bingham, John A., reports on immunities of citizens, 105; concerning Tennessee, 105; amendment to resolution on President's policy, 111.

Blockade, proclamation concerning, 7, 9, 13.

Boutwell, George S., resolution respecting trial of Jefferson Davis, 113.

Brooks, James, Representative in thirty-ninth Congress, 108; unseated, *note*, 108.

Brownlow, William G., President Johnson's telegram to, 27.

Cabinet of President Johnson, 107.

Campbell, John A. parole of, 14.

Canby, E. R. S., telegram forbidding meeting of rebel legislatures, 19.

Census Tables, on Representation, population, &c., 125.

Citizenship of United States, proposed Constitutional amendment respecting, 102; legislation upon, 78; President Johnson's views, 74.

Civil Rights, proposed amendment to secure, 102–106.

Civil Rights Bill, President Johnson's veto of, and votes on passing and re-passing, 74–80.

Clark, Charles, parole of, 14; attempt to call rebel legislature and General Canby's order forbidding, 19.

Clay, Clement C., reward for arrest, 8; parole of, *note*, 8.

Codes, Freedmen's, orders, and legislation, 12, 13, 29–44.

Colorado, bill for admission of, veto and votes, 81–83.

Colored People, of District of Columbia, President Johnson's address to, 63; conventions and action of, in insurrectionary States, 18, 20, 21–24.

Colored Soldiers, President Johnson's addresses to, 49–52.

Colored Suffrage, President Johnson's telegram to Prov. Gov. Sharkey on, 19, 20; President Lincoln's letter to Governor Hahn on, *note*, 20; President Johnson's allusions to, 24, 49, 52–55; proposed in District of Columbia, 114–116; in the Territories, 116; proposed in Connecticut and vote, 120.

Commercial Intercourse, President Johnson's orders respecting, 7, 9, 13.

Congress, resolution on duty of, to guarantee a republican form of government, 112; President Johnson's telegram to Provisional Governor Perry on organization of 39th, 24; members of 39th, 107, 108.

Connecticut, election of 1865 on colored suffrage, and election of 1866, 120.

Constitution of the United States, copy of, 1–6; Mr. Seward's certificate of ratification of anti-slavery amendment, 6; President Johnson's message on proposed amendment to, 83; votes on propositions of amendment, 102–106.

Convention, proposed National Union, 118; resolution of Democratic National, 118; of Pennsylvania Union and Democrat, 123; Union National, 117; Maryland Union, 124; Southern Unionist, 124.

Cooper, Edmund, telegram respecting peace proclamation, 17; claimant of seat in Congress, 108.

Davis, Jefferson, President Johnson's order for arrest of, 7; resolution for trial of, 113.

Defrees, Joseph H., resolution on elective franchise, 110.

Democratic National Platform of 1864, 118; Address of Democratic Congressmen, 119, 120; platform of Penna., 123.

Dennison, William, Postmaster General, 107.

Direct Taxes, proposed constitutional amendment on, 104.

District of Columbia, President Johnson on proposed suffrage in, 52; bill on suffrage, 114–116.

Dodge, William E., qualified as representative, *note*, 108.

Douglass, Frederick, interview with President Johnson, 52–56.

Edmunds, George F., qualified as Senator, *note*, 107.

Elections of 1866, returns of, 120.

Elective Franchise in the States, resolution concerning, 110; in Territories, to be no discrimination on account of color, 116; President Johnson's allusion to, 19, 20, 24, 49, 52–55; President Lincoln, *note*, 24.

Fenians, President Johnson's proclamation respecting, 17, 18; Attorney General Speed's order for arrest of, *note*, 18; resolution on, 113, 114.

Florida, provisional governor appointed, 12; General Gillmore's order annulling the call of acting Gov. Allison for meeting of rebel legislature, 24; reconstruction, steps in, 24, 25; Freedmen's code, 38–41; claimants in Congress, 107, 108.

Foot, Solomon, Senator, death of, 107.

Forney, John W., Secretary of the Senate, 107; allusion of President Johnson to, 61.

Freedmen, orders respecting, 12, 13; laws concerning, 29–44.

Freedmen's Bureau, President Johnson's veto of bill for, and votes on passing and repassing, 68–74; number of rations issued by, to April 1, 1866, *note*, 69.

Georgia, General Gillmore's order annulling Gov. Brown's call for a meeting of the rebel legislature, 20; reconstruction, steps in, 20, 21; laws on freedmen, 32, 33; claimants in Congress, 107, 108.

Grant, Ulysses S., General, report on condition of insurrectionary States, 67, 68; surrender of Lee to, 120, 121; orders of, to protect loyal persons and suppress disloyal newspapers, 122, 123, 124.

Habeas Corpus, annulling suspension of, in certain States, 15; resolution on, 112; bill respecting, 116.

Hale, Robert S., amendment to District of Columbia suffrage bill, 114.

Harlan, James, Secretary of the Interior, 107.

Henderson, James H. D., resolution on punishment of treason, 109.

Hill, Ralph, resolution on test oath, 110.

Holden, William W., appointed provisional governor of North Carolina, 11; President Johnson's telegram to, respecting rebel debt, 19; defeated for Governor, 19.

Homestead Act, bill extending the, votes on, 116.

Howard, O. O., orders of, as Commissioner of Freedmen's Affairs, 12, 13.

Insurrectionary States, President's proclamations concerning, 7, 9, 11, 13–17; reconstruction steps in, 18–28; legislation respecting freedmen, 29–44; President Johnson's messages, concerning, 64–67; Lieutenant General Grant's report, 67, 68; President Johnson on representation of, 57–66, 71, 72; votes in Congress upon, *note*, 72; reports and propositions, 102–106; claimants from, for seats in Congress, and memoranda respecting, 107, 108.

Johnson, Andrew, Cabinet of, 107: inauguration of, 44.

Johnson, Andrew, Interviews and Speeches—To citizens of Indiana, 44–47; Nashville speech of June 9, 1864, *note*, 46, 47; to Virginia refugees, 47, 48; with George L. Stearns, 48, 49; to colored soldiers, October 10, 1865, 49–51; with Senator Dixon, 51–52; with colored delegation respecting suffrage, and reply of, 52–55; with committee of the Virginia legislature, 56–58; speech of February 22, 1866, 58–63; speech to colored people of District of Columbia, 63.

Johnson, Andrew, Messages of—Annual, 64–66; special, on the condition of the insurrectionary States, 66, 67; veto of Freedmen's Bureau bill, 68–72; veto of civil rights bill, 74–78; veto of Colorado bill, 81, 82; on proposed constitutional amendment, 83.

Johnson, Andrew, Orders and Proclamations of, 7–18; on commercial intercourse and blockade, 7, 9, 13; for trial and punishment of Abraham Lincoln's assassins, 7; for arrest of Jefferson Davis, Clement C. Clay, and others, 7; for release of latter, *note*, 8; recognizing Pierpoint's administration in Virginia, 8; respecting rebel cruisers receiving hospitality in foreign ports, 9; of amnesty, 9, 10; appointing provisional governors in North Carolina, Mississippi, Georgia, Texas, Alabama, South Carolina, Florida, 11, 12; respecting freedmen, 12, 13; for return of property to pardoned persons, 13; respecting the State of Tennessee, 13, 14; Passports for paroled prisoners, 14; paroling certain State prisoners, 14; withdrawing martial law from Kentucky, 15; annulling the suspension of the *habeas corpus*, 15; announcing that the rebellion has ended, 15, 16; President Johnson's interpretation thereof, *note*, 17; in relation to appointments to office, 17; in relation to trials by military courts and commissions, 17; forbidding the invasion of Canada by the Fenians, 17, 18.

Johnson, Andrew, Telegrams of, to Provisional Governor Holden on repudiating rebel debt of North Carolina, 19; to Provisional Governor Sharkey, on colored suffrage in Mississippi, 19, 20; to Provisional Governor Johnson on repudiating rebel debt of Georgia, 20, 21; to Provisional Governor Perry of South Carolina on ratifying anti-slavery amendment, 22, on annulling ordinance of secession, 23, on Representatives elected to Congress presenting their credentials, 24; to Provisional Governor Marvin of Florida, 25; to Governor Brownlow of Tennessee on sustaining and enforcing the election laws of that State, 27; to Governor Murphy of Arkansas, 28.

Johnson, Andrew, thanks of House to, 113; sundry resolutions respecting, 111, 112.

Johnson, James, appointed provisional governor of Georgia, 12, telegrams from and to, 20, 21.

Johnston, Joseph E., agreement with General Sherman, 121, 122.

Joint Reconstruction Committee, majority and minority reports of, 84–101; various propositions of, and votes upon, 102–106.

Kelley, William D., bill to regulate suffrage in District of Columbia, 114.

Kentucky, withdrawal of martial law, 15.

Kirkwood, Samuel J., qualified as Senator, *note*, 107.

Lee, R. E., surrender to General Grant, 120, 121.

Lincoln, Abraham, orders for trial and punishment of assassins of, 7; letter of, to Governor Hahn on colored suffrage, *note*, 20; telegram to General Weitzel forbidding the meeting of the rebel legislature of Virginia, 26.

List of Congressmen and Claimants, 107, 108.

Longyear, John W., resolutions on public affairs, 111–113.

Louisiana, J. M. Wells elected Governor, 28; James T. Monroe mayor of New Orleans, and pardon of, 28, 29; legislation on freedmen, 43, 44; claimants in Congress, 107, 108.

Marvin, Wm., appointed provisional governor of Florida, 12; claimant of seat in Senate, 107.

Maryland, Unconditional Union platform, 124.

McCulloch, Hugh, Secretary of Treasury, 107.

McPherson, Edward, Clerk of House, 108; telegrams of Provisional Governor Perry, as to action of, 24.

Messages of President Johnson, annual, 61–66; on condition of insurrectionary States, 66; vetoes of Freedmen's Bureau, Civil Rights, and Colorado bills, 64–82; on proposed constitutional amendment, 82.

Military Courts, effect of peace proclamation upon, *note*, 17; order in relation to trials by, 17.

Mississippi, rebel legislature forbidden to assemble, 19; reconstruction steps in, 19, 20; President Johnson's telegram to Provisional Governor Sharkey on colored suffrage, 19, 20; convention of colored people of, 20; laws on freedmen, 29–32; claimants in Congress, 107, 108.

Morrill, Lot M., amendments to District of Columbia suffrage bill 115.

Nebraska, election of 1866, 120.

New Hampshire, election of 1866, 120.

New Jersey, Senator from, unseated, *note*, 107.

North Carolina, provisional governor appointed, 11; steps taken in reconstruction, 18, 19; claimants for seats in Senate and House, 107, 108; convention of colored people of, 18; laws concerning freedmen, 29.

Office, President Johnson's order respecting appointments to, 17.

Orders, Military, of General Sickles, setting aside Freedmen's code for South Carolina, 36–38; of General Terry in Virginia, 41–42; President Johnson declined to interfere, 42; of General Grant to protect loyal persons and suppress disloyal newspapers, 122, 123, 124.

Oregon, election of 1866, 120.

Pardoned Rebels, order for return of property to, 13.

Paroled Prisoners, passports ordered for, 14, 15.

Parsons, Lewis E., appointed provisional governor of Alabama, 12; claimant of seat as Senator, 107.

Pennsylvania, resolutions of Union and Democratic conventions, 123.

Perry, Benjamin F., appointed provisional governor of South Carolina, 12; telegrams on sundry topics, 22, 23, 24; claimant of seat as Senator, 107.

Phillips, Wendell, allusion of President Johnson to, 61.

Platforms of 1864, Union and Democratic, 117, 118.

Provisional Governors appointed, 11, 12.

Public Debt, resolution respecting inviolability of, 109; proposed constitutional amendment respecting, 102, 103; amount of, 126.

Public Lands, legislation on, 116.

Randall, Samuel J., resolution on public debt, 109.

Rebel Cruisers, proclamation concerning, 9.

Rebellion Suppressed, proclamation announcing the, 15, 16.

Rebels Pardoned, order for return of property to, 13.

Rebel Debt, proposition to repudiate, 102, 106; resolution concerning, 109; action of legislatures of insurrectionary states on rebel State debt, 19, 21, 23, 24, 28.

Reconstruction Committee, majority and minority reports of, 84–101; votes upon propositions of, 102–106.

Representation, proposed constitutional amendment on, 102–105; census tables on, 125.

Representation of Insurrectionary States, President Johnson's allusions to, 57–63, 71, 72, 82; concurrent resolution upon, *note*, 72; majority and minority reports upon, 84–101; bills and propositions relating to, 102–106; resolution concerning, 109.

Representatives in Thirty-Ninth Congress and Claimants, 108, 109.

Resolutions on Political Subjects, 109–114.

Rhode Island, election of 1866, 120.

Schenck, Robert C., propositions on representation, 104, 105; on Fenian resolution, 114; on suffrage in District of Columbia, 115.

Senators in Thirty-Ninth Congress, and Claimants, 107, 108.

Seward, William H., Secretary of State, 107; certificate of ratification of anti-slavery amendment, 6; telegrams to provisional governors, 21, 23, 24, 25; report on transmission of proposed constitutional amendment, 83, 84.

Sharkey, William L., provisional governor of Mississippi, 12; action as, 19, 20; President Johnson's telegram on colored suffrage, 19, 20; claimant as Senator, 107.

Sherman, William T., agreement with General Joseph E. Johnston, 121, 122.

Sickles, Daniel E., order of, setting aside South Carolina's code, 36–38.

South Carolina, provisional governor appointed, 12; reconstruction, steps in, 22–24; General Gillmore's order annulling Governor Magrath's call for legislature, 22; President Johnson's and Secretary Seward's telegrams, 22, 23, 24; failure to repudiate rebel debt, *note*, 24; form of ratifying anti-slavery amendment, 23; laws on freedmen, and order of General Sickles relating thereto, 34–37; claimants in Congress, 107, 108.

Speed, James, Attorney General, 107; order for arrest of Fenians, *note*, 18.

Stanton, Edwin M., Secretary of War, 107.

Stearns, George L., President Johnson's interview with, 48, 49.

Stephens, Alexander H., parole of, 14; claimant in Congress, 107.

Stevens, Thaddeus, allusion of President Johnson to, 61; resolution on representation, *note*, 72; propositions from Reconstruction Committee, 103–105; resolution on test oath for lawyers, 111; motion not to recognize the North Carolina State government, 113.

Stockton, John P., Senator, 107; unseated, *note*, 107.

Suffrage in District of Columbia, 114–116; in territories, 116, 117; vote in Connecticut, 120; President Lincoln upon, *note*, 20; President Johnson, 19, 20, 24, 49, 52–55.

Sumner, Charles, allusion of President Johnson to, 61.

Taber, Stephen, amendment to homestead act, 116

Tabular Statements, on representation, tariff, debt, 125, 126.

Tariff, votes on all, since 1816, 126.

Tennessee, President Johnson's proclamation respecting suppression of insurrection in, 13; franchise acts in, 27, 28, and President Johnson's telegram concerning, 27; legislation on freedmen, 42, 43; joint resolution concerning, 105.

Territories, elective franchise in, 116.

Terry, General, order setting aside vagrant act of Virginia, 41, 42; sustained by President Johnson, 42.

Test Oath, action of North Carolina requesting repeal of, 19; of Mississippi, 20; vote in House on, 110, 111.

Texas, provisional governor appointed, 12; action of convention, 28; legislation on freedmen, 43.

Thornton, Anthony, resolution on elective franchise, 110.

Treason, Punishment of, resolution respecting, 109.

Trenholm, George A., parole of, 14.

Virginia, order to re-establish authority of United States in, 8, 9; call for meeting of rebel legislature, 25; Mr. Lincoln's telegram forbidding it, 25; legislation, &c., in, 26, 27; freedmen's code, and General Terry's order setting aside vagrant act, 41, 42; claimants in Congress, 107, 108.

Voorhees, Daniel W., Representative in Thirty-Ninth Congress, 108; unseated, *note*, 108; resolution endorsing President Johnson's policy, 111.

Warren, Gouverneur K., General, telegram of General Canby to, prohibiting the meeting of the rebel legislature of Mississippi, 19.

Washburn, Henry D., qualified as Representative, *note*, 108.

Welles, Gideon, Secretary of the Navy, 107.

West Virginia, bill, votes on, 116; election of 1866, 120.

Willey, Waitman T., amendment to District of Columbia bill, 115, 116.

Williams, Thomas, resolution on withdrawal of military force, 111.

Wilson, James F., proposition relative to rebel debt, 106; resolution on representation, 109, 110; amendment to District of Columbia bill, 114.

www.ingramcontent.com/pod-product-compliance
Lightning Source LLC
LaVergne TN
LVHW021416110826
845150LV00007B/1956
9781425509378